JOSEPH McDONNELL

Text Donald Kuspit   *Photographs* David Finn and Rebecca Binder

JOSEPH McDONNELL

Introduction Andre Emmerich

Text Donald Kuspit

Photographs David Finn and Rebecca Binder

Published by The University of Washington Press in association with Ruder Finn Press, New York

To my girls, Drew, Julia, Ellie, Kate, Sophia, and to Maryann

TABLE OF CONTENTS

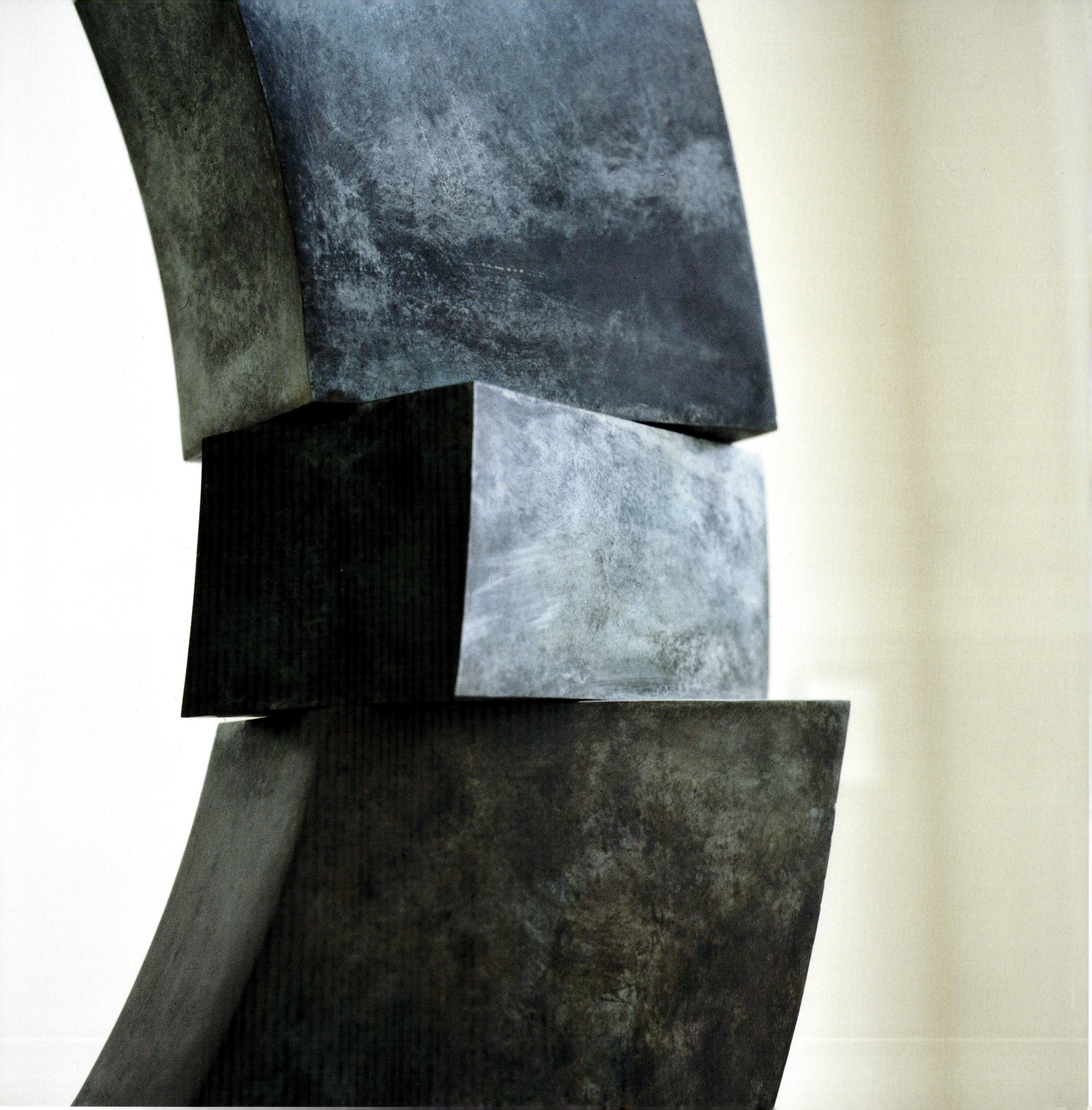

INTRODUCTION

Andre Emmerich

I have long been an admirer of Joe McDonnell's sculpture. However, it was only when he lent me some sculptures for Top Gallant, my 150-acre sculpture park in Dutchess County, that I came to appreciate fully the strength and beauty of his work.

As is well known, the eye is a lazy organ. It is usually only when circumstances require a careful analytic look that most of us make such an effort. In the case of the McDonnell sculptures at Top Gallant, I needed to find sites that would allow these works to be seen to their best advantage. While the installation cranes and their operators were still on hand, I engaged in a dialogue with the sculptures, turning them this way and that, installing some in the shade of great trees and others in open fields, all the while discovering the strength of each work.

I learned to remember that when a sculpture is installed and lit in an indoor setting, that setting remains constant, unlike sculptures placed out-of-doors, where the trajectory of the sun lights the sculpture differently each hour of the day and with the coming and going of each season. Equally important were decisions on which angle would be the best choice for a catalogue photograph, and which side should be first presented to a viewer. More importantly, I learned to appreciate the rich variety of aesthetic experiences McDonnell's sculptures presented as nature's light changed—like the varnished look matte sculpture assumes in the rain. While logic would lead one to think that black painted steel sculptures would look their best in sun-bathed open spaces, trial and error led to the discovery that black sculptures are often seen at their best in the shade of great trees, while white sculptures will do equally well in sunlight and in shade. Most importantly, as I kept working with McDonnell's sculptures, moving them about until I found the most ideal site for each work, I came to see and enjoy the very special qualities which time and familiarity revealed to me.

McDonnell's work has kept on growing and evolving. My own favorites to date are the monumental entrance gates that Jon and Mary Shirley commissioned for their waterfront estate near Seattle. The majestic elements of the gates are a powerful reference to the geological history of the site they so splendidly occupy, and evoke the giant boulders strewn across the Washington landscape in the last Ice Age. McDonnell reveals his eclectic artistic affinities in titling this work, *The Second Gates of Paradise*, a clear reference to the most famous bronze gates of the Renaissance, Ghiberti's early fifteenth century doors of the Baptistery in Florence. Other chosen ancestors subtly referenced in his work include the second millennium B.C. megaliths of Stonehenge, and McDonnell's contemporary, Andy Goldsworthy, the Scottish sculptor best known for what he has called running fences, beautiful laid low stone walls that meander through fields and forests.

McDonnell's sculptures competed with the work of some of the best known and admired sculptors of our time in their installation at Top Gallant. Tough competition, indeed. McDonnell's work, in its richly unfolding complexity and strength, more than held its own.

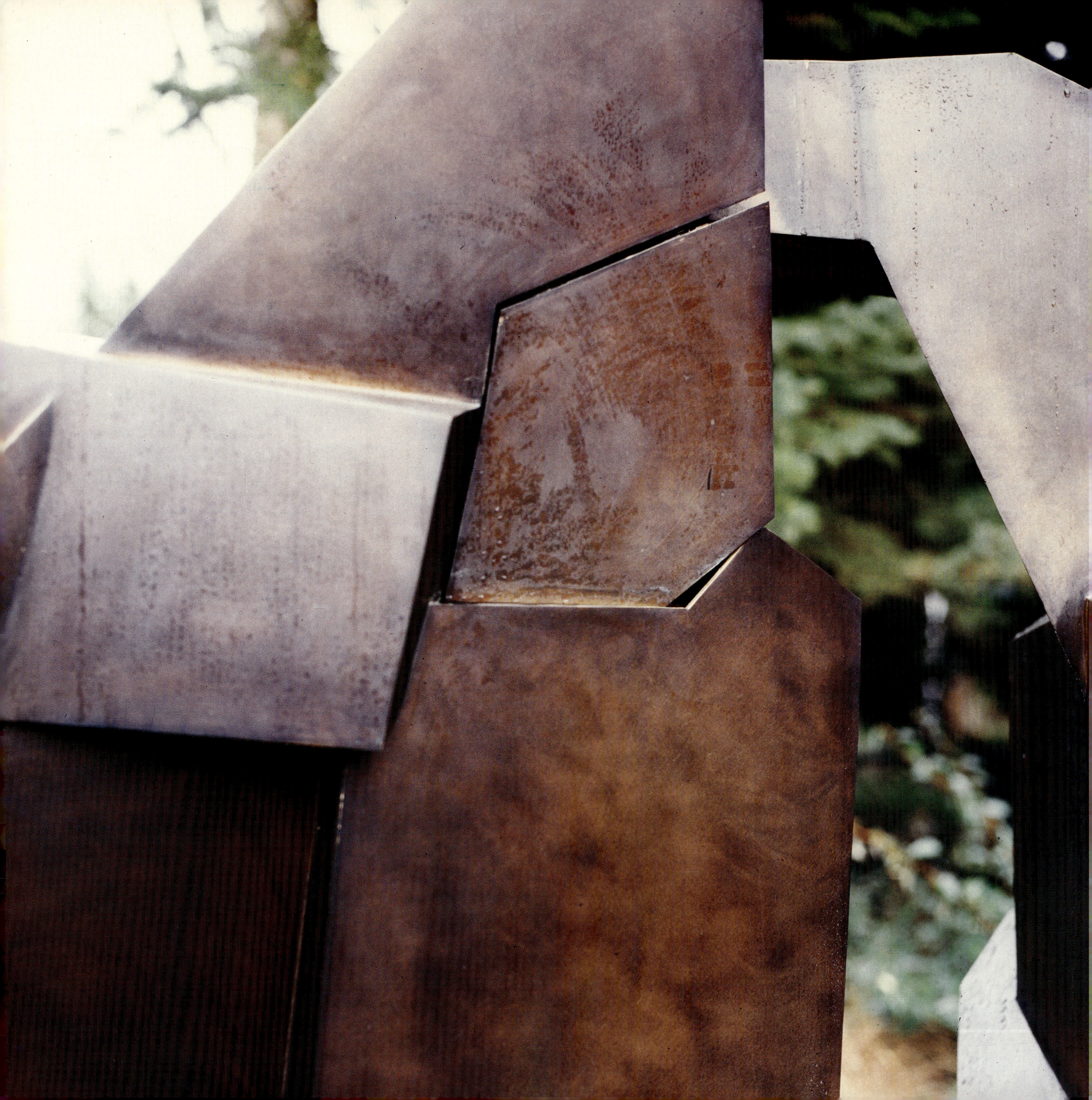

THE SCULPTURE OF JOSEPH McDONNELL

Donald Kuspit

Joseph McDonnell is clearly a master of what might be called late modern sculpture—cubist/constructivist complexity and an expressionistic sense of drama. Their surface richness suggests a painter's sensibility—but there is much more to them than their stylistic subtlety. To take a cue from the title of one of his most monumental works, *The Second Gates of Paradise*, 2003, they are about the restoration of paradise in hellish times. They are about faith in the possibility of perfection in an imperfect and unperfectable world. They are about the second coming of paradise after the apocalypse.

Or, to come at his sculpture in another way, it is about pulling "horrific beauty"—the phrase he used to characterize *Hurricane*, 2001—from destructive energy. Like that work, many of his sculptures are constructions of geometrical dice that seem to have been thrown at random—unlike those in Malevich's aerodynamic suprematist works, which seem prearranged. Unexpectedly and luckily, McDonnell's works come out right, conveying a winning sense of "off perfection." This is as close as we can get to paradise—certainly to artistic paradise (what Charles Baudelaire called an "artificial paradise")—on earth. In both *Hurricane* and *The Second Gates of Paradise*, disruptive contrasts are resolved in a bizarre coherence, suggesting that destructive energy has been put to constructive purpose, resulting in a subliminal sense of perfection. A great lack in the world has been remedied by art. *Hurricane* is less massive and intimidating than *The Second Gates of*

Paradise—the void at the center of the former contrasts rather starkly with the density of the latter—but both are constructed of fragments that cohere only through the sheer force of the artistic will to perfection. To put this another way, if, as the philosopher Francis Bacon famously said, there is always something strange in the proportions of beauty, then in both of McDonnell's works the strangeness is just as conspicuous as the beauty.

The paradox of McDonnell's sculptures is that they seem to be falling apart and coming together simultaneously. This is true even of the minimalist *Solar Discs* of the early eighties: what look like rays of the sun are also fault lines. The luminous works have a tragic undertone, as the black lines incised in their surfaces suggest. Thus, signs of death appear even in the source of life. The tragic aspect of McDonnell's sculpture is dramatically explicit in the *Alba Rosa Fountain*—a red granite disk marked by parallel bands of white striations. It is an entropic form brought to artistic life, but it remains a three dimensional black hole—a flattened abyss in which there are spectral traces of light, no longer life-giving. Or, to put this another way, a perfect circle ironically marred by imperfect light. McDonnell's works may be autonomous—absolute art—but they are also fraught with unexpected emotional implications and disturbing power, sometimes impacted, as in the *Solar Discs*, sometimes all but explosive, as in *The Second Gates of Paradise* and *Hurricane*.

In his remarkable essay, *Notes on the Dissolution of Object-Representation in Modern Art*, the psychoanalyst Michael Balint observes that in modern art "objects are dismembered, split, cruelly twisted, deformed, messed about; the dirty, ugly qualities of the objects are 'realistically' and even 'surrealistically' revealed;… less and less regard is paid to the object's feelings, interests and sensitivities; kind consideration for, and 'idealisation' of, the object becomes less and less important."[1] For another psychoanalyst, George Frankl, such ruthless sadism is the inevitable consequence of the modern tendency to "regressive desublimation." It is an attack on "the cultural Superego, a demand

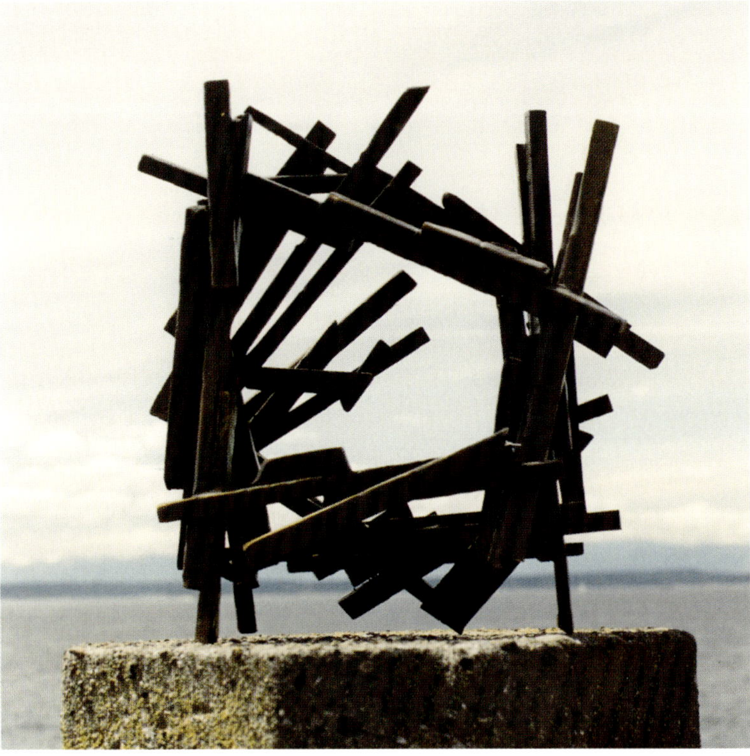

Hurricane

for a right to express any impulse previously considered taboo."[2] Indeed, it is an anarchistic attack on "sublimation itself, the foundation of culture." The nihilistic result is what the psychoanalyst Janine Chasseguet-Smirgel calls the "reconstitution of Chaos."[3] It is the immature universe of the "anal-sadistic phase" of development—the decadent "anal universe" in which all difference is obliterated, or at least not respected.

What I admire about McDonnell's sculpture is its maturity. It renews our sense of the sublime: each of his sculptures is an ideal object—even those that seem to be chaotically constituted. They make it clear that one can use the fragmentary, arbitrary forms—each an instance of what Chasseguet-Smirgel calls "indifferentiation"—that are the remainder of disintegrative desublimation to sublime effect. His sculpture shows that modern art may initiate chaos but it need not end there. The daring next step is to reconstitute wholeness—to show that chaos is the modern way to a more complicated sense of wholeness and harmony than existed in tradition: a wholeness that remains ideal—urgently harmonious—however flawed, and however tentative and improvised the wholeness may seem. McDonnell shows us the ideal in the process of aesthetic formation, as it were, so that it seems unresolved however resolved, unstable however ultimate. The ideal may seem more evoked than realized—is it ever?—in McDonnell's work, yet its presence is indisputable, as both aura and geometrical form.

McDonnell himself is aware of the ironic dialectic of chaos and ideality—entropy and transcendence—in his works. The "grooves and channels" found in each of his bronze *Stele* are flaws of imperfection in their monumental integrity—signs of disintegration like "those etched by [the] time and weather" the "inroads" are meant to evoke. But however marred by forces beyond their control, the stelai remain triumphantly upright, symbols of civilization holding its own against nature, implicitly forever. Clearly these works symbolize the strength of McDonnell's ego—his will to survive. He has in fact called his works "personal statements of my faith in man's profound determination to survive." Thus, the stele also symbolizes the cultural superego—resurrects it, as it were—with its will to social perfection and immortality, evident in its long, reflective memory. The stele, then, suggests the triumph of civilization over transient impulse, visible in the grooves and channels. Or rather their uneasy balance. McDonnell's stele is a subtle condensation of internal conflict and the conflict between man and nature. More dramatically, the "assemblages of large beams and disks" that form the series *Breaking Away* "express the cycle of deconstruction and rebuilding in life's constant evolution." That is, the conflict between death and life, destruction and creativity. Ironically, without the sense of breakage and slippage McDonnell's sculptures would lose their majesty and mastery.

I think it is because of his training in traditional object-representational art and his Catholic convictions—however latent they may have become—that McDonnell was able to resolve the destructive tensions evident in his late modernist sculptures. "Even in those formative years of high school in a Catholic seminary for the priesthood," McDonnell has written, "I knew my 'calling' was to be an artist. Had I known the life of [Fra] Filippo Lippi I might have continued in both." Clearly, he never lost his faith—even when his "subject matter was Freudian," as it was in his youth—suggesting that it continues to inform his art. It is a faith in the sublime and ideal, as I have suggested, of which God is the symbol. God is crystallized numinosity, which is one way one can understand McDonnell's idealistic sculpture.

McDonnell attended the University of Notre Dame, "the best Catholic college with an art department," as he said. He learned fresco painting from Jean Charlot, a well-known French/Mexican muralist. Charlot had worked on Diego Rivera's gigantic frescos in the Detroit Institute of Art. A respect for the gigantic—a sense of the instant impact large size could have—remains a constant of McDonnell's art. More crucially, he became aware of the "fascinating world of pre-Colombian art, especially sculpture. This latter hit me over the head like a baseball bat." It was clearly a revelation, indeed, a kind of conversion experience. It was in fact the discovery of a new religion— a religion much more primitive than Catholicism. More generally, McDonnell's religious feeling spontaneously transferred to "the primordial objects of life: the sun, the column, and the arch, created from the oldest sculptural materials, bronze and granite." They are all pure forms, geometrically self-contained yet expansive and "moving"— ideal examples of dynamic integrity. McDonnell wanted an art that dealt with the grand themes of existence, as Catholicism did, but in a much more fundamental way. He wanted to make art that would be as permanent, compact, expressive, and public as the pre-Colombian

art in the National Museum of Anthropology in Mexico City. It would embody the aspirations of the civilization in which it was made and convey the vitality of eternal truths.

McDonnell was determined to become a sculptor. At Notre Dame he was a student of, and eventually assistant to, Ivan Mestrovic, a major figurative sculptor who had worked with Rodin. The Yugoslavian Mestrovic taught at Notre Dame from 1955 through 1962 (the year of his death), producing major religious art. McDonnell must have seen Mestrovic's *Moses* in the Memorial Library at Notre Dame, and his *Madonna and Child* in front of Lewis Hall. The latter, like many of Michelangelo's sculptures, seems to have been carved from a stone block, while the former has a dramatic intensity worthy of Rodin as well as Michelangelo. Both are grand, emotionally profound works, at once monumental and intimate. They are also public sculptures dealing with universal themes—like McDonnell's sculptures. In a

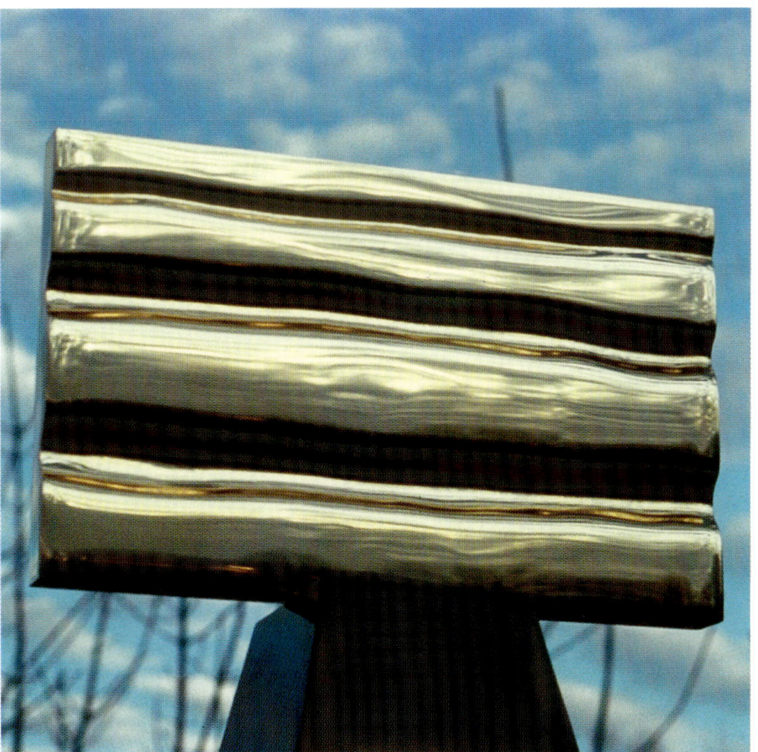

Cross River

sense, McDonnell's sculpture translates Mestrovic's intense public figures (he did many more, with political as well as religious import) into strictly formal terms. The abstract geometrical painter Joseph Albers, a former teacher at the Bauhaus, had offered McDonnell a scholarship at Yale, which he turned down. Nonetheless, he must have been aware of Albers's systematic study of the "interaction of colors" and modernist belief in "less is more," both of which found their way into McDonnell's sculpture. Indeed, Mestrovic's worship of the living, expressive body, vulnerable yet powerful, comes together with Albers's worship of geometry, emblematic of the eternal—the axiomatically true—in McDonnell's work. It is the tension generated by this reconciliation of opposites—the contingent, flexible body and absolute, fixed form—that gives McDonnell's sculptures their dramatic force. As he writes, "many of my sculptures suggest organic flux in the play of bending geometric shapes, provoking a sense of internal force or magnetic movement."

Mestrovic's elaboration of "motifs which have historical analogies in ancient Egyptian, Assyrian and Cretan civilizations,"[4] also clearly influenced McDonnell, as his interest in pre-Colombian sculpture indicates. The sense of rhythmic patterning, archetypal statement, and mythic import that informs the sculpture of ancient civilizations carries over into Mestrovic's figuration and McDonnell's formalism. They are both visually codified and materialized religion—like pre-Colombian art. It was also Mestrovic's idealization of art, along with his religious idealism, that put the finishing touch on McDonnell's conviction that art "should lift the mind and soul." "Art," Mestrovic said, "has always been part of what is finest in man and gone in step with his greatest aspirations in the idealistic and moralistic sense."[5]

Looking at McDonnell's works, one realizes that for all their drama and excitement they are carefully framed. Conflict is contained, which is as close to paradise as it is emotionally possible to come on earth. *Oracle II*, 2002 may be expressionistically agitated, but it is also insular, indeed, almost hermetically enclosed. A series of concentric circles, each impulsively "drawn" in space, it seems to curl in on itself and expand at once, as though uncertain of its power. Self-enclosure and

self-contradiction are evident in many of McDonnell's works, whether they deal with human relationships, as *Love Ain't Easy*, 2001 does—in effect two bodies locked in intercourse but at odds with each other—or are strictly formal, as in the *Cube* series of the seventies, a tour de force of cubes merging and diverging, that is, emerging from one another and collapsing into one another simultaneously. They are daring acrobatic performances, heroic yet risky constructions, precariously balanced on one angle and thus always in danger of tipping over. But some inner gyroscope keeps them steady. The variegated textures of McDonnell's cubes show his painterly sensitivity, adding to the energy of their movement.

Even the *Discs* are disjunctive and conjunctive at once, as *Horizontal Disc Fountain*, 1983, makes clear. Disk after disk—perhaps most dramatically in *Magma I*, 1981, and *Magma II*, 1999—is disrupted while remaining self-contained, suggesting its precarious state. Magma

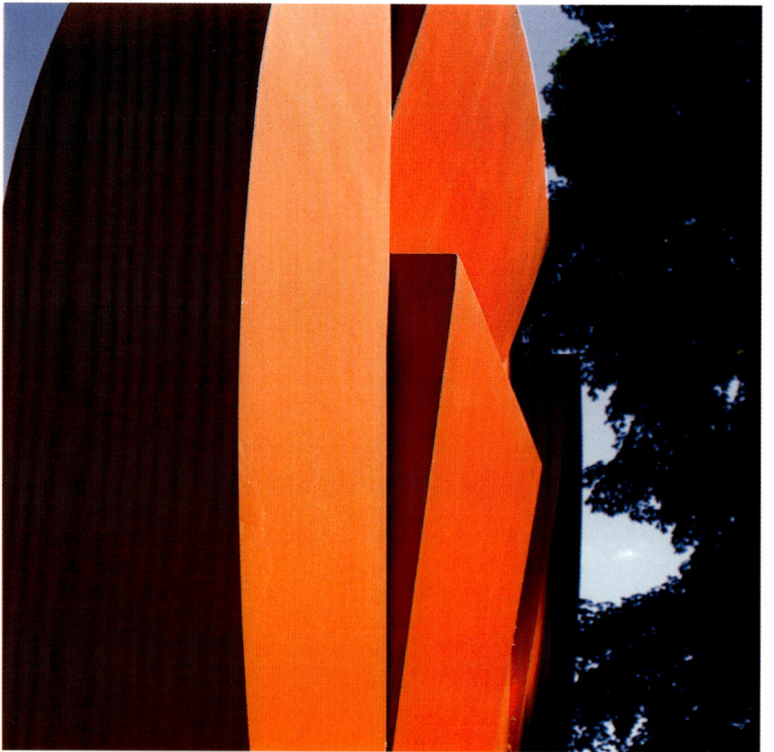

Magma I (detail)

is the material flow from a volcanic eruption, suggesting the impacted violence of McDonnell's works. It is as though the flaming red magma externalizes his inner fire, even as its containment in the circular disk suggests its sublimation into spiritual aspiration. Constructed of painted planes, the disks are in a perpetual process of assembling themselves, giving them an abstract expressionist intensity as well as suggesting their constructivist irony. *Spirit of Jazz*, 1998, seems particularly expressionist as well as constructivist, all the more so because the circular disk seems to be an incomplete reconstruction of fragments. The disk has had a bad fall, and has not been properly put together again, as the conspicuous fractures suggest. McDonnell's sculpture may seem as improvised as jazz, but it is also a broken whole. Even his *Solar Disc* is split down the middle—light is self-deconstructing. The tonalities of the sun's surface suggest dusk as well as dawn, confirming the disk's dynamic, "moody" character.

McDonnell's *Oracle* series and *Stele* series are overtly archaic as well as modernist. *Stele I*, 1980, seems like a modernized ancient hieroglyph—a three-dimensional inscription, inscrutable yet emotionally meaningful, and eloquently streamlined. The holes that appear in the smooth surfaces remind one of Henry Moore, but McDonnell's pierce planes rather than bodies, suggesting that they are more purely aesthetic, however symbolic they may also be. They not only enliven the plane but add to its mystery by incorporating the surrounding space into the work—a space already reflected in its mirror-like surface. Ambient space is particularly crucial for public sculpture, and McDonnell tries to include it in the work while establishing the work in a space of its own. His object is not only in space, but of space. Thus the *Cross River* pieces of the early eighties suggest the fluidity of space by letting it flow through the river's channels, even as the pieces stand alone in geometrical aloofness, unswayed by the currents of air and light that inform space. Many of McDonnell's works incorporate space in their movement, suggesting its inherent restlessness and inescapability, even as they resist its emptiness by standing firm in it. Strange as it may seem to say so, McDonnell's sculptures have a certain affinity with modernist buildings. They open to the outside while also being open inside.

McDonnell's *Breaking Away* sculptures—perhaps his most expressionistic (energetic) as well as cubist (autonomous) works—depend for their drama on the tension between so-called negative (immaterial) space and positive (material) space. The view through them into the infinite beyond them is crucial to their primordial import. Like the

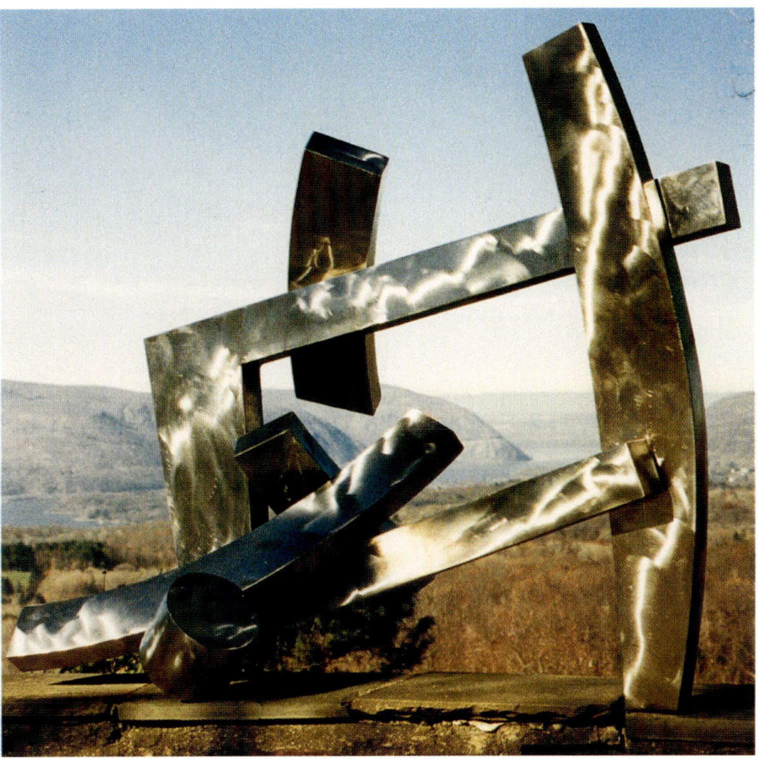

Muscoot

arches at Stonehenge, they are gateways to the sky—passages to a higher world, as it were. They frame the landscape and sky, as though inviting the gods into a temple. Indeed, they are free-standing entrances to a temple that exists only in the religious imagination. Nature is also part of their structure, however unstructured it may seem in comparison. But their form seems in flux, however grand their over-all design, so that they look like living landscapes as well as engineering feats.

Virtually all of McDonnell's *Breaking Away* sculptures are meant to be exhibited outdoors. Interaction with natural light is crucial to them.

As McDonnell says of *Breaking Away: White*, 1992, "on a 'soft' day, the shadows are just right. With bright sun it is black and white." In this work the "break away" is completely contained in a rectangular frame, however much individual geometrical elements project out of it. Like David Smith's early sculpture, the work is a kind of compromise formation: a three-dimensional sculpture and a two-dimensional picture in one. The frame turns the sculpture into an exciting picture, all the more so because of its relief-like flatness (whatever its density). This is true even when some of the geometrical elements project beyond the frame, as in the dark brown *Breaking Away* sculpture installed at 733 Third Avenue in New York City. The projecting plane is a grand gesture opening the work to the space beyond it without destroying the frame. Interior space and exterior space seamlessly merge in the *Breaking Away* sculptures. It is not only a modernist idea of harmony, but, emotionally, what Balint calls a "harmonious mix-up"—a dialectically successful integration of usually incommensurate individuals.

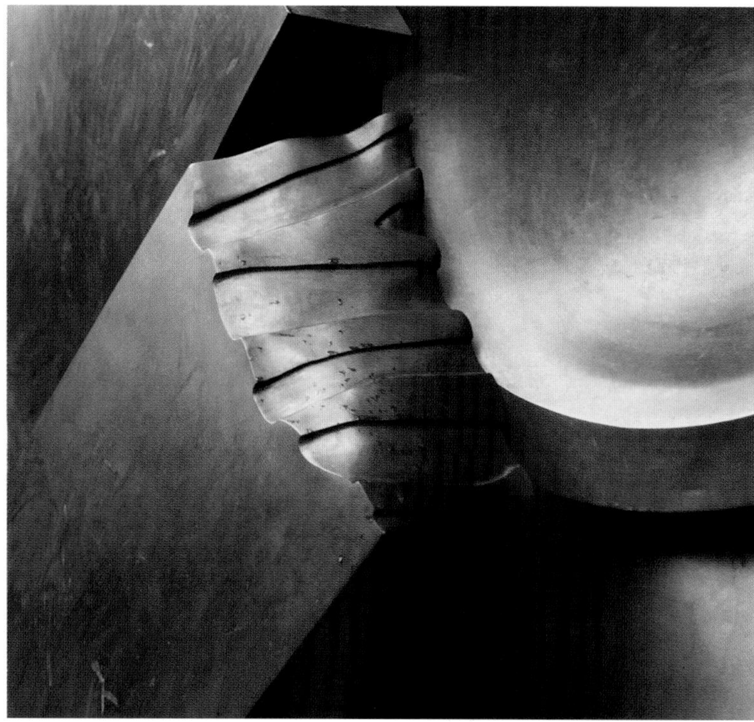

Breaking Away (detail)

McDonnell prefers to work with bronze and granite, as noted, but sometimes he uses wood, as in several *Breaking Away* works made of two-hundred-year-old chestnut beams. Thus the organic becomes the literal substance of the sculpture, adding to the sense that it is a living construction—a construction that has grown itself, as it were. The chestnut wood pieces are examples of another tendency in McDonnell's sculpture, already evident in *Hurricane*: instead of cluttering the center with geometrical elements, as though in *horror vacui*, it is left empty. This is not simply to let in nature—open the work to the surrounding space—nor is it a way of "idolizing" negative space by enclosing it in positive space, although it does do that. Rather, I would argue, it symbolizes what the art historian Hans Sedlmayr calls the loss of the center—the sense of durable human presence—evident in modern art. Even more, McDonnell's open-centered works are a kind of jerry-built monstrance waiting to exhibit the wafer that is the sign and substance of God. But God is absent and unknown—the ultimate mystery. I am suggesting, perhaps all too speculatively, that McDonnell's sculptures, particularly the *Breaking Away* pieces and *The Second Gates of Paradise*, acknowledge what mystics call the *deus abscunditas*, the hidden God—the God latent in all things and sometimes idiosyncratically manifest.

It is as though McDonnell expects God to appear in the empty center, a revelation framed by art, indeed, invited by art. The light that bathes the sculpture, adding emotional subtlety to its strong physical presence, anticipates revelation. As in primitive temples, the open center will fill with divine light at "the right time," confirming God's cosmic presence. The open center is a kind of invitation to the infinite to make itself felt in finite form. There is clearly something theatrical about McDonnell's *Breaking Away* sculptures, but it is sacred theater. They are proscenium arches suggesting that all the world is a stage for God. It is worth noting that Albers's *Homage to the Square* series, which McDonnell certainly knows, also has a monstrance-like character, suggesting its religious import. They are square disks, as it were, and thus related to McDonnell's disks, and, more broadly, his *Breaking Away* pieces, which are often square in form. They are also a kind of little theater, in contrast to McDonnell's big theater. Albers's concentric squares are imbued with light, suggesting that they are a kind of sun, like McDonnell's disks: a modern sun in contrast to the natural sun that Malevich's Suprematist square—from which Albers's square derives—triumphed over in his avant-garde *Victory Over the Sun* play. I am suggesting that, however unconsciously , McDonnell was deeply influenced by Albers.

The religious import of McDonnell's sculptures is all but explicit in his brilliant *The Second Gates of Paradise*, a private commission for a property in Medina, Washington. The first gates were made by Lorenzo Ghiberti for the Baptistery of the Cathedral of Florence, (1425-52). *The Second Gates*, more than a continent away in the new world, not only modernize the first gates—which, like Mestrovic's works, represent biblical figures—by reconceiving them in abstract terms, but suggest a second chance for salvation. They imply the possibility of spiritual rebirth: to go through the gates is to enter the temple of God and prepare to experience his living presence. Setting foot on sacred grounds, one shows one's faith. One is ready to be re-baptized. If the first baptism cleansed one of original sin, the second baptism will purge one's accumulated sins, readying one for death. Thus *The Second Gates of Paradise* are a metaphor for salvation, or at least express faith in its possibility. This faith is demonstrated more subtly by their peculiarly theodician character. As McDonnell says, they combine two *Breaking Away* sculptures. Their fragmentation is subsumed in a new wholeness. That is, their brokenness is made good, which is the argument of theodicy. Being the fundamental miracle, it is the ultimate justification for faith.

For McDonnell, the gates are a "running fence" made of stonelike shapes. This is no doubt appropriate to their rural context, certainly in contrast to the urban context of Ghiberti's gates. Unlike those gates, which admit the public at large, McDonnell's gates exist to protect privacy. But like Ghiberti's gates their point is spiritual not physical: suggesting that inert, earthbound matter can be transformed into sacred geometry and thus in effect lifted up—have a higher purpose, as it were. They show that art can perform miracles, and thus is divine.

Notes

[1] Michael Balint, *Notes on the Dissolution of Object-Representation in Modern Art*, Problems of Human Pleasure and Behaviour (London: Maresfield Library, 1987 [1957]), p. 123

[2] George Frankl, *Civilisation, Utopia and Tragedy* (London: Open Gate Press, 1992), p. 169

[3] Janine Chasseguet-Smirgel, *Perversion and Creativity* (London: Free Association Books, 1985), p. 10

[4] Lawrence Schmeckebier, *Ivan Mestrovic: Sculptor and Painter* (Syracuse: Syracuse University Press, 1959), p. 25

[5] Quoted in *Ivan Mestrovic: The Notre Dame Years* (South Bend, Indiana: University of Notre Dame, 1974; exhibition catalogue), p. 2

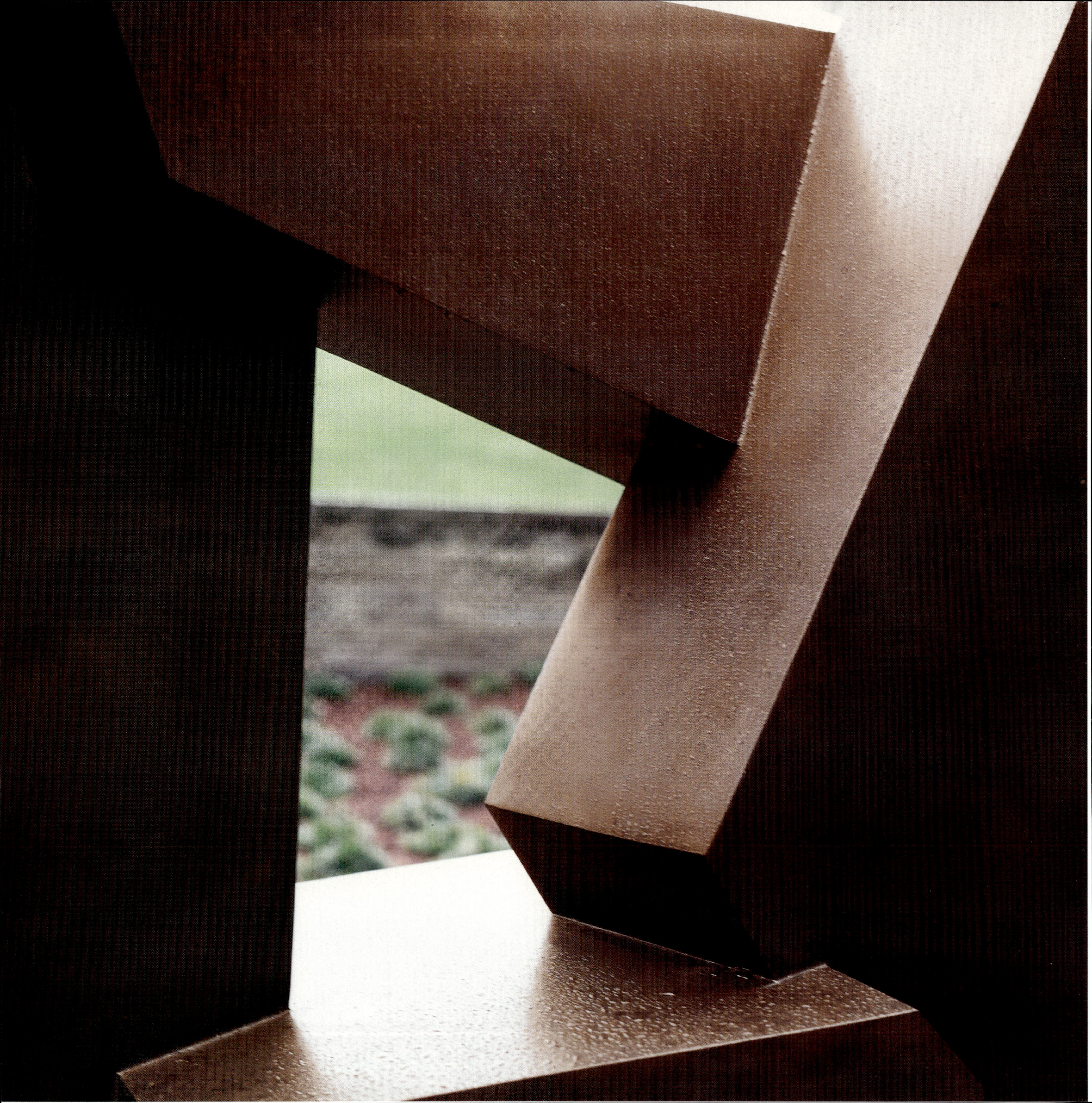

PHOTOGRAPHING JOSEPH McDONNELL'S SCULPTURE

David Finn

My adventures as a photographer began almost forty years ago when I discovered that I could express my love for sculpture by showing the different images I could uncover in outstanding works of sculpture. Recently, I found to my delight that my seventeen-year-old granddaughter, Rebecca "Becky" Binder, had a similar eye and love for three dimensional works of art. So when my friend, Joseph McDonnell, asked if I would take the photographs for a book on his work, I said I would be delighted to do so if Becky could be my co-photographer. Joe was delighted, as was Becky, and so we embarked on what proved to be a most delightful and rewarding adventure for all of us.

Becky and I loved the idea of approaching a sculpture with our cameras, each of us walking around, looking through our viewfinders on our own, and snapping away as we found intriguing views. We never bothered to separate the film we exposed, so when it was developed we never knew for sure who had taken which shots. Our camera eyes complemented each other, and working together gave us an opportunity to reveal different aspects of the sculptural forms and the environments in which the sculptures were located.

As we worked with Joe on this project, we found that there is something unusually friendly and open about both Joe personally and his works of art. Although he seems to be constantly exploring different forms and ideas, there is a consistency and continuity that is clearly his own. He is modest and unassuming about himself, and there is not an ounce of pretension in his sculpture. It is what it is — clear and honest statements about forms, spaces, materials, surfaces. When Joe describes how concepts come into his head for one or another sculpture, the process seems so simple, so direct, so straightforward, one can only admire the way his creative mind works.

The sculptures themselves are a delight to photograph. They are like landscapes with twists and turns and forms that both stimulate and surprise the searching eye. What may seem like straightforward geometric shapes turn out to have many secrets in the details. One has to look carefully to discover the variety of lines and surfaces and spaces he has created.

Joe is constantly experimenting and developing original ideas. Sometimes discarded remnants of old sculptures in his studio become the basis for something he has never done before, and an archetypal form evolves that is very different from his earlier work. This in turn can become the beginning of a new series in which each sculpture is a variation of the others. Different concepts are developed around a central theme and his work moves in the same direction until he feels he has exhausted all its possibilities.

Many of the sculptures that we photographed were commissions from collectors or developers. It is not hard to understand why those who see his work in one setting are moved to ask him to create another work for themselves. His sculpture seems to fit well into both urban and country landscapes. In the former, they echo the shapes of surrounding buildings, in the latter, they provide an accent for the fields in which they are placed and a striking image against nearby trees and bushes.

One of the first sculptures of Joe's we photographed was *Horizontal Disc*. It was on the lawn of a private home in New York, and we were fascinated with the way the different forms fitted into each other. Although it seemed simple at first glance, we found as we moved around the piece and looked at it through our camera lenses that there were constantly new discoveries to be made in the way the forms fitted into each other. It turned out to be a delightful visual adventure for Becky and me.

In a different location on the same property was one of Joe's polished stainless steel sculptures called *Breaking Away*. Fortunately the weather was fine when we were there, and we not only had a blue sky as background but the sun lit up the designs on the surface of the

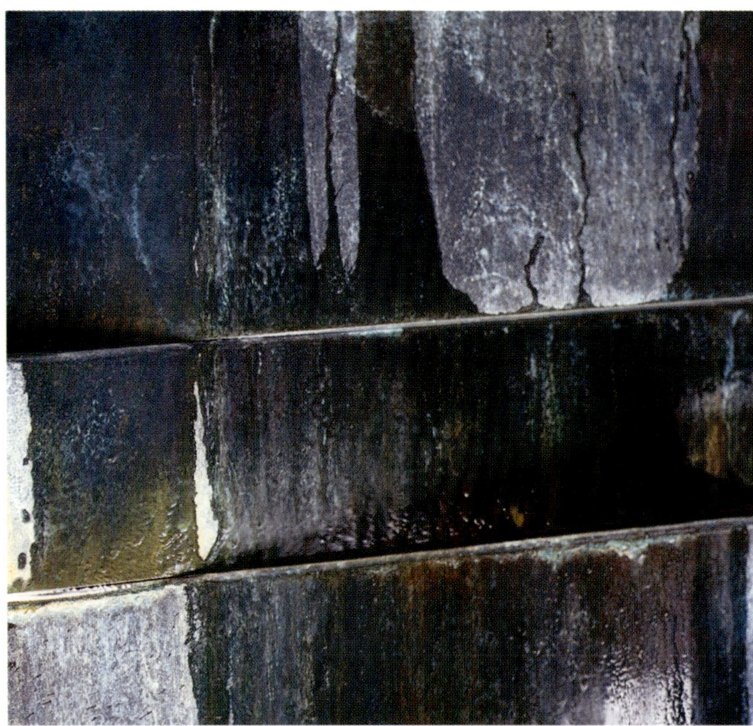

Horizontal Disc Fountain (detail)

metal. Joe had created spaces between and around the forms, and there we discovered many intricate compositions with our cameras. The sunlit designs on the surfaces of the sculpture were like paintings and we were inspired to photograph them as works of art in themselves.

A similar sculpture, called *Muscoot*, was in an open field where again we could walk around with our cameras and discover a wide variety of intriguing views. Here, too, the brilliant lines on the surface created lovely compositions, and seeing them through our lenses against the trees and sky, with the sun lighting the different shapes and forms, proved to be an exciting adventure.

In other sites we photographed Joe's large round objects. Some were solid, like the *Magma* sculptures, which we photographed in Connecticut and Seattle. There were well-composed elements within the circles, creating different abstract shapes with variations on the sides and the ends of each work. An especially inventive version of these works, called *Horizontal Disc Fountain*, was created as a fountain with water flowing down the sides of the forms and creating its own pattern against the bronze. Others, in a series called *Etruria*, were circular forms with open spaces in the middle and intriguing breaks on each side. Still another variation was *Locking Piece,* which was a square form with round corners and a space in the middle mirroring the outer form, enriching the work with a variety of breaks on all sides.

In early works that we photographed, *Pan* and *The Bather*, we could see the beginning of Joe's abstractions in their naturalistic images. Arms and legs and bodies were shaped in ways that created well-composed forms. The subjects seemed less important than the opportunity to shape spaces in the special way that became Joe's hallmark.

In White Plains, New York there was an intriguing departure from Joe's circles called *Stele XII*. A monumental steel form rose from a pyramid-like base, curved on bottom and flat on top. Within the form were three carefully placed round openings through which one could look at the sky, and on the surface of one side there was another circle marked with lines and squares within the image. Other sets of lines appeared on the surface—three of them horizontal and one at an angle. On top of the figure there was a curve at the edge as if

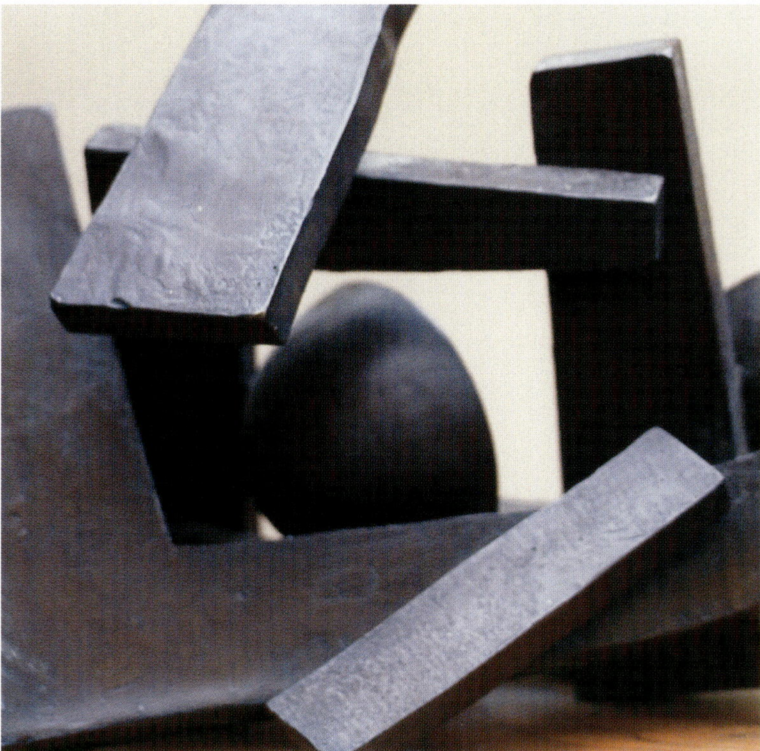

The Source (detail)

the number of impressive photographs that can be taken of its forms, and on that basis the gates deserved very high marks. Becky and I took roll after roll of film of this extraordinary sculpture and had a hard time deciding when to stop. There seemed to be an endless number of images we could discover. The gates are, in fact, the entranceway of a lovely home on the waterfront, which the owners open when they are leaving or entering their driveway by the press of a button. Besides being convenient ways to protect their privacy, they are superb sculptures, and it was thrilling for us to have had the opportunity to photograph them. We took so many photographs that we felt a book could be published just on that one sculpture!

When an exhibition of Joe's sculpture opened at a gallery in Scarsdale, it gave Becky and me an opportunity to photograph a number of his smaller pieces. We found them as impressive as his larger works, and delightful to look at from many different angles. There were also painted works that were visually stimulating in the way they related to the sculptural forms.

When we were finished, we felt that we had had a great adventure together exploring fine works of art. We were grateful that the images we produced revealed the qualities of Joe's sculptures and are pleased to see our photographs published together in this book on his work.

another circle was about to be created. We photographed it in the late afternoon when the light was beginning to fade, but the striking details were still visible.

One of Joe's monumental works, *Breaking Away*, was on the campus of the University of Washington. Here we had to cope with pouring rain, and although we got soaked it didn't affect our enthusiasm for the many different forms we discovered in the sculpture. Rectangles, circles, curves, angles, see-through spaces; unusual surfaces, frames, patterns—we kept finding more and more intriguing elements to photograph. We took many rolls of film to capture as many details as we could, and when we were finished we felt we had thoroughly explored one of Joe's most impressive works.

Of all the works we photographed, the one that we found most overwhelming was *The Second Gates of Paradise*. I have often thought that one measure of the impact of a monumental work of sculpture is

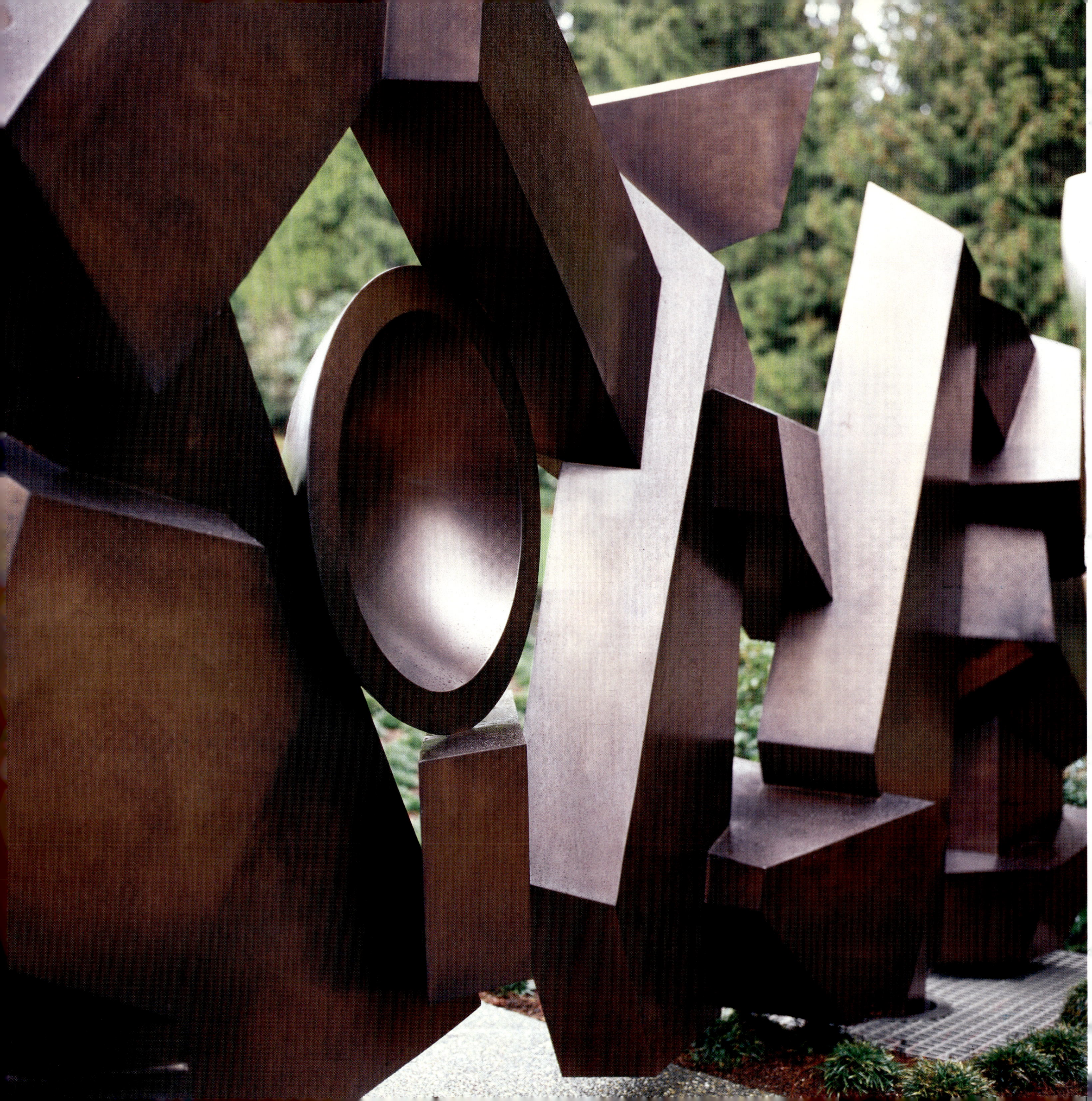

A LIFE IN ART

Joseph McDonnell

From my earliest recollection, even in those formative years of high school in a Catholic seminary for the priesthood, I knew my "calling" was to be an artist. Had I known the life of Fra Filippo Lippi I might have continued in both. All my spare time, and much of my school time, focused on drawing and making things. Looking back I sense a Freudian element to the subject matter—naked ladies in canoes, bucking horses, and contact sports.

A chance visit to the sculptor Marshall Frederick's studio outside Detroit profoundly affected my youth. Frederick had modeled a heroic eagle in clay, in high relief, for the facade of the Veterans' Memorial Building. The specter of a small model enlarged to monumental proportions blew my mind. Little did I dream that I would some day make nine large bronze eagles (measuring up to twenty-five feet) for the John Wanamaker stores in the Philadelphia area.

I decided to attend the University Notre Dame for the study of art because of its reputation as the best Catholic college with an art department. Fortunately, one of my first courses was fresco painting with the noted French/Mexican muralist Jean Charlot. Previously, he taught the technique to Diego Rivera, Orozco, and Siqueros. Rivera's work was very familiar to me because of his gigantic frescos in the Detroit Institute of Art. A trip to Mexico to see the murals first-hand opened my eyes not only to their aesthetic but also to the fascinating world of pre-Colombian art, especially sculpture. This latter hit me

over the head like a baseball bat. An onyx monkey jar, a standing Aztec figure with folded arms, and, of course, the Mayan Choc-mols (which were my favorites) at the National Museum of Anthropology, were overwhelming.

At that point I decided that I had to sculpt. Back at University, through the intersession of the president, Reverend Theodore Hesberg, I became a student of Ivan Mestrovic. A world-renowned figurative sculptor from Yugoslavia, Mestrovic had worked with Rodin. There were only four students in his course, and eventually I had the good fortune to become his assistant. I studied under him for three years, earning my BFA ('58) and MFA ('59) degrees.

While under Mestrovic's tutelage not only did I learn the basics of figure modeling and wood and stone carving, but I also became proficient in the building of armatures and plaster casting. I built and cast into plaster for him figures up to eighteen feet in height. Perhaps the most important thing that I took away from those years was the courage of his example to take on large sculptural projects. While working somewhat in his style I was, nonetheless, inclined to make my work more cubistic. The work of Jacques Lipchitz, Ferdinand Leger and Georges Braque seemed to be pulling me.

For graduate school I turned down a scholarship offered to me by Joseph Albers at Yale. Making the leap to total abstraction seemed more than I was willing to undertake at the time. Albers paid me a

Opposite page: The Second Gates of Paradise (detail)

backhanded compliment by saying that my work "had a lot of poetry and that he took poetry out of art." Actually, I believe he was putting me on. Thinking back I realize that my contemporaries at Yale would have been Nancy Graves, Richard Serra, Chuck Close, Claus Oldenburg, and many more of today's established contemporary artists.

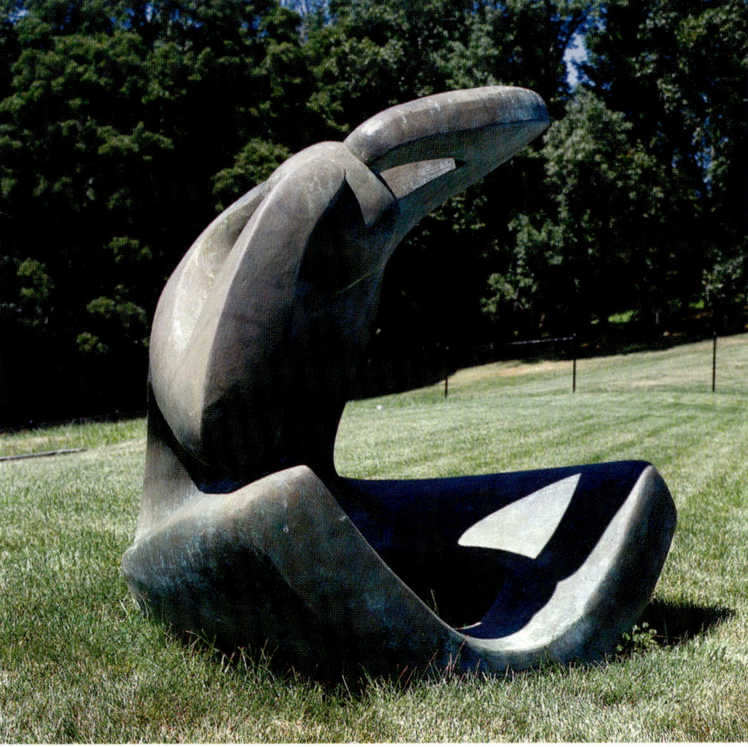

The Bather

On the other hand, my hope for a scholarship to Italy was not fulfilled. Subsequently, and much influenced by the romantic novel *The Charterhouse of Parma*, I took money from war bonds that my parents had saved for me ($2,500) and purchased the least expensive berth aboard the SS United States ($127) and sailed off to Europe. Landing in Southampton, I spent several weeks sightseeing before arriving in Florence.

Italy was the most wonderful place to be in the fall of 1959. A fantastic late summer had made everything warm and golden. For wines it was the best vintage of the century and I felt it would be great for me, too. Domenico Modugno was singing "Volare," one could stay in a pensione for a couple of dollars a day, food and wine were cheap and the daily cost of labor a little over a dollar.

I enrolled in the Accademia di Belle Arti. My instructor, a sweet gentle man, Antonio Berti, checked the class about once a week. Usually the class worked on figure studies. Our model was a chubby sixteen year old who would stand so close to the wood-burning stove that her sides would turn bright red. Another model was an old horse (a la Marini), which we would occasionally ride around the halls. This seemed appropriate as the Accademia had once been the Medici stables. On Wednesdays we would go to the hospital at Correggi for anatomy lessons from corpses.

The biggest lesson I learned at the Accademia was to break away from a rather tight approach to sculpture. I began modeling with plaster and carving directly into stone and wood. These materials appealed to me more than clay. Often I would first create in clay, cast the piece into plaster, and finish it by carving, filing, and sanding.

During these years I maintained a modest studio near Piazza Donatello, in which I created small works for casting into bronze. Around the corner was a stone-carving studio where I improved my skills in that medium. Most of these early efforts were very imaginative and fantastic. I experimented with many forms and approaches, never feeling that any was an end in itself. These early works were displayed and sold by galleries in Florence, Rome, Milan, Venice, and Spoleto. I also sold pieces from my studio— especially to the many Americans and British who came through Florence. Within a few years I was actually able to sustain myself. My wife (we had met on my first day as a student at the Accademia!) and I rented a small villa, drove a Volkswagen Beetle, and even hired a young farm girl, Angelina, as a housekeeper. My sculptures had a strange otherworldliness that, looking back on them, makes me realize just how special those years were. I was groping to find my own personal statement and "style." I would take one idea, develop it, and then move on. While in Florence, I often visited the Archeological Museum, with its collection of Etruscan bronzes and sarcophagi. These pieces were of special interest to me—the elongation of the bronzes and the compactness and sense of well-being of the sarcophagi greatly appealed to my aesthetic.

My sojourn in Italy was a wonderful existence that lasted approximately five years. It ended because I felt I had to become involved in a more current art scene, and I realized that there would be greater opportunities if I returned to the U.S.

I sold several works in New York, and felt very positive about the city, however, when it came to deciding to move back to the States I chose to move back to my roots in the Midwest. We first moved to Detroit, not only because it was my hometown but also because Bruno Bearzzi, consultant to the Uffizi Gallery in Florence, was advising a local industrial foundry about the techniques of fine art casting. I situated my studio in this foundry so that the architects and real estate developers that came to the foundry would see my work. As a result, I received a commission to do a large suspended bronze piece for a Detroit bank and a number of pieces for some new shopping malls. A fountain I had done in Milwaukee led to another commission there, and smaller works were sold directly from my house or, in a few cases, through local galleries.

Throughout, my work became more and more abstract. I discovered one could take heavy plates of bronze or brass and cut them into interesting forms; actually bend or roll them, and polish them. Material became very important to me. I was fortunate to receive commissions for large-scale works from shopping center developer Alfred Taubman, and also from the JL Hudson Company and the First Federal Savings Bank of Michigan. However, in time the Detroit foundry arrangement did not work out. The prices became too high and the quality was not to my liking. So for the small pieces I joined forces with another sculptor who decided to start his own foundry. We built a basic lost wax ceramic shell operation in a small industrial garage. I produced many pieces under twelve inches, which sold rather well. That small foundry has since grown into one of the major art foundries in the country, Mengel Foundry, now located in Atlanta.

For the larger work and commissions I decided, like many other Americans, to work in Italy. While in Florence I heard about Pietrasanta, a small town about an hour due west, where the techniques involved in the making of sculpture thrived for centuries. Michelangelo secured his marble from the nearby quarries and such sculpture luminaries as Jacques Lipchitz, Henry Moore, Isamu Noguchi and Marino Marini spent time there. I arranged to have a studio and plaster caster available for what soon became my regular visits. I would devote about half the year in staggered forays, usually casting works in bronze but occasionally carving a work in marble.

Despite these successes, I still had many difficulties to face. Three of our four children were born severely handicapped, and my wife disliked the idea of living in a big city. We made a decision to move to the country, and by chance found a wonderful, large coach house on several acres in Bedford, New York, about forty mines north of Manhattan.

My approach to sculpture was also changing again. I felt myself more and more influenced by constructivism as it had been developed in the fabricated works of David Smith, Alexander Calder, Anthony Caro, Richard Lippold, Tony Smith, and Mark DiSuvero. Soon I was working in this vocabulary, using fabricating shops in Brooklyn and Detroit and moving away from cast work. Instead of making a model in clay, then into plaster and having it cast at a foundry, I conveyed a small maquette often made of balsa wood to an industrial fabricating plant to have it executed at full scale in sheet or plate metal.

For a while this approach seemed to be a success. However, after a few pieces executed in this manner, I began to feel that I was losing control of the final work. Changes demanded a different approach from that of the model. I also discovered that while fabricating was less expensive than bronze casting it could still be quite costly. Only if I had control of the execution and supplied my own labor would I be satisfied. So I decided to fabricate my own pieces even though my knowledge of such metal work was still peripheral. I rented an industrial garage space, and hired a welder/metal worker. Our first commission was an enormous eagle in deep relief to be fabricated in bronze over a stainless steel armature. It measured twenty-five feet in width and fifteen feet in height. The client was the John Wanamaker store in Philadelphia and eventually eight other eagles were commissioned for their various new stores.

We had tremendous technical problems with this first fabricated sculpture, beginning with the fact that my welder had never worked in bronze! Nor did I own the necessary equipment to cut and finish bronze. Nonetheless, we worked our way through this piece and I received the best learning experience of my life. It took six months and, of course, there was no profit. After that, however, work started coming in, and my need for extra help increased to the point where I often had five, six, even seven workers, usually art students, with me. These commissions consumed my time. A few of these fabricated works were motorized while others were suspended so as to move freely. Looking back it all seems rather adventurous.

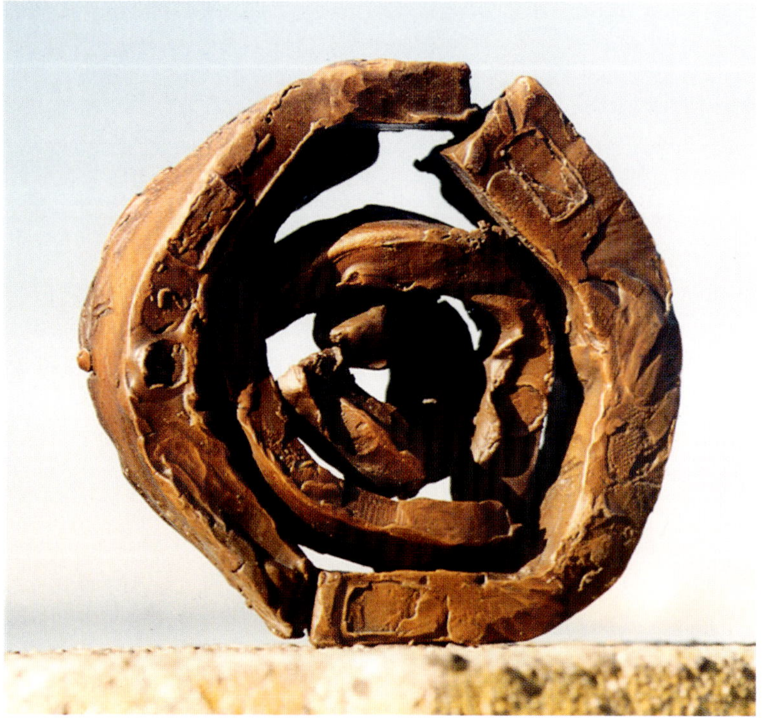

Oracle

With the seventies coming to a close, a real recession set in. High interest rates prohibited building and there was the oil crisis. In addition, my Swedish welder/fabricator decided to retire. I took courses at night to improve my knowledge of the various methods of welding and metal work. I also decided to build a studio on my property in Bedford, and give up my rented industrial garage shop. In six years at that location I produced more than forty large-scale sculptures for public spaces as well as many smaller works.

One of my close friends, and a former neighbor in Bedford, was Harry Parker, director of the Dallas Museum of Fine Art. Another friend, Don Vogel, owned a well-established gallery in Dallas. Since Texas was booming at the time, it seemed well worth the plane fare to visit them. Once in Dallas, Don put me in touch with Trammell Crow himself, the owner of the company that bears his name. At the time it was perhaps the largest development company in the United States. I was privileged to receive a commission to do ten large sculptures for his buildings. With these new sculptures my work turned a corner. My forms became stronger and more simplified, elegant and with certain overtones of ancient cultures. The studio I built on my country property in Bedford was equipped with the latest welding equipment. My assistants were able young artisans. Art consultants and dealers began calling. As with Noguchi, I began to work in several directions at once, one of which was developing kite forms and suspended, moveable works. Another was wall reliefs. Jack Welch, CEO of General Electric, acquired six pieces for the GE headquarters in Fairfield, Connecticut. Life was looking up.

However, at about this time my marriage came apart. The children were all away in special schools. The act of selling my house and studio in Bedford proved devastating. Eventually I resettled in the little Hudson River town of Cold Spring, situated across from West Point. I purchased a small 1840s house with a lovely garden and then an old factory building to use as my studio. Several New York galleries began handling my work. There was a steady flow of commissions from dealers and art consultants. I found myself taking one idea and evolving many variations of it such as the *Locking Piece* series and the *Solar Discs*. Scale seemed more and more important. Some work just looked better large.

About two years before moving to Cold Spring the Irish virus caught up with me, and I stopped drinking. At about the same time, I began exploring a design for a sculpture that was inspired by a piece of jewelry. Basically, it resembled a picture frame, still together but rather broken apart. From it and through it forms and pieces were cascading. I called the piece *Breaking Away*, as it so reflected what was going on in my life. I gave the first interpretation of this theme, a small bas-relief, to the Century Association in New York as my artist's gift to its collection. Subsequently a real estate developer, David Durst, saw this small maquette and commissioned an eleven foot bronze version for the lobby of one of his Manhattan office towers. There were other versions of *Breaking Away* to follow. These became freestanding pieces. Some versions began with found bronze cut-offs, others from recycled works. Recently I was commissioned by the University of Washington to create an eleven by fifteen foot version for the campus. All told I have created about a dozen versions on the "Breaking Away" theme. In fact, a recent and probably my grandest sculpture, a twenty-five foot gate for the Jon and Mary Shirley residence in Medina, Washington, consists basically of two *Breaking Away* designs that swing open. However, I call them *The Second Gates of Paradise,* after Ghiberti's Baptistery doors in Florence.

Another theme I have used extensively is the *Locking Piece*. This series was seeded by the recollection of an Etruscan bracelet seen in the Archeological Museum of Florence. My original concept consisted of an oval formed by two sets of arcs cut in half. Another cut created a link to lock the two arcs. All the pieces were arranged slightly askew. The largest of the series is ten feet tall and is located in front of the state office building in Trenton, New Jersey.

The *Stele* and *Solar Disc* series evolved at the time I made contact with the Trammell Crow family. They commissioned the first of each of these series for their building projects in Texas. The pieces have a definite '80s look about them. *Stele I* is a twenty-foot tall flat plinth with striations and piercings. It stands outside Waterway Tower, a building in the Los Colinas development. *Solar Disc I*, a six-foot disc, resides in the lobby of the Trammell Crow headquarters. Both these series have a very basic, clean, contemporary, geometric look with surfaces etched or gouged in a primeval manner.

In 1984, shortly after my move to Cold Spring, I was introduced to a young lady from Manhattan, Maryann Jordan, who was assistant to the director of the New York Public Library. We dated for several years and were married in nearby Garrison, New York. With her apartment in the city and my home and studio in the country we had a very good arrangement. Then, six years ago, she was offered the position of deputy director of the Seattle Art Museum. We both thought this would be an exciting opportunity to move into a new,

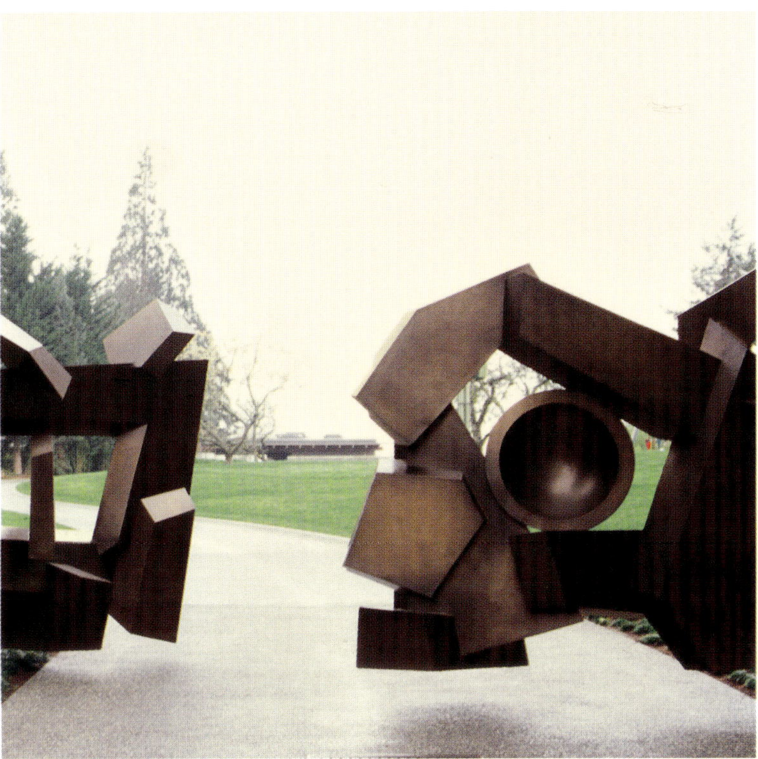

The Second Gates of Paradise (detail)

expanding location. Many things were happening in Seattle. In addition, it seemed a better environment in which to raise our then two-year-old daughter, Sophia. Maryann fit into her job and surroundings like a hand into a glove. I, on the contrary, felt quite lost. I liked to say it was as if I was in an FBI witness protection program. During those first years most of my time was spent returning to New York to deal with various clients and galleries.

Then the situation changed, and I received several major commissions in Seattle and began exhibiting with local galleries. This is where I am today. Constantly experimenting, changing, growing, and thoroughly enjoying this latest chapter in my artistic life.

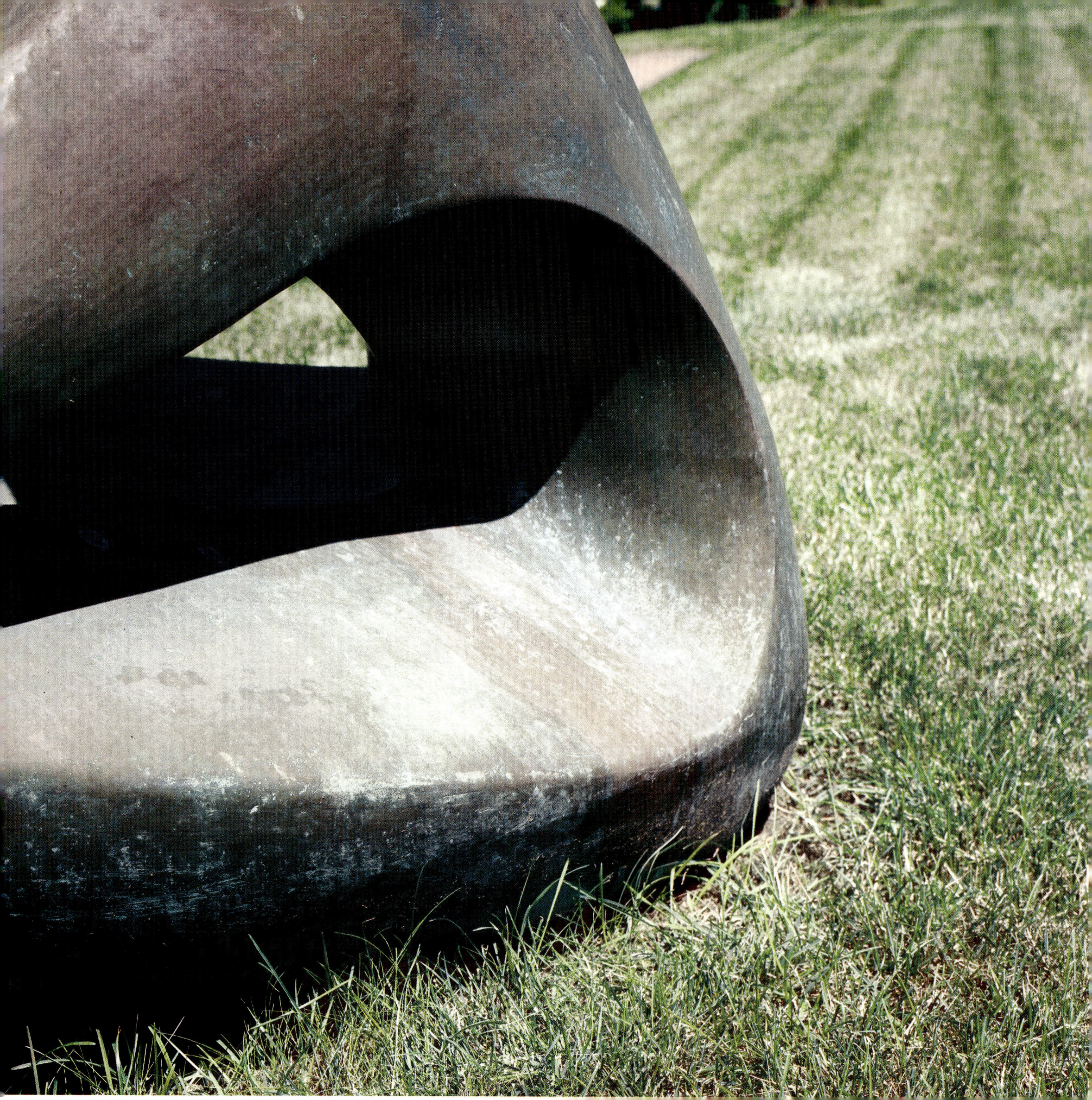

EARLY FIGURATIVE

My early figurative work was an attempt to move away from Ivan Mestrovic's style. However, his influence can still be seen in my early wood carvings, like the large *Madonna* and *Orpheus*.

At the Accademia in Florence, I felt the influence of Marino Marini, which was still strong years after he stopped teaching there. His technique of battering the clay and slicing it with saws and knives proved very liberating to me in developing new forms while retaining the strengths and intense feeling of Mestrovic's work.

The small *Meditation* had as its inspiration the famous monkey jar from the Archeological Museum in Mexico City. Subsequently, I closed the form somewhat to make the marble *Contemplation* and even more so in the bronze *Condemned*. *Pan* developed from opening the closed form.

Done at the same time, *Acrobat* became a more cubistic rendering of the figure, while *Woman in the Wind* showed elements of deconstruction.

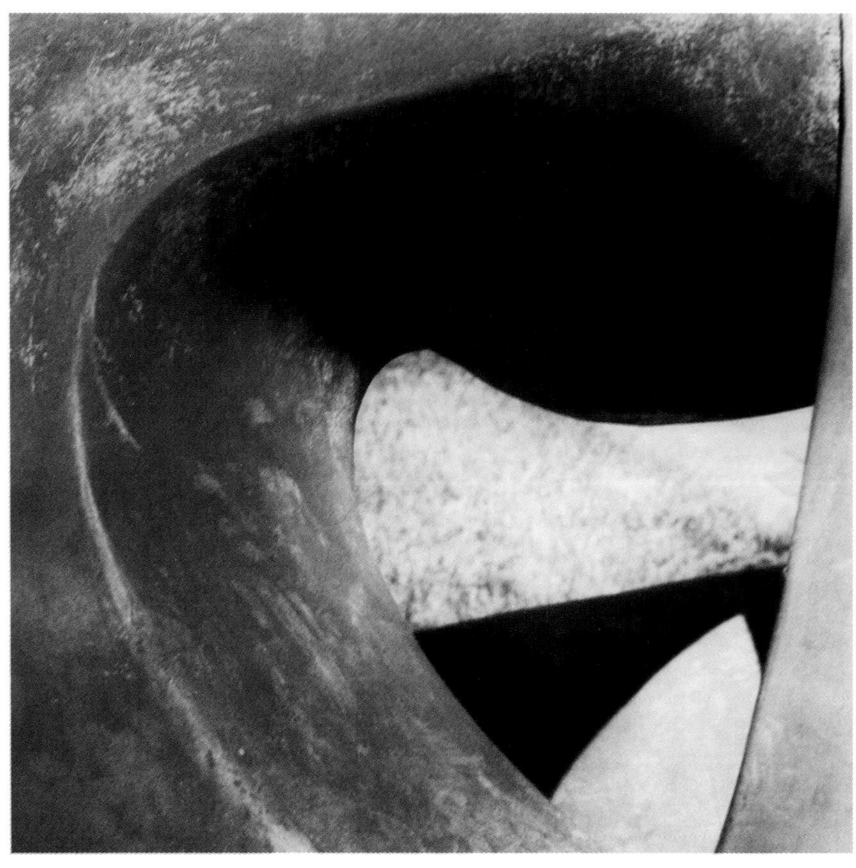

THE BATHER

1967, enlarged 1991
Bronze
50" x 48" x 42"
Collection of Judy and Anthony Evnin, Greenwich, CT

I originally did the small version of this in 1967 while I was still living in Detroit. The concept was to build a figure around a nonexistent sphere. I found that the negative spaces were so interesting that I concentrated on developing the triangular openings between the arms and legs and the body. The few details, the face and the toes, were understated to emphasize the overall design. It was done in plaster, which I polished so that it was smooth and had an almost machine-like finish. It has been enlarged several times. This is the biggest.

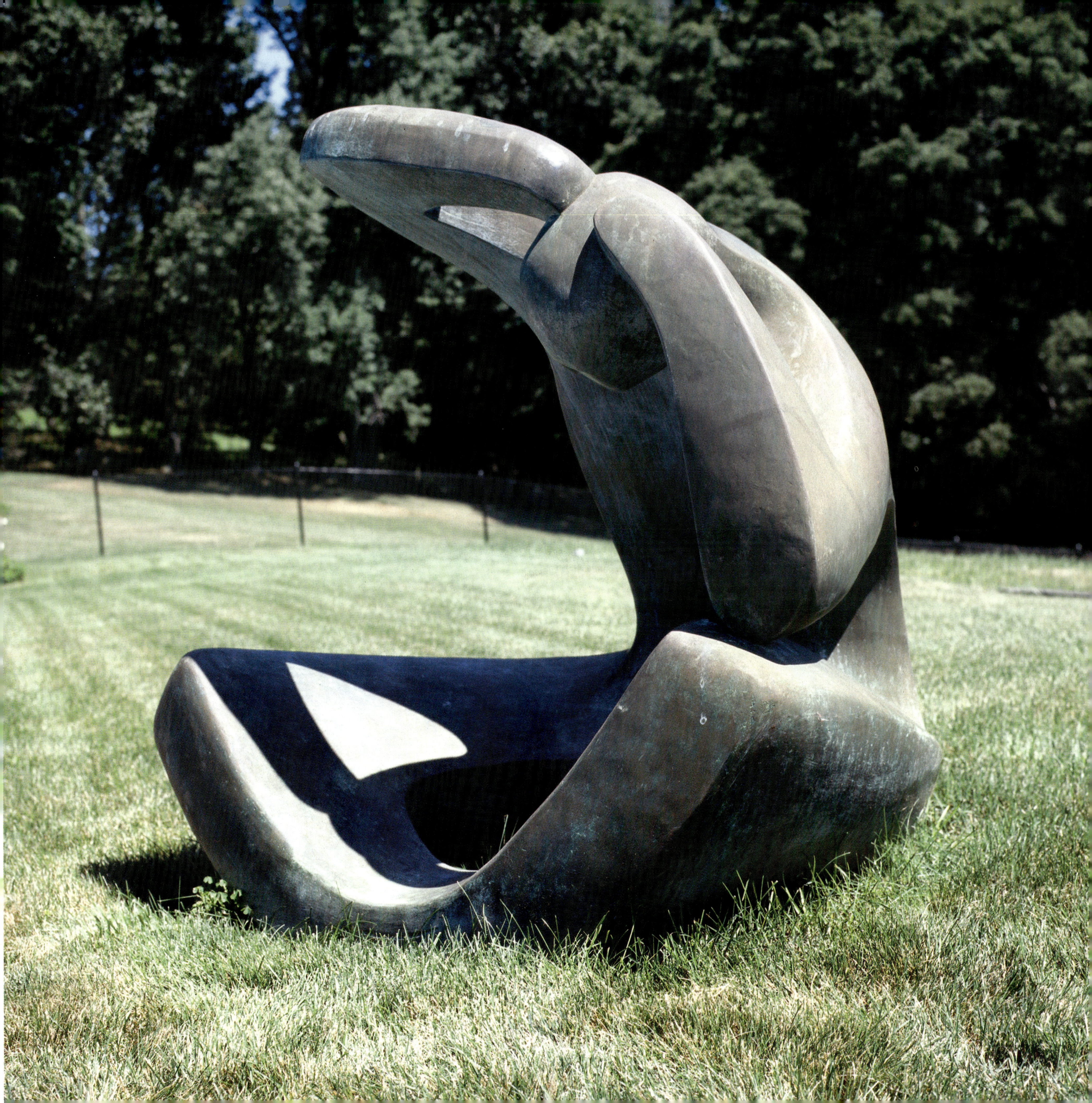

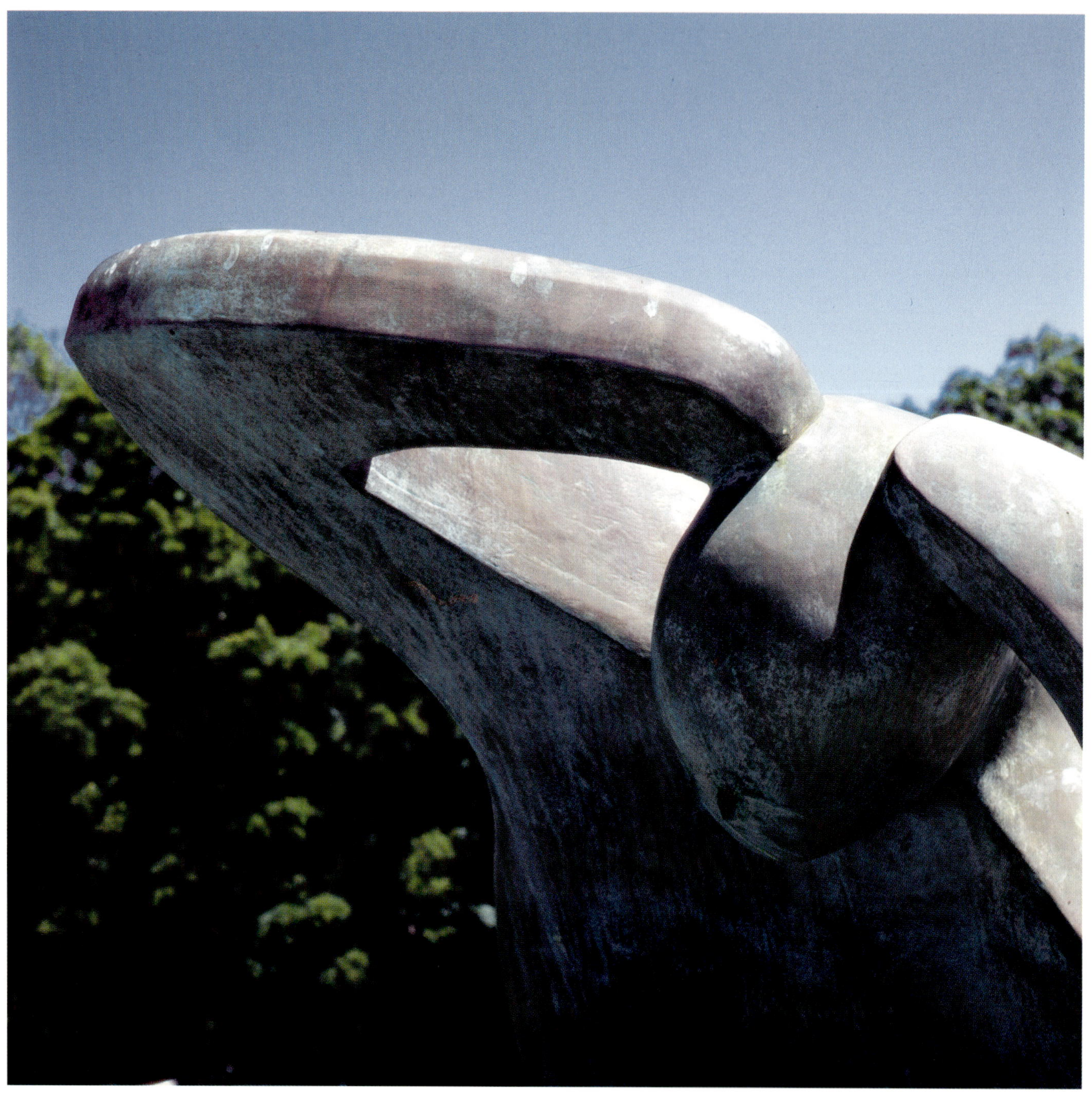

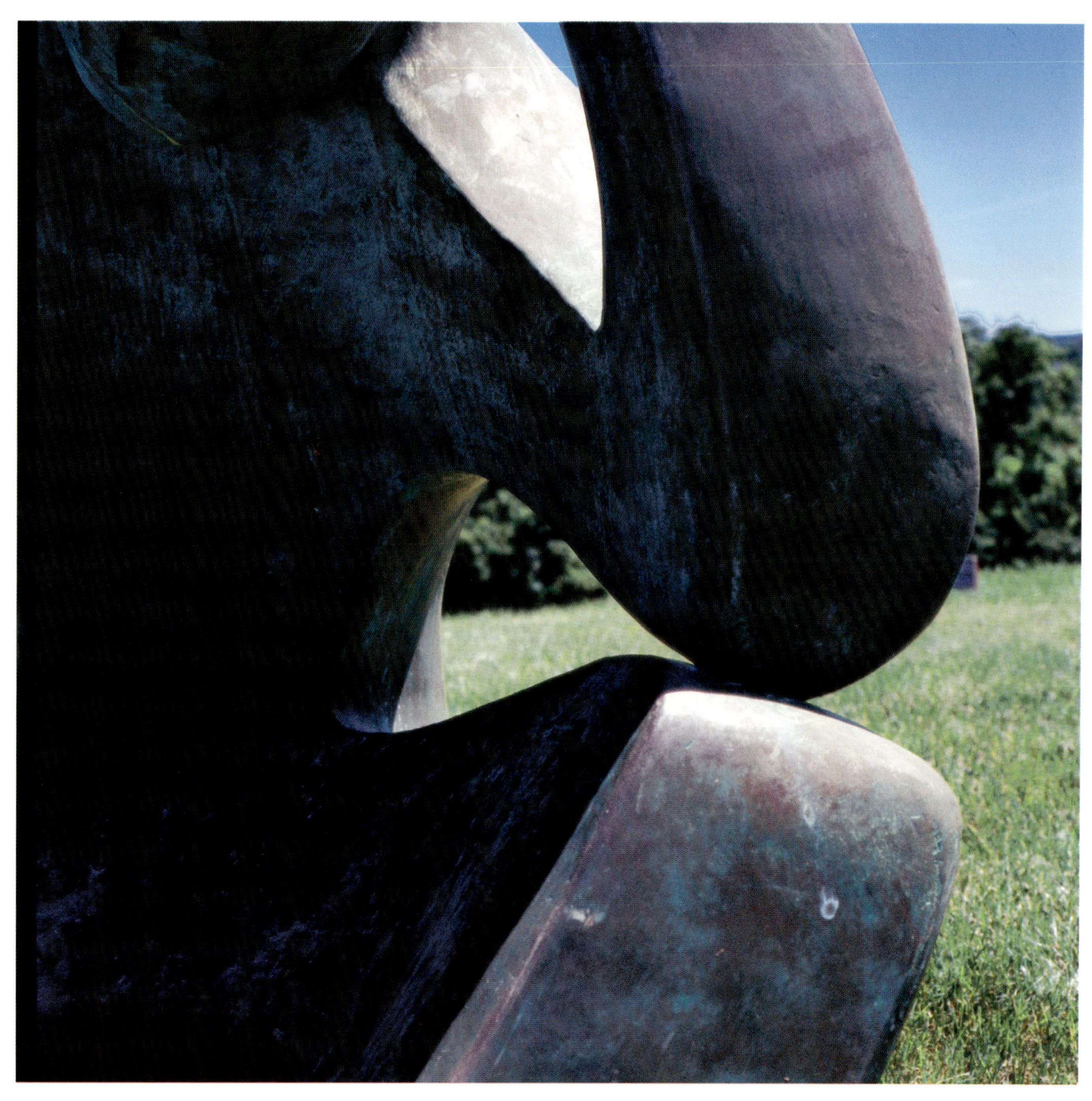

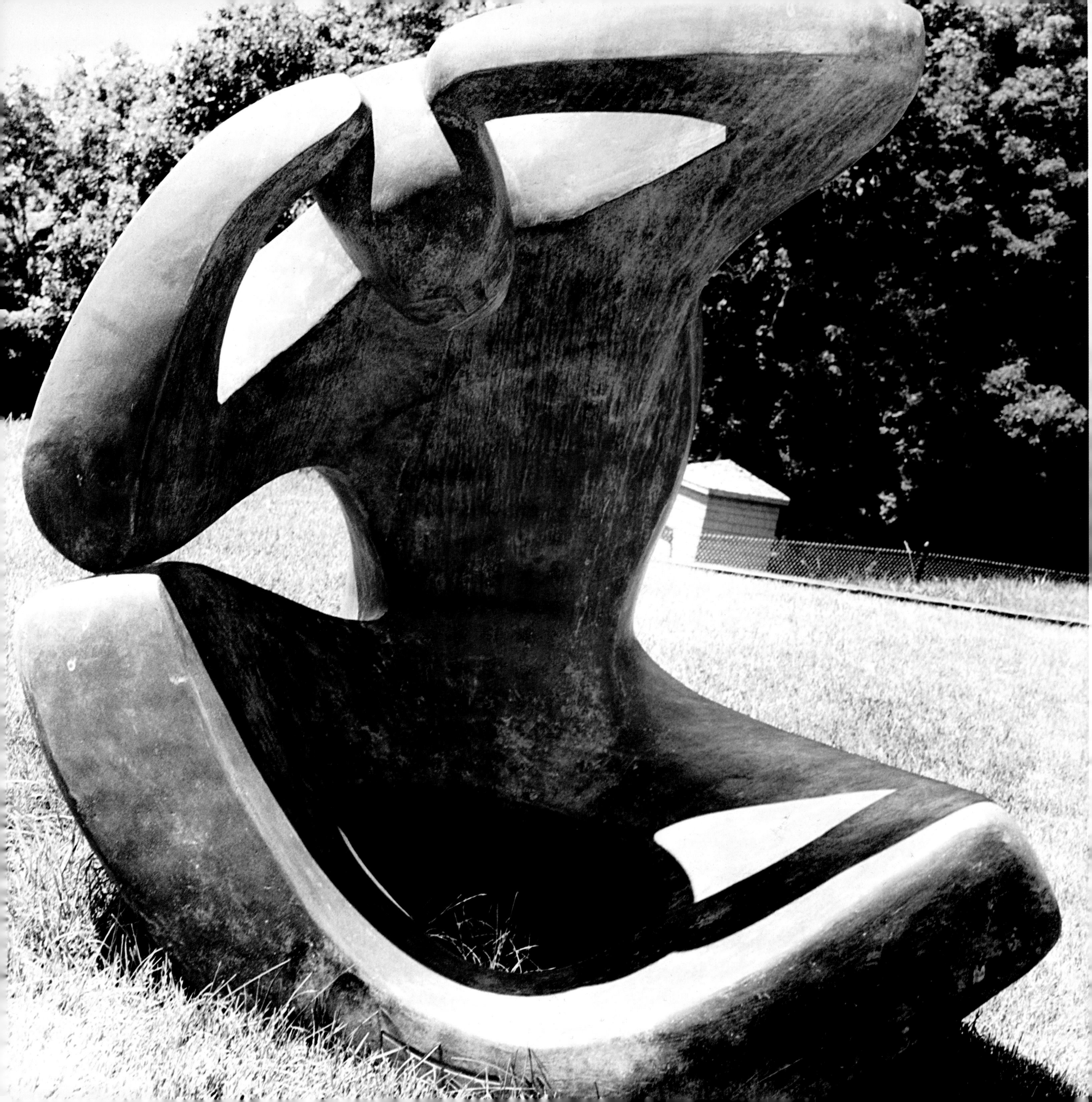

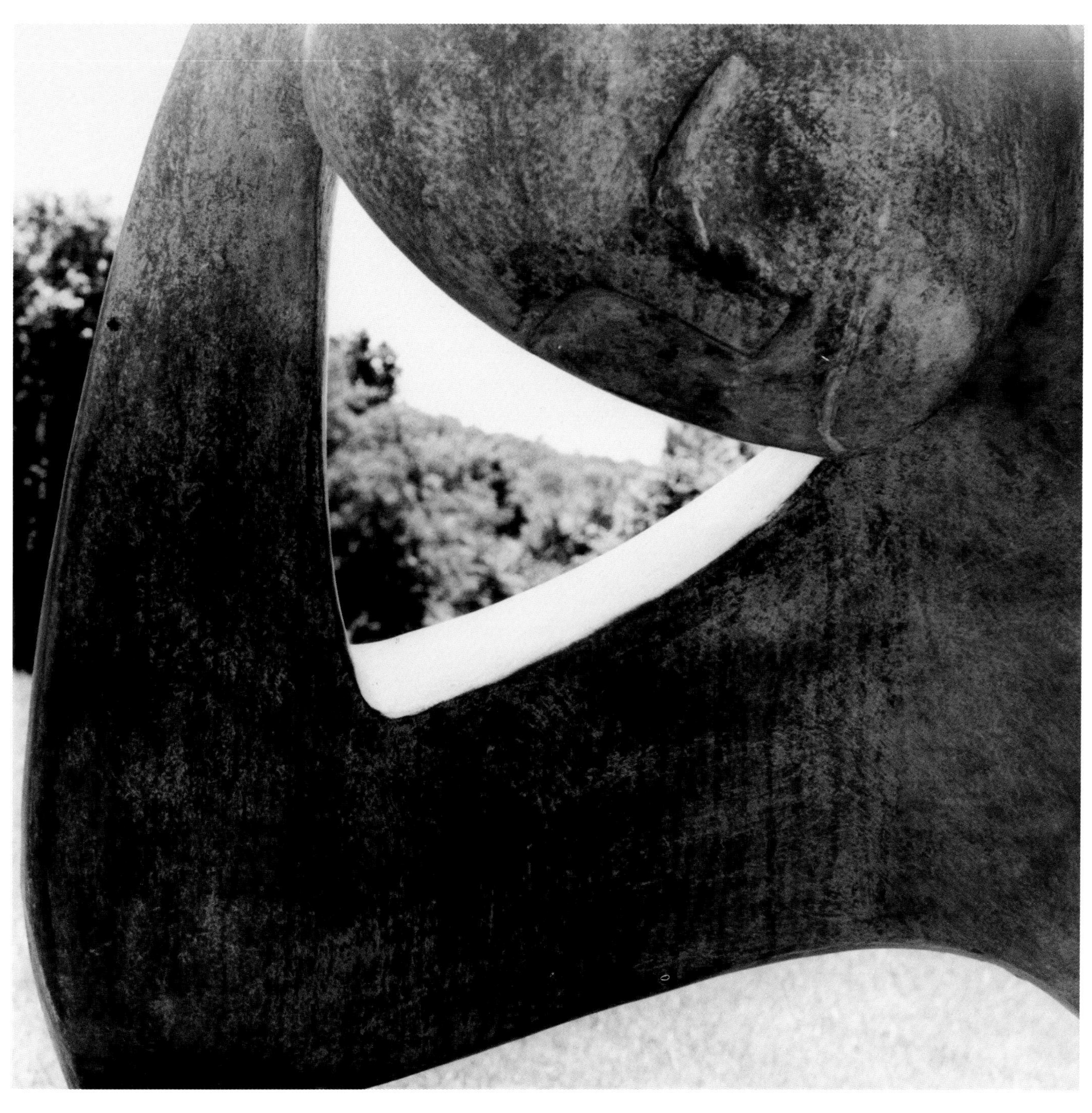

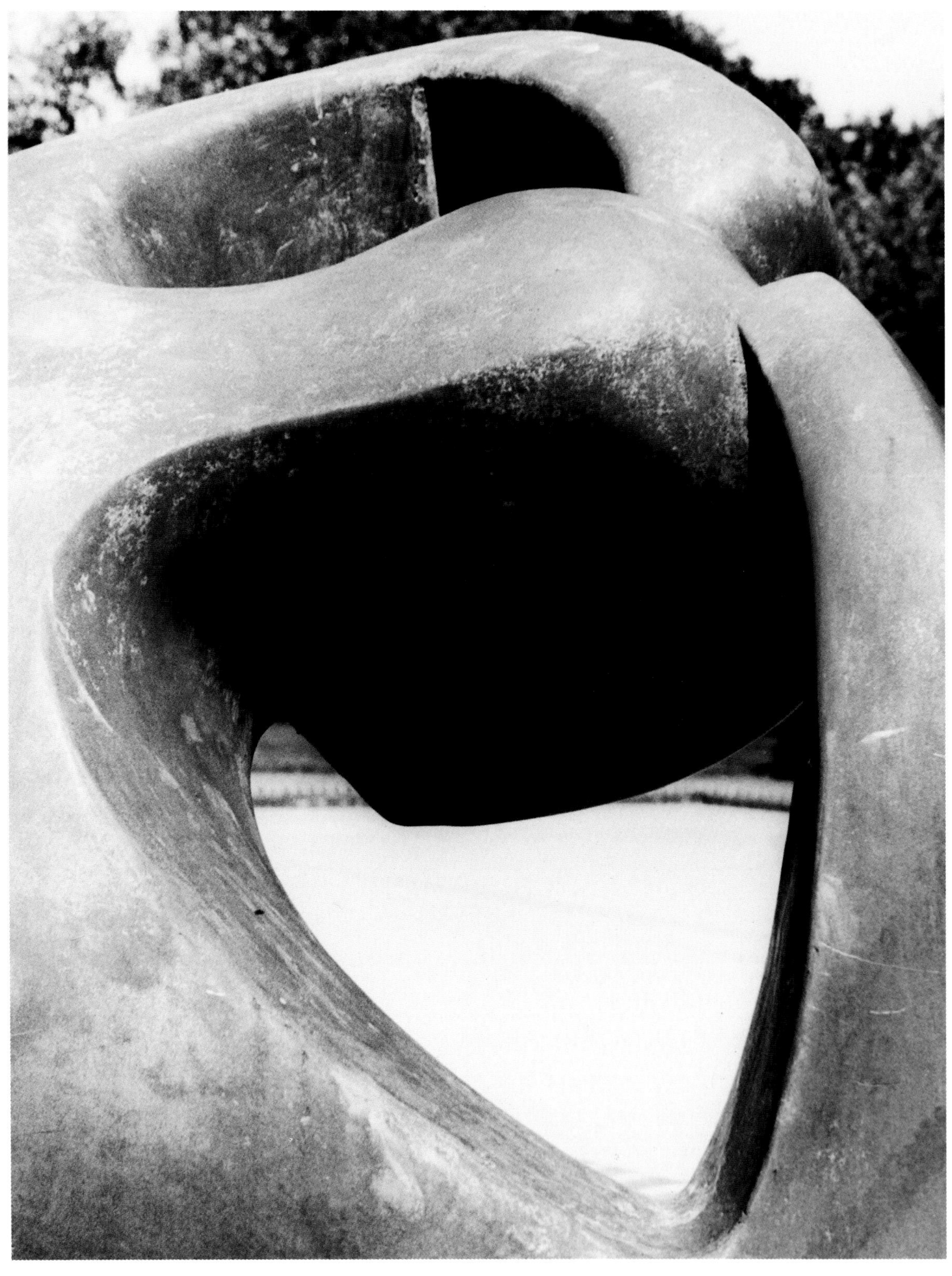

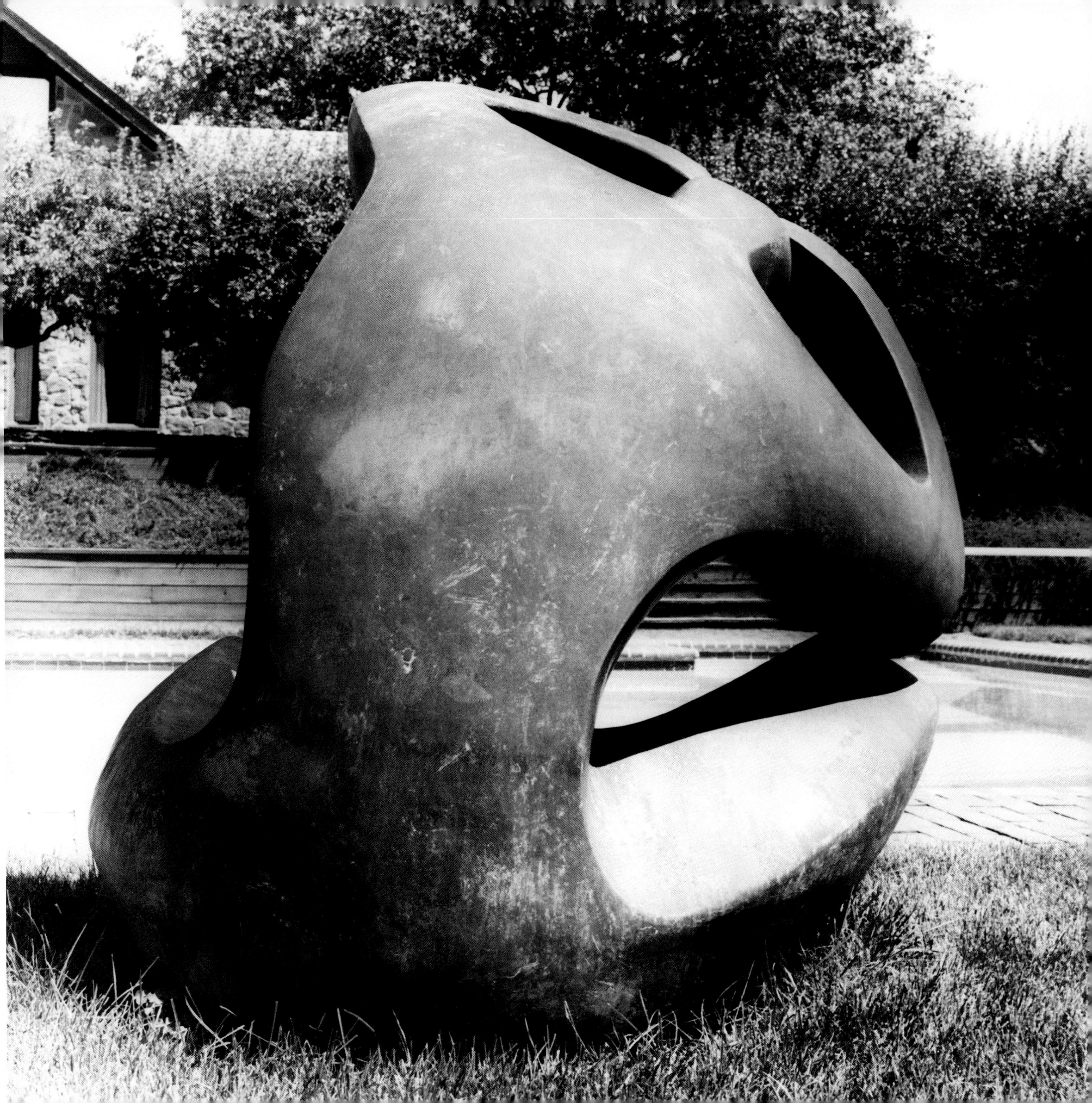

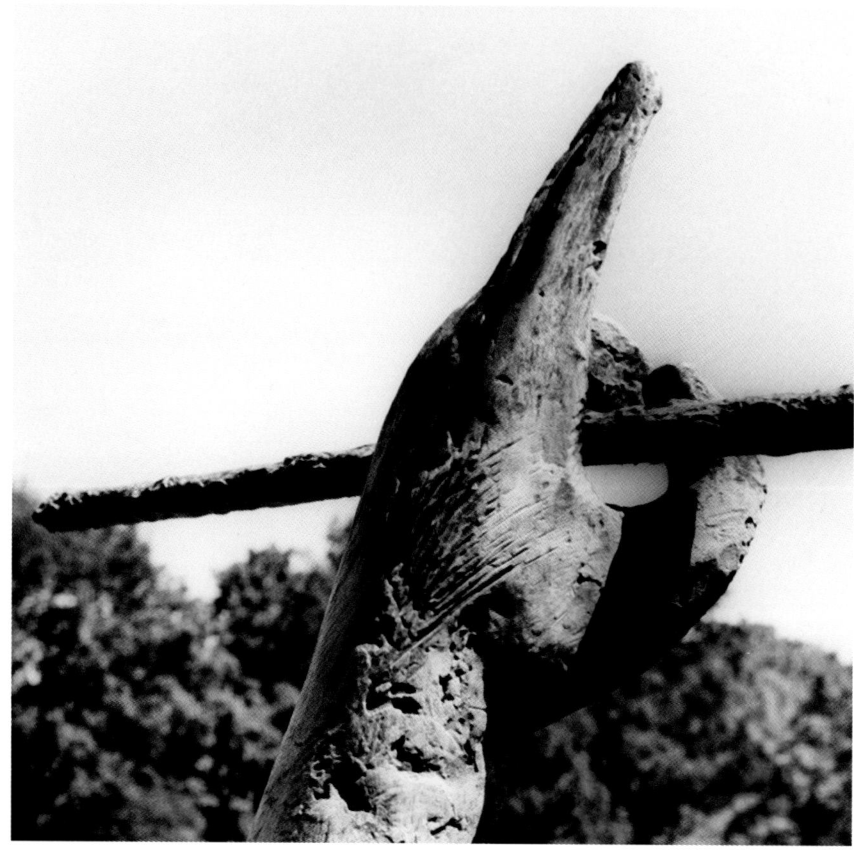

PAN

1970, enlarged 1997
Bronze
66" x 40" x 42"
Collection of Judy and Anthony Evnin, Greenwich, CT

I first made a small sculpture of this in wax and cast it into bronze. Everyone liked it so much that I cast a series of small ones. Judy Evnin, who loves music, saw the little one and asked me if I could enlarge it. This was difficult, as I wanted it to look very modern and yet it still had to look like a goat. Pan was the only Greek god that actually didn't live on Mt. Olympus—he lived down in the swamps. In order to placate those who were angry with him, he turned reeds into musical pipes and charmed everyone.

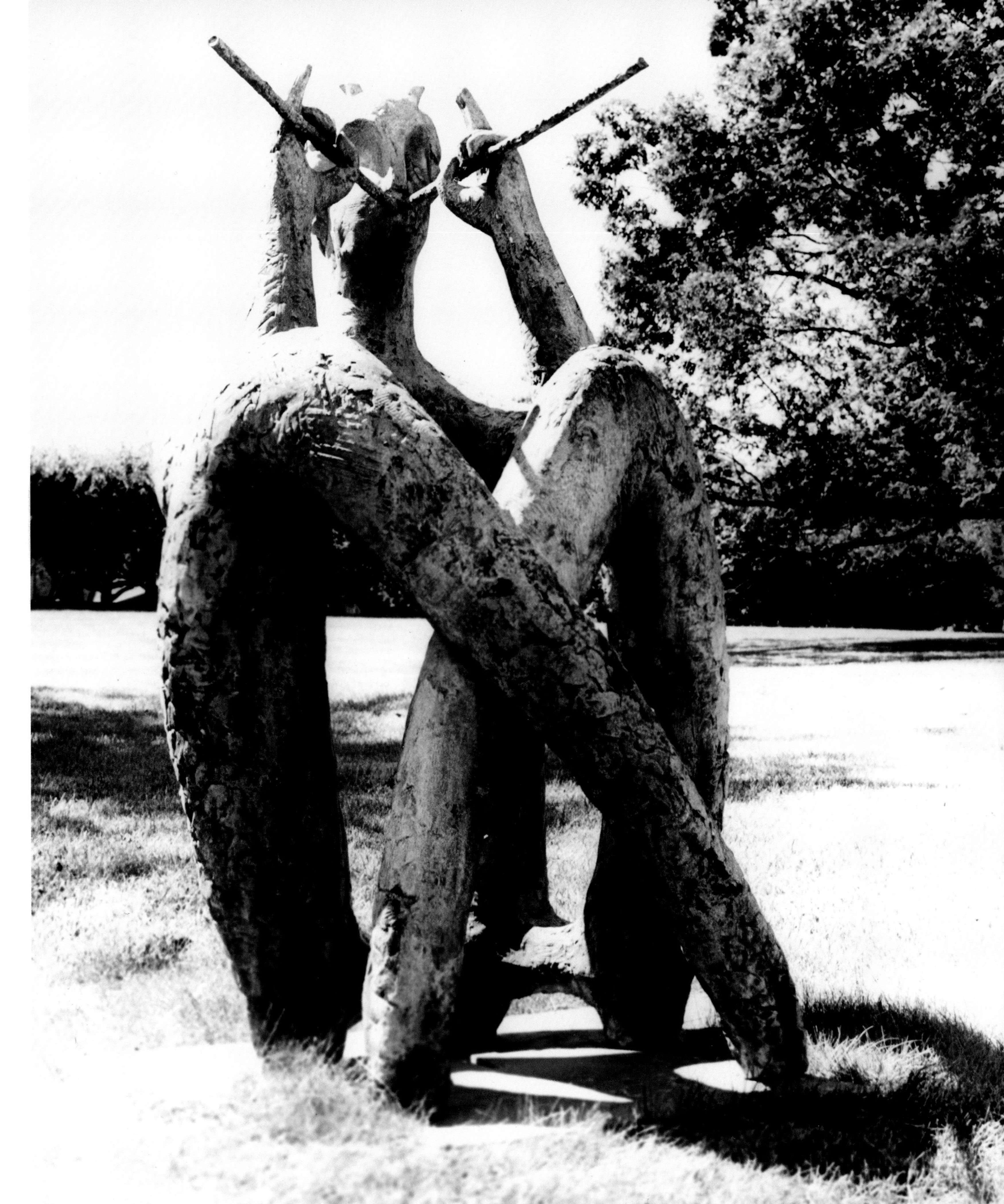

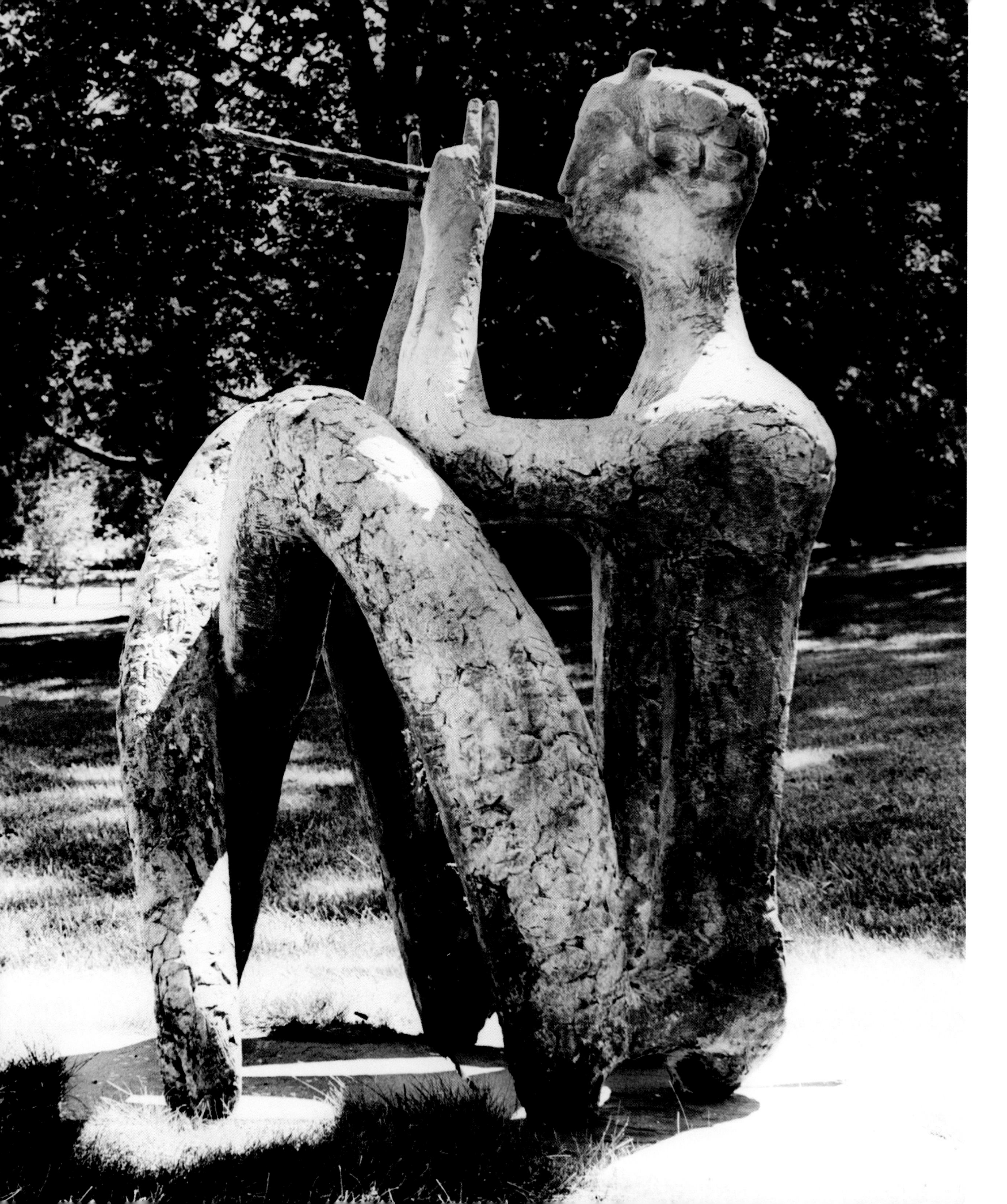

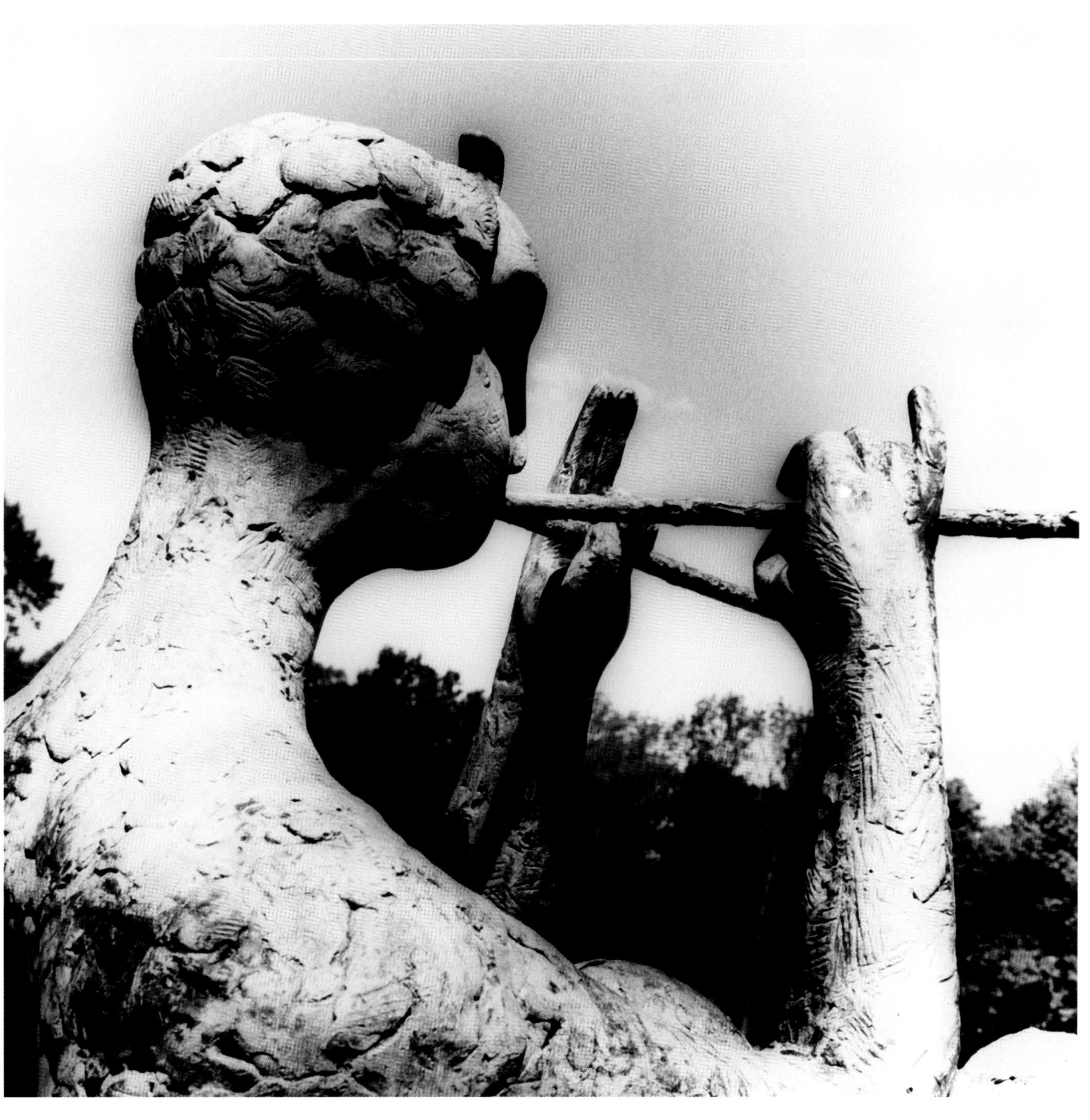

MADONNA WITH CHILD AND DOVE

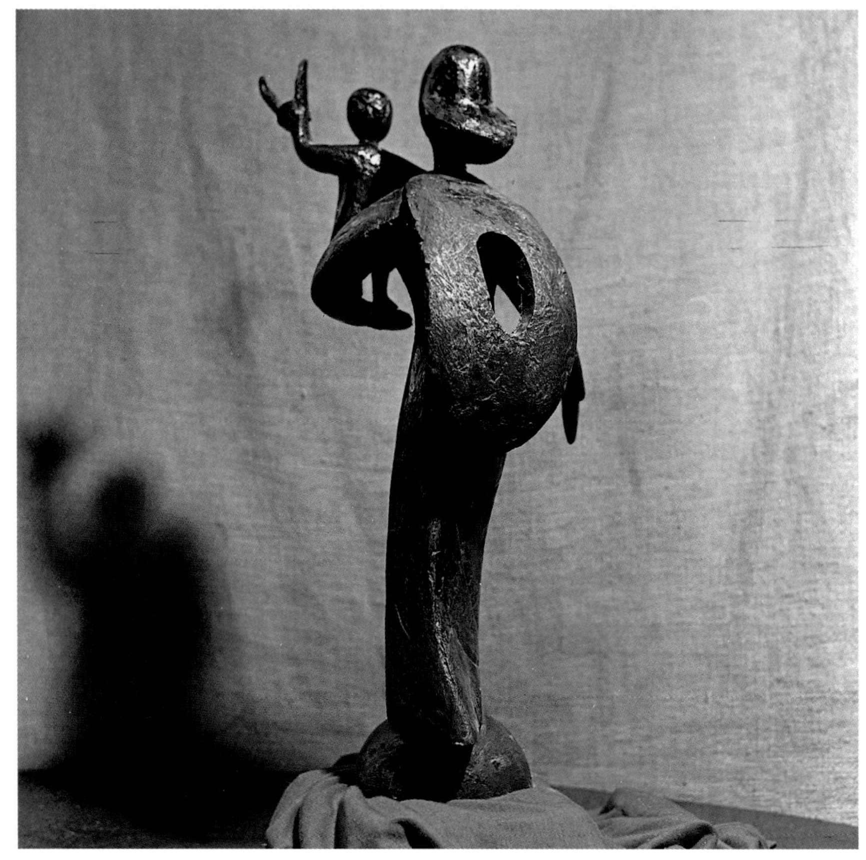

1961
Bronze
20"
Collection of Carleen Gunther, Milwaukee, WI

This work evolved as one of my first pieces directly modeled in plaster. It is a striding woman, much like Jacopo Della Quercia's wood carvings. It was my first constructed work, and it evolved piece by piece. The child was added, then the dove, the hair and finally the cape with the see-through hole.

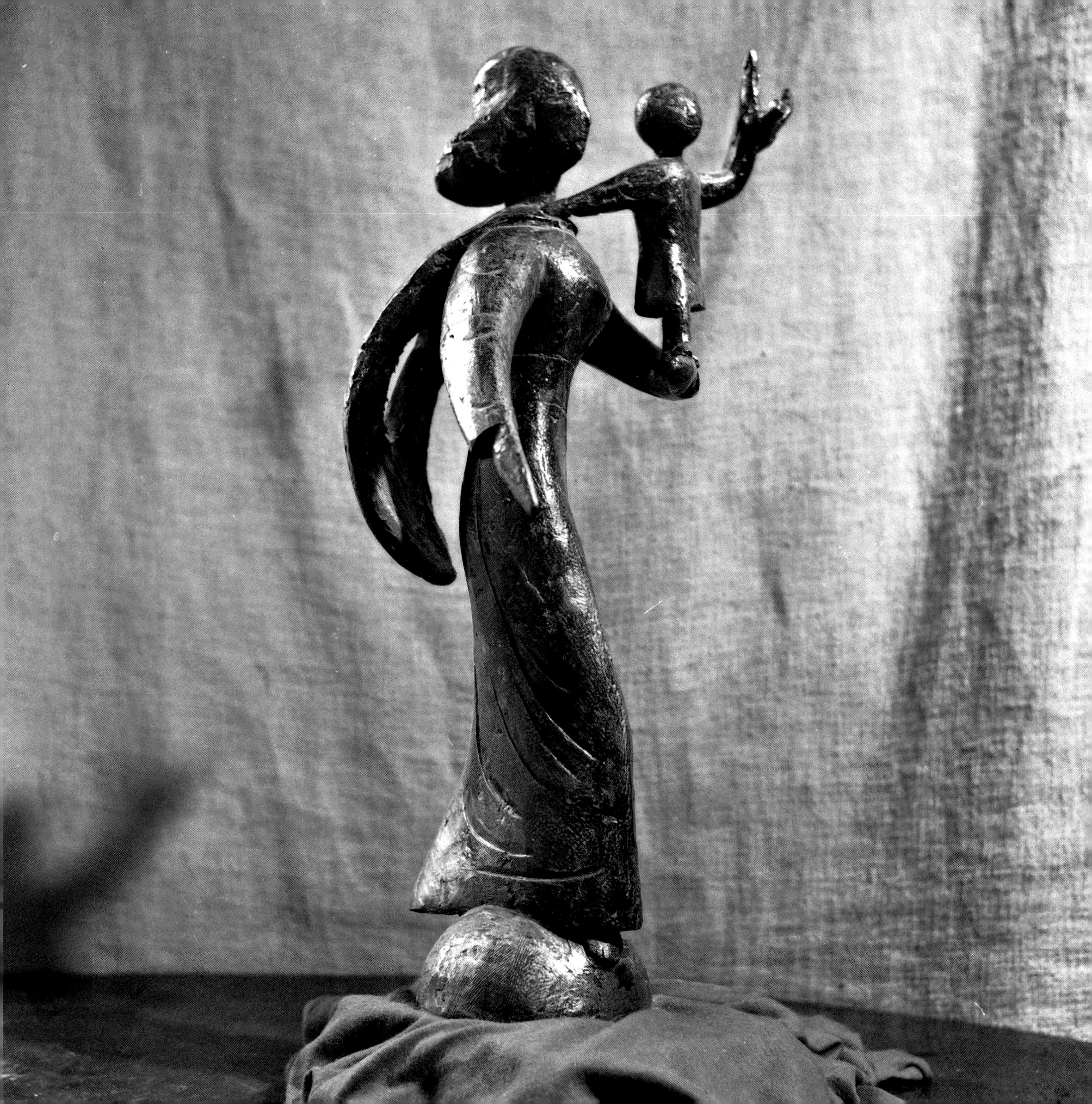

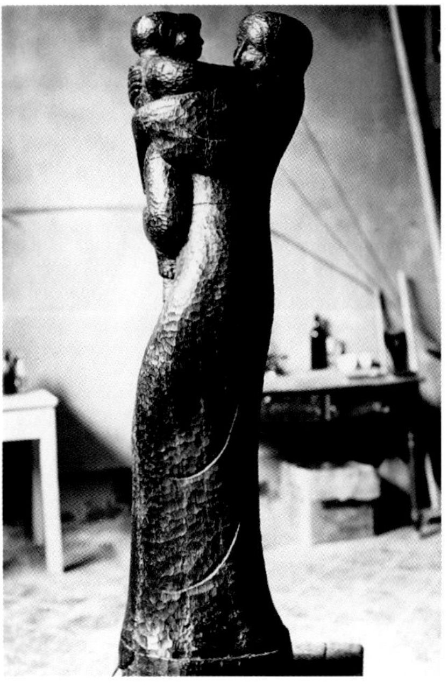 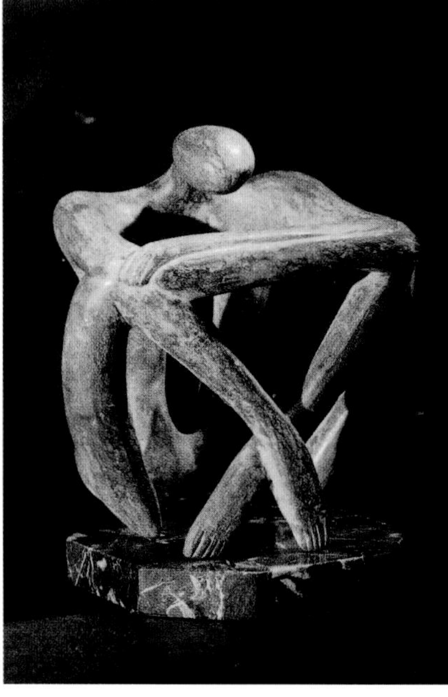 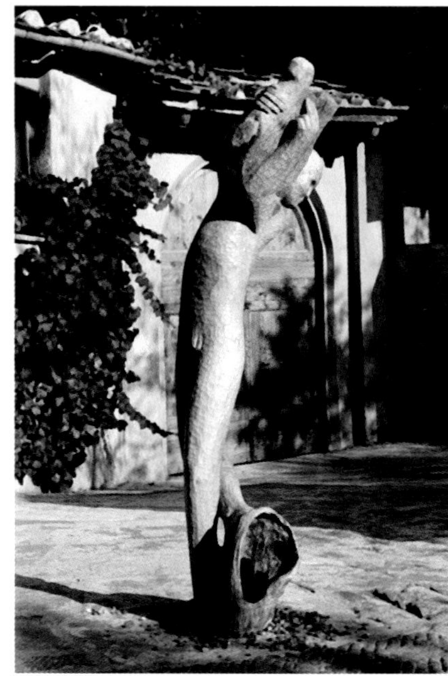

MADONNA AND CHILD
1960
Apple wood
65"
Collection of Gene Albert, Burlington, VT

MEDITATION
1960
Bronze
6"x 6" x 6"
Collection of Lucy Epley, Milwaukee,WI

ORPHEUS
1962
Apple wood
74"
Whereabouts unknown,
last seen in Italy

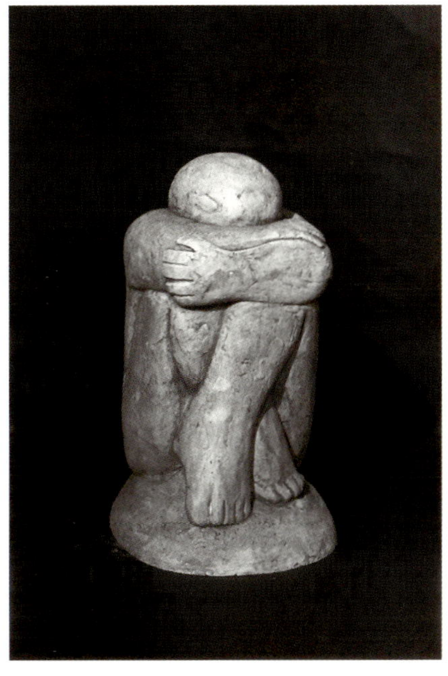

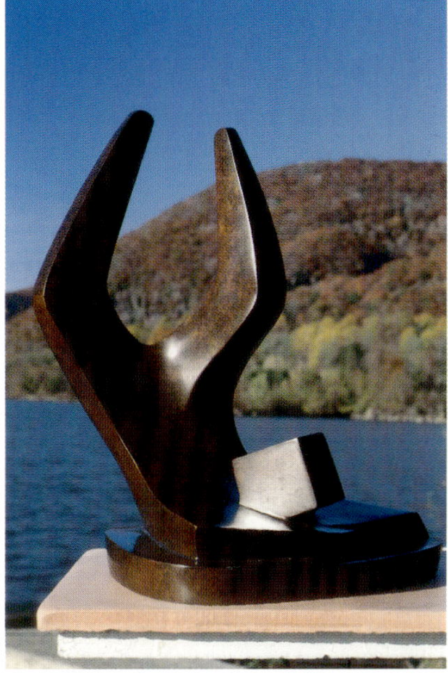

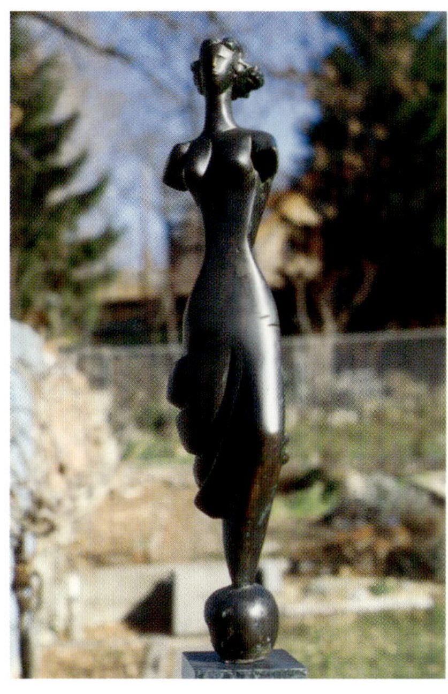

THE CONDEMNED
1963
Plaster for bronze
9"
Owner Unknown

ACROBAT
1968
Bronze
11"
Collection of A. Alfred Taubman,
Troy, MI

WOMAN IN WIND
1963
Bronze
26"
Collection of the artist

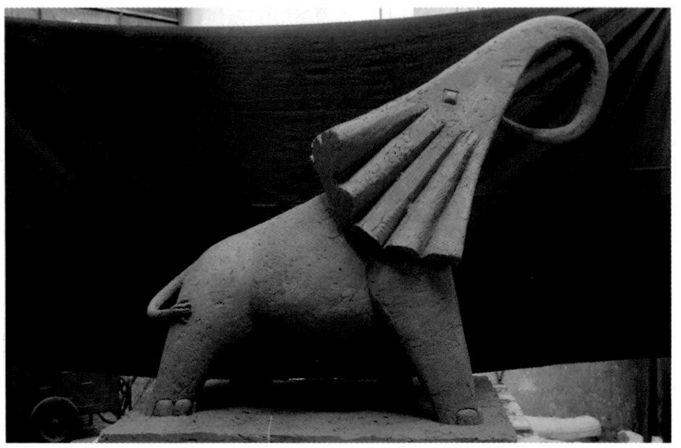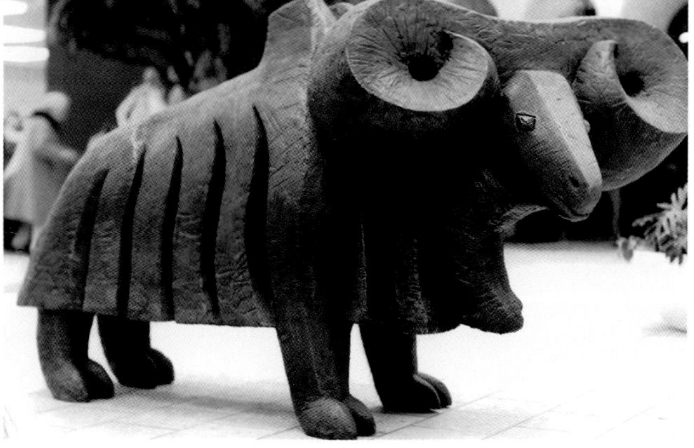

ELEPHANT
1967
bronze
48" X 58" X 40"
Children's Hospital, Detroit, MI,
Woodland Mall Grand Rapids, MI, Taubman Co.
Turfland Shopping Center, Lexmgton, KY

RAM
1967
bronze
60" X 70" X 72"
Woodland Mall, Grand Rapids, MI, Taubman Co.
Sun Valley Shopping Center, Concordia, CA, Taubman Co
Woodland Mall, Grand Rapids, MI, Taubman Co.

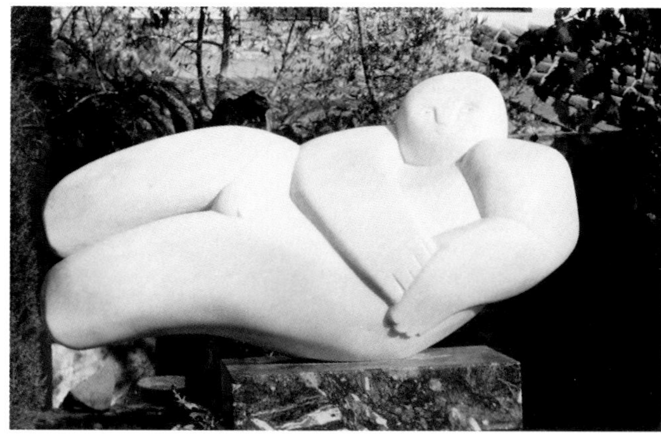

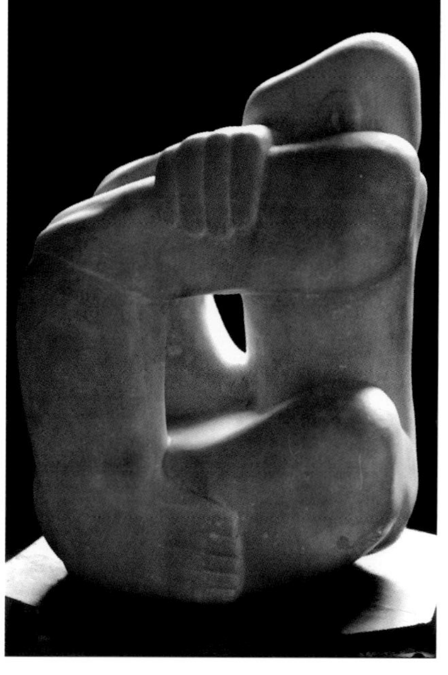

HOMAGE TO ETRUSCANS
1961
Carrara marble
10" x 23" x 8"
Collection of A. Alfred Taubman,
Troy, MI

CONTEMPLATION
1961
Carrara marble
12" x 8" x 10"
Collection of Gerald LaCost, London

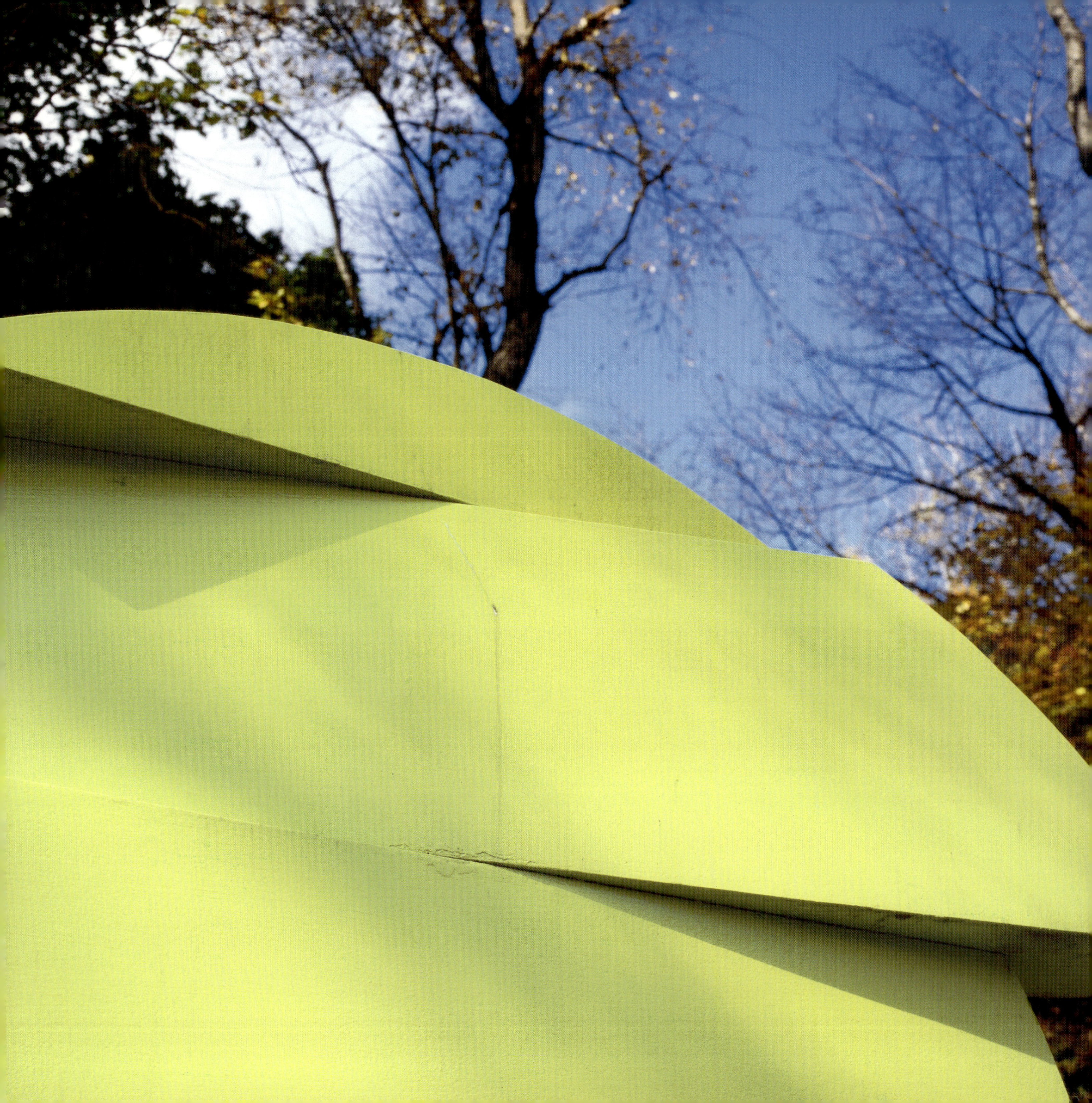

DISCS AND STELAI

The inspiration for my Solar Discs was twofold. First, from studying the little Italian telephone tokens called *gettoni*, which had several grooves cut into them. Second, from a fabric design used in the cabins of American Airlines jets, consisting of a rising/setting sun with recessed, horizontal cloud-like shapes extending across the surface.

The stele idea evolved from my wish to create a monolithic sculpture from a chunk of solid brass found in my studio. I carved deep horizontal lines and several deep divots into the plinth. Then the whole piece was highly polished. In some of the later variations, I completely pierced through the brass with round holes, and in others I crosshatched it as if an entablature had been removed.

Opposite page: Horizontal Disc

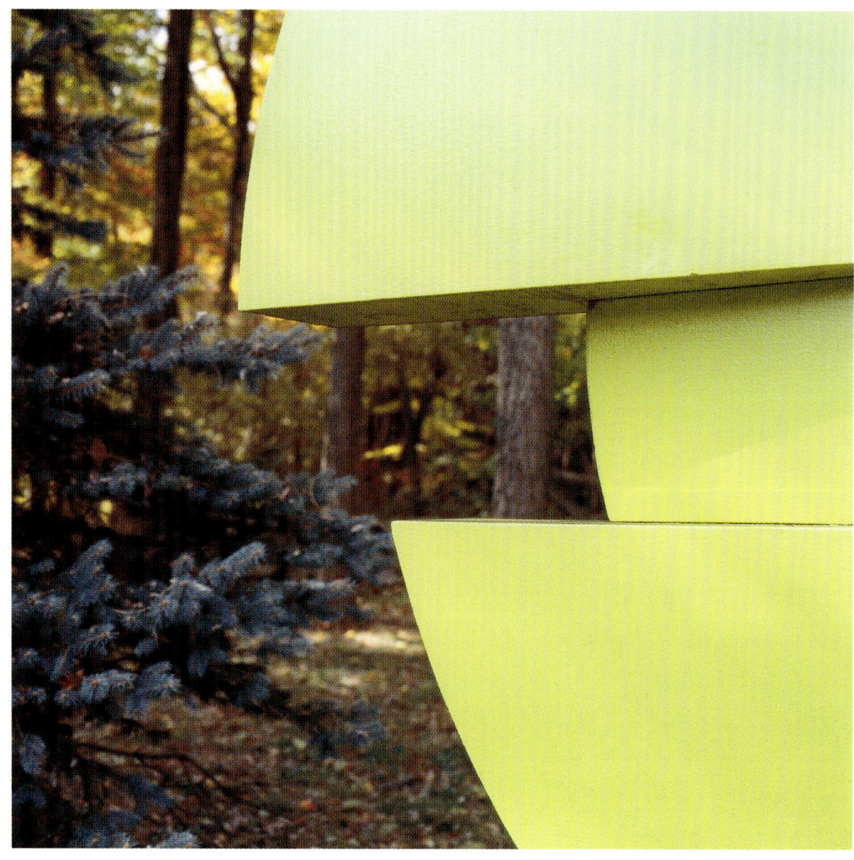

HORIZONTAL DISC

1983
6' in diameter
Enamel on steel
Collection of Robert Stahmer, Yorktown Heights, NY

Horizontal Disc was a variation of the *Solar Disc* series. However, I decided to divide the circle by cutting it into various horizontal sections and assembling them in an interesting manner.

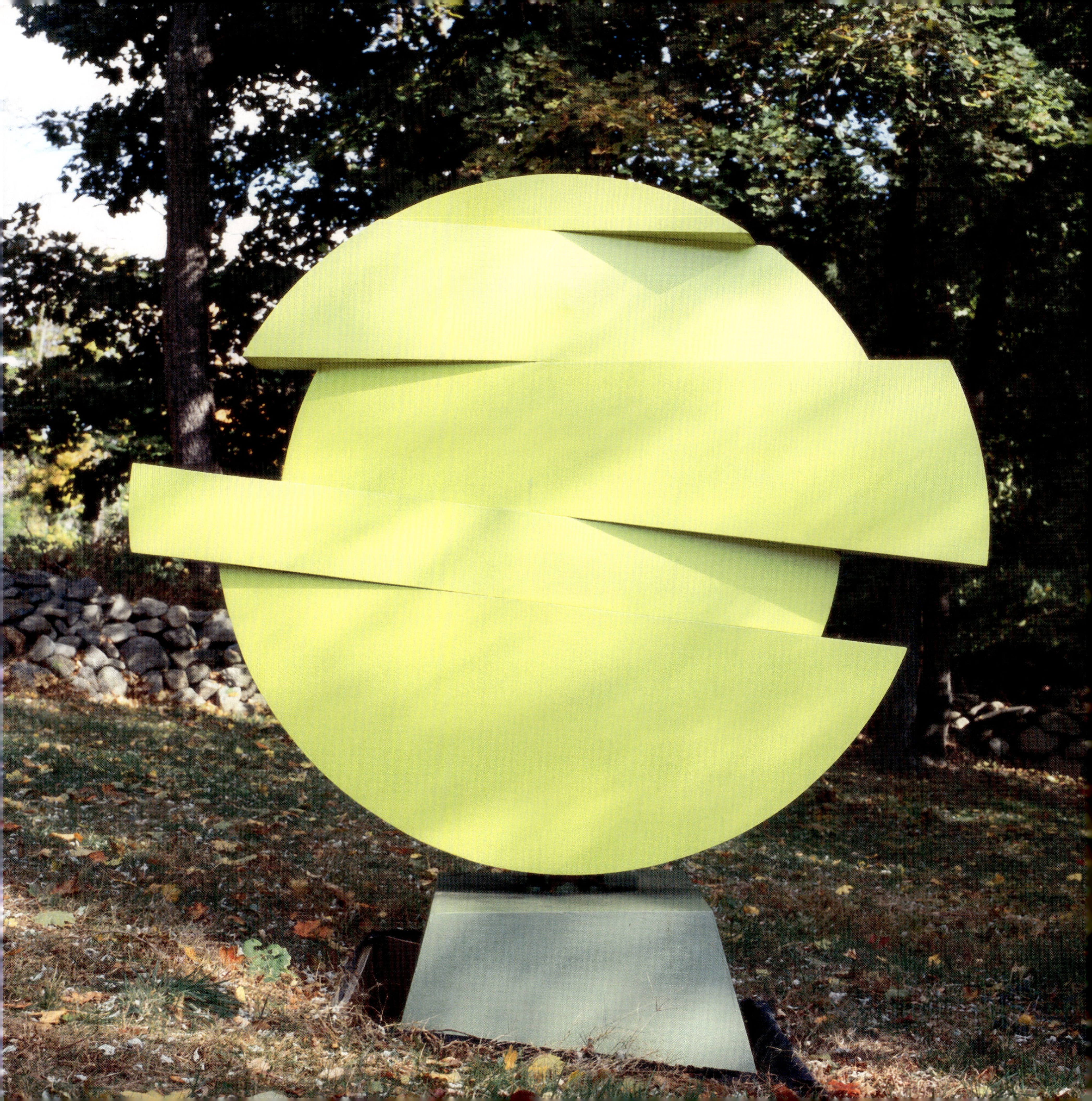

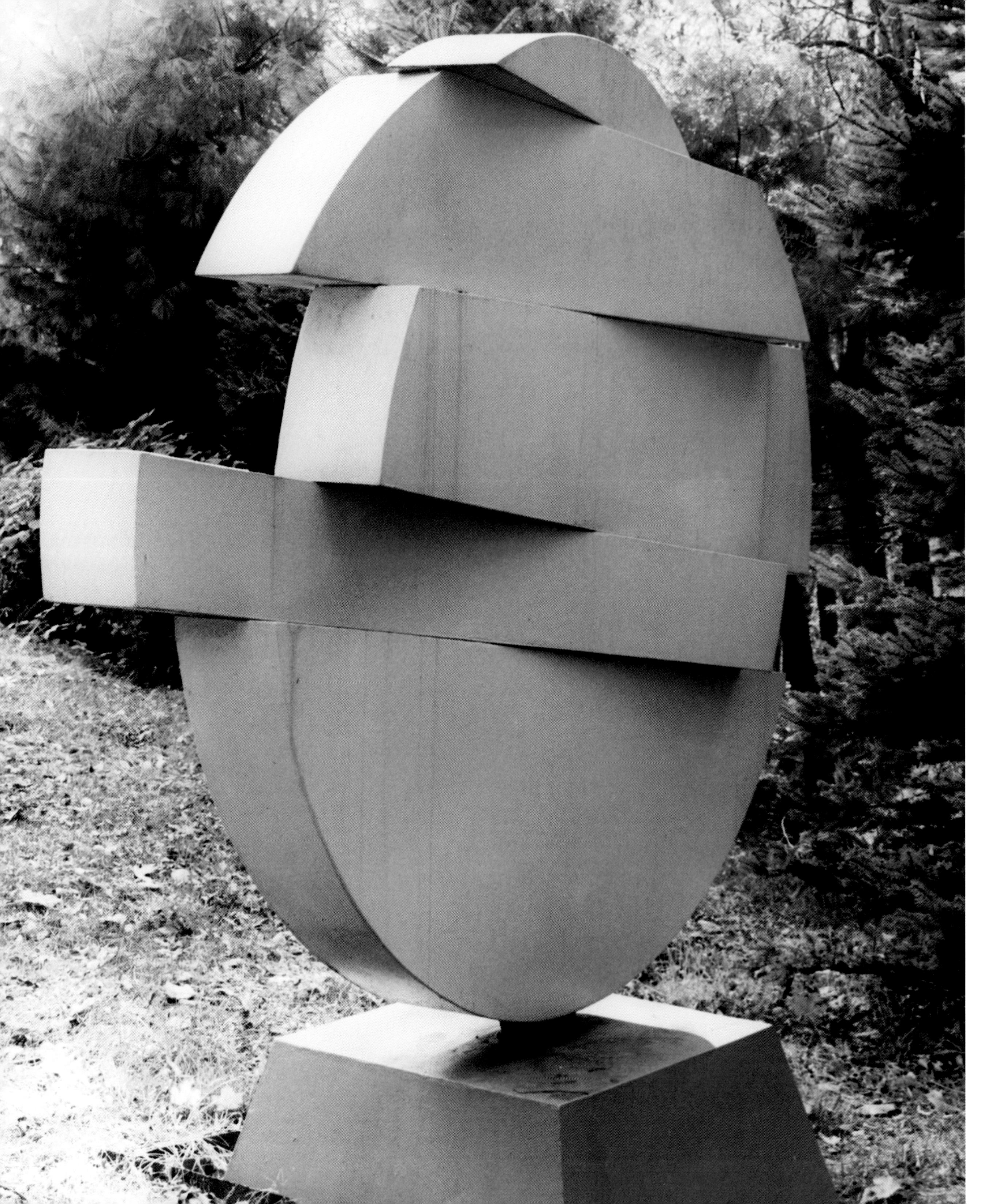

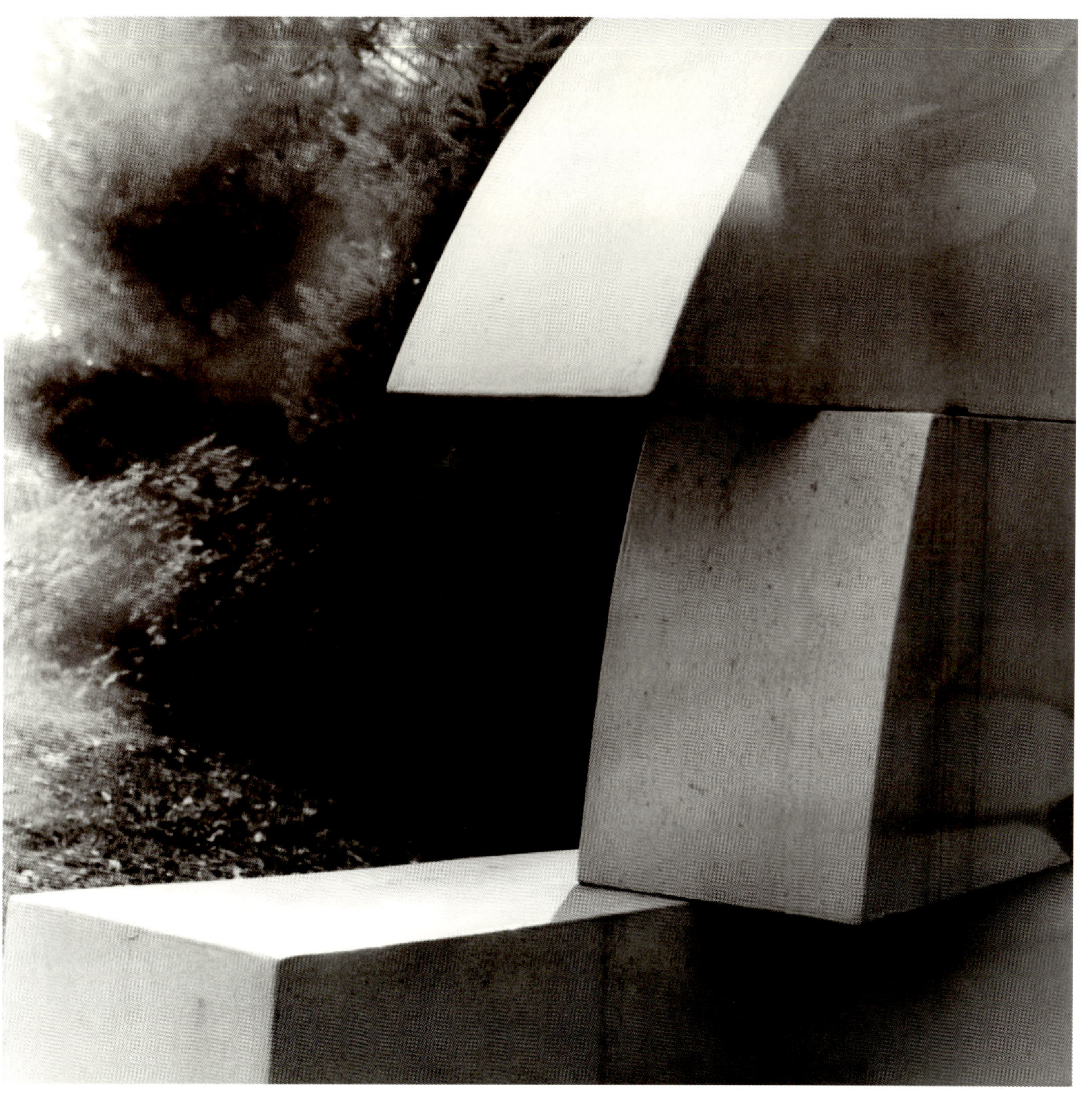

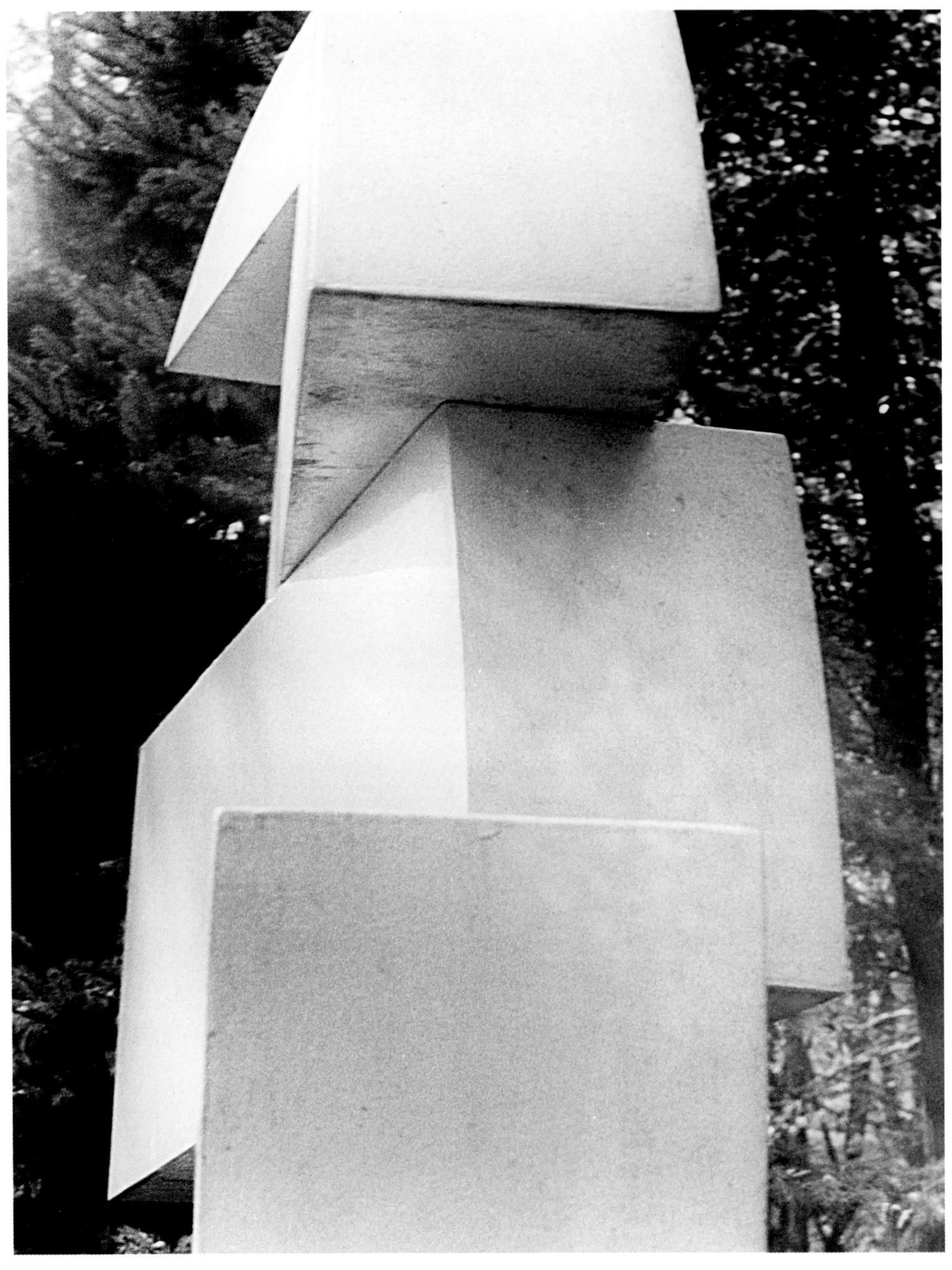

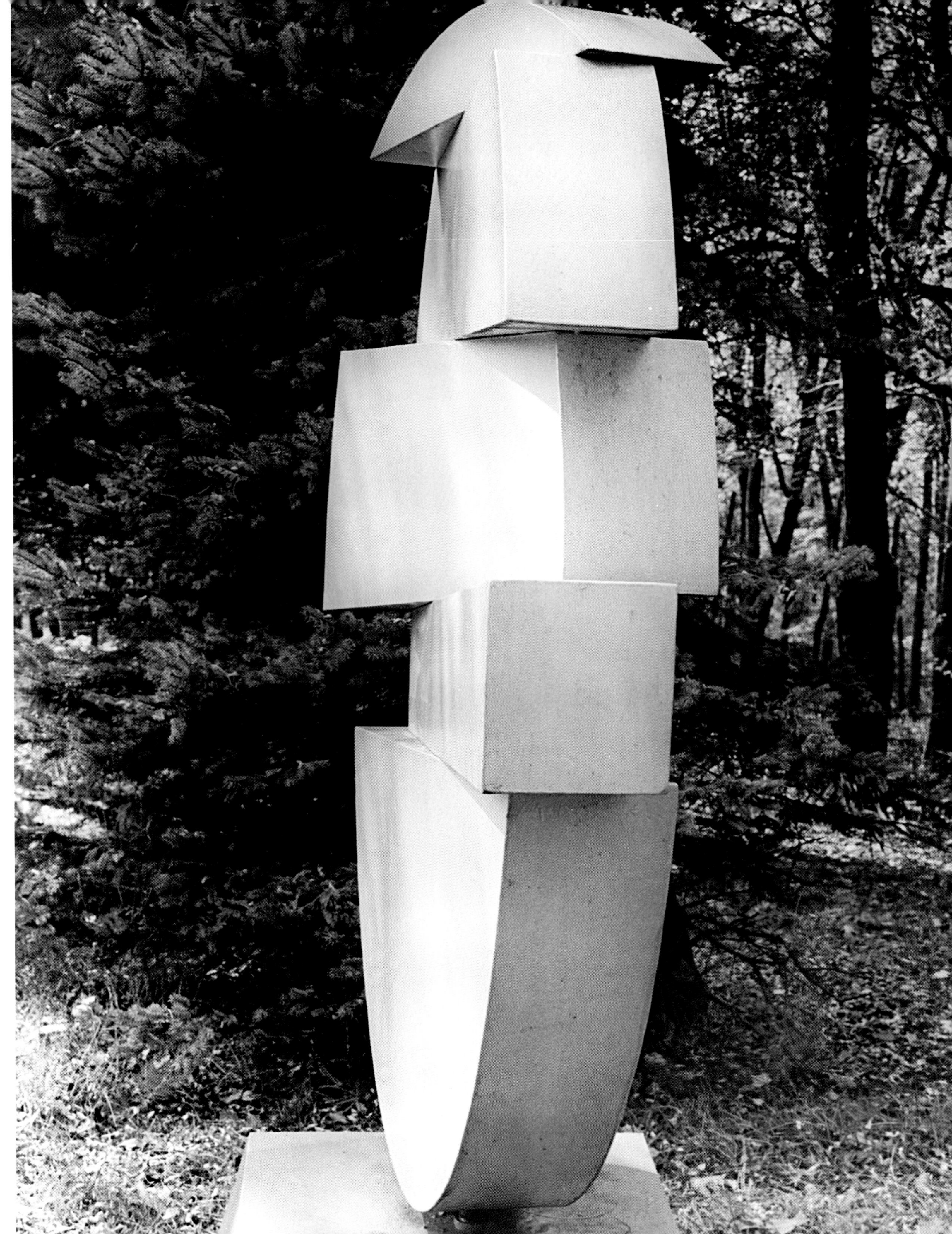

MAGMA I

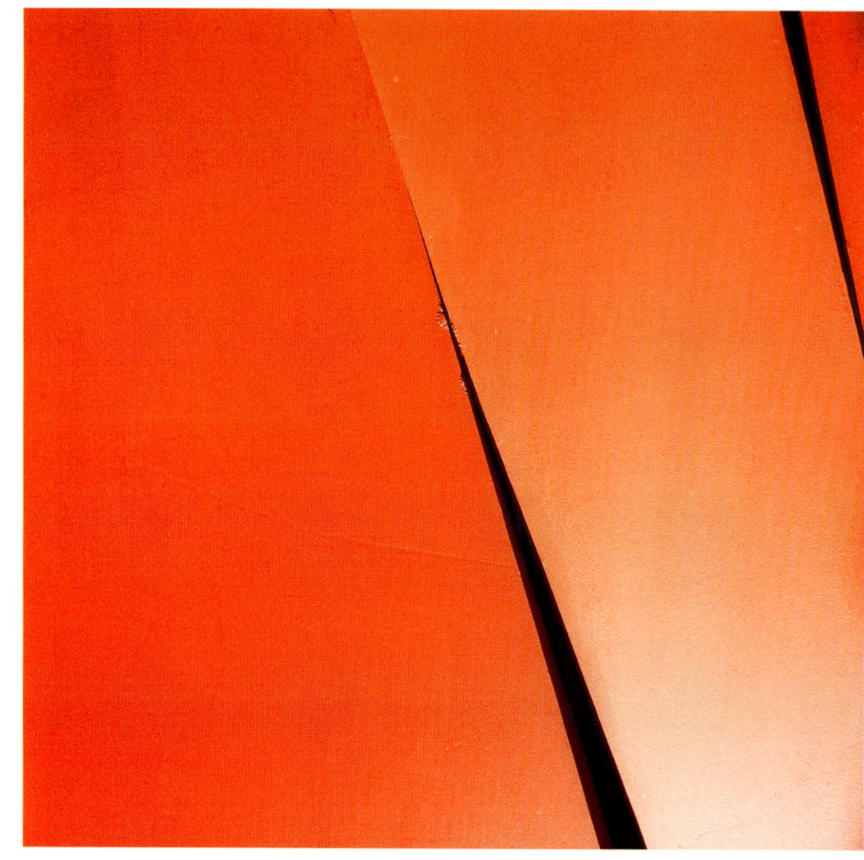

1987
Painted steel
10' x 10'
Collections of Judy and Anthony Evnin, Greenwich CT
and Kelly Simpson, Katonah, NY

Magma involves a further breaking up of the *Horizontal Disc*. The pieces are almost the same, except for two divisions.

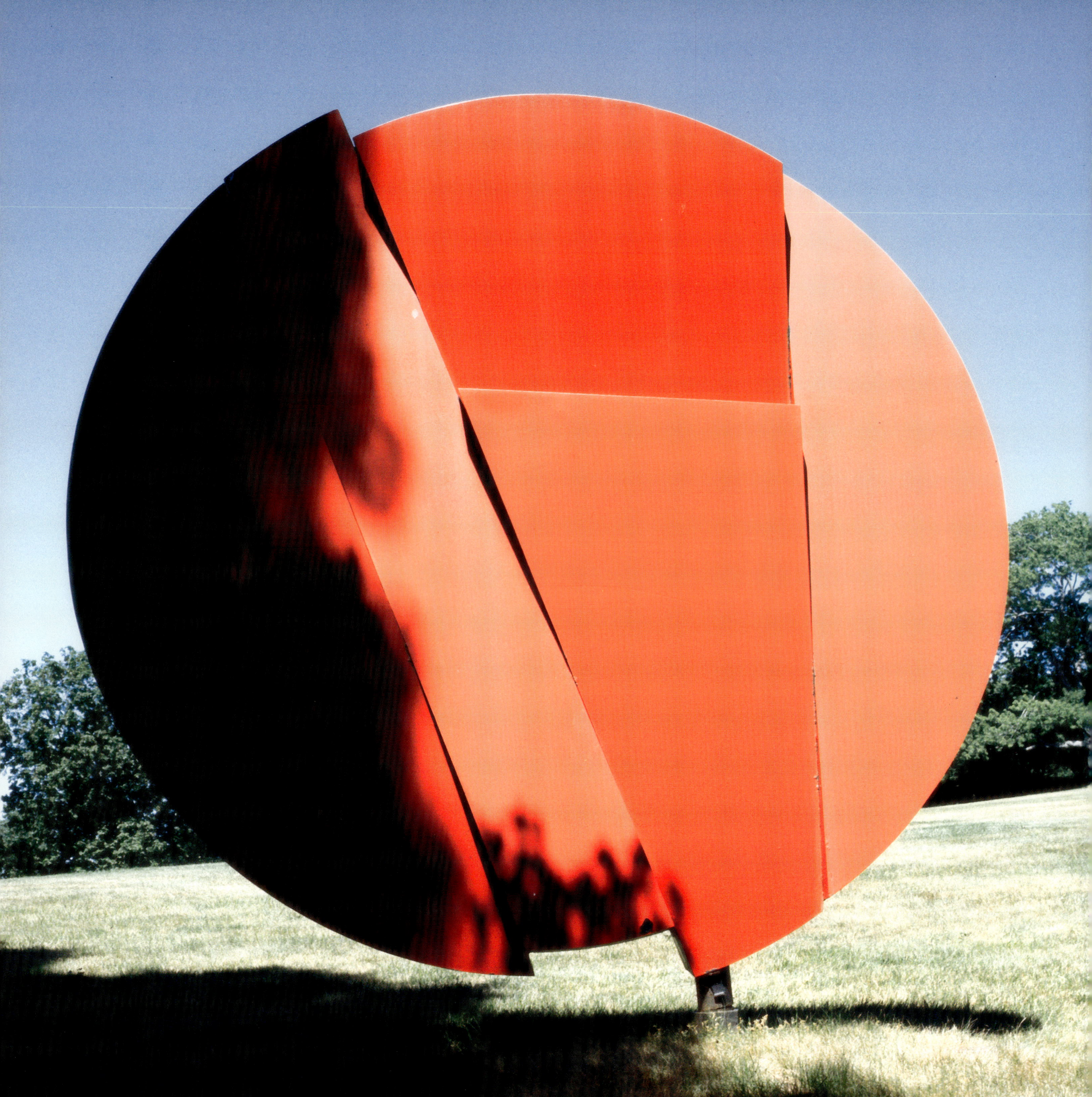

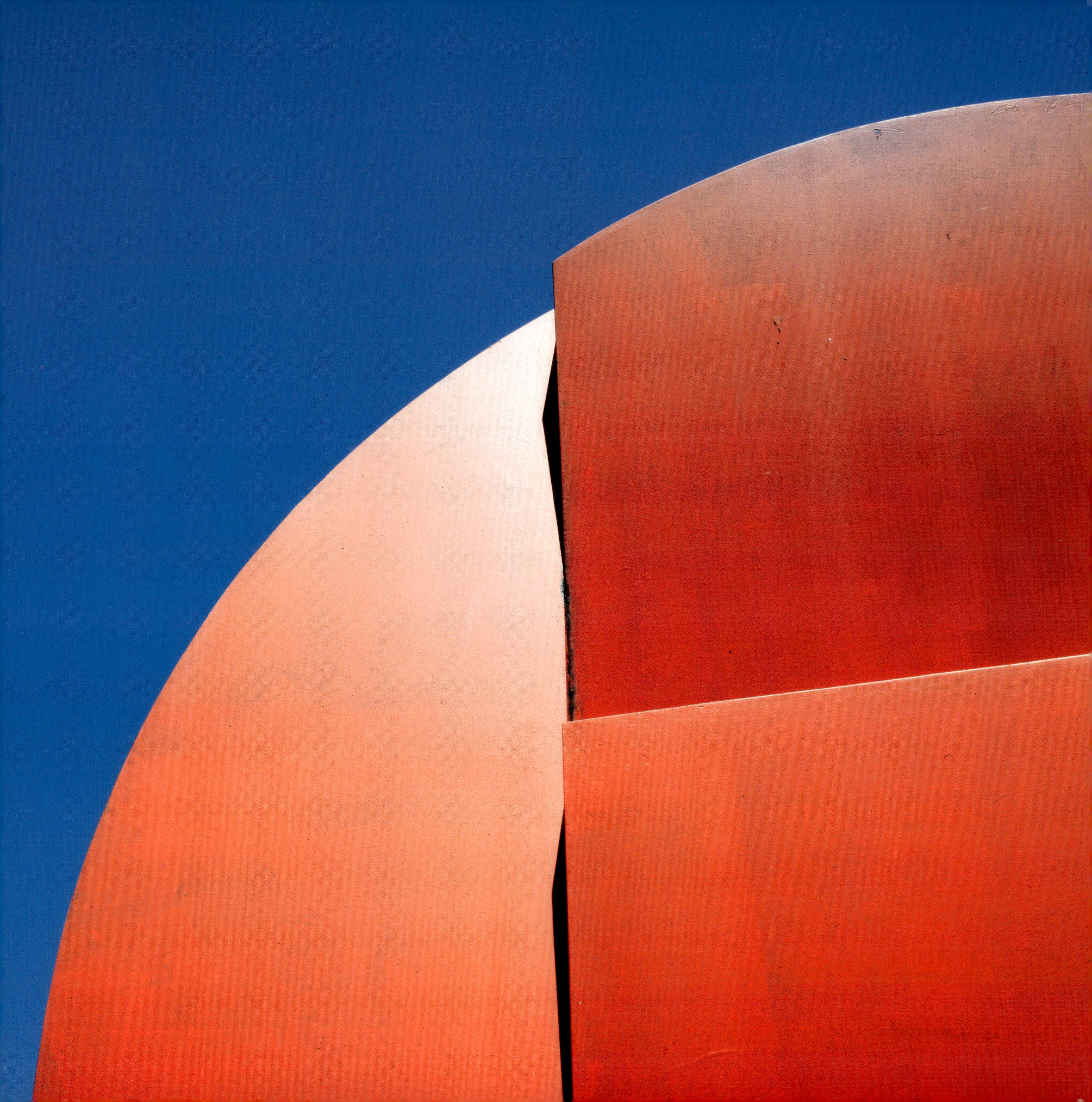

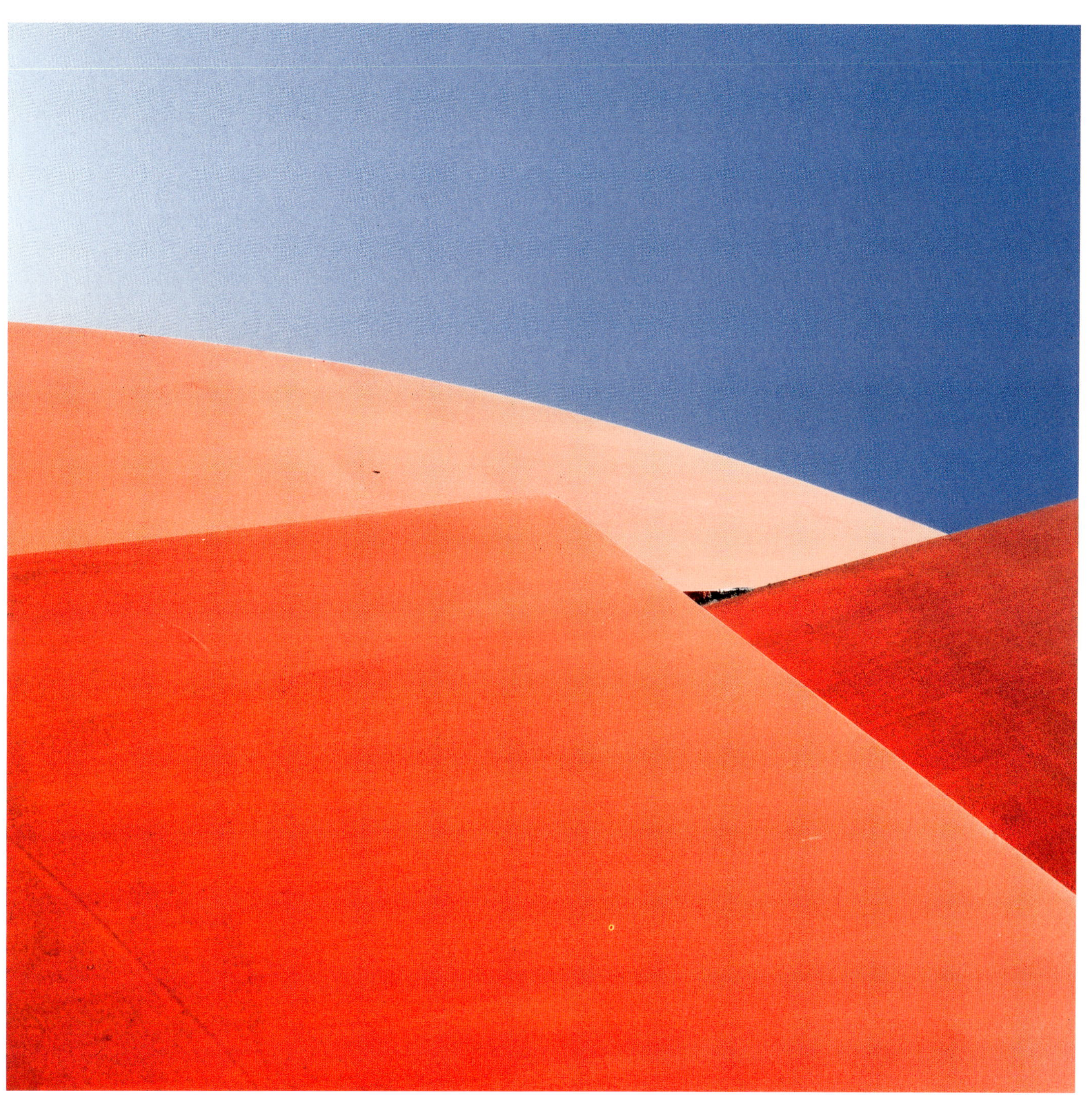

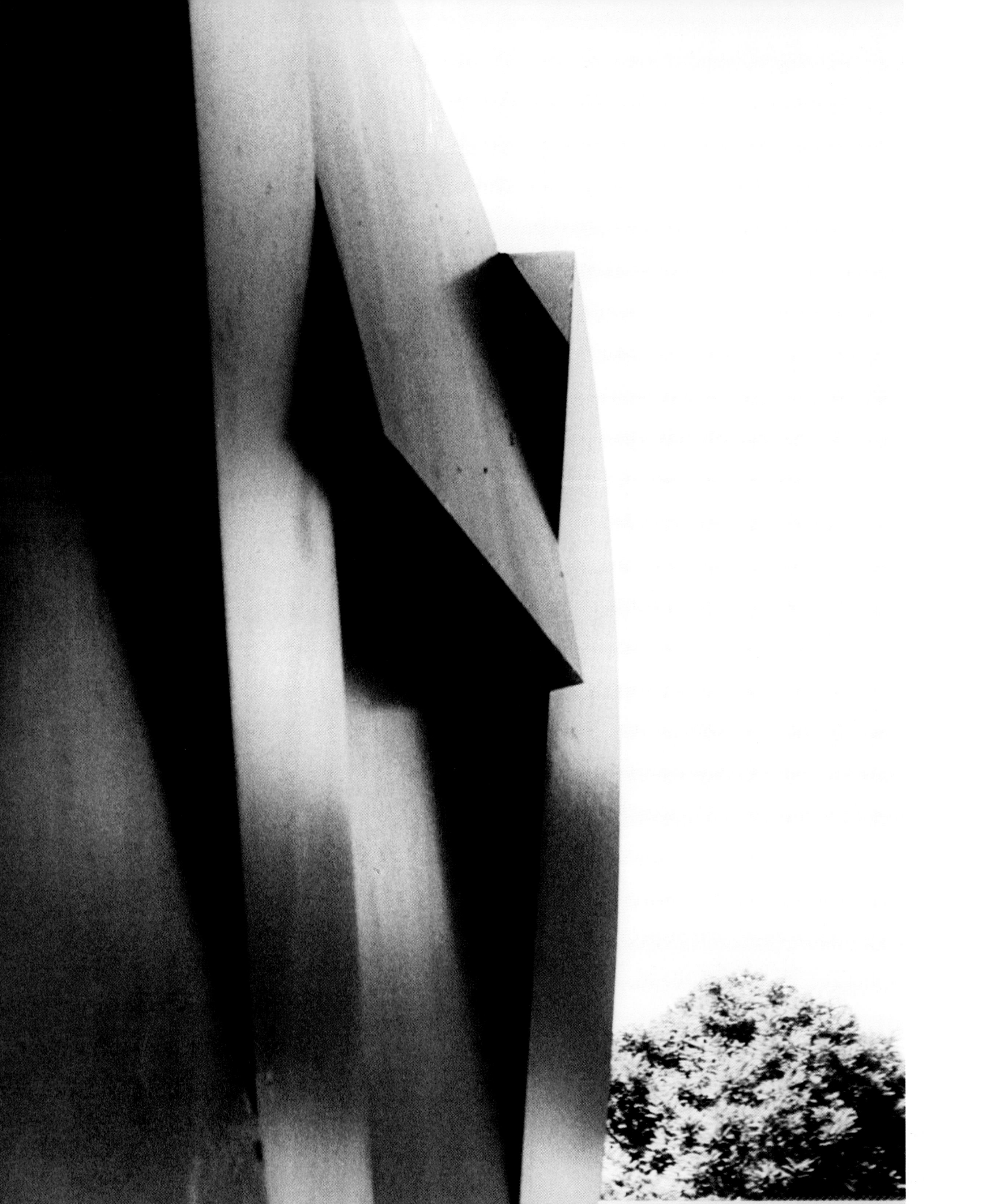

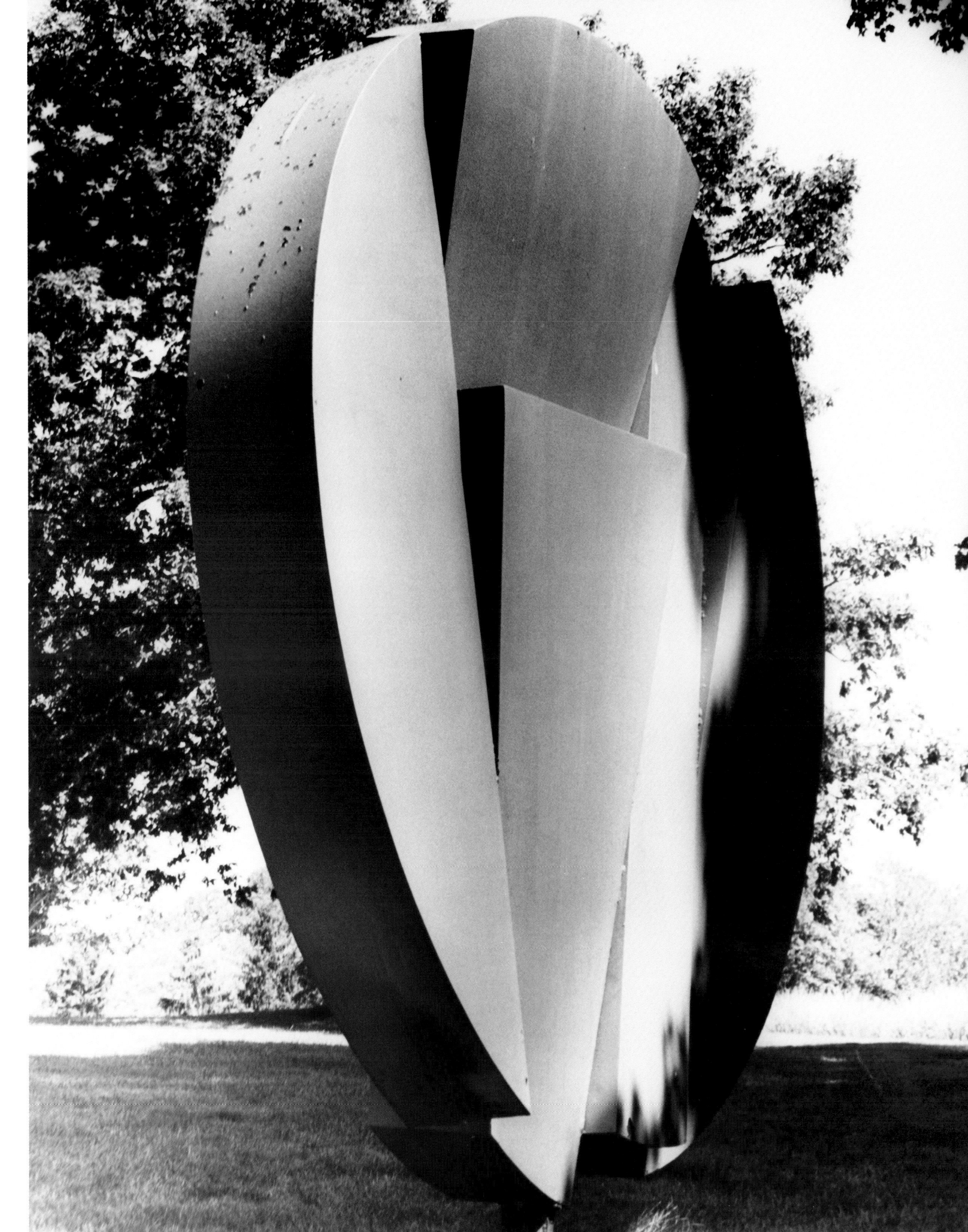

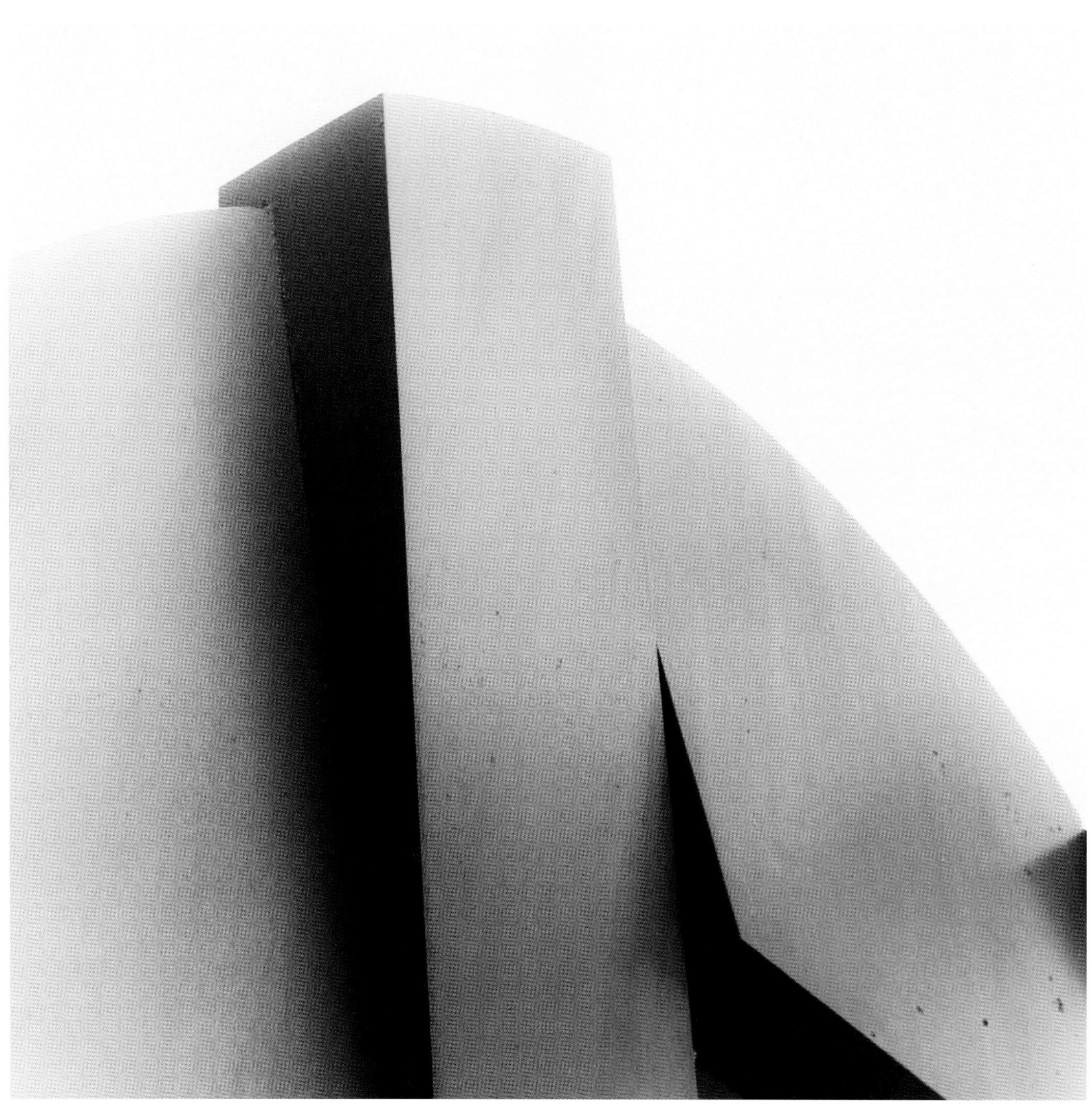

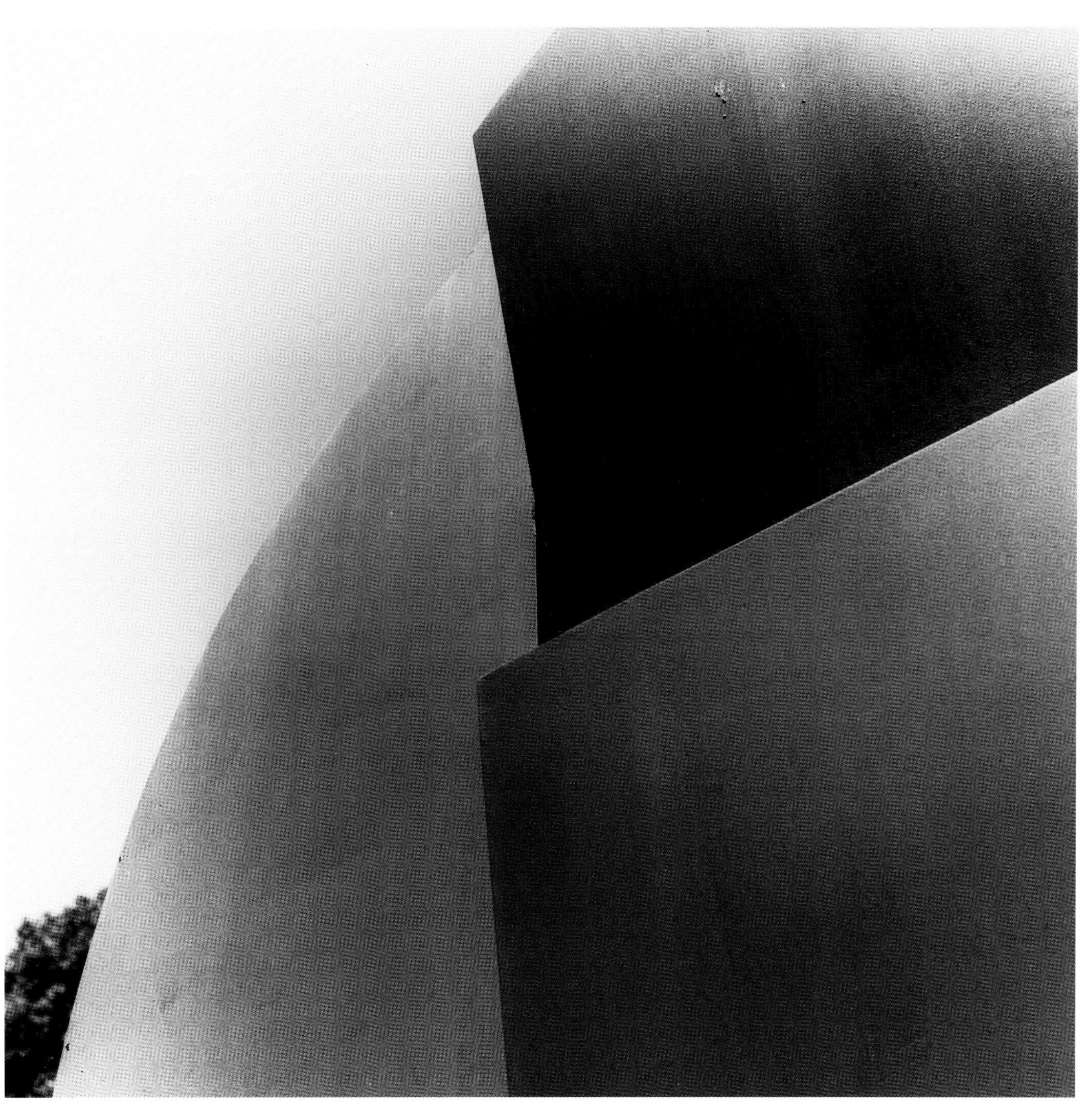

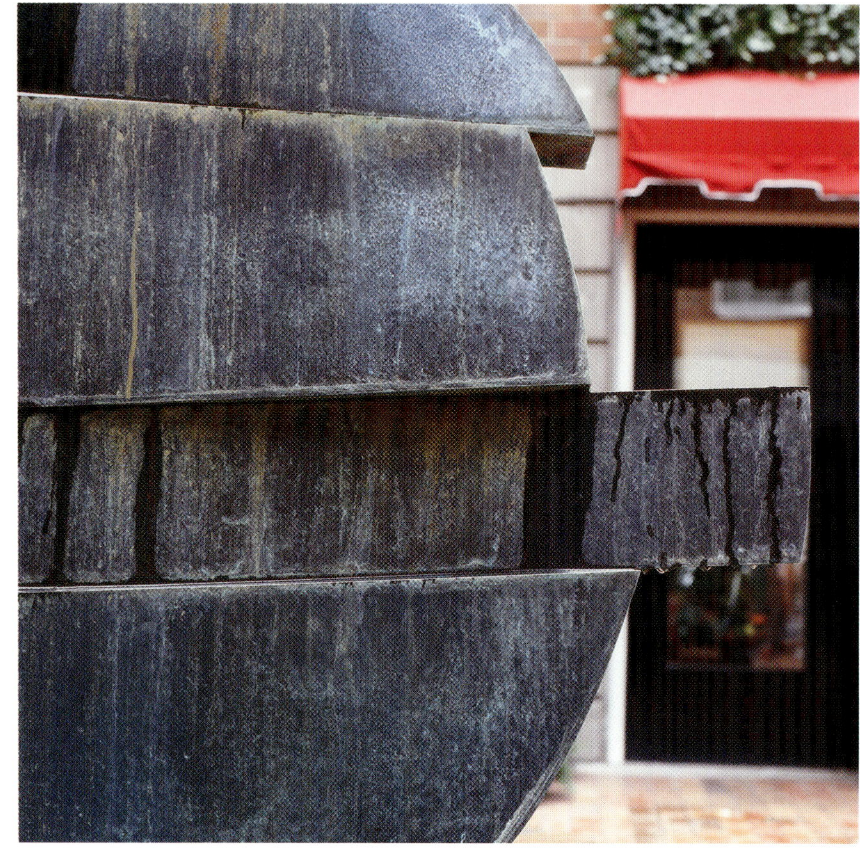

HORIZONTAL
DISC FOUNTAIN

Original 1983, this version 2000
Bronze
4' diameter
Nine West Office Building, Fort Lee, NJ
and Inn at the Market, Seattle, WA

This sculpture was designed as a fountain even though I have also executed it without water. The idea evolved from my Solar Disc sculptures, which had striations cut into solid forms. The forms are offset in such a way that the water flow creates interesting patterns, leaving part of the surface dry and part wet. It has a very oriental feeling.

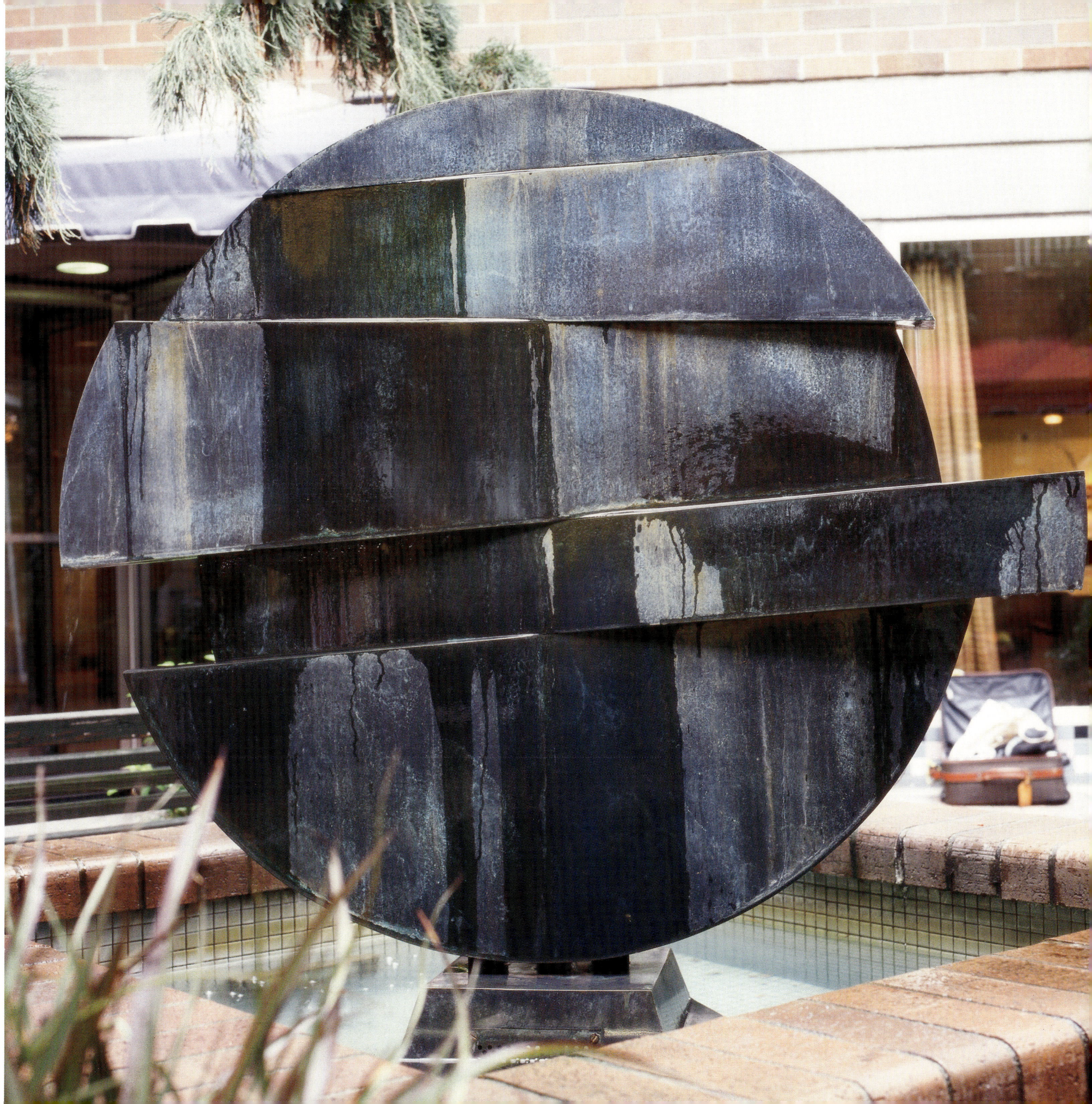

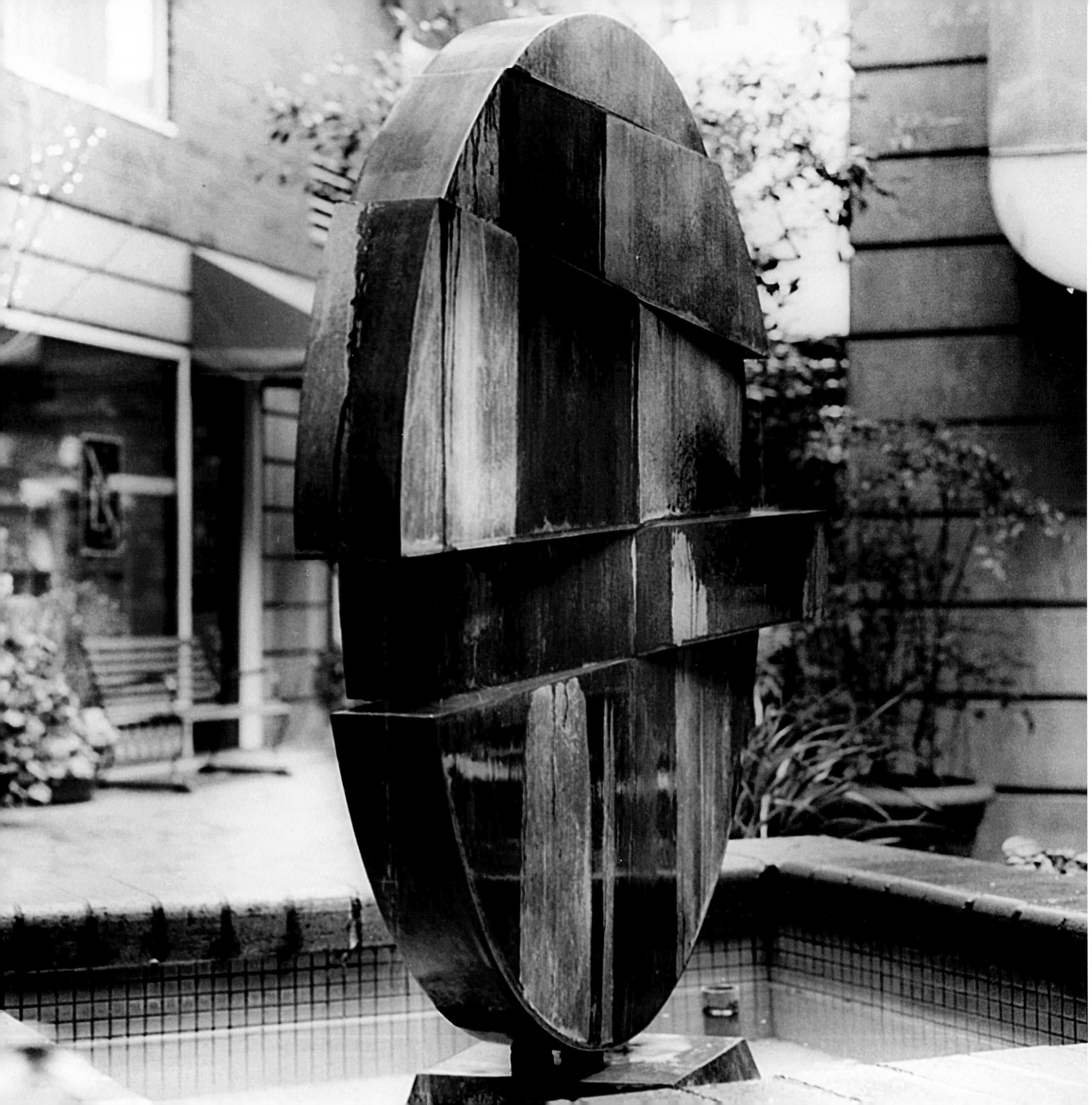

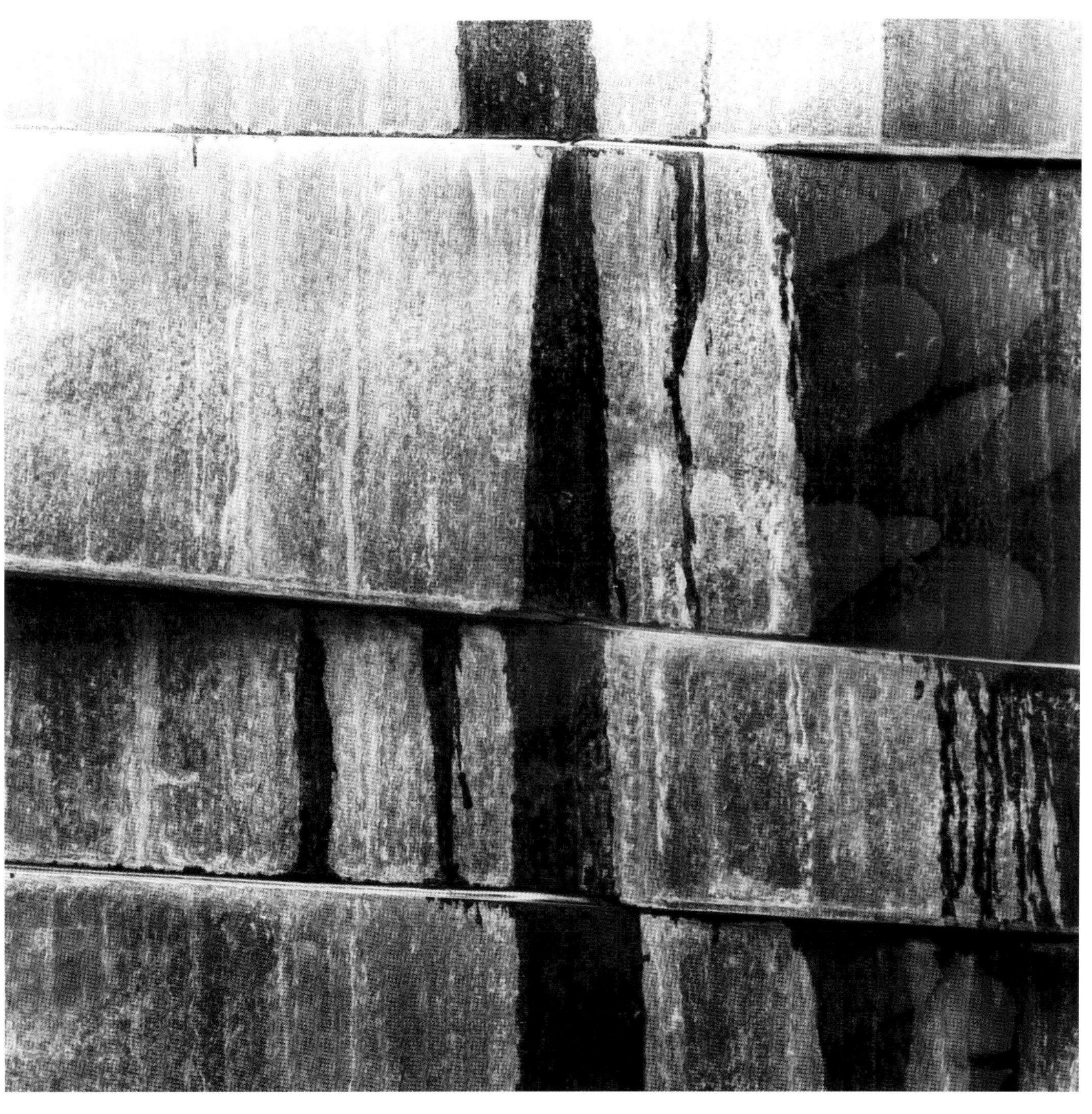

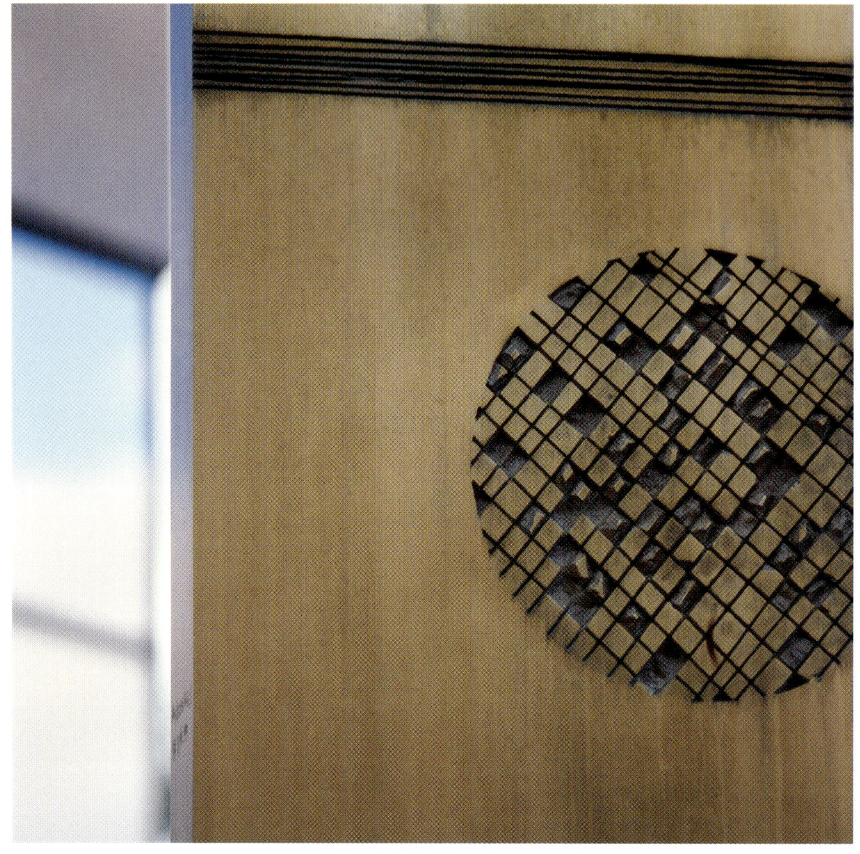

STELE 12

A stele is usually a large vertical form, used as a marker. Historically, it would have been engraved with some type of identification. When I first started doing the Stele group, I had just seen the movie *2001, A Space Odyssey*. It starts out with apes discovering a large, tall, totemic piece of metal in a barren wasteland. I had a similar piece of metal in the studio and began carving it with my grinders. That was my first of about 15 sculptures on the same theme. The largest is 24 feet tall. They are all very modern, and yet have overtones of ancient civilizations. I like to think the lines and crosshatching resemble what one might see on the remnants of ancient columns. The holes suggest what one might see in an old wall shot at by cannon. This one is number 12 in the series, and was made for an office building in White Plains near the Court House.

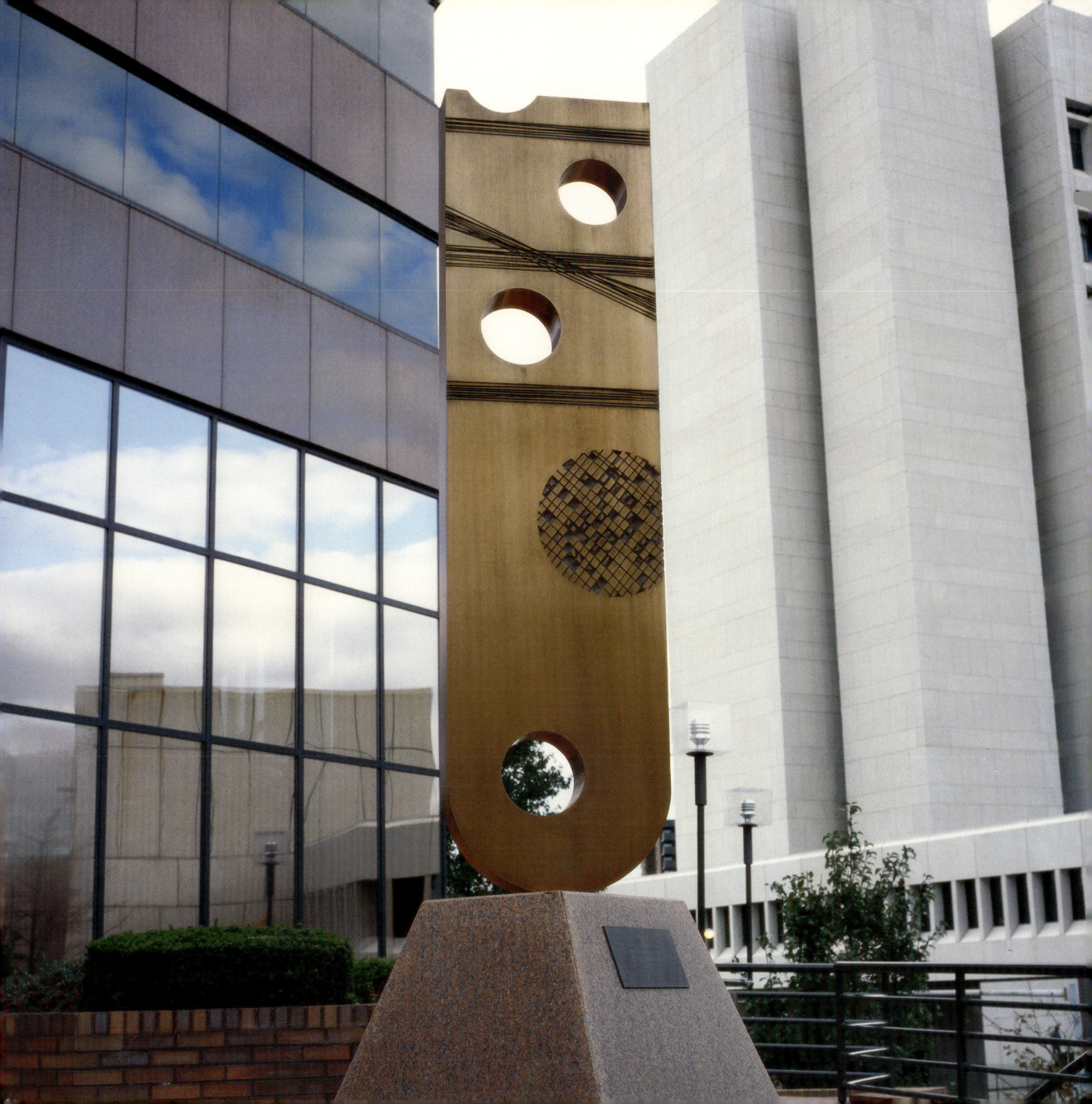

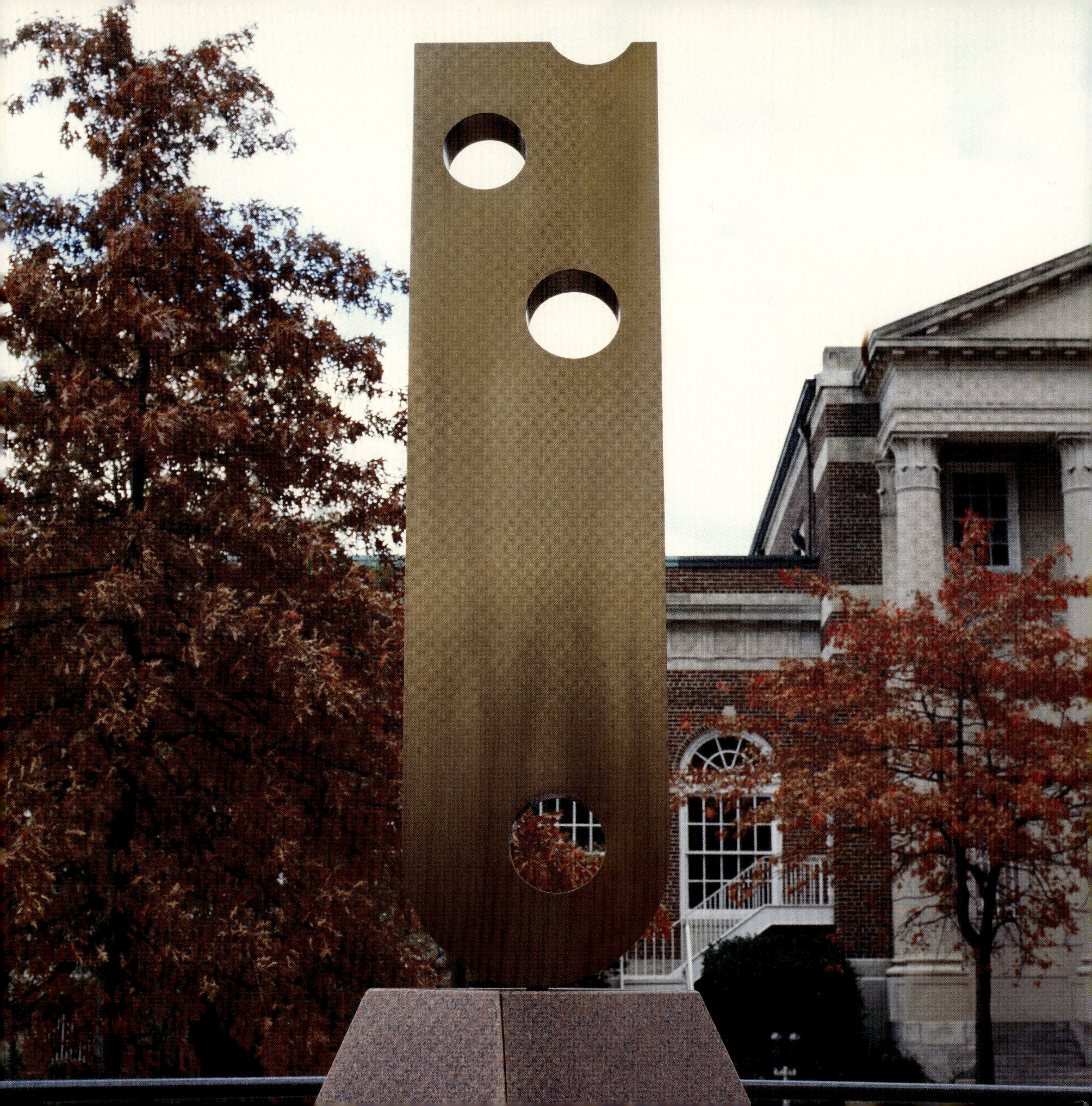

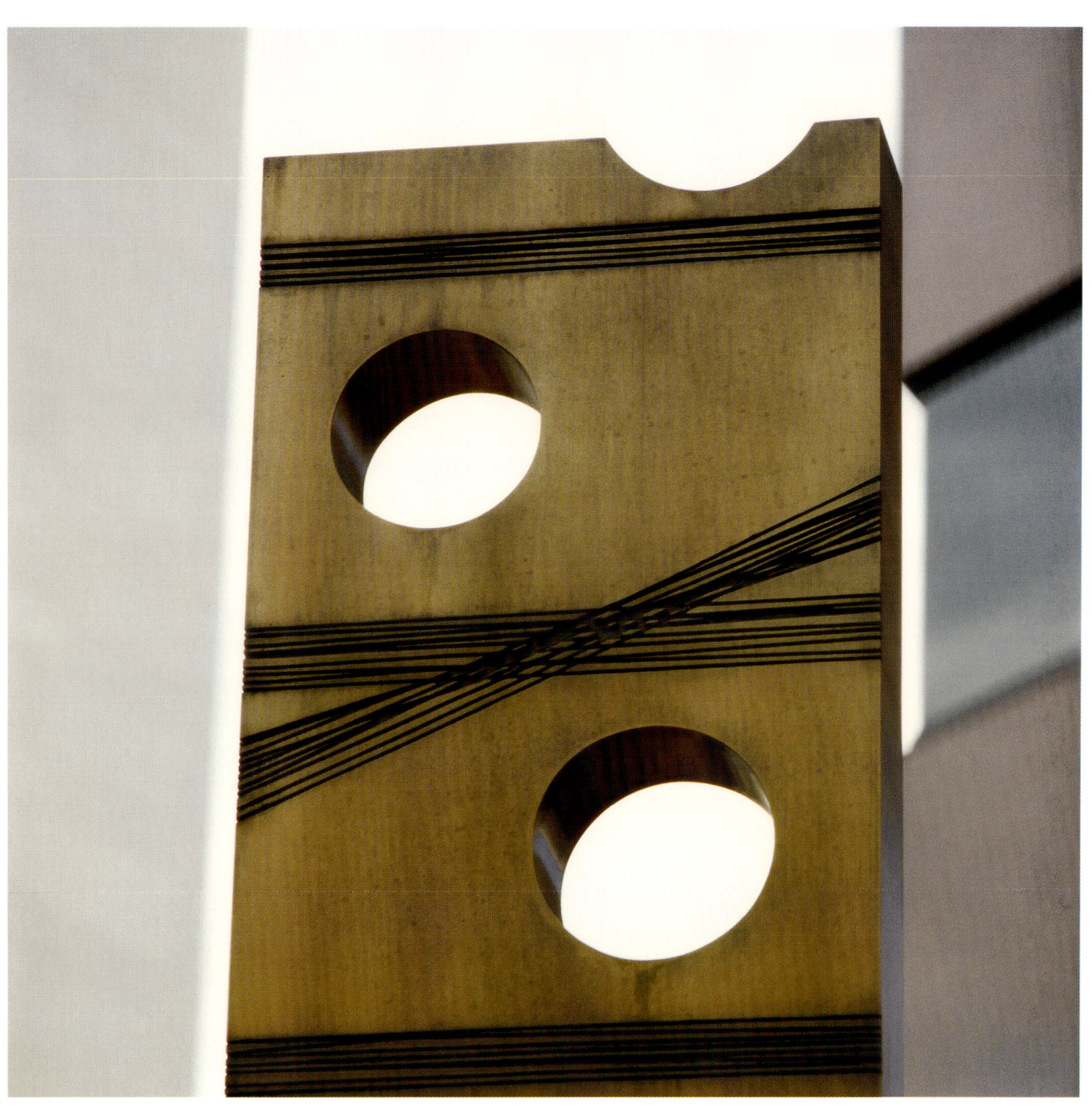

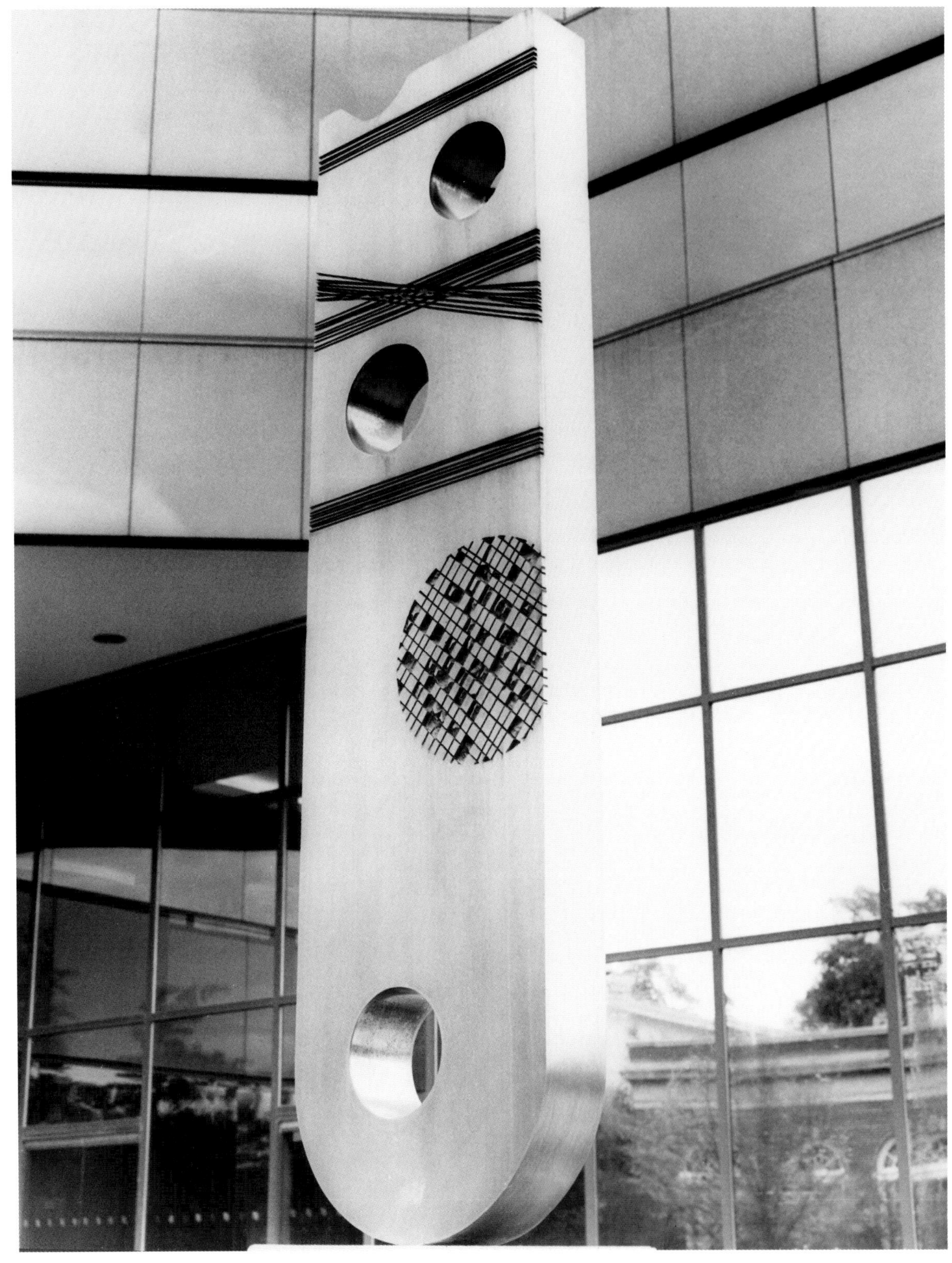

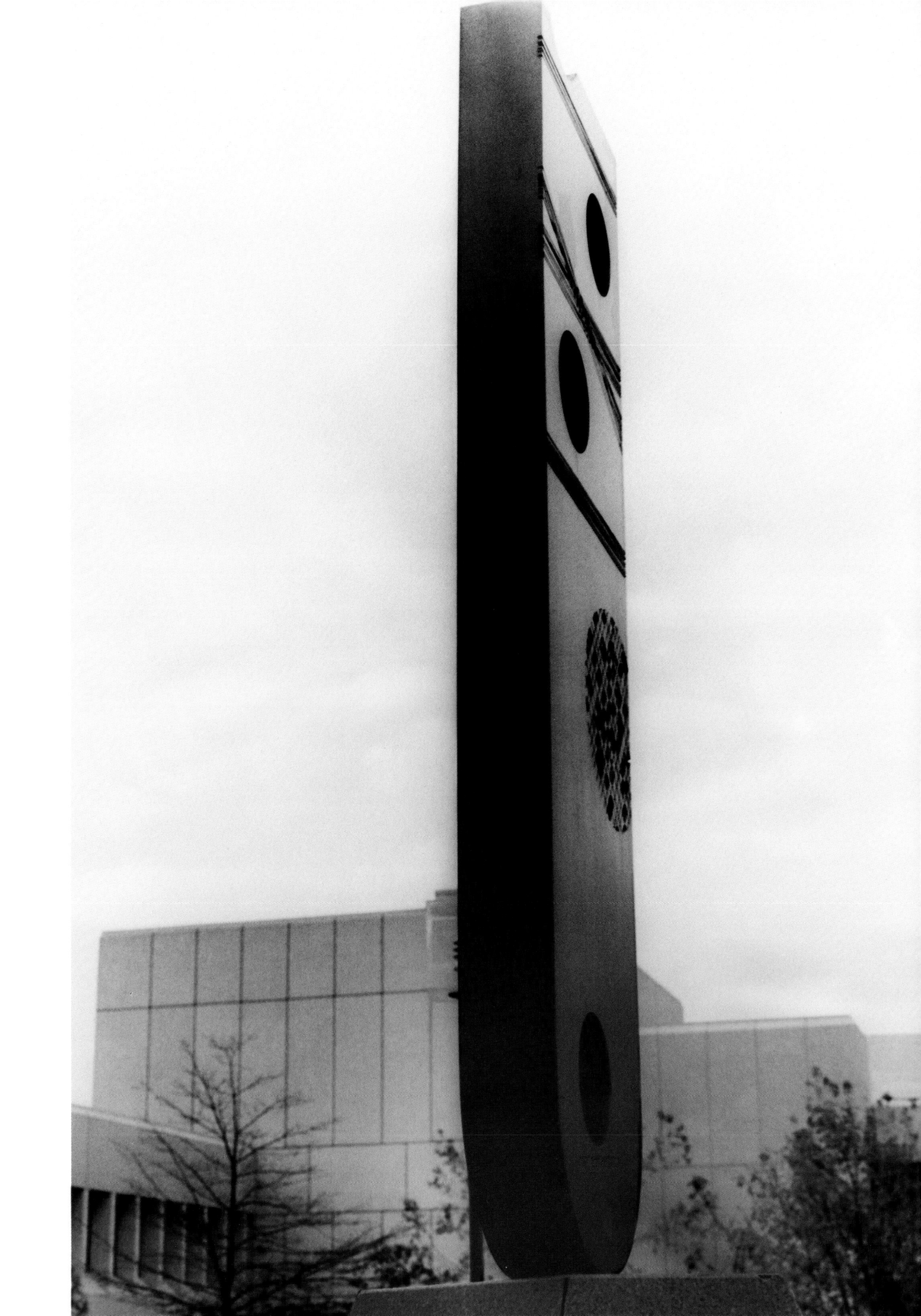

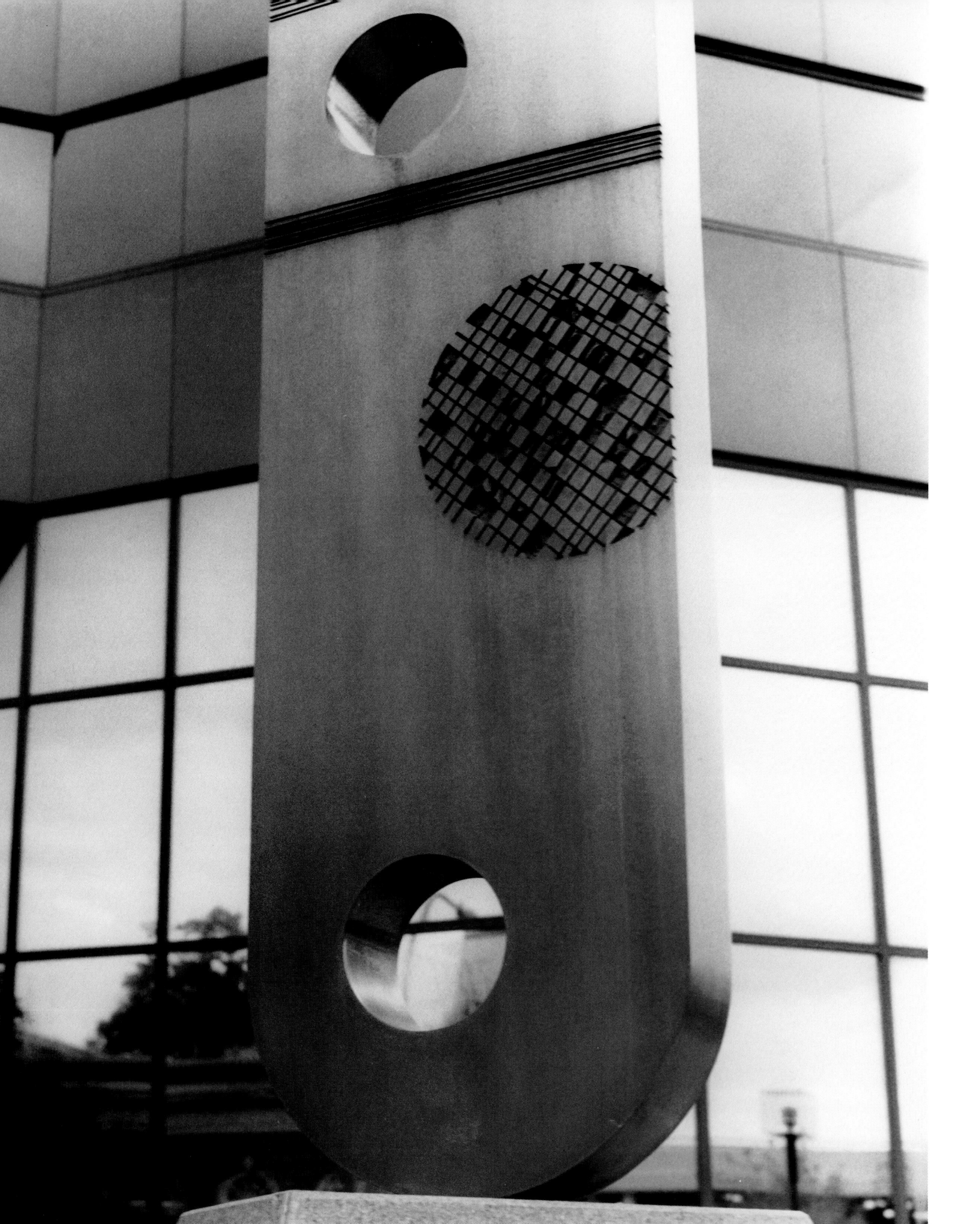

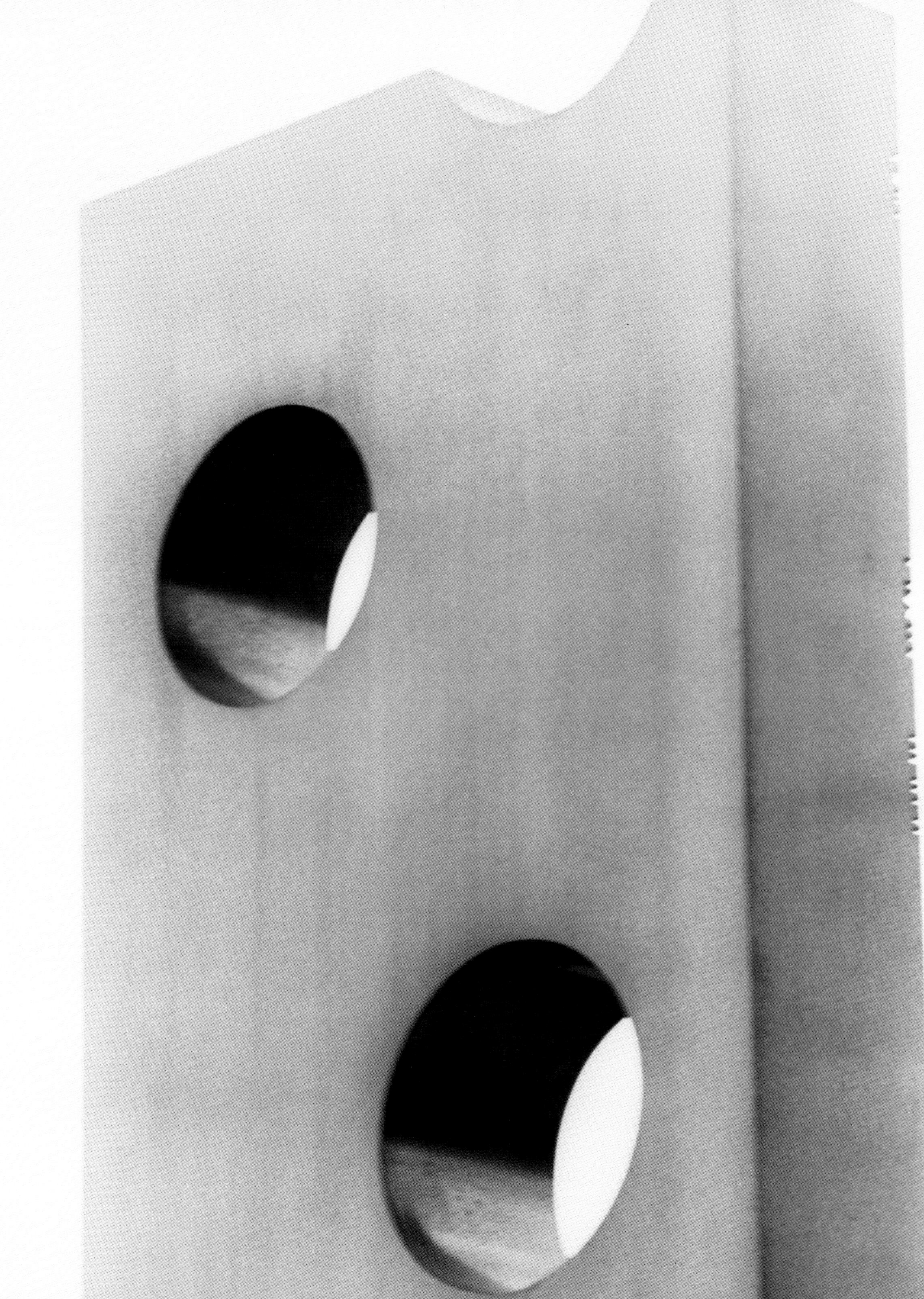

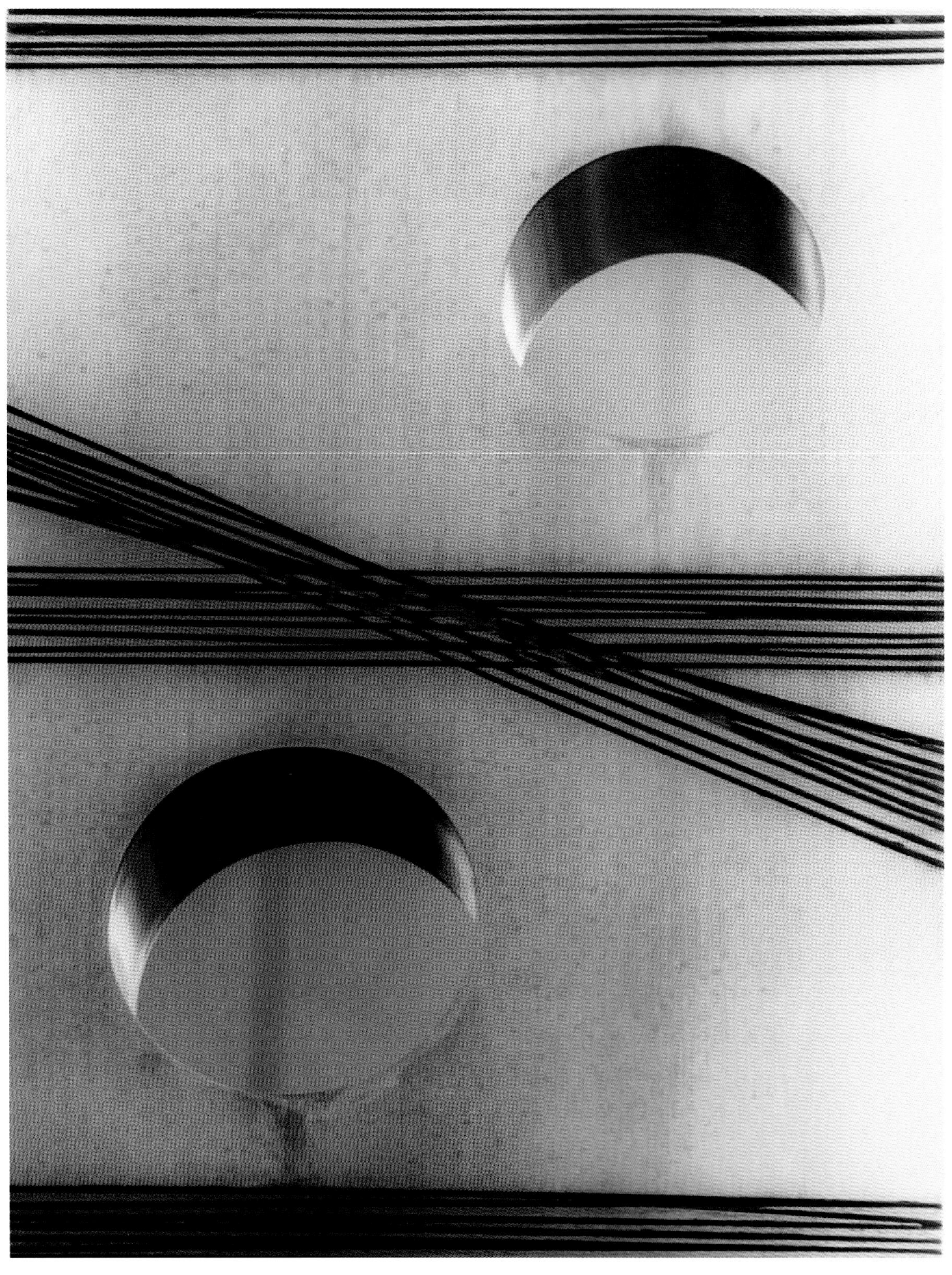

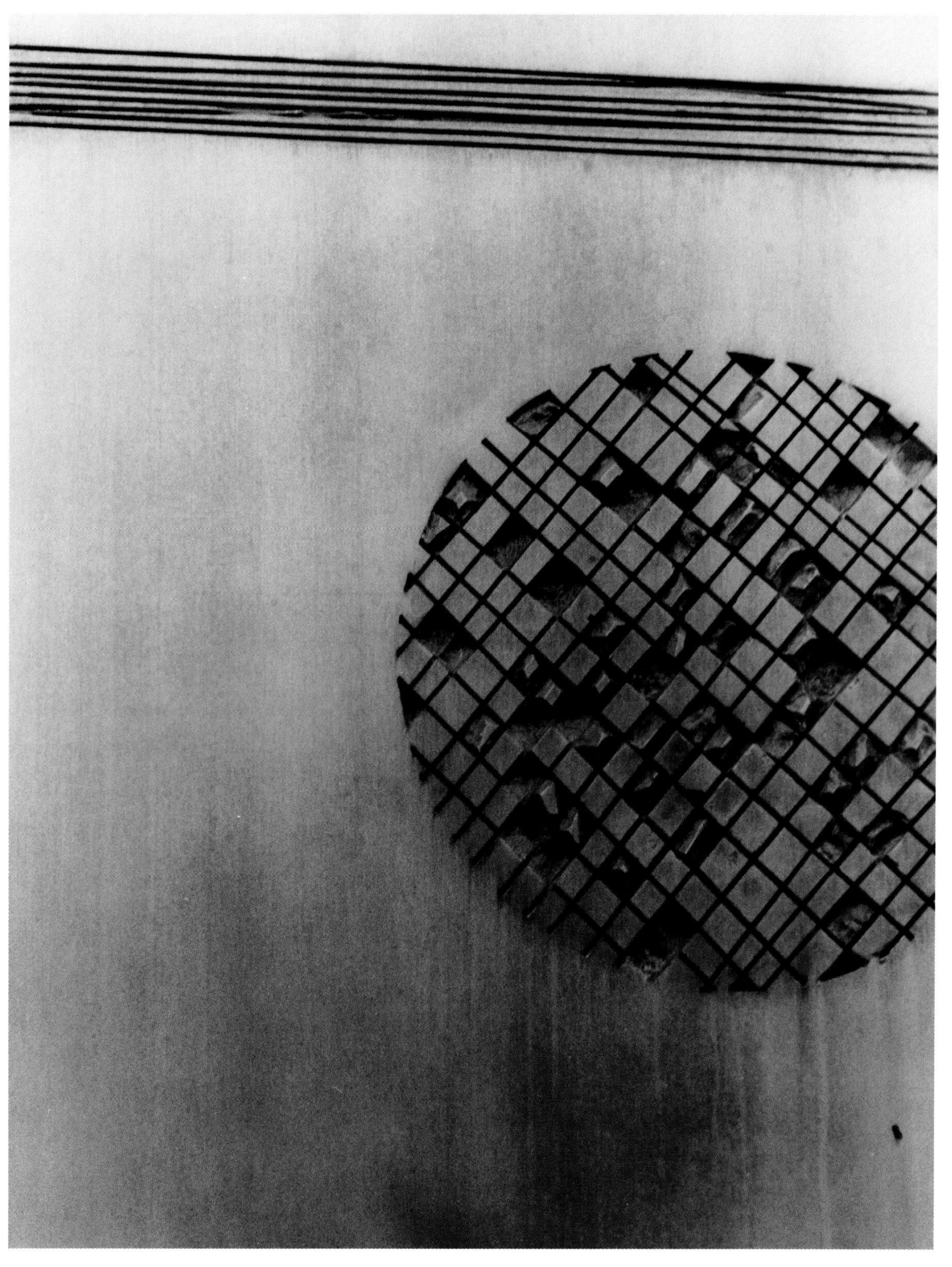

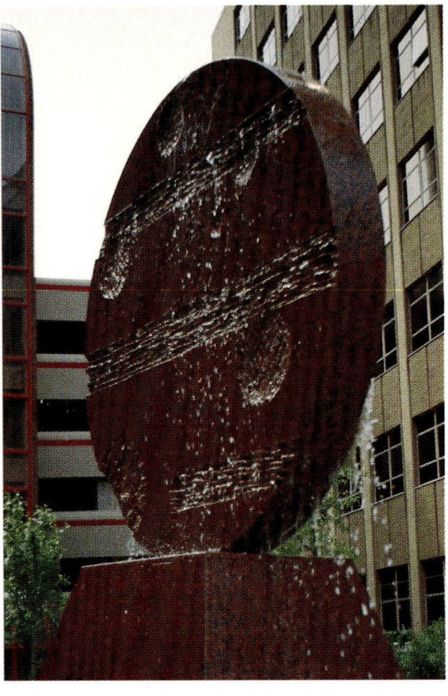 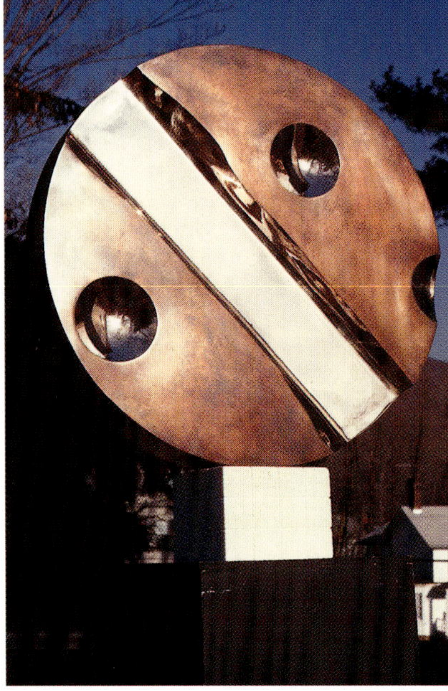 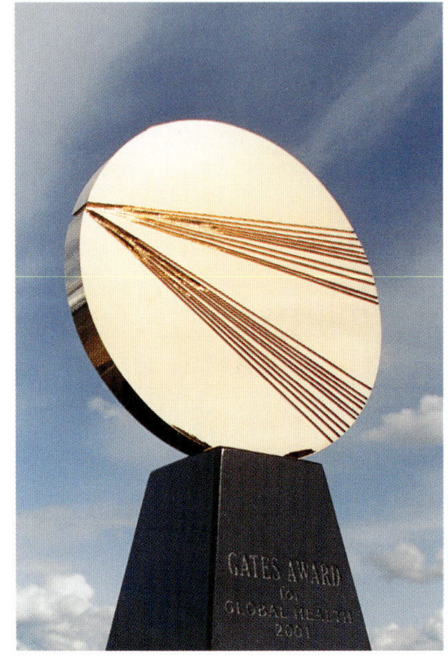

ALBA ROSA FOUNTAIN
1986
Red granite
6' 6" in diameter
Fenwick Park, Silver Spring, MA,
commissioned by Montgomery
County, MD

SOLAR DISC DAYBREAK
1987
Bronze
30" in diameter, on 4" base
Collection of the Artist

GATES AWARD
2001
Gold plated aluminum
11" in diameter, on 7" base
The Bill and Melinda Gates
Foundation, Seattle, WA

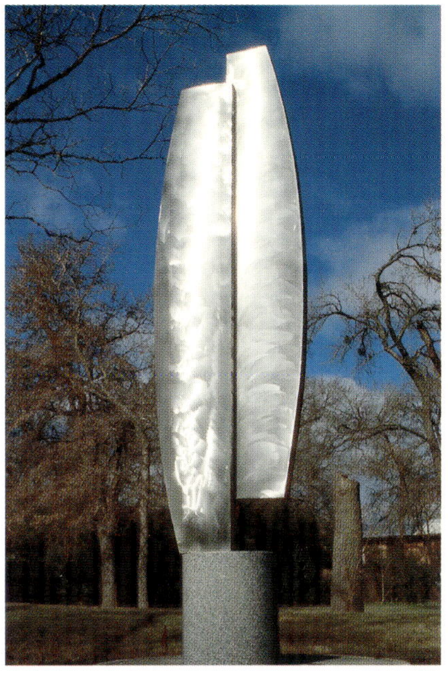 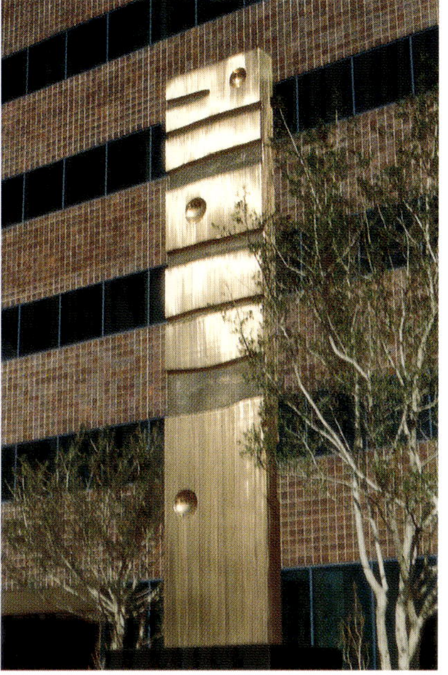 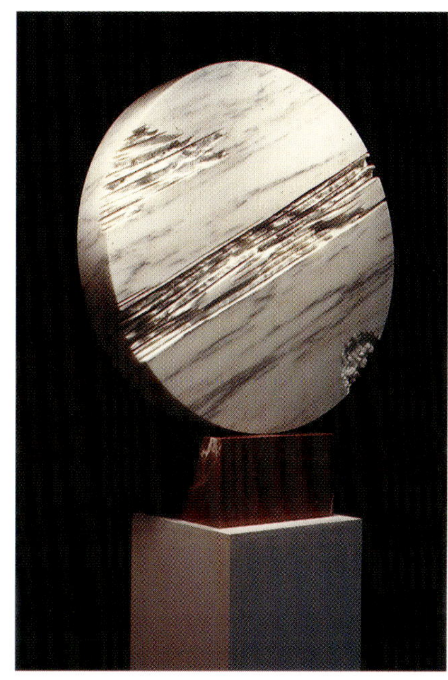

WE NEVER SAID GOODBYE,
or SOARING PIECE
1980
Stainless steel
76"x 18" x 6"
Collection of Dr. and
Mrs. Jerry Dersch, Redding, PA

STELE I
1980
Bronze
20' x 4'x 8"
Waterway Tower, Las Colinas,
Irving, TX

CARRARA DISC
1985
Carrara Marble
36" X 36" X 5"
General Electric Headquarters,
Fairfield, CT

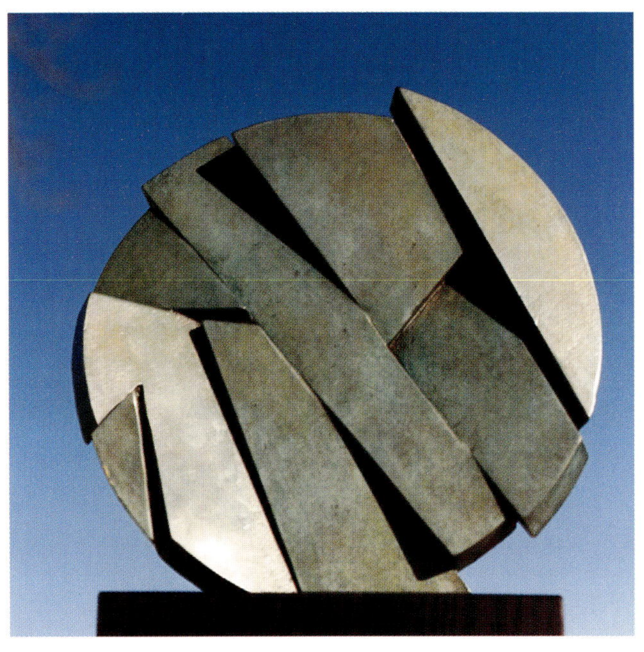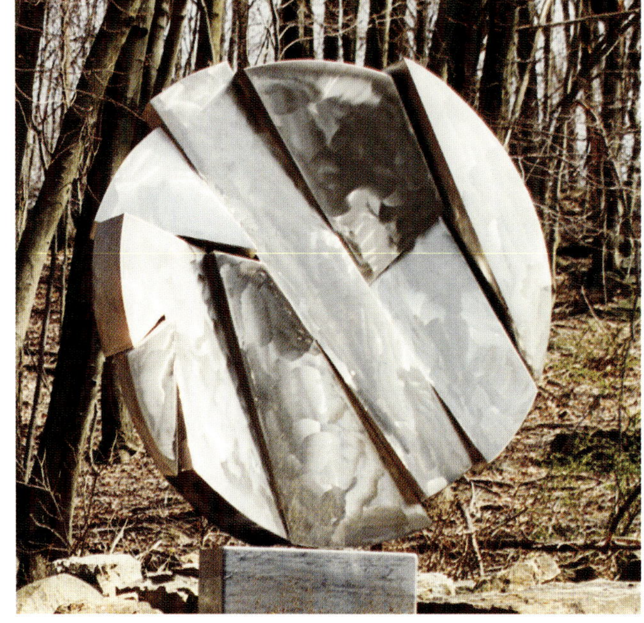

SPIRIT OF JAZZ
1994
Bronze
9" in diameter, on 4" base
Collection of Jazz at Lincoln Center

SPIRIT OF JAZZ
1996
Stainless steel
40" in diameter, on 6" base
Collection of Ann Wycoff,
Seattle, WA

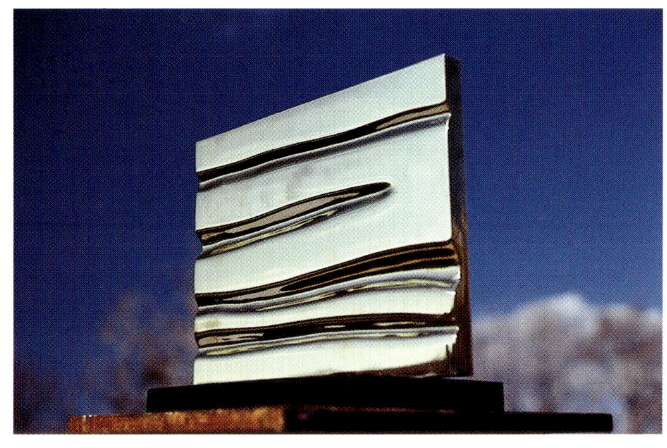 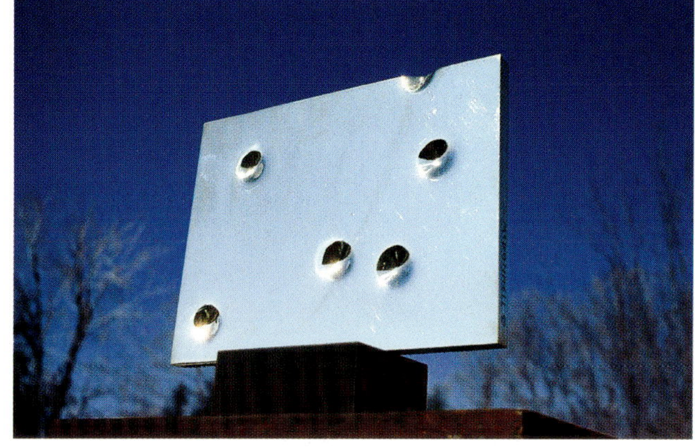

CROSS RIVER 3
1982
brass
12" X 15" X 1"
whereabouts unknown

CROSS RIVER 5
1982
brass
12" X 15" X ¾"
whereabouts unknown

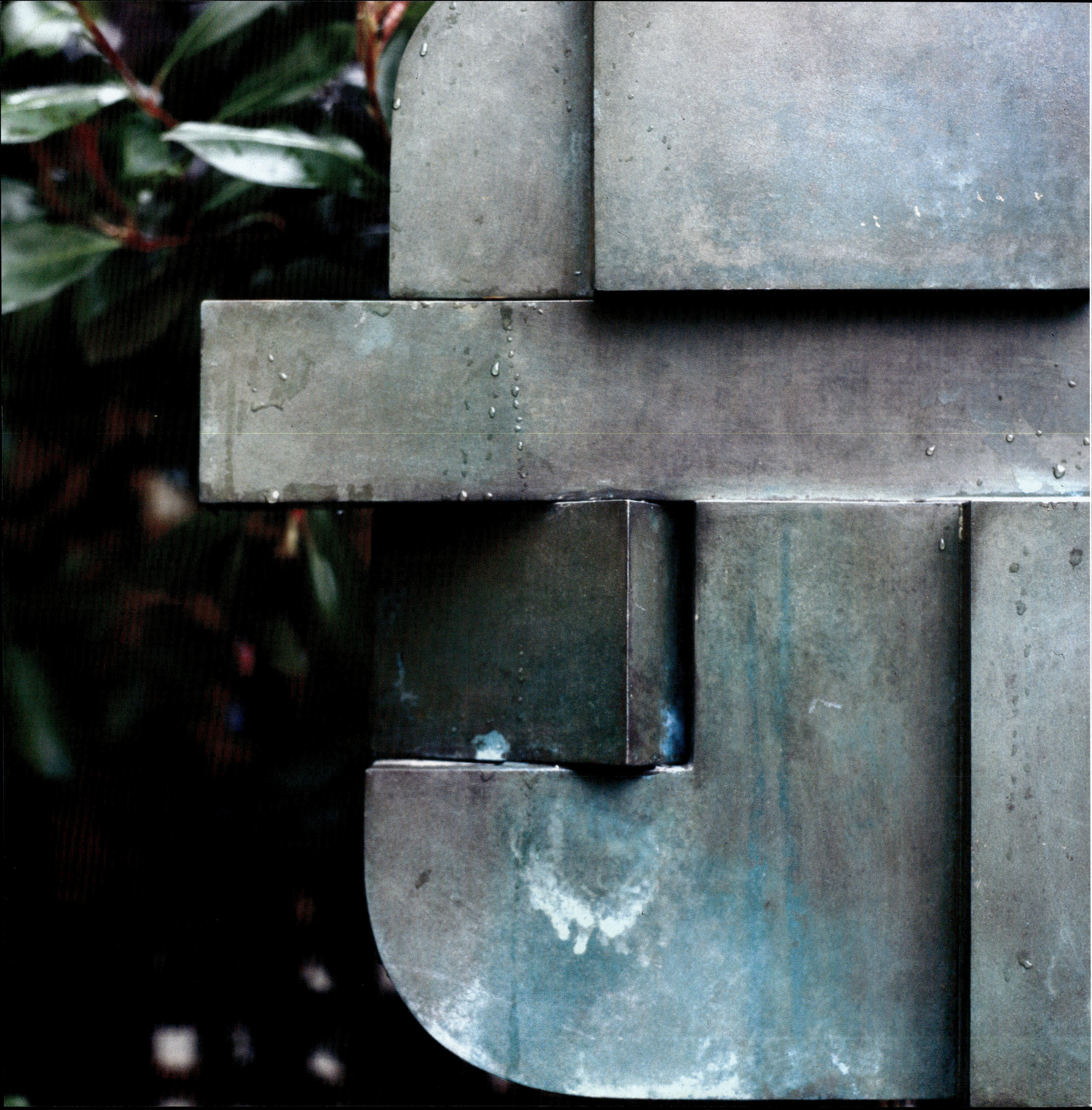

LOCKING PIECES

As I experimented with the *Locking Piece* sculptures, working through various sizes and different materials, I discovered that although the small bronze model, *Locking Piece II*, and the much larger, *Locking Piece IV,* and *Etruria (Locking Piece I)* were almost identical in the design of their shapes and forms, the "personality" of the sculptures changed radically according to the medium I used. The dark surface of the small bronze gave a sense of solidity and an implication of heaviness; the burnished surface of the more monumental stainless steel version subtly reflected the surrounding trees, sky, and clouds and, as Christopher Youngs, director of the Freedman Gallery at Albright College stated, made one sculpture seem to "float like a smoke ring."

Opposite page: Mayan Fountain

MAYAN FOUNTAIN

2002
Bronze
23" x 20" x 4"
Collection of the artist

The *Mayan Fountain* reminded me of ancient Mayan glyphs. Its basic shapes are square with rounded corners, divided into varied sections that are arranged in an interesting manner allowing the water to flow over it in a very poetic and gentle way. The hole helps to make the piece visually float on the water. I like the idea of having several moveable sections.

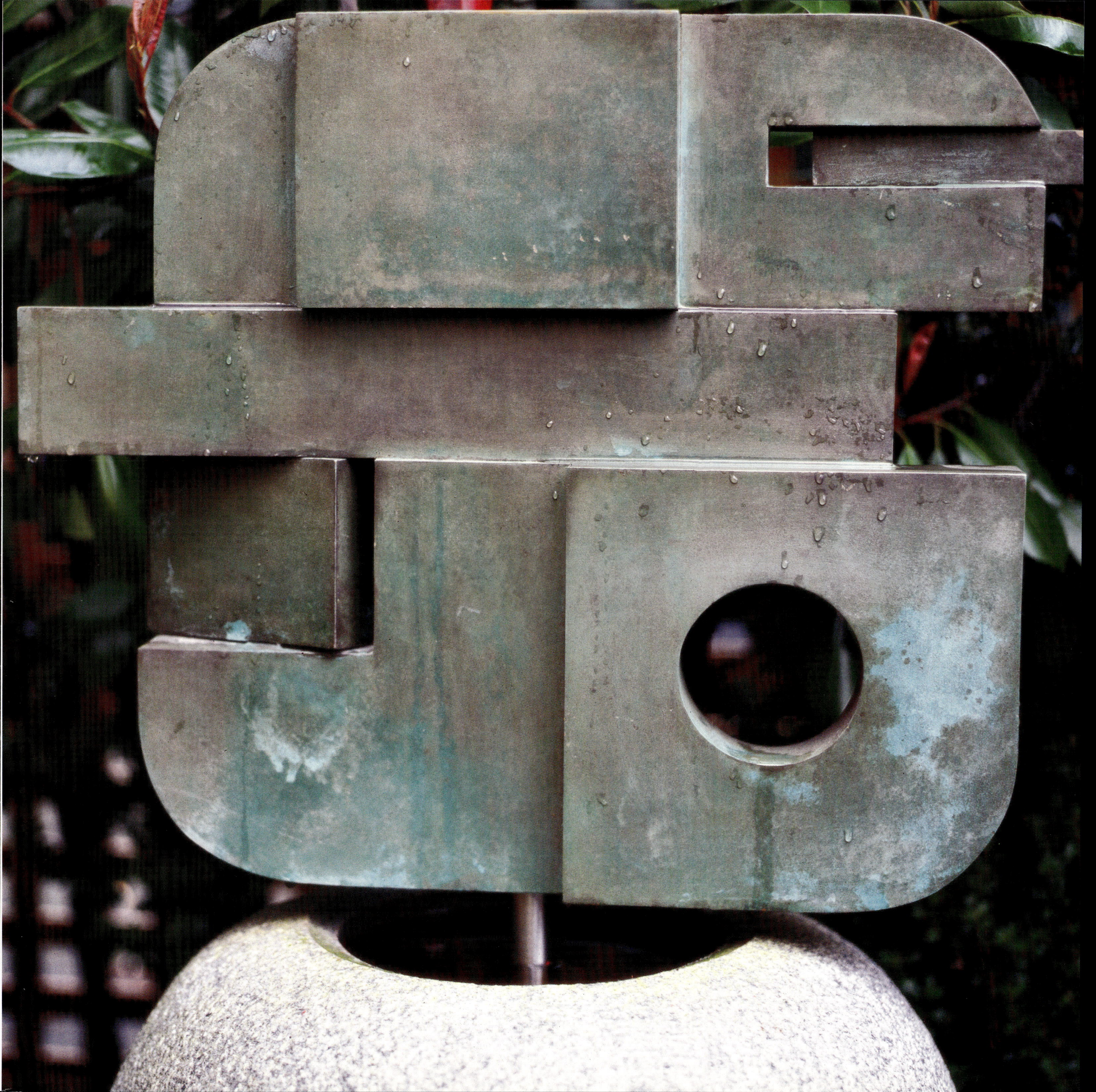

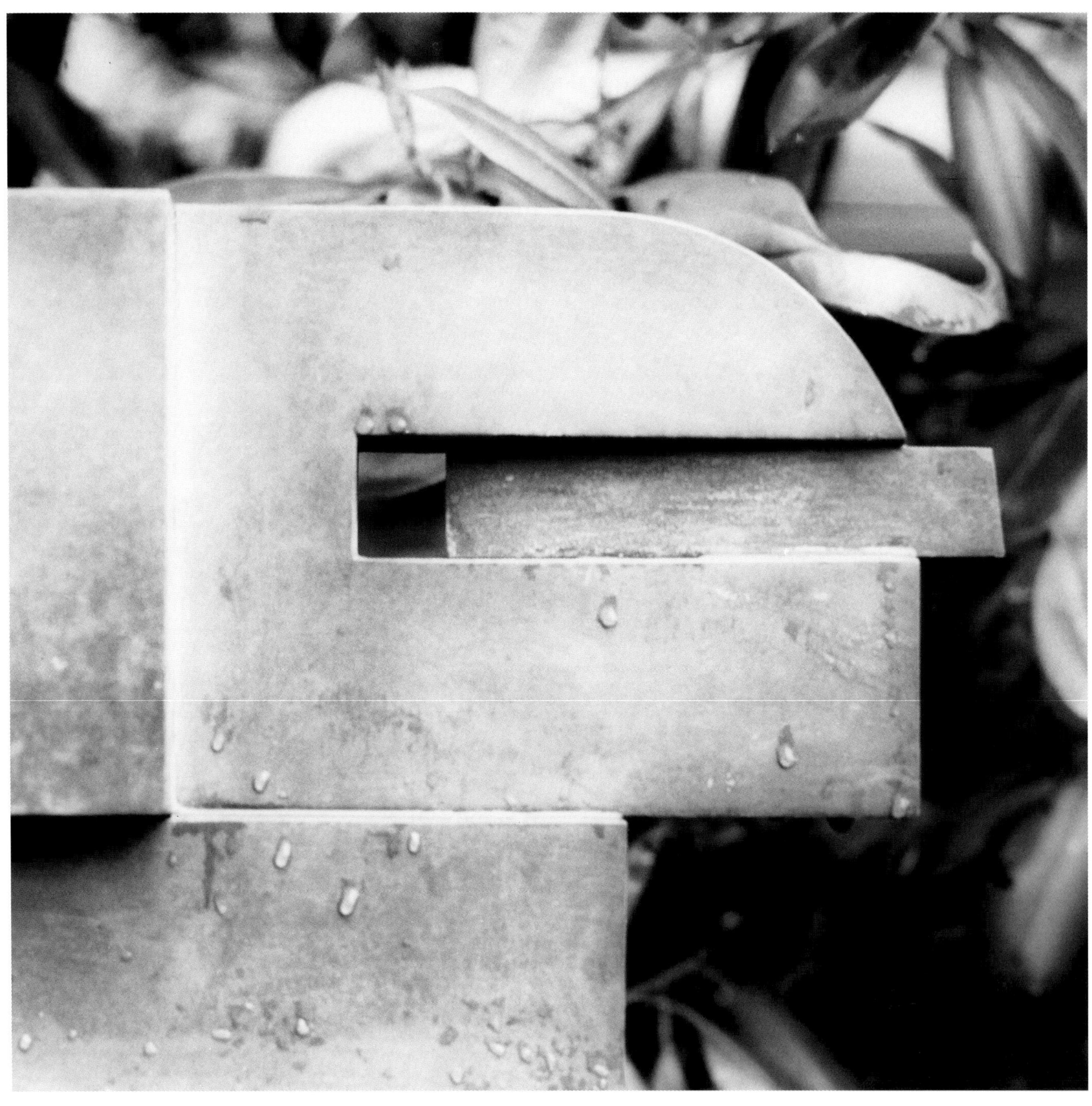

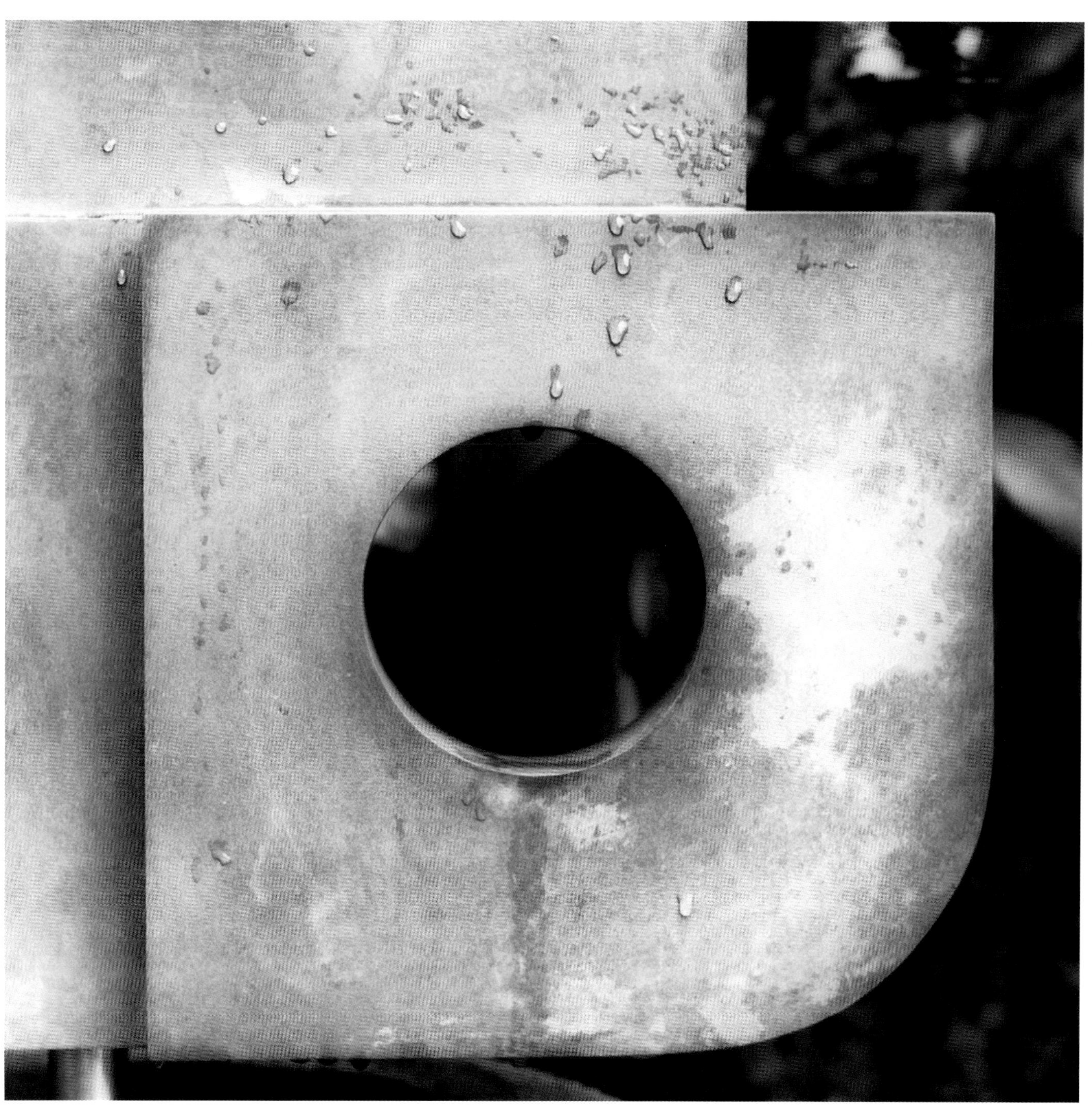

LOCKING PIECE II

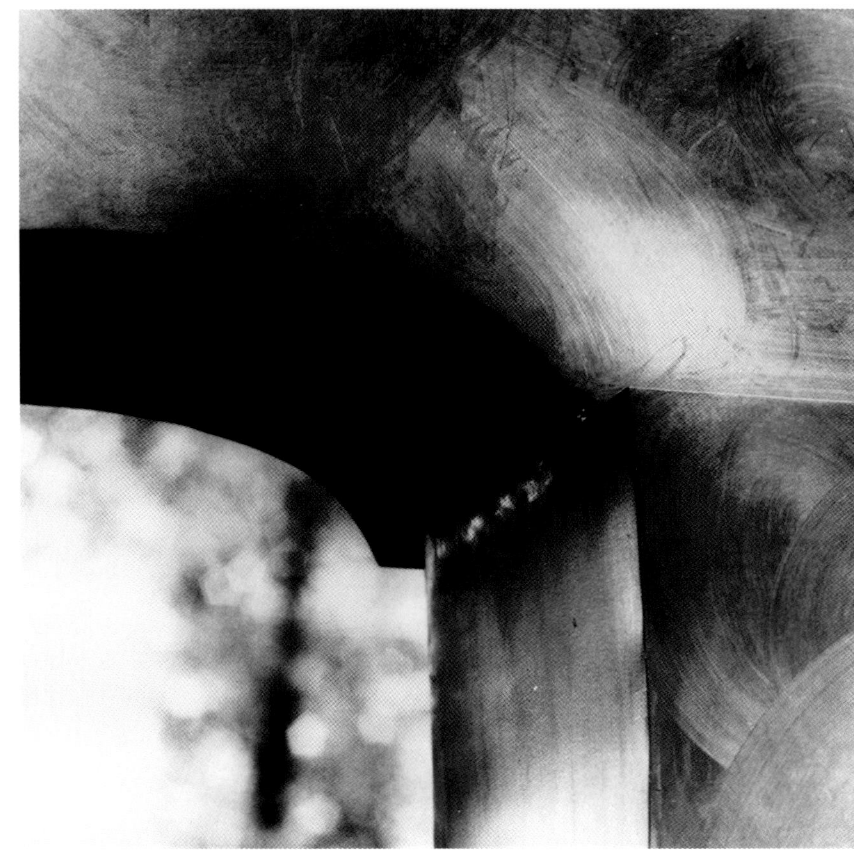

1994
6' x 6'
Bronze
Robert and Pamela Goergen, Greenwich, CT
and Jerry and Rhoda Dersch, Mohuton, PA

I charted a shape that was 2/3 of the way between a
square and a circle. I quartered it into unequal sections,
and assembled them offset with a slight opening left at
the bottom. This opening, or "passage," reminded me
of the openings in the Anasazi cliff dwellings of the
Southwest.

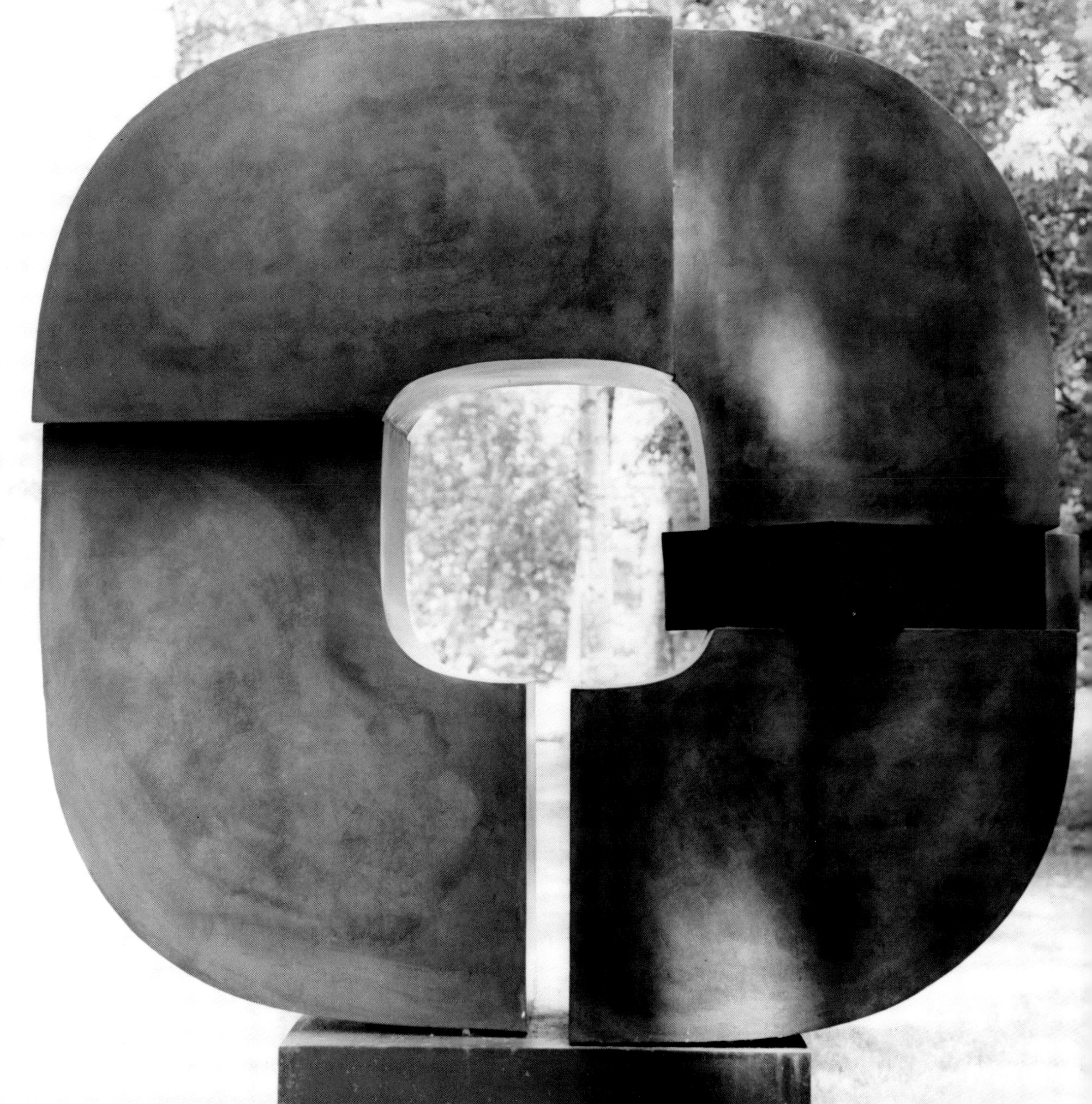

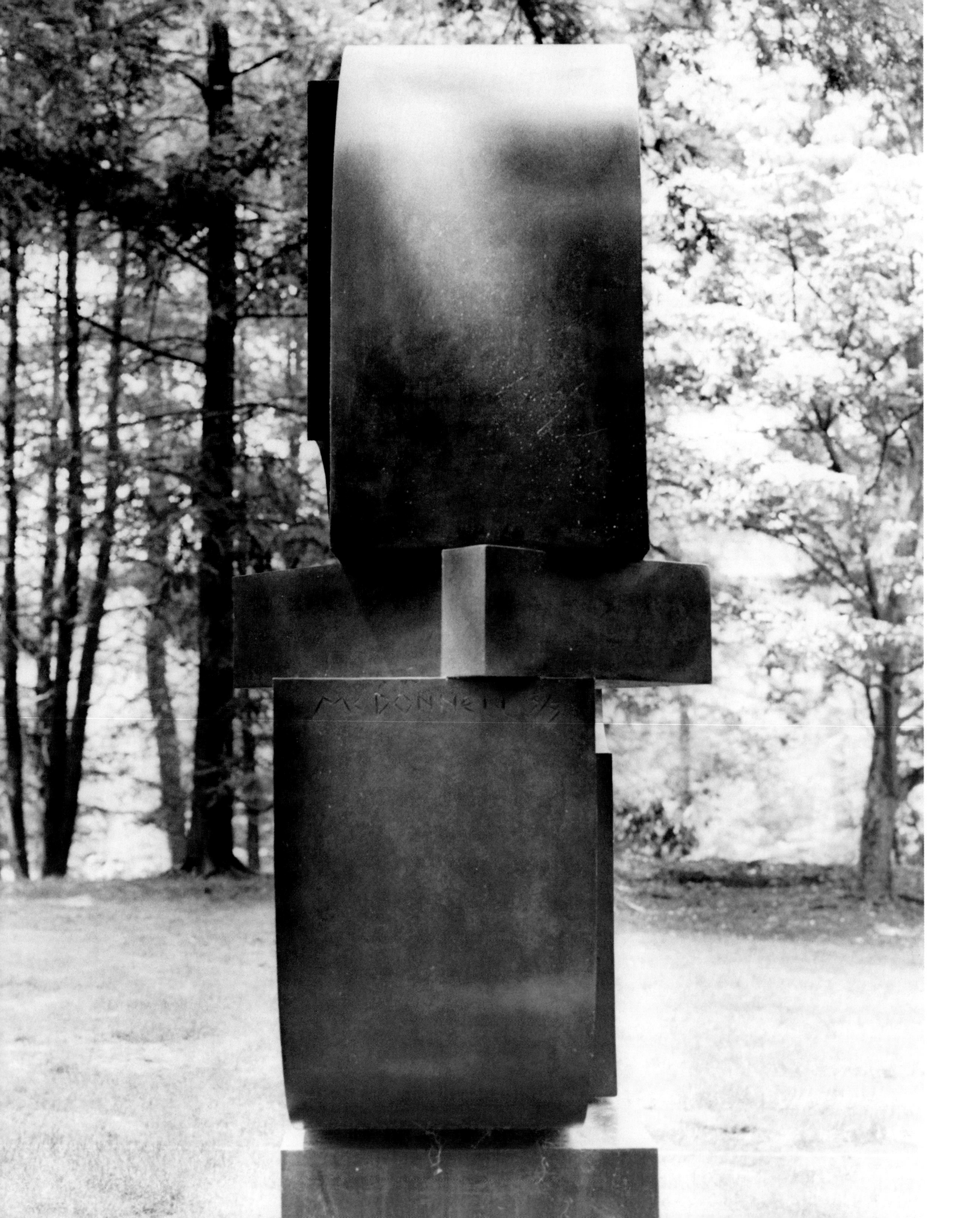

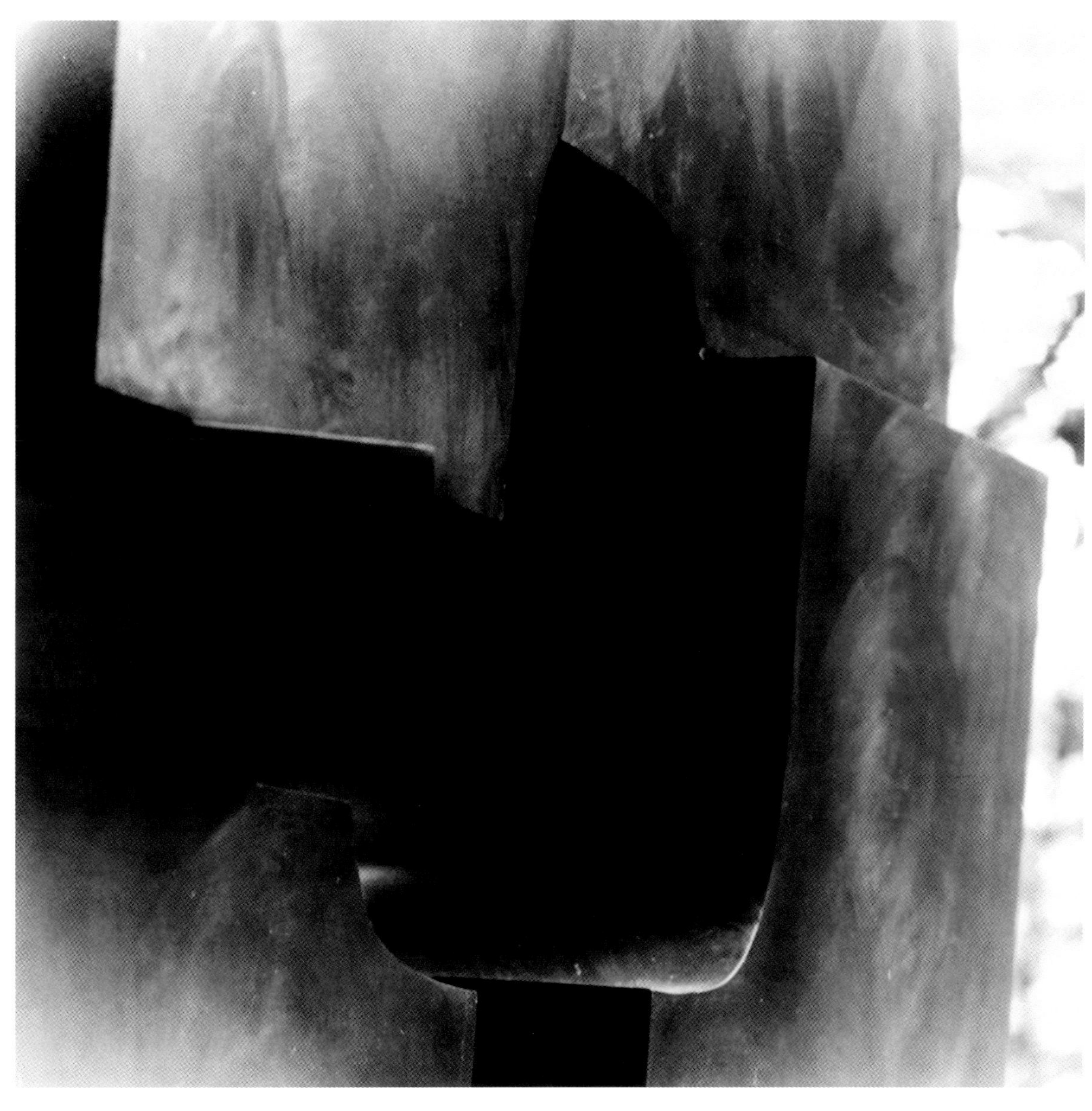

ETRURIA:
LOCKING PIECE I

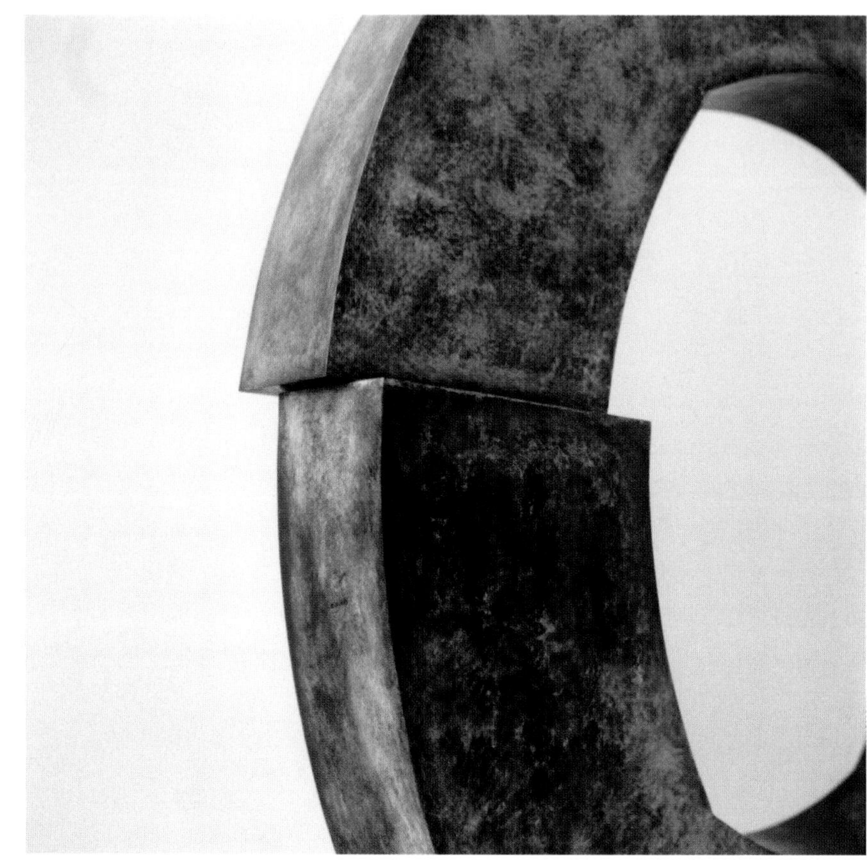

Bronze
48" x 38" x 6"
collections of Marybeth and Bob Cresci, Garrison, NY
Susan and Jeffery Stern, Scarsdale, NY
Judy Evnin Greenwich, CT

Etruria is the Italian word for Tuscany. The sculpture was inspired by an Etruscan bracelet I saw in the Archeological Museum of Florence. In my interpretation a set of arcs form the top and bottom. They are, if connected, actually sections of the same circle. The sides are arcs from a larger circle whose center lies outside the sculpture. The small locking piece section was added to make the work more interesting. Its proportion is the thickness of the circle.

There are several versions of this particular design. The original was about 18" tall. The largest is 10' and is sited in front of the State Office Building in Trenton, NJ.

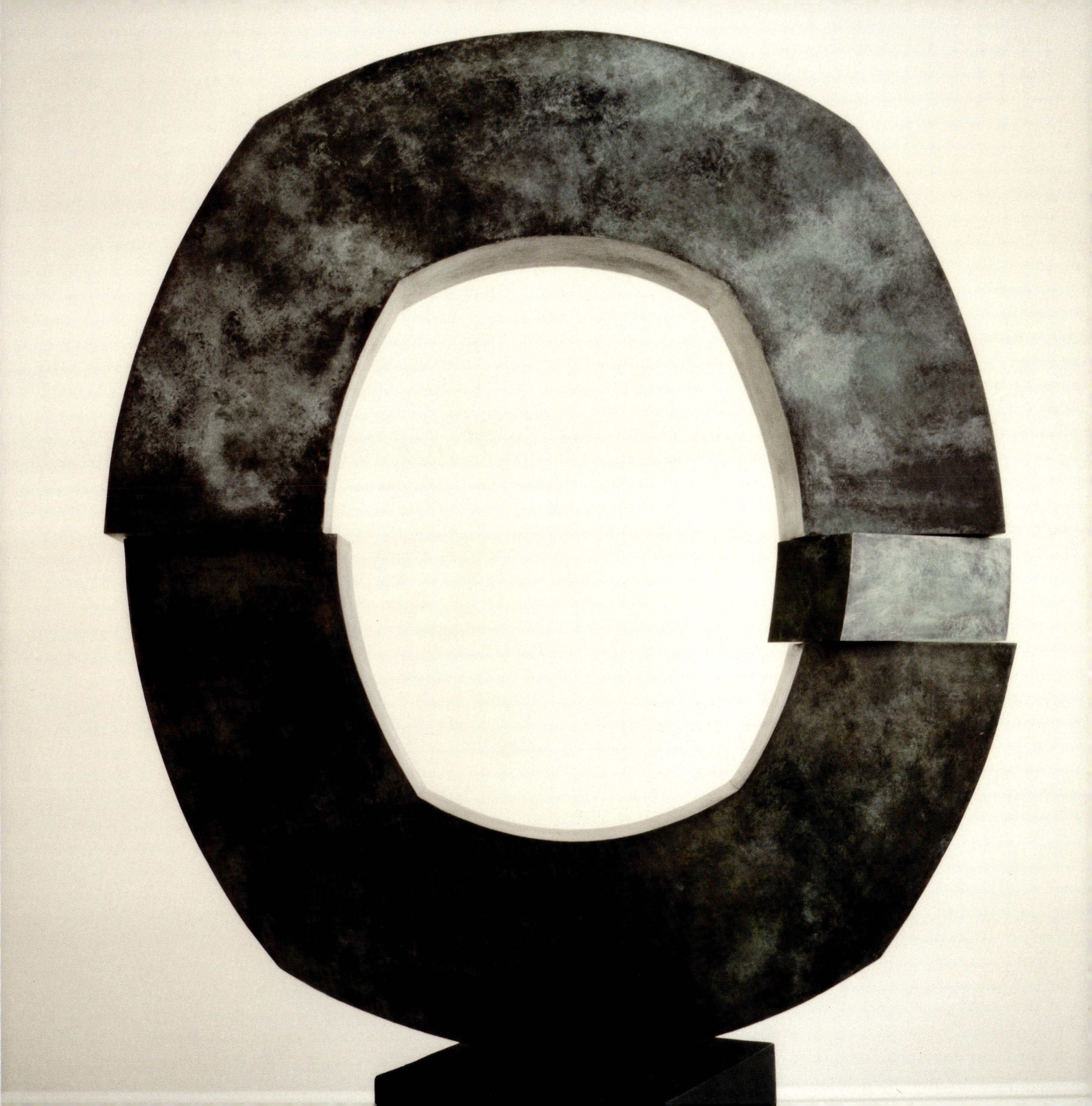

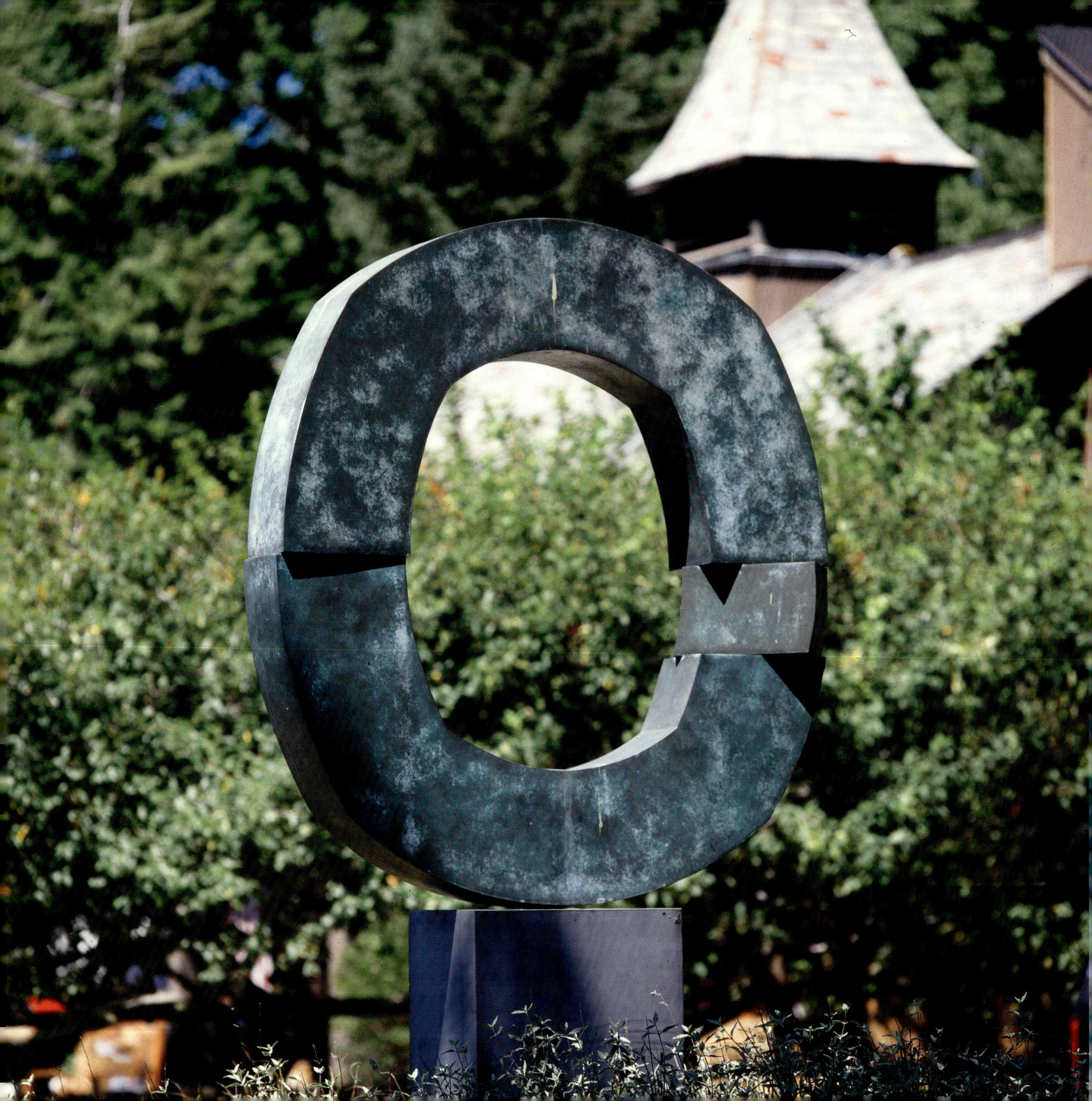

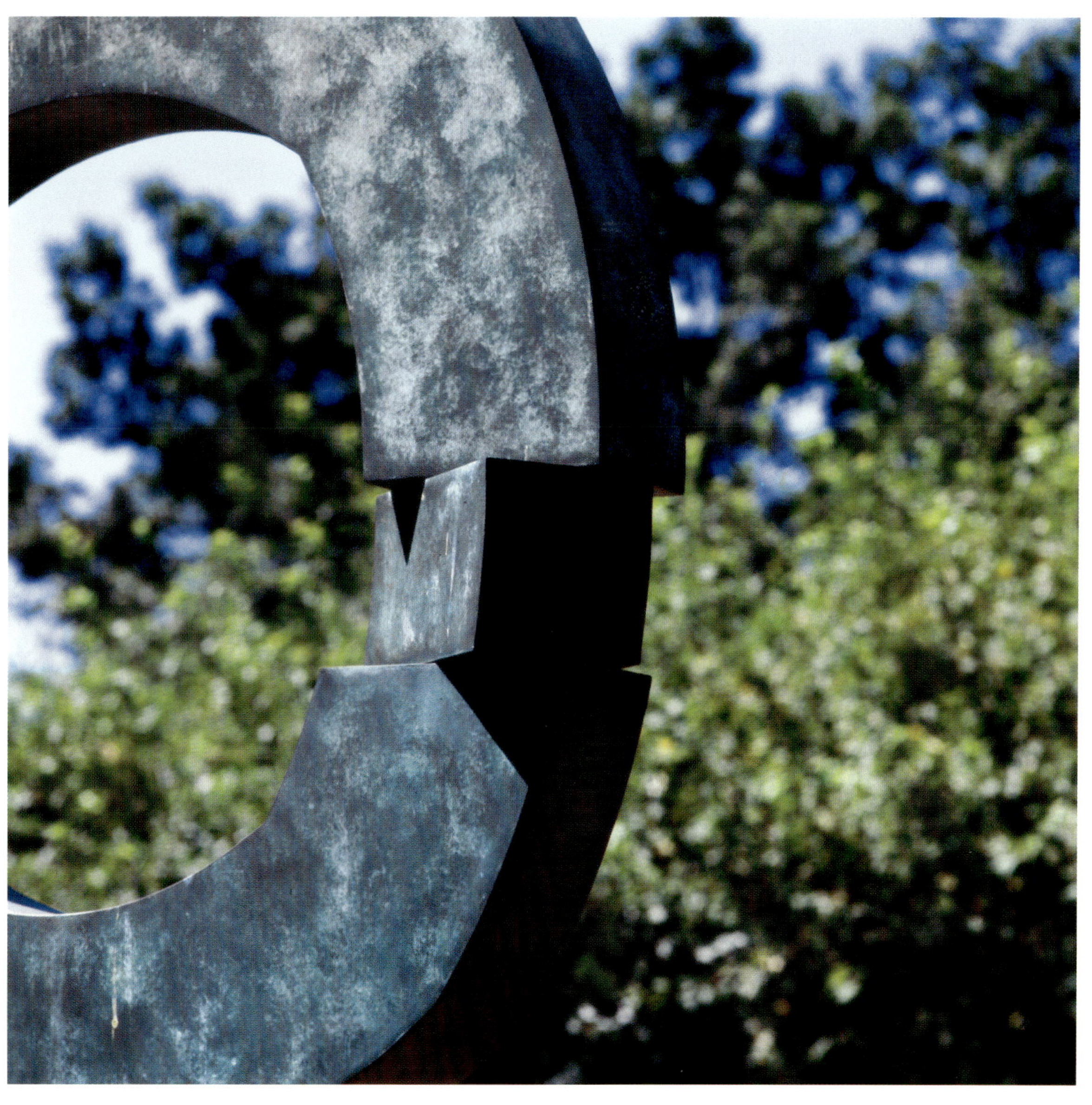

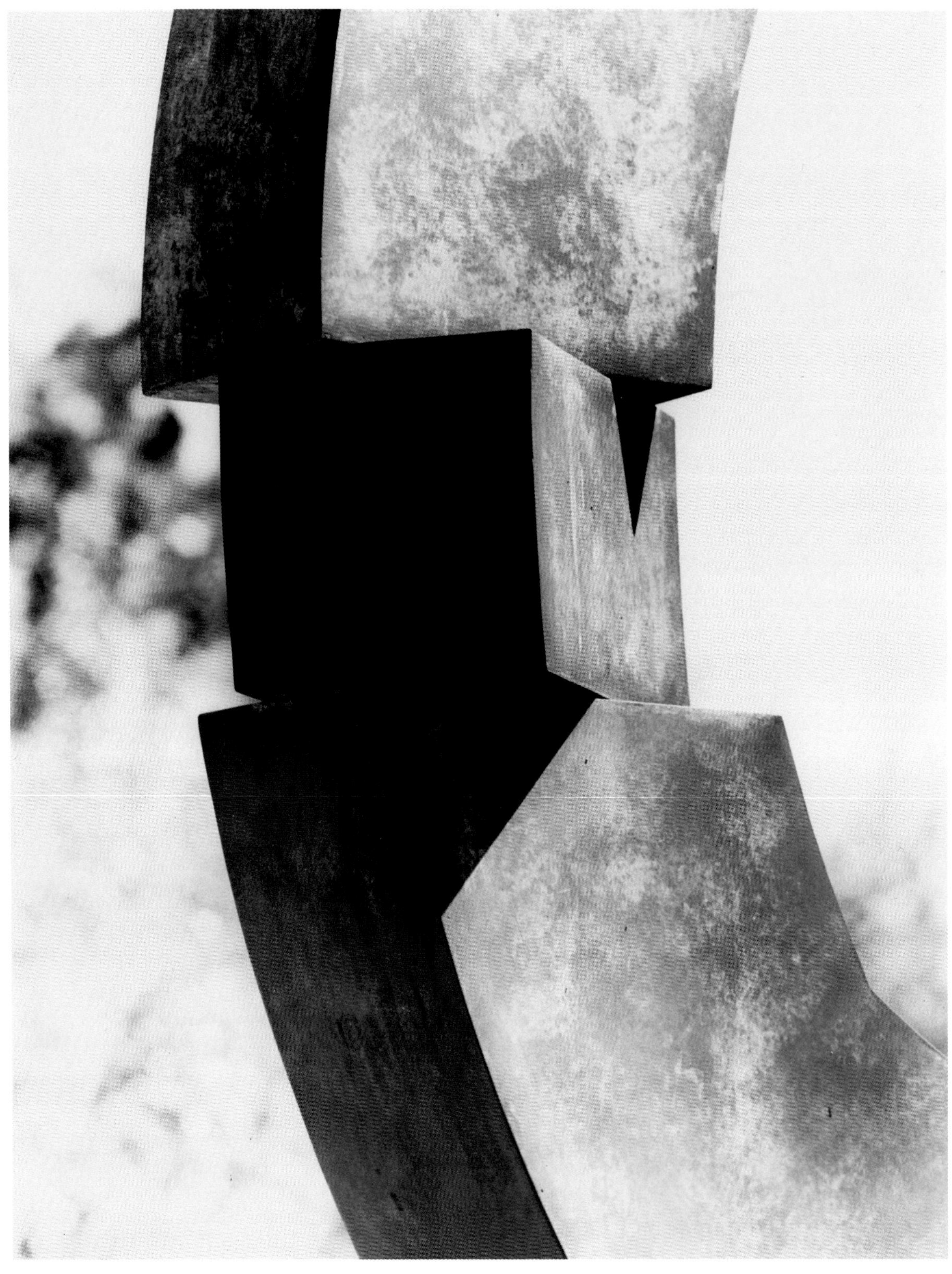

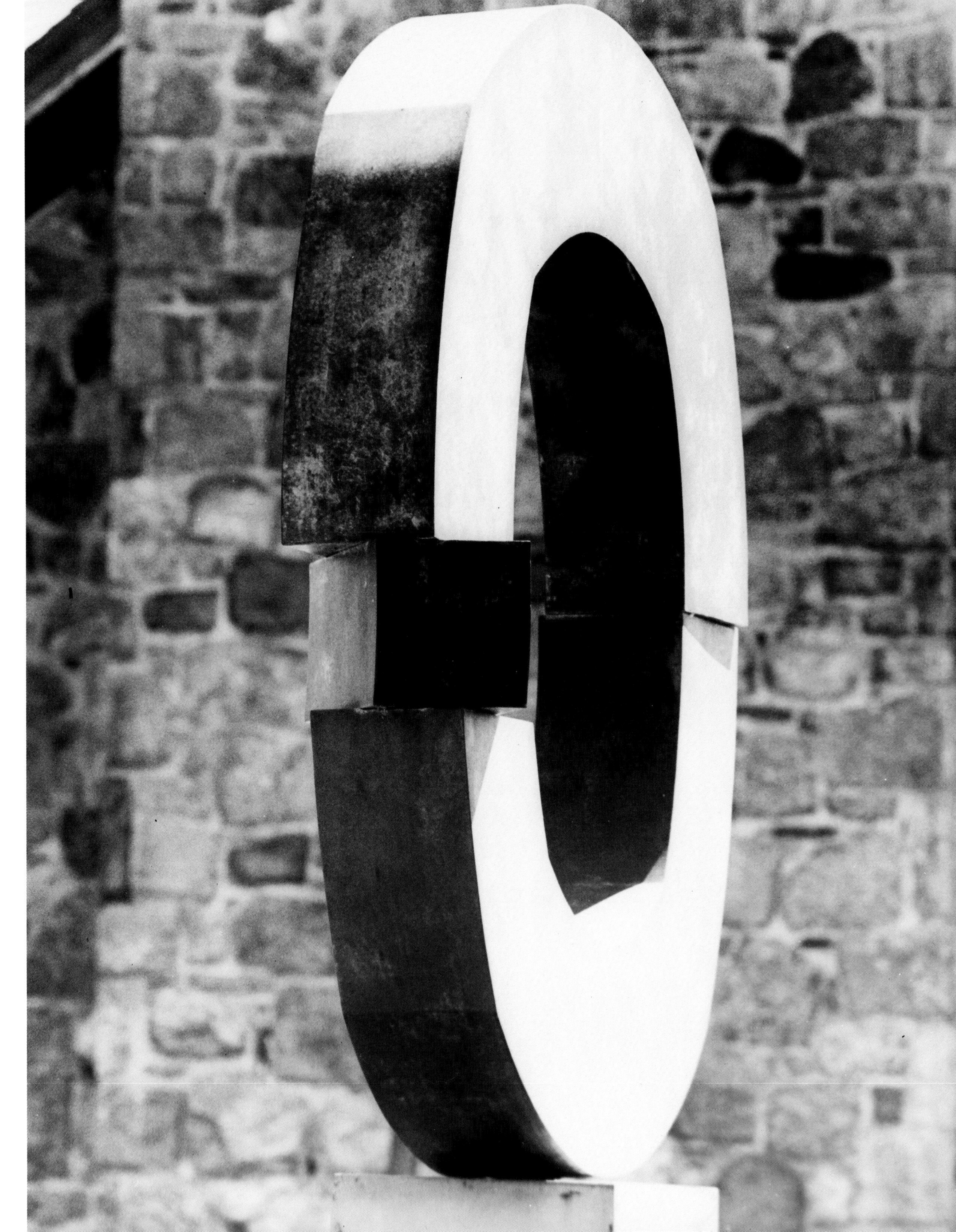

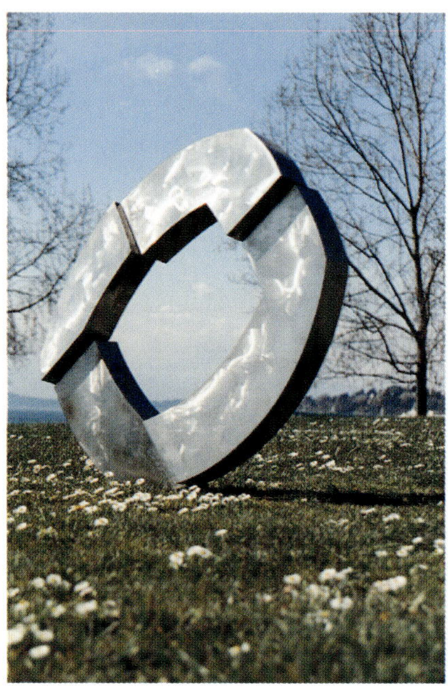

LOCKING PIECE IV:
ANGLE OF REPOSE
1997
Stainless Steel
8' x 10'
Collection of the artist

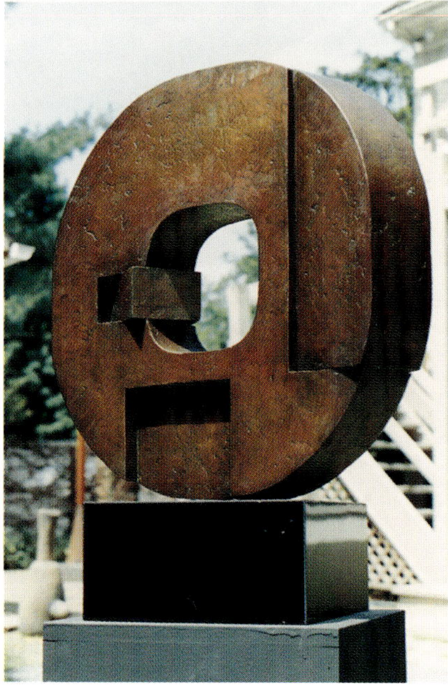

LOCKING PIECE III
1996
Bronze
18" x 18" x 4.5"
Collection of Faye and Herman
Sarkowsky, Rancho Mirage, CA

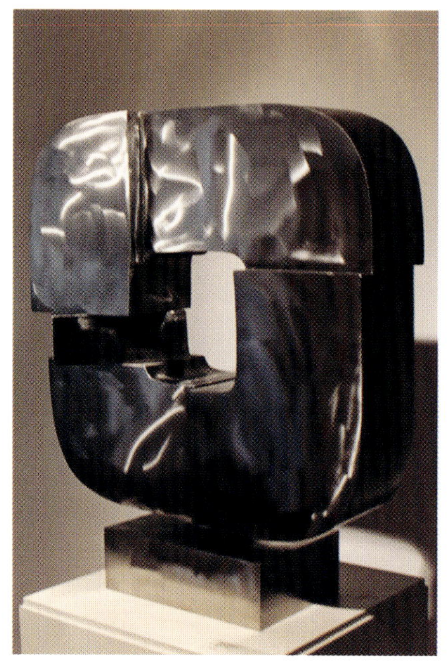

LOCKING PIECE II
2001
Stainless Steel
20" x 20" x 6"
Collectioin of Bill Gates, Sr.
Seattle WA

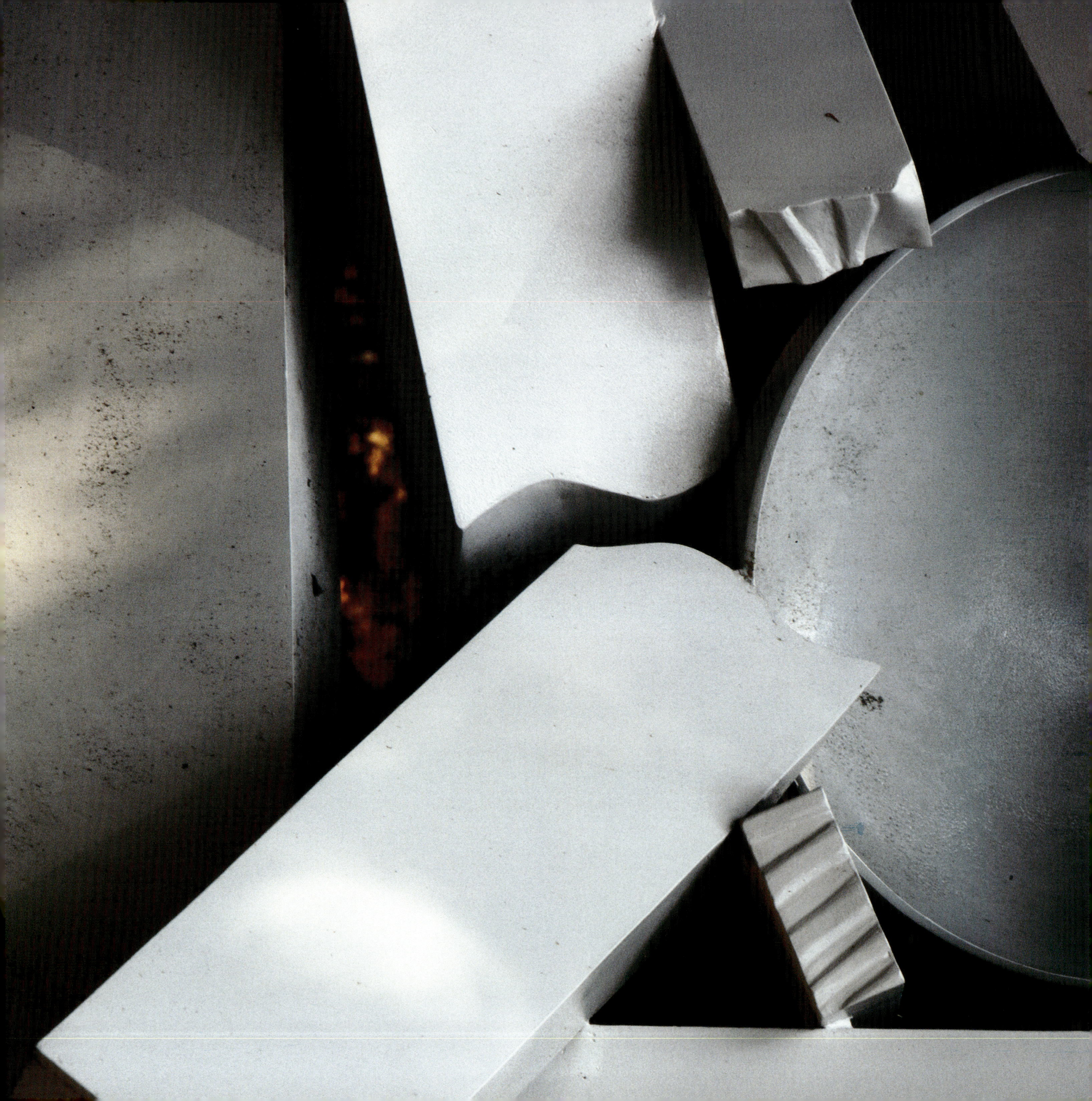

BREAKING AWAY

In 1980 a dramatic change took place in my life. My drinking had gotten out of control and I had to put "the plug in the jug." About the same time, I saw a broken picture frame. Chunks of wood, and bits of bowls, and other small forms broke through the splintered structure. It felt like my life, so many things coming apart that I would have to reconstruct. Like me it was breaking from the past. That composition inspired me to commence what I consider a very important series.

The original *Breaking Away* maquette hangs in the Century Association in New York.

Opposite page: Breaking Away: White

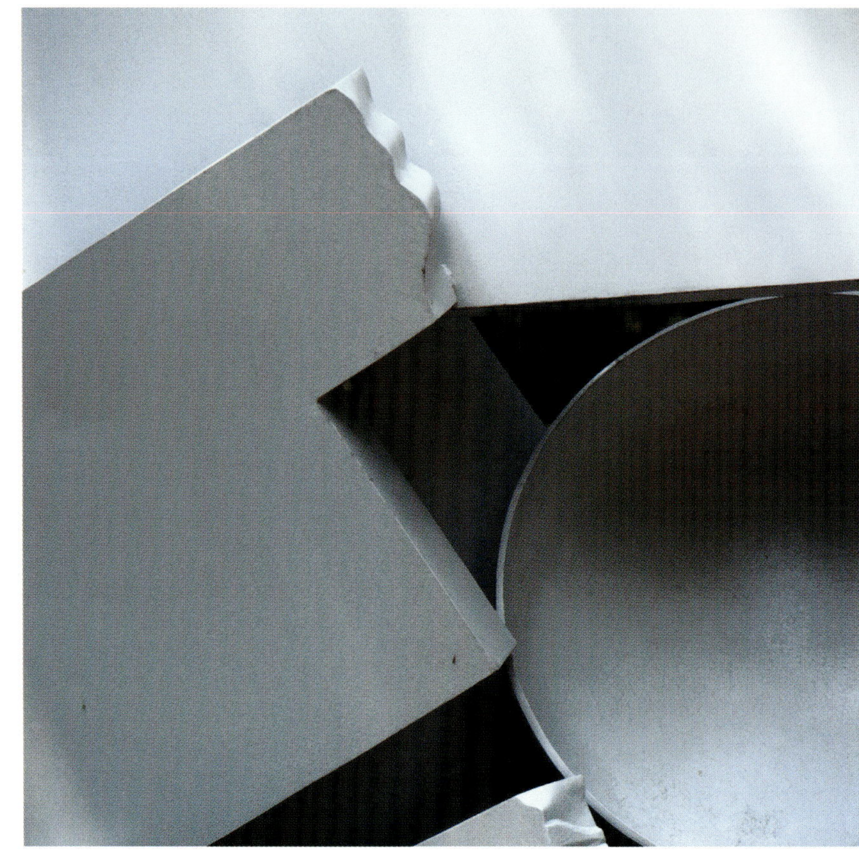

BREAKING AWAY: WHITE

1984
11' height, 14' width
Fabricated steel
Collection of Robert and Pamela Goergen,
Greenwich, CT

It is amazing how dramatically the feeling of a piece of sculpture is affected by changing the color. Especially when it has been changed from bronze to a pearly white. Shadows show off the forms more and the work has an almost weightless quality. I especially like this work in winter when the snow settles around and on it.

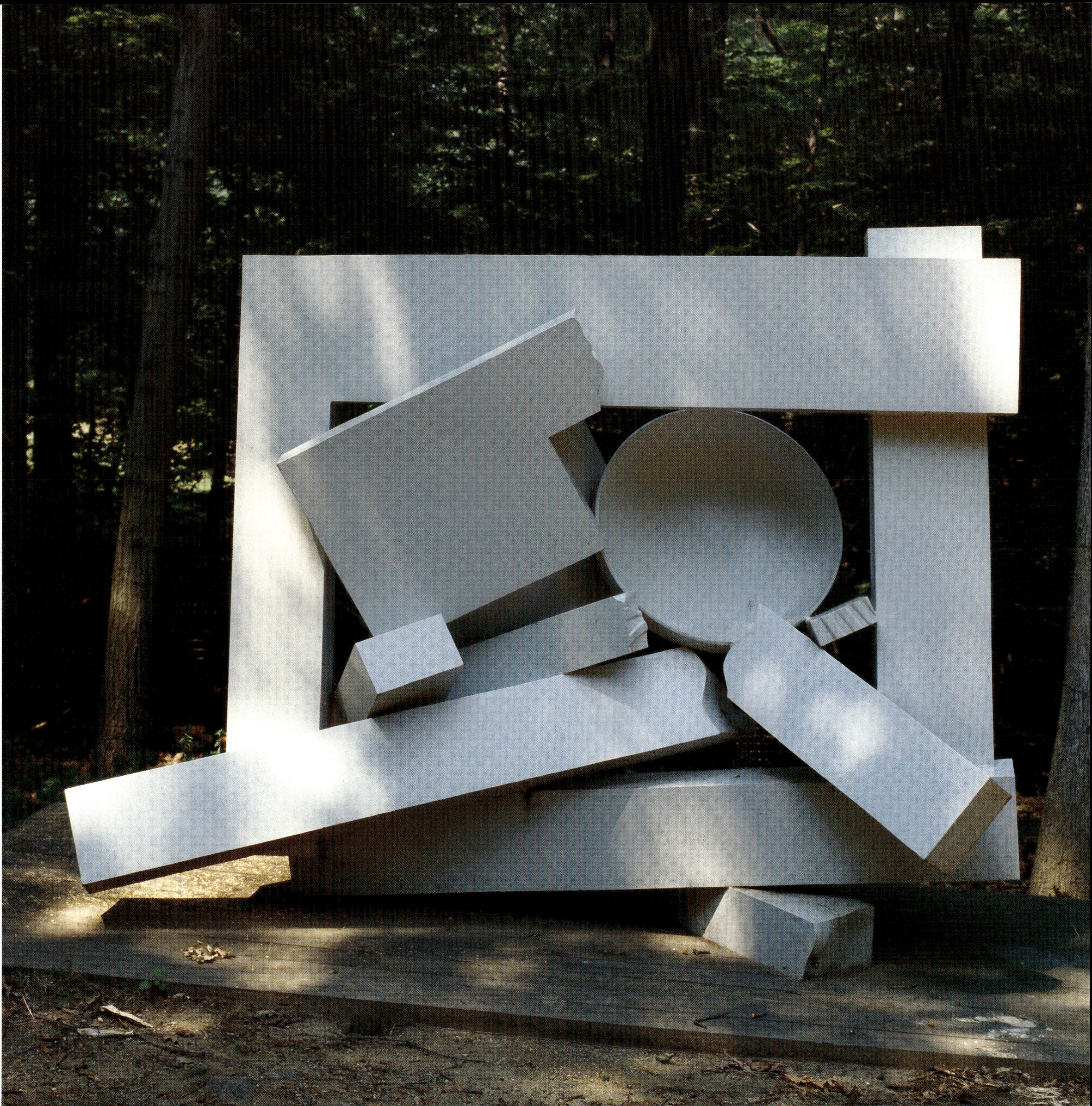

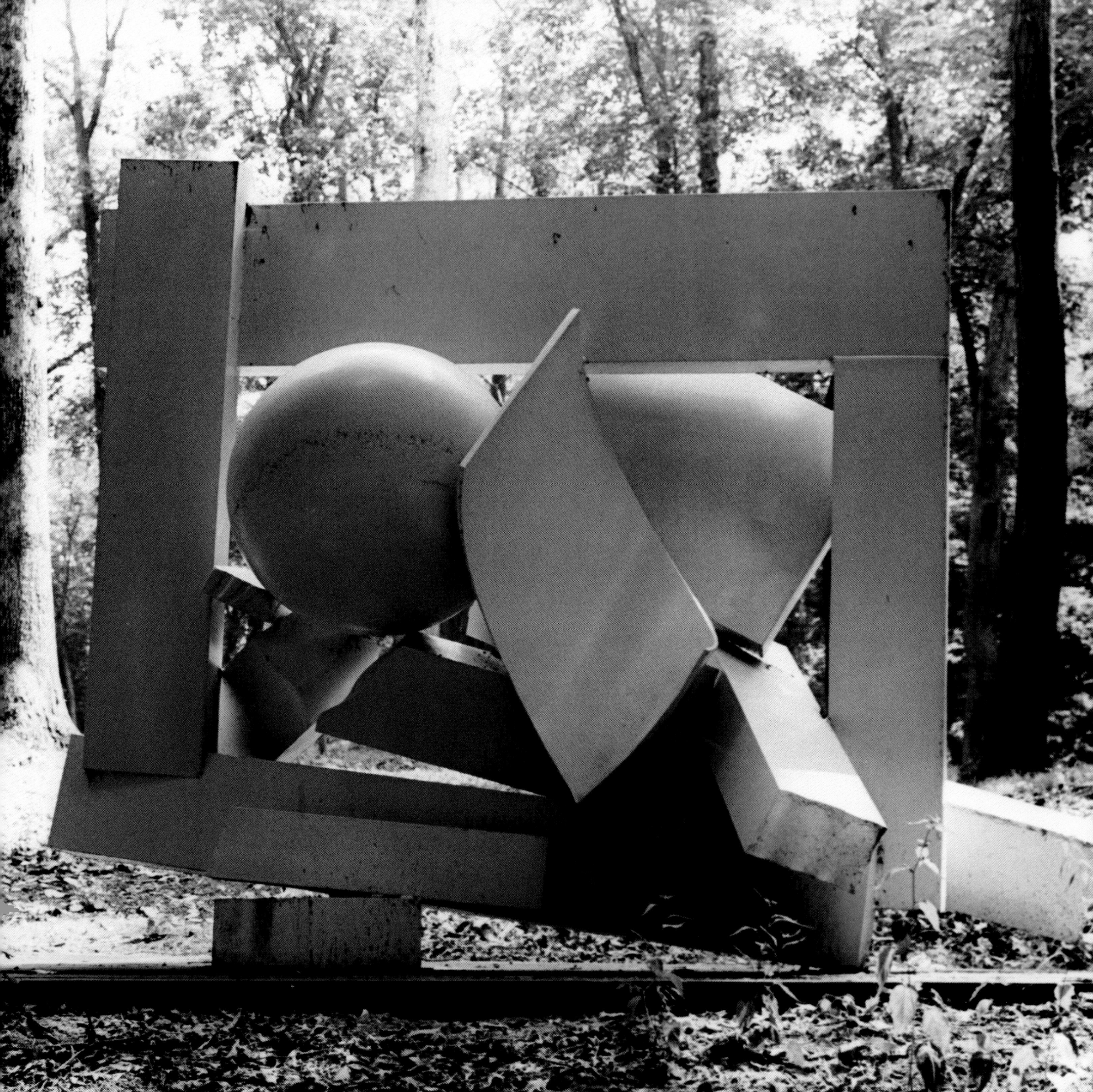

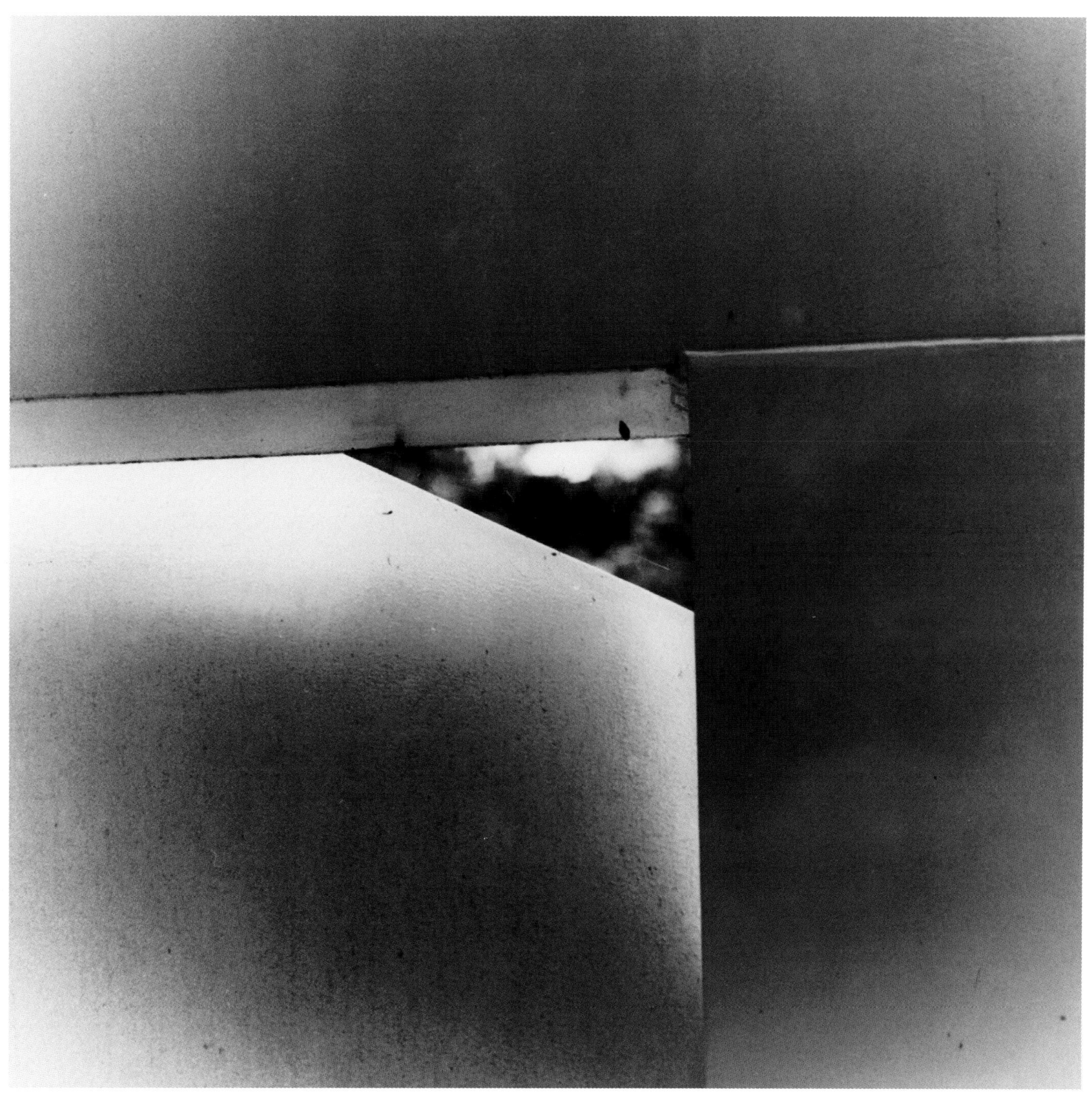

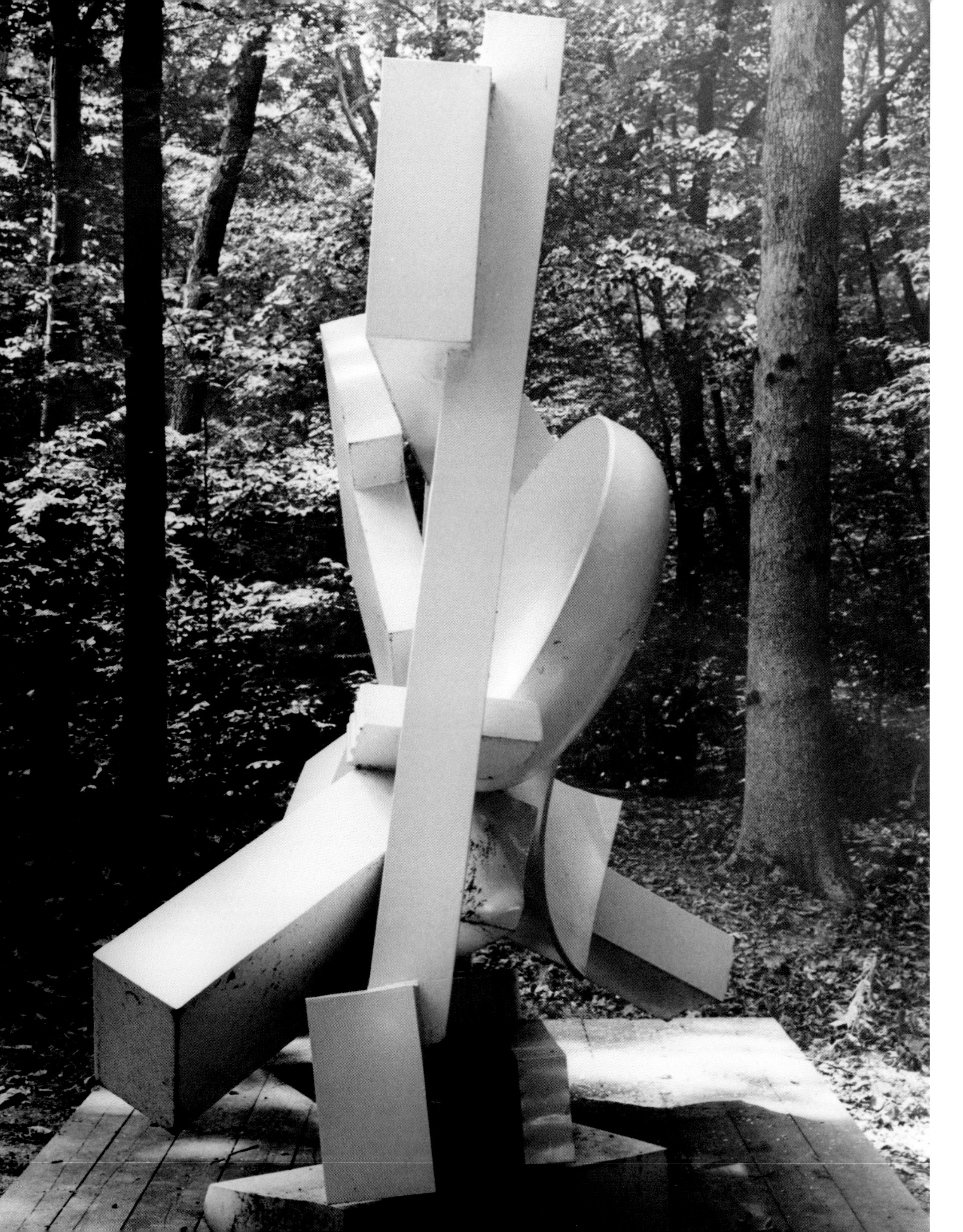

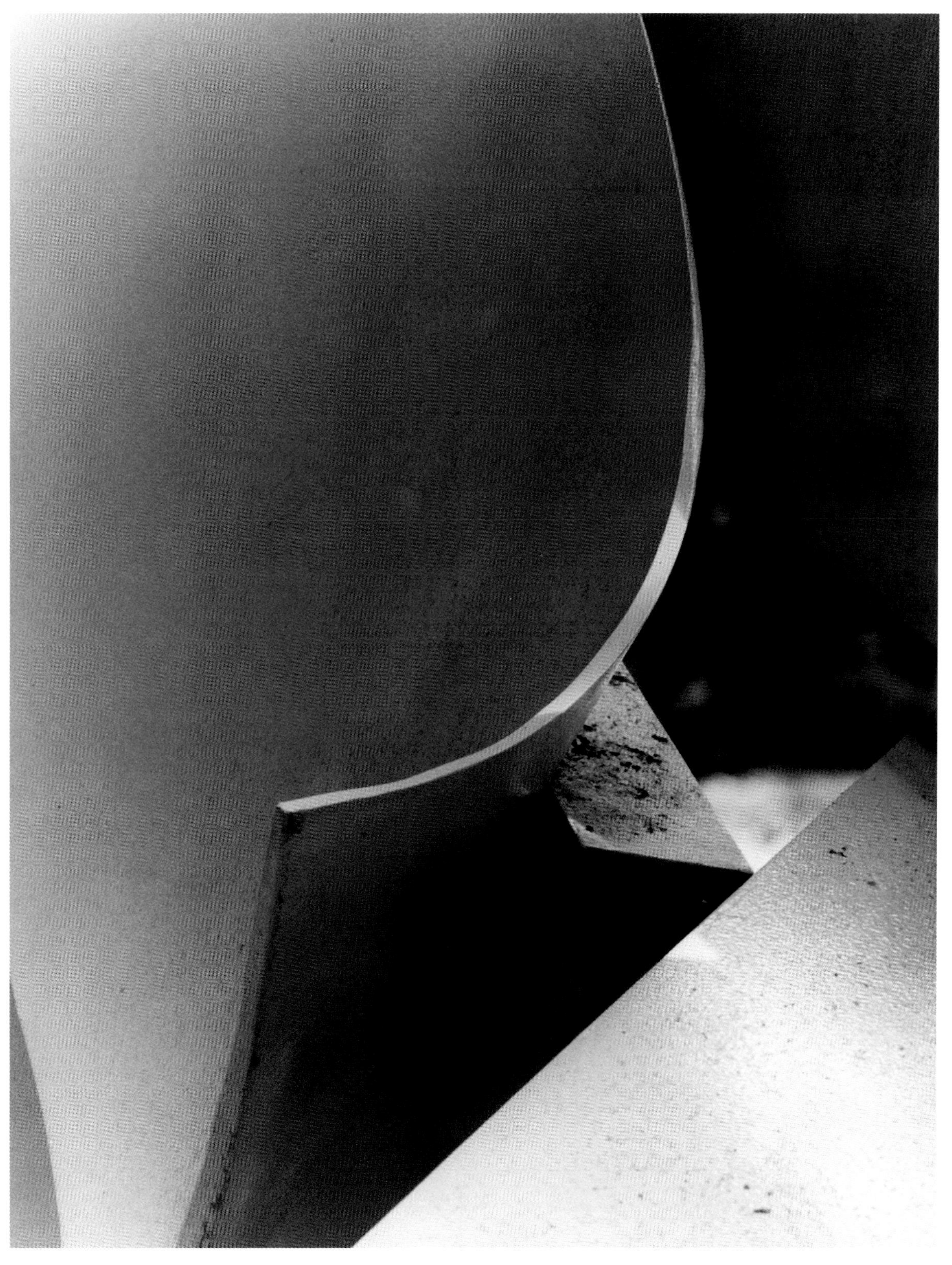

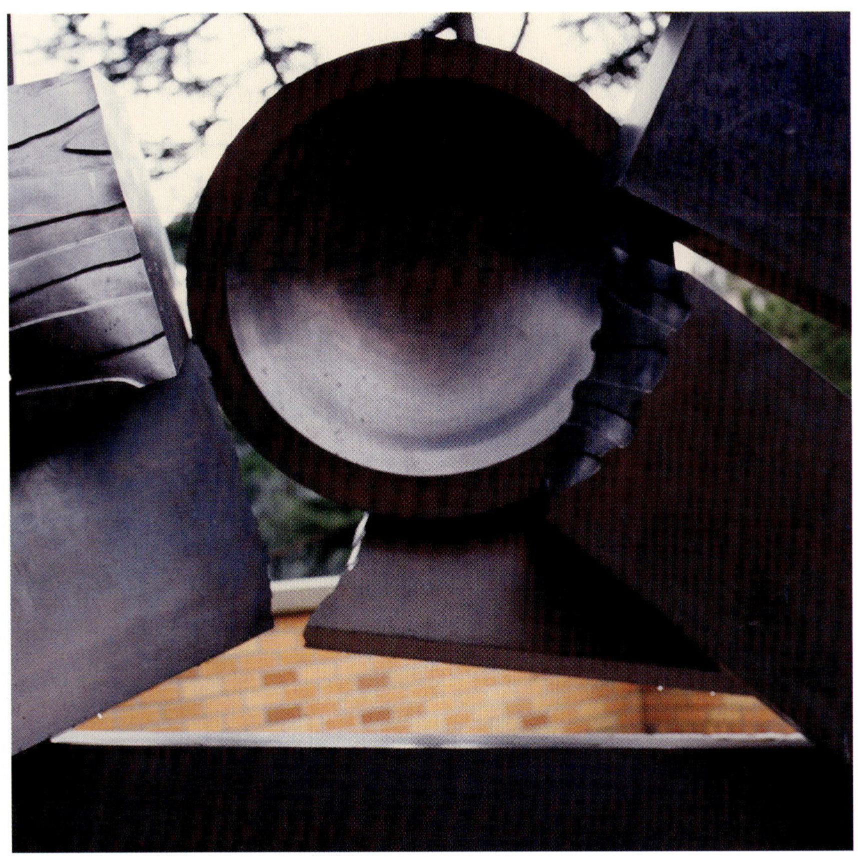

BREAKING AWAY

2001
Bronze
11' x 14' x 7'
University of Washington, Seattle, WA

The original *Breaking Away* was a wall relief. I was honored by a request to make a large freestanding sculpture for the University of Washington campus by Kayla Skinner, a major patron of the arts in Seattle, WA. Its theme was most appropriate, as "breaking away" is certainly something most parents hope their offspring will do when they head off to college.

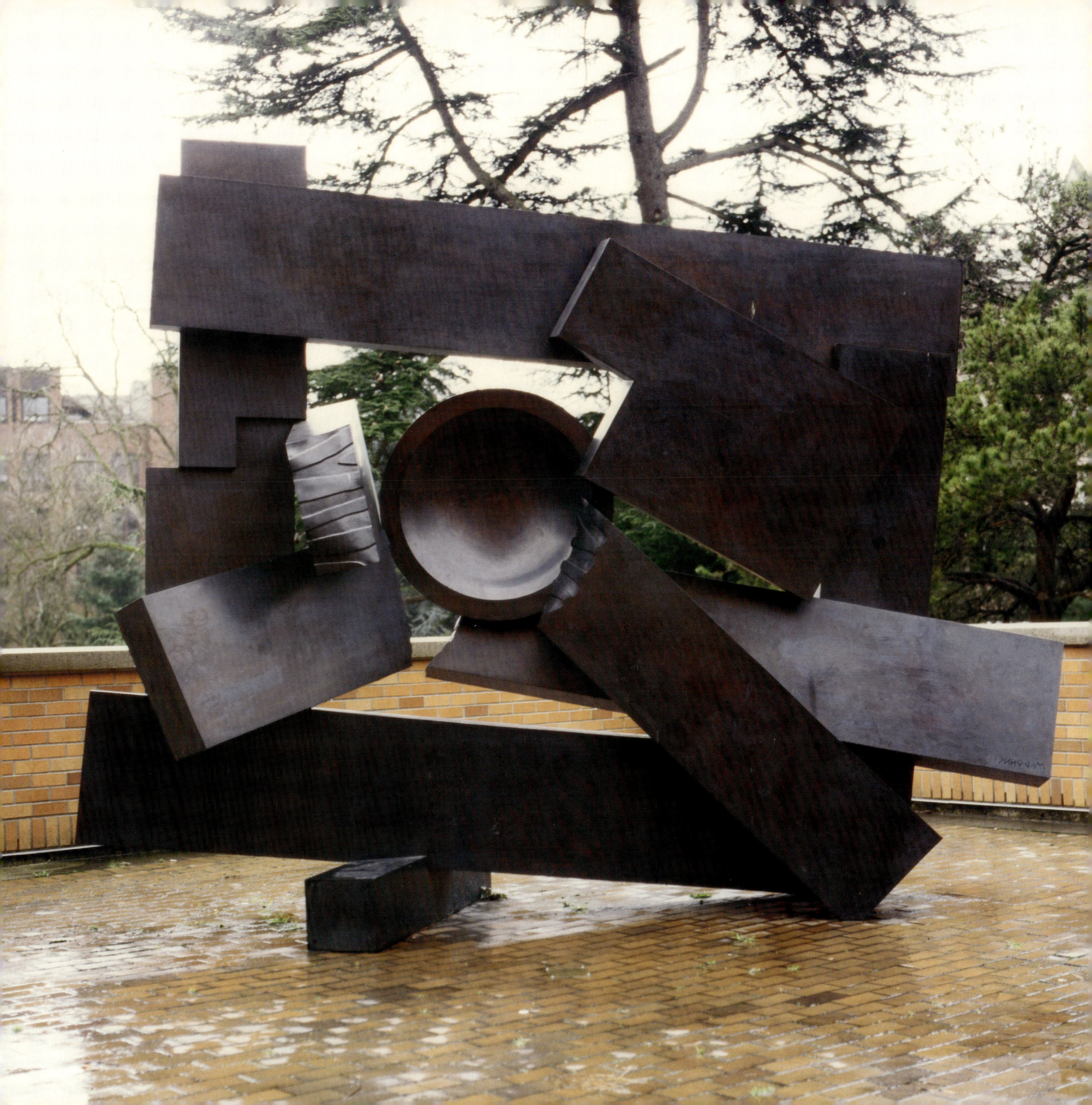

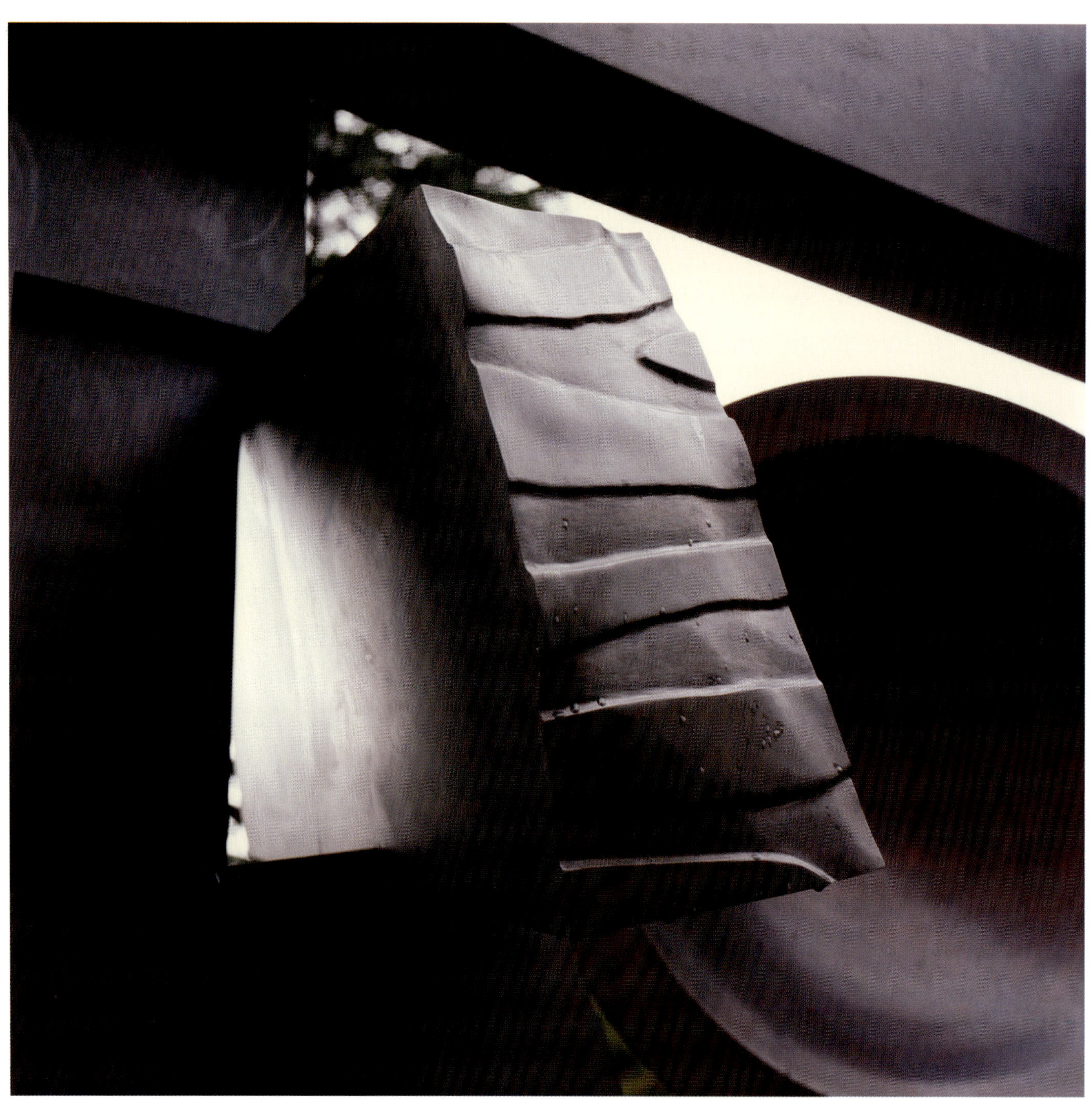

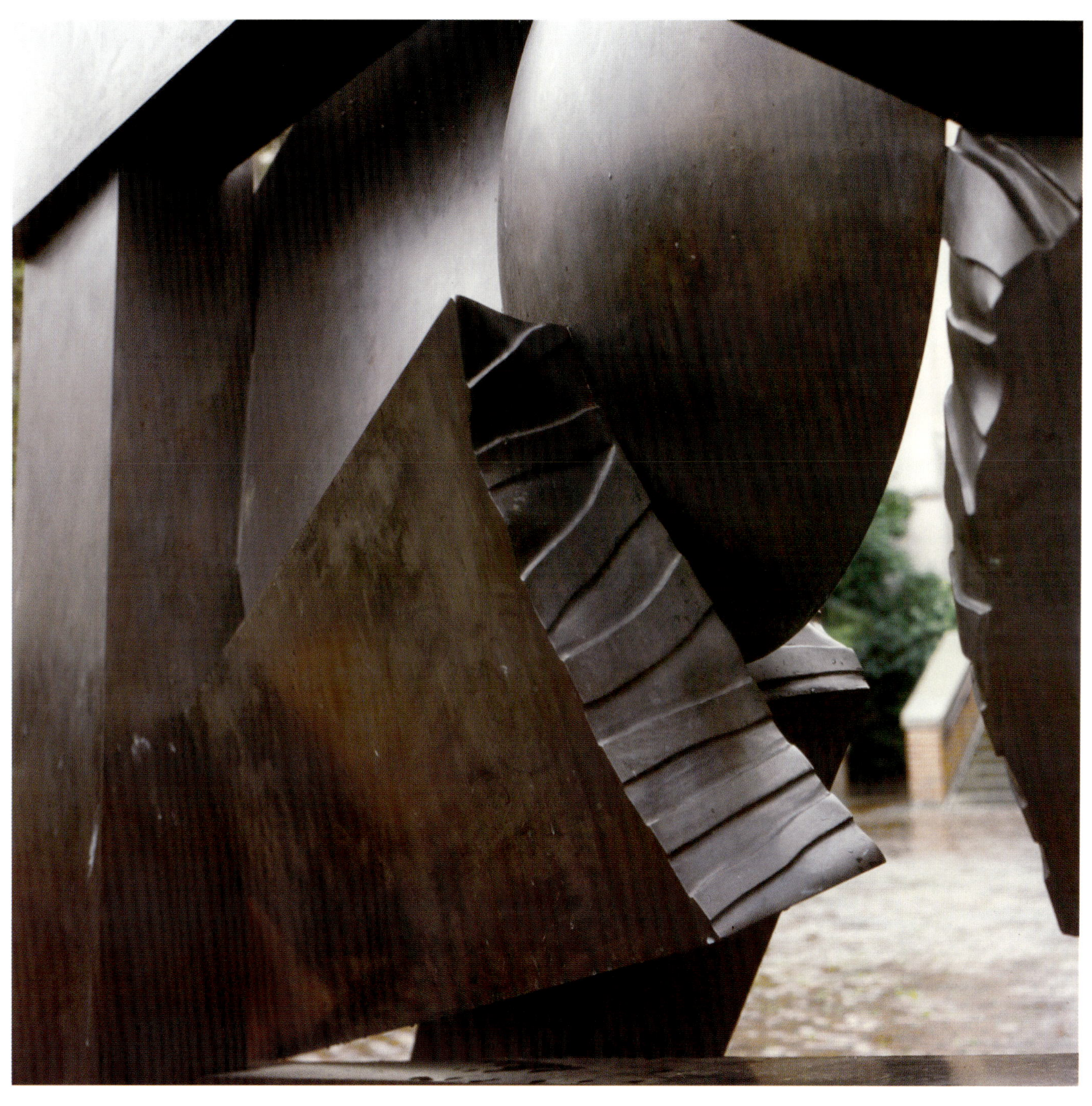

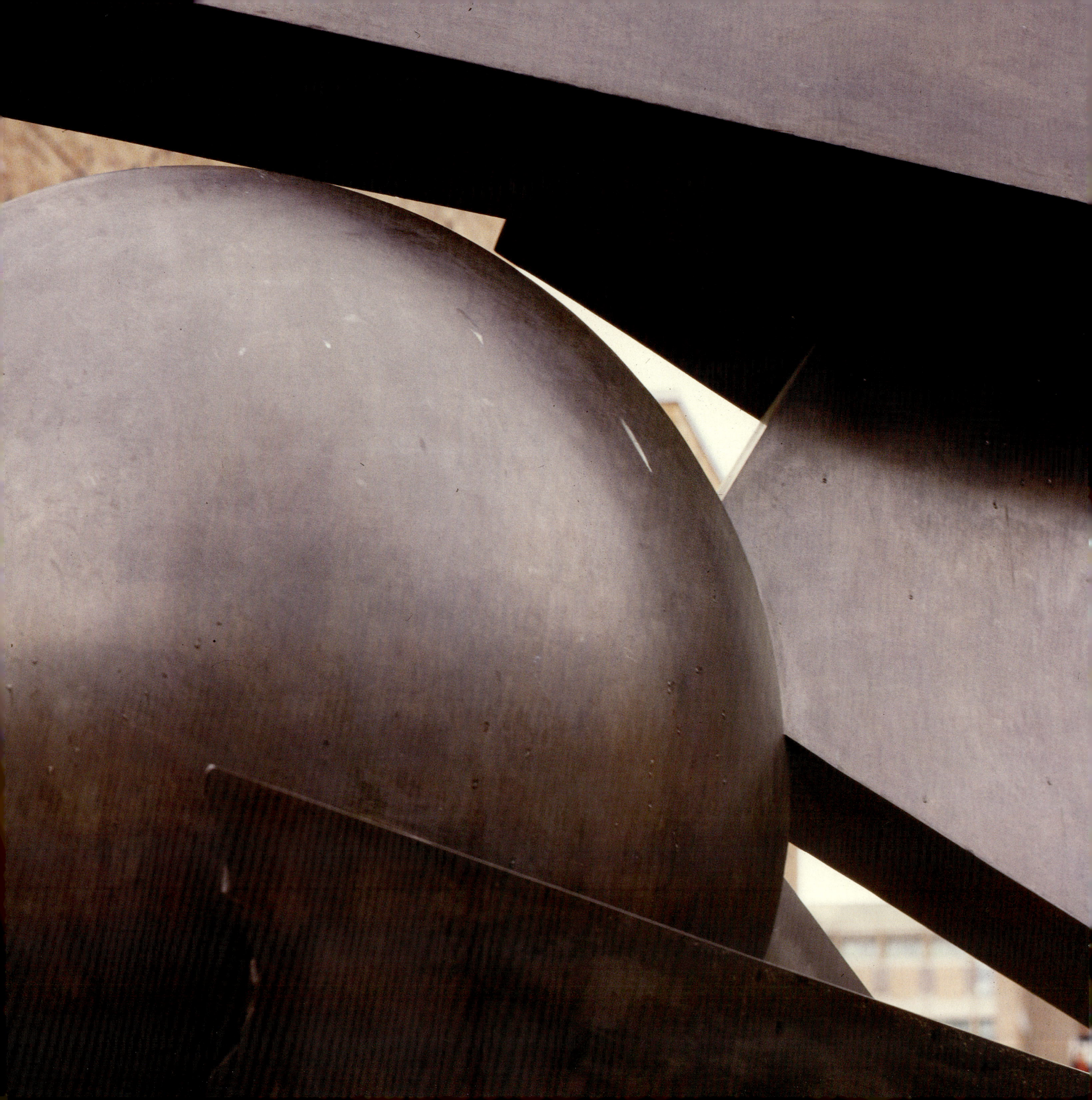

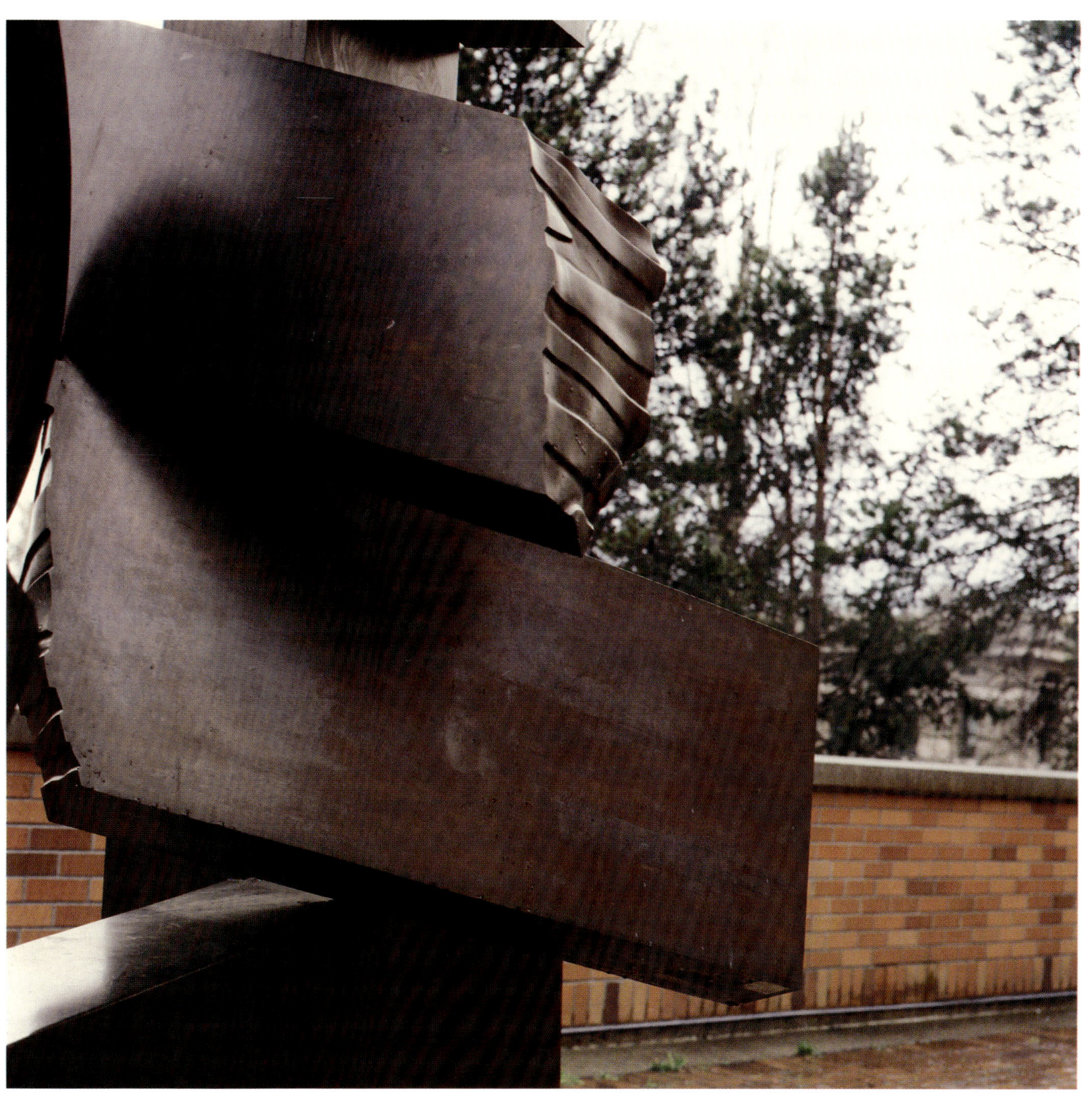

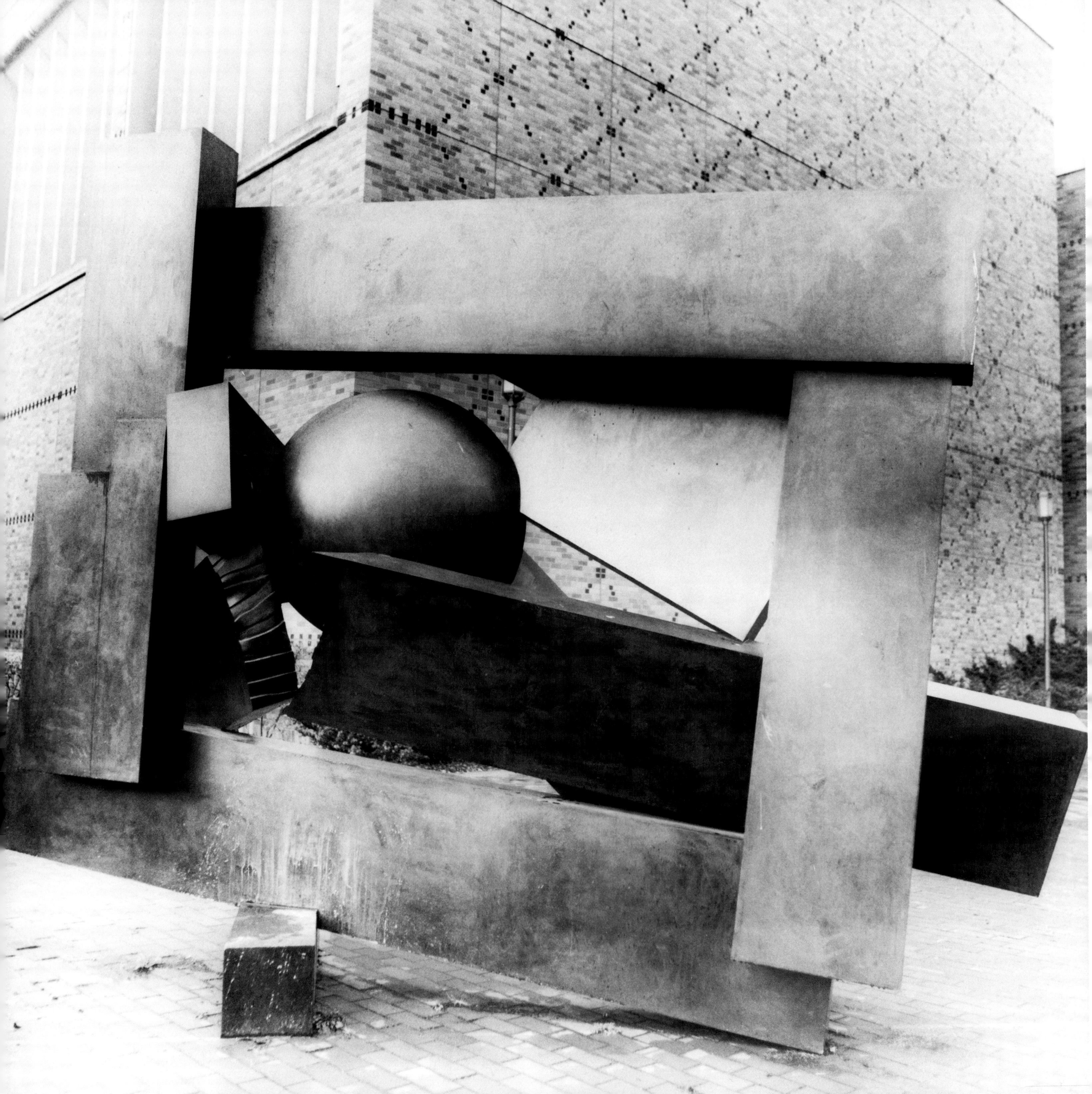

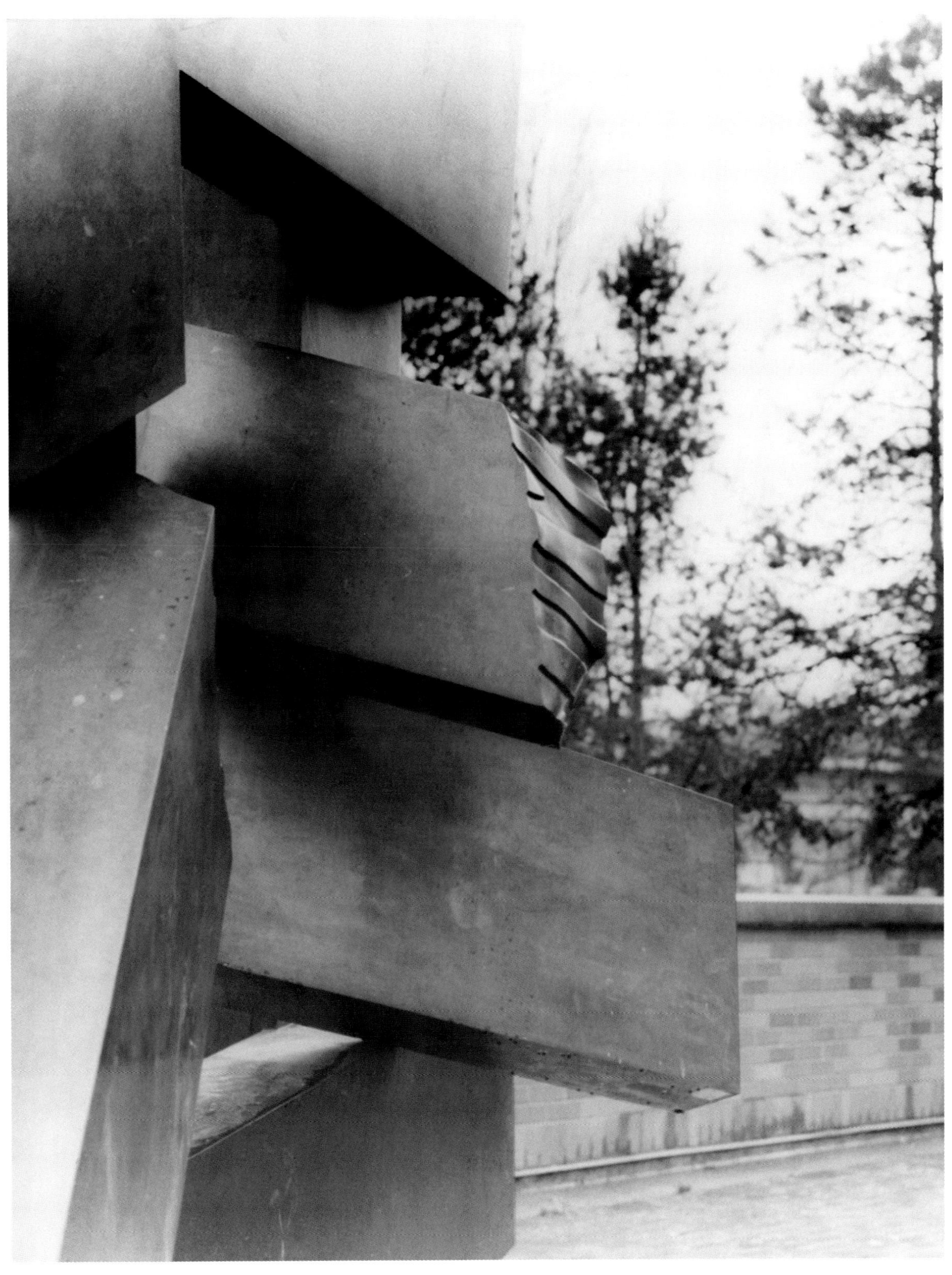

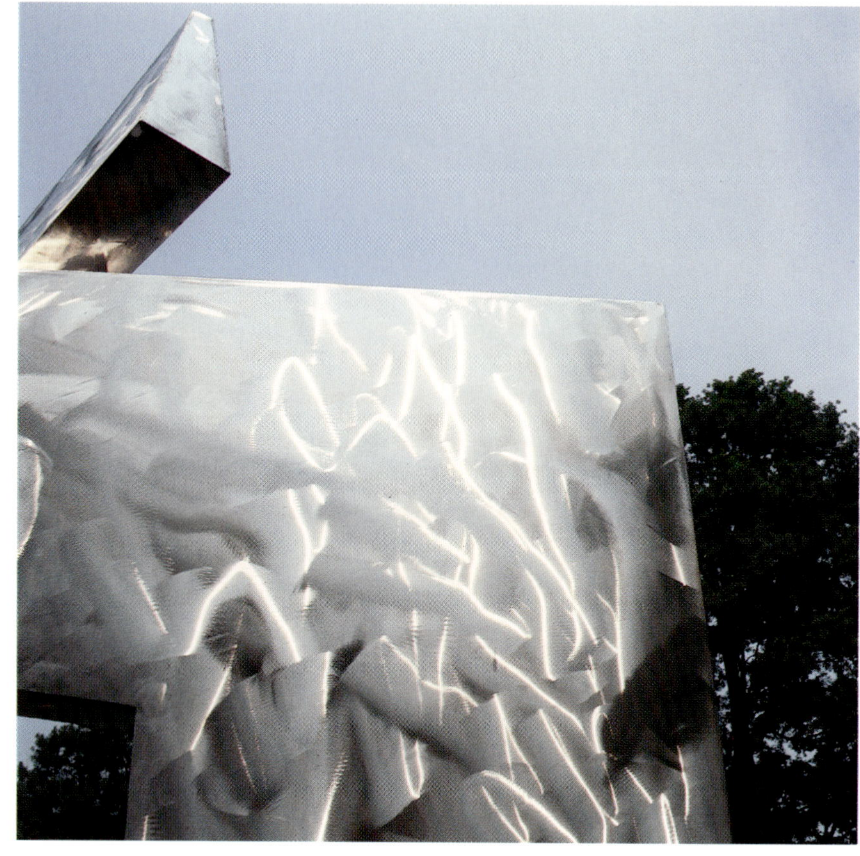

BREAKING AWAY II

1996
Stainless steel
7' height, 9' width
Collection of Arnold Cohen and
Bren Robbins, Scarsdale, NY

The model for this was composed of pieces from another sculpture, *Triad*, which I decided to cannibalize. Its pieces just seemed to work well together. The same idea of a frame with pieces breaking through is maintained in this composition.

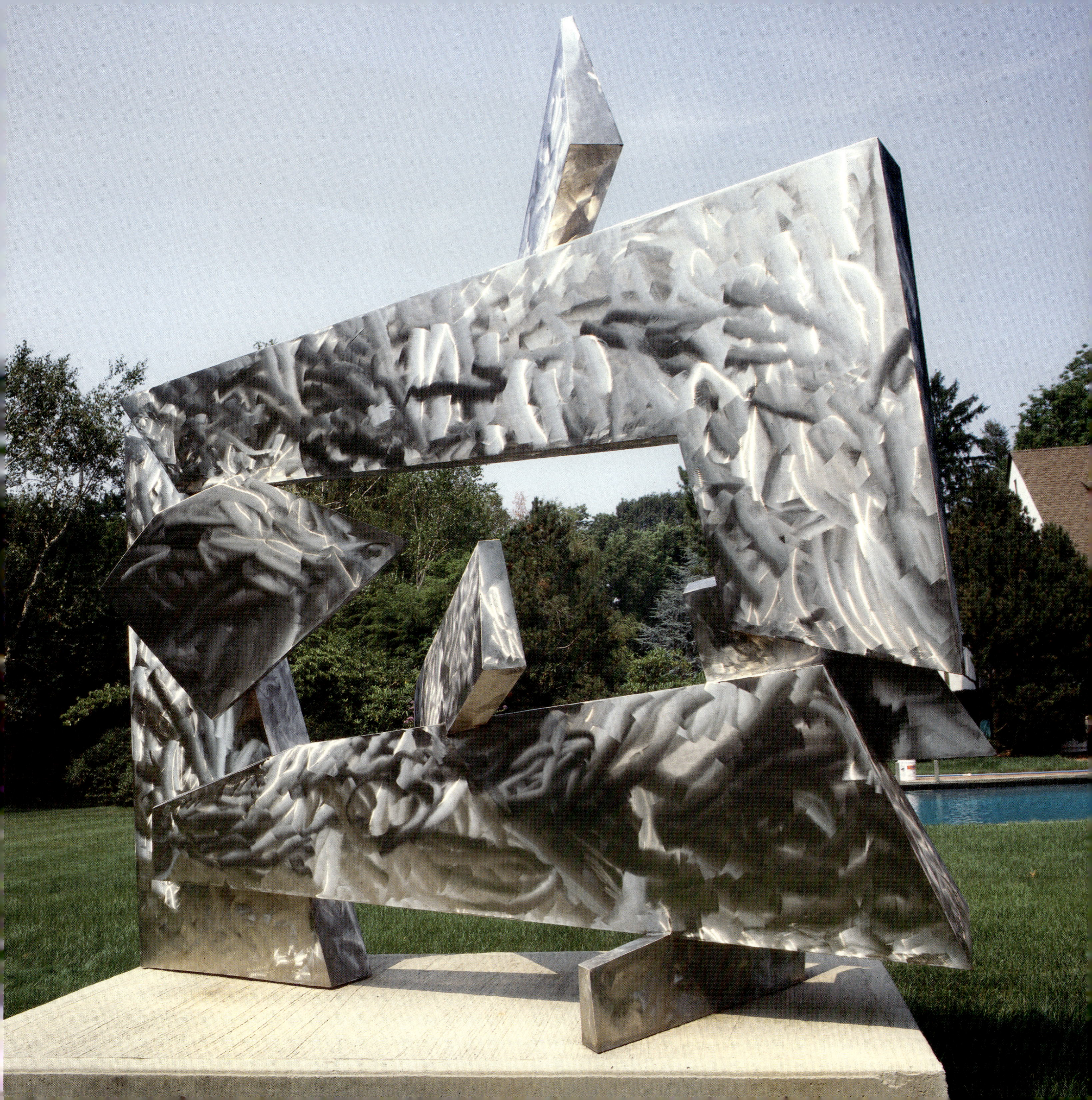

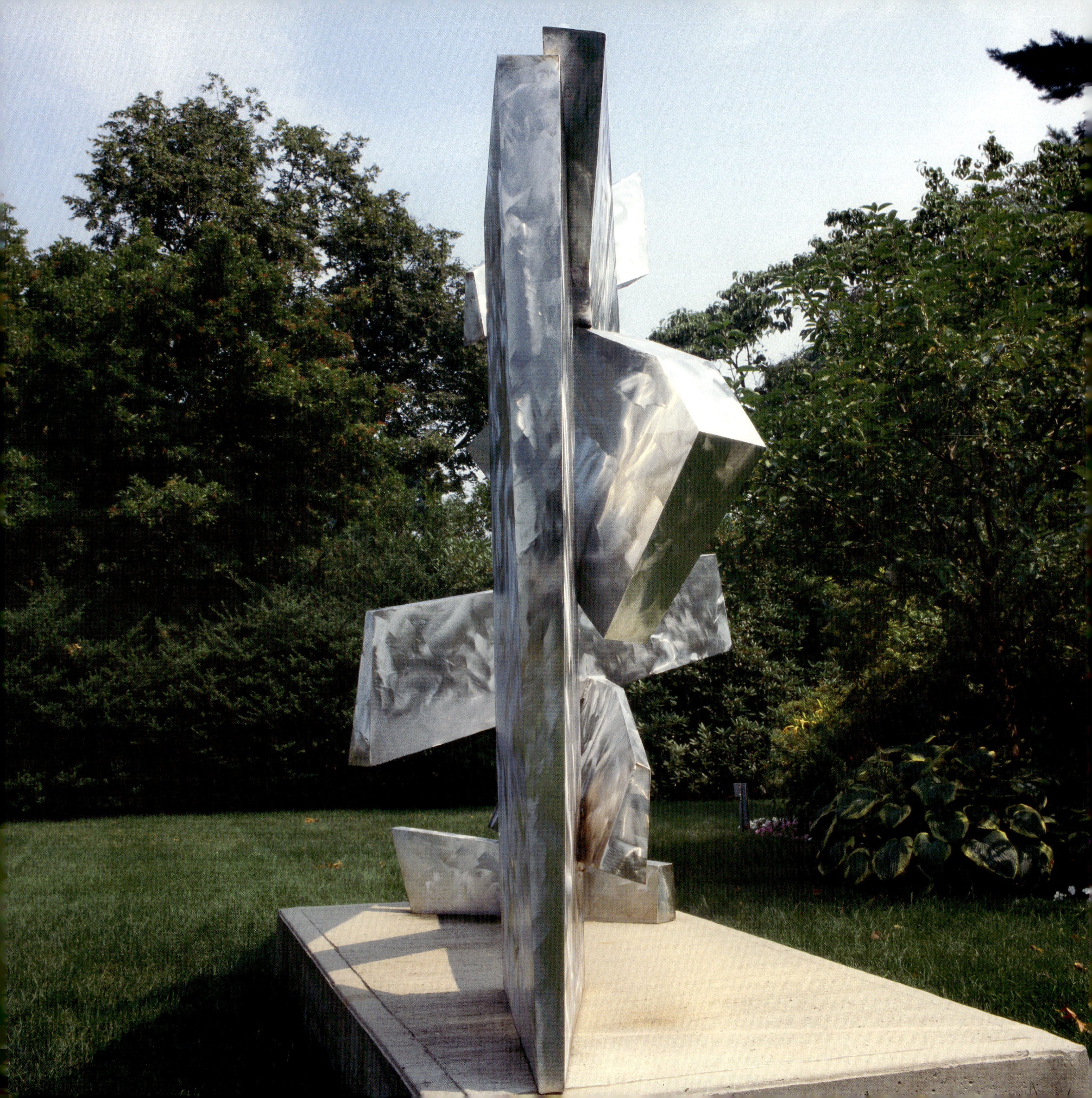

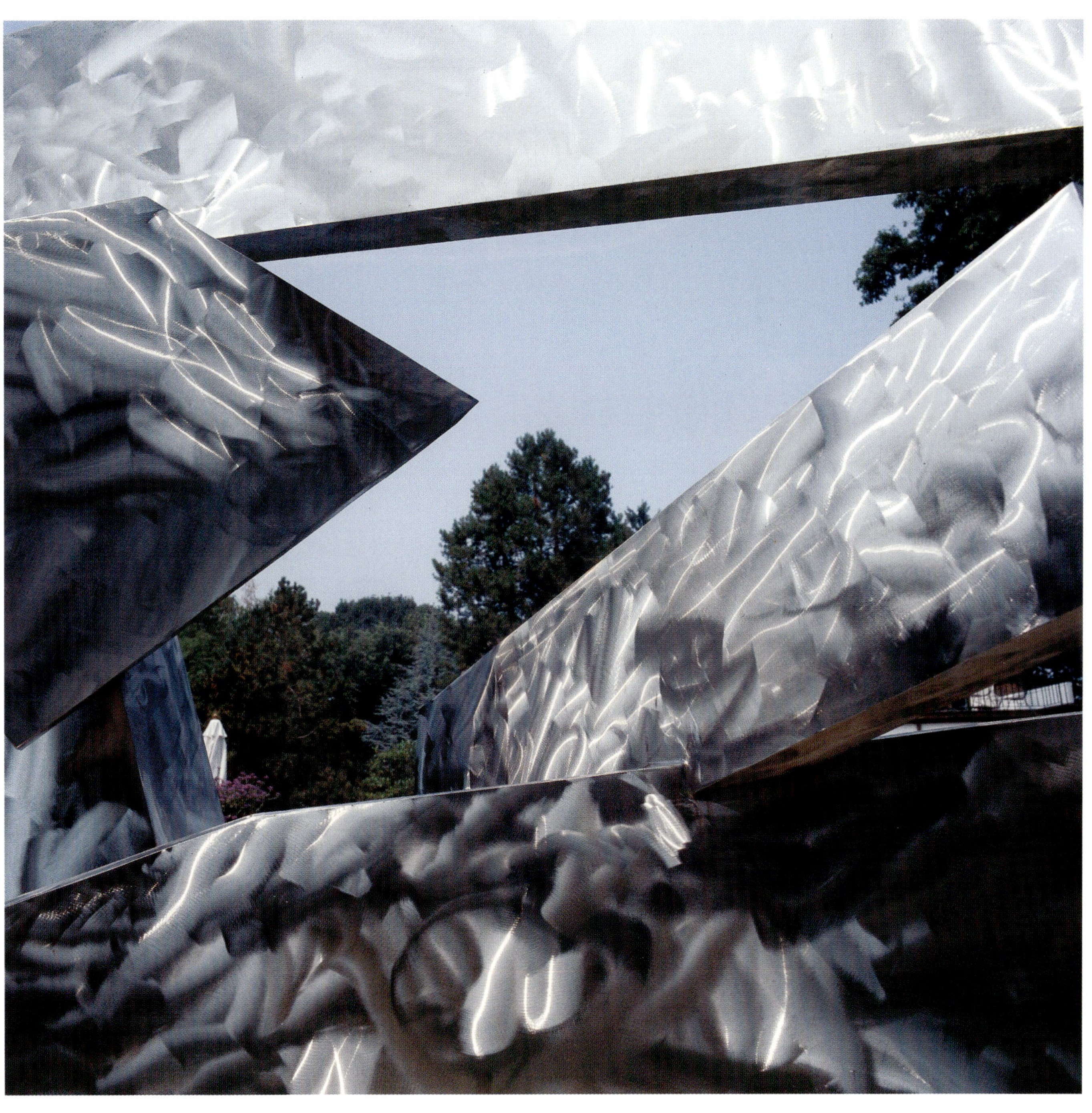

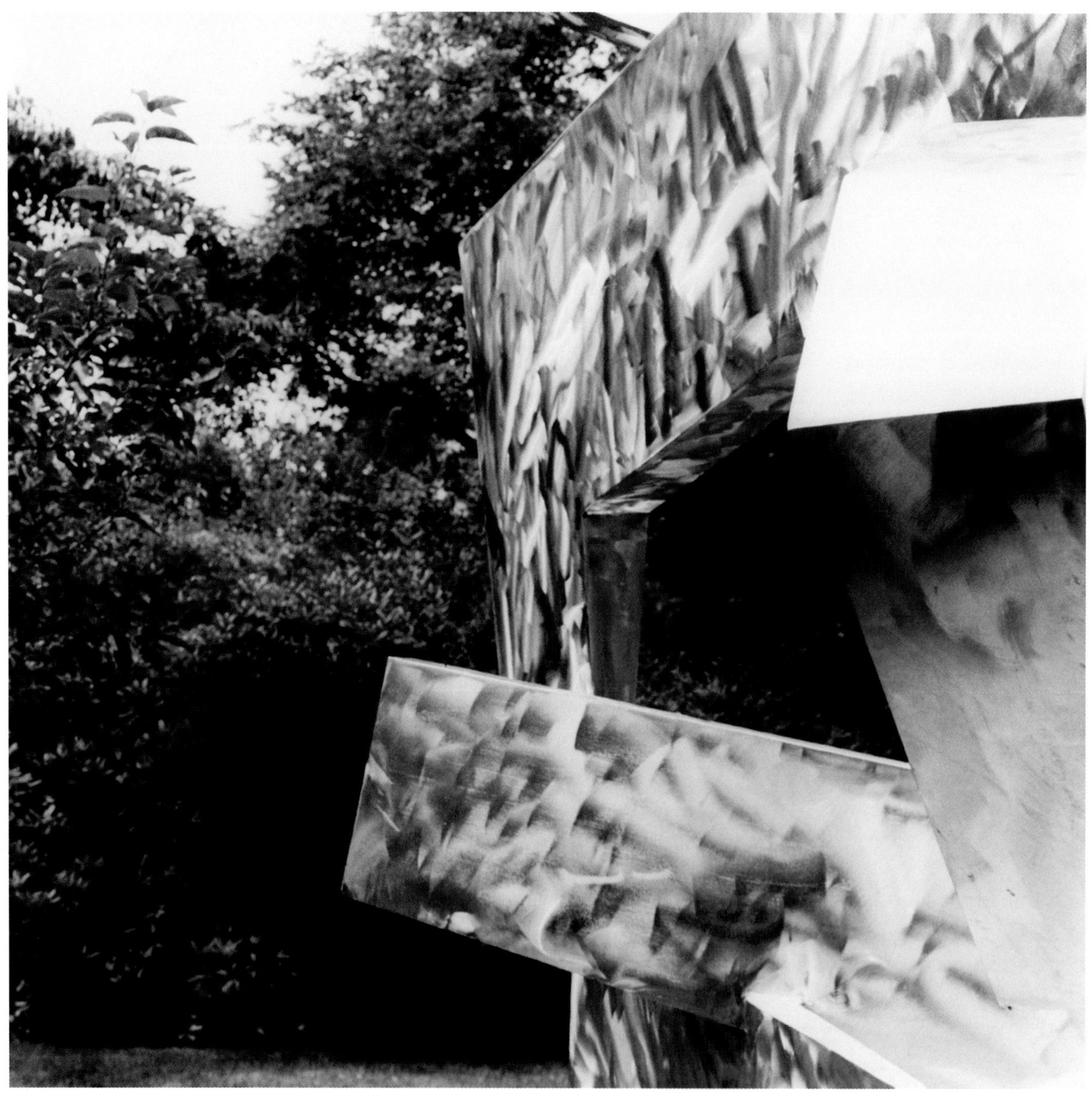

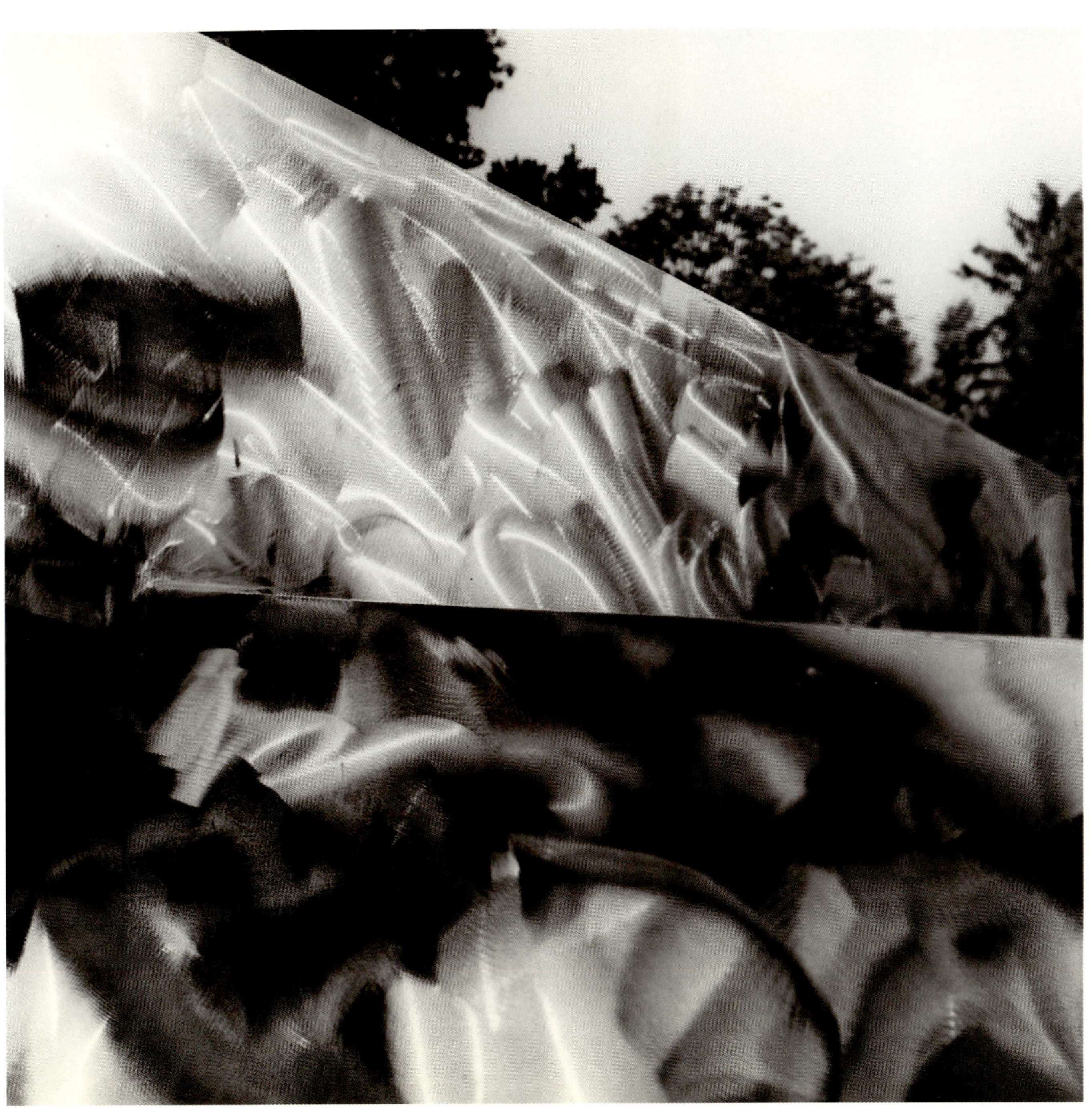

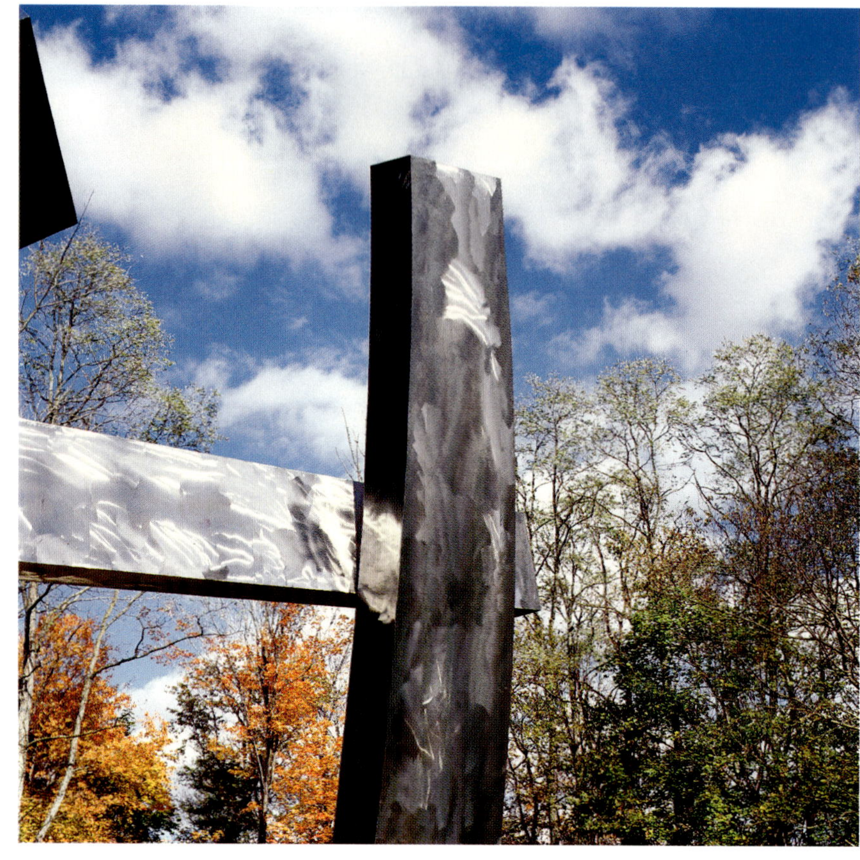

MUSCOOT

1996
Stainless steel
11' height 14' deep, 7' width
Collection of Robert Stahmer,
Yorktown Heights, NY

The model for this piece evolved from several cut-off shapes in the studio. It was named after the nearby Muscoot reservoir, 40 miles north of Manhattan. I wanted to stay with the *Breaking Away* composition but wished to open it up and relax the forms. The wonderful spacious setting enhances the reflective stainless steel.

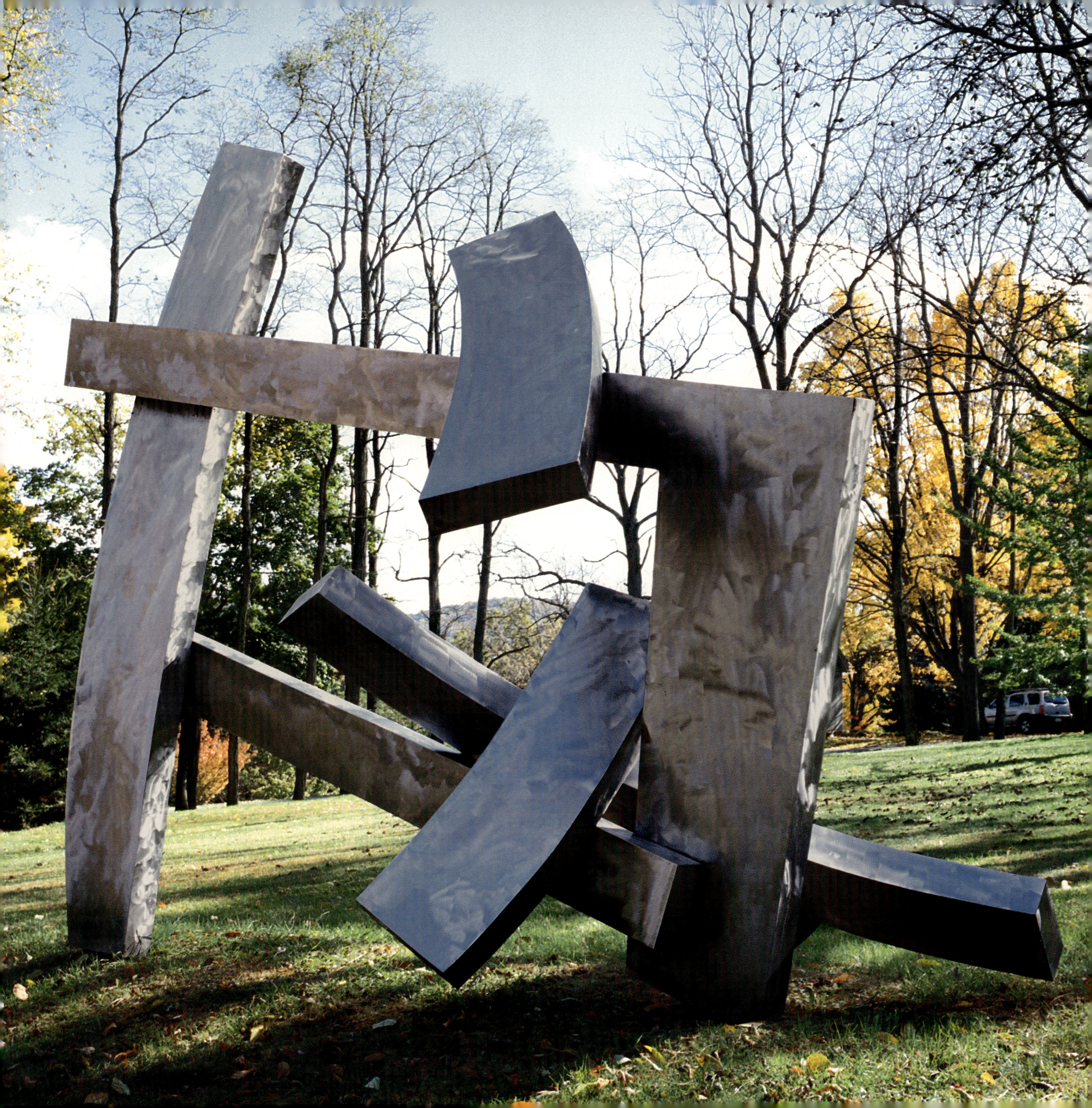

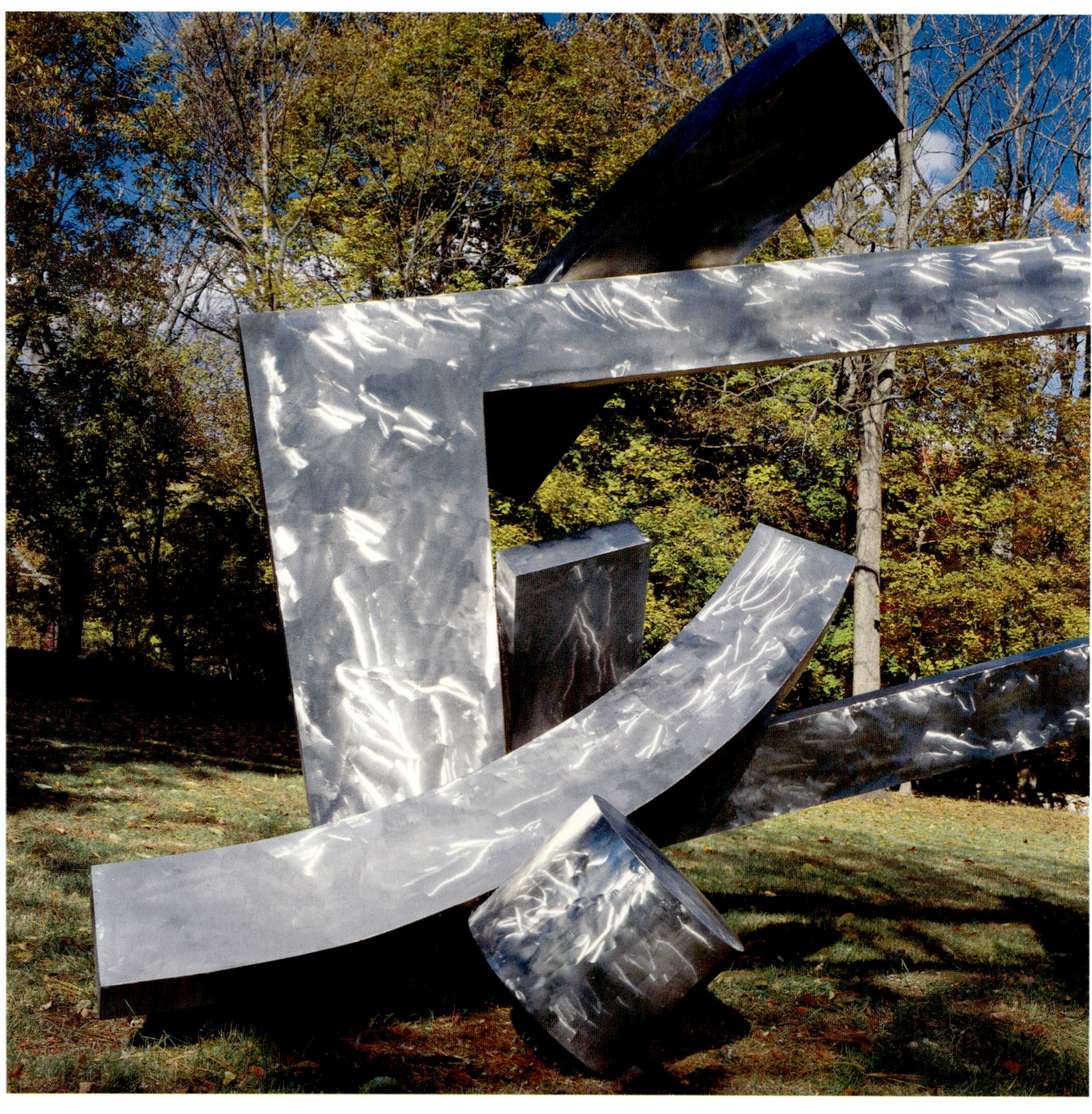

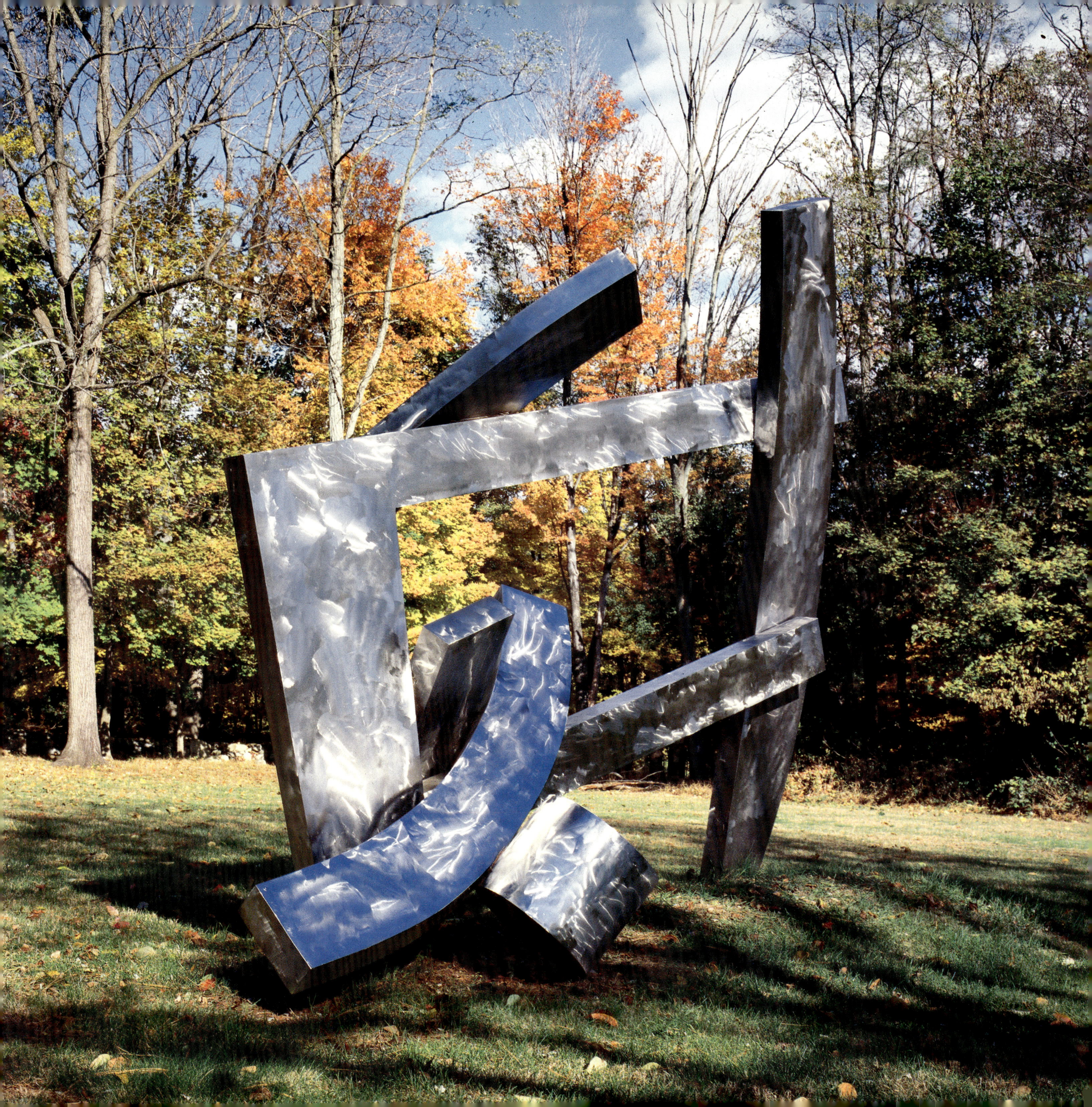

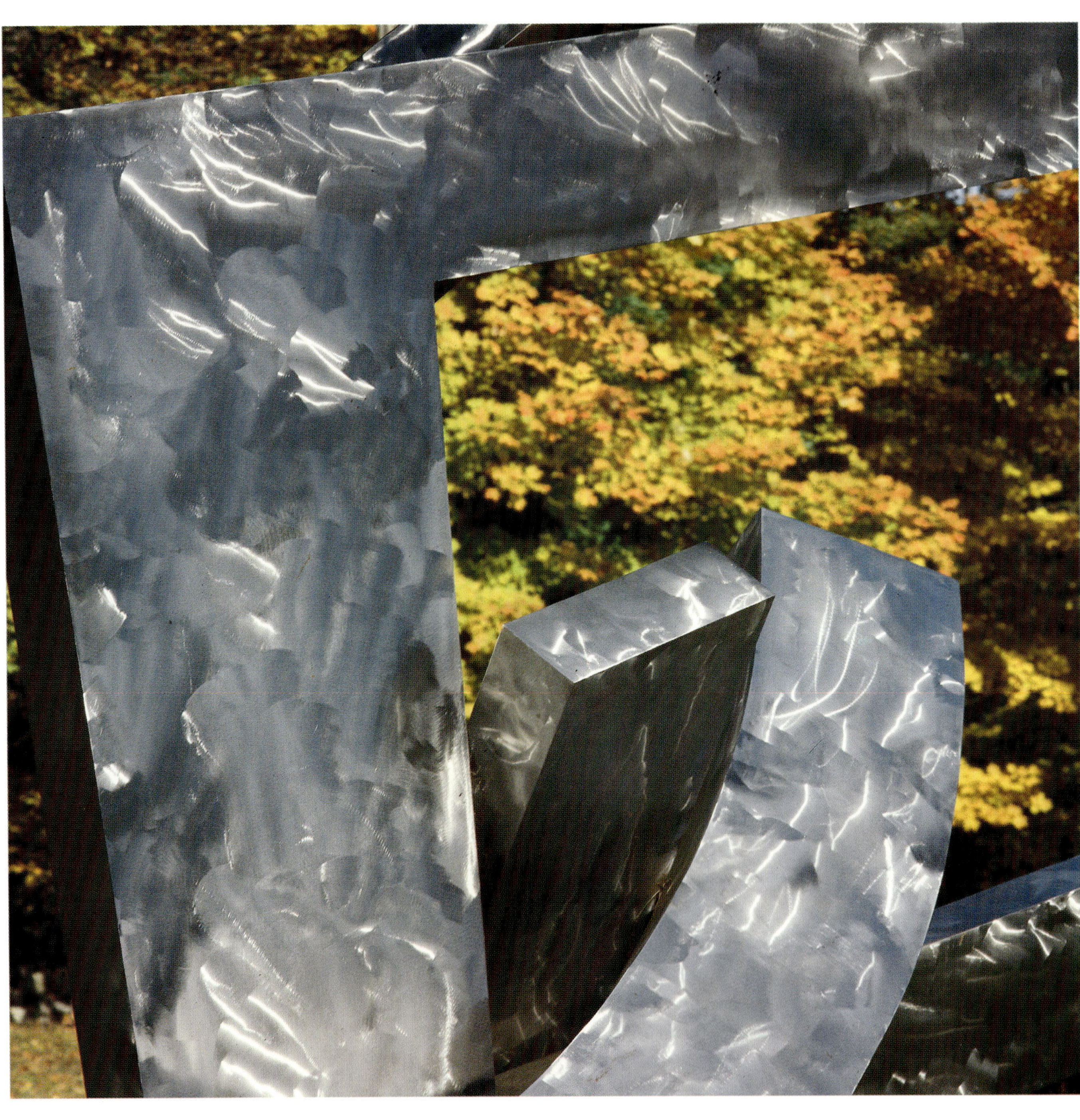

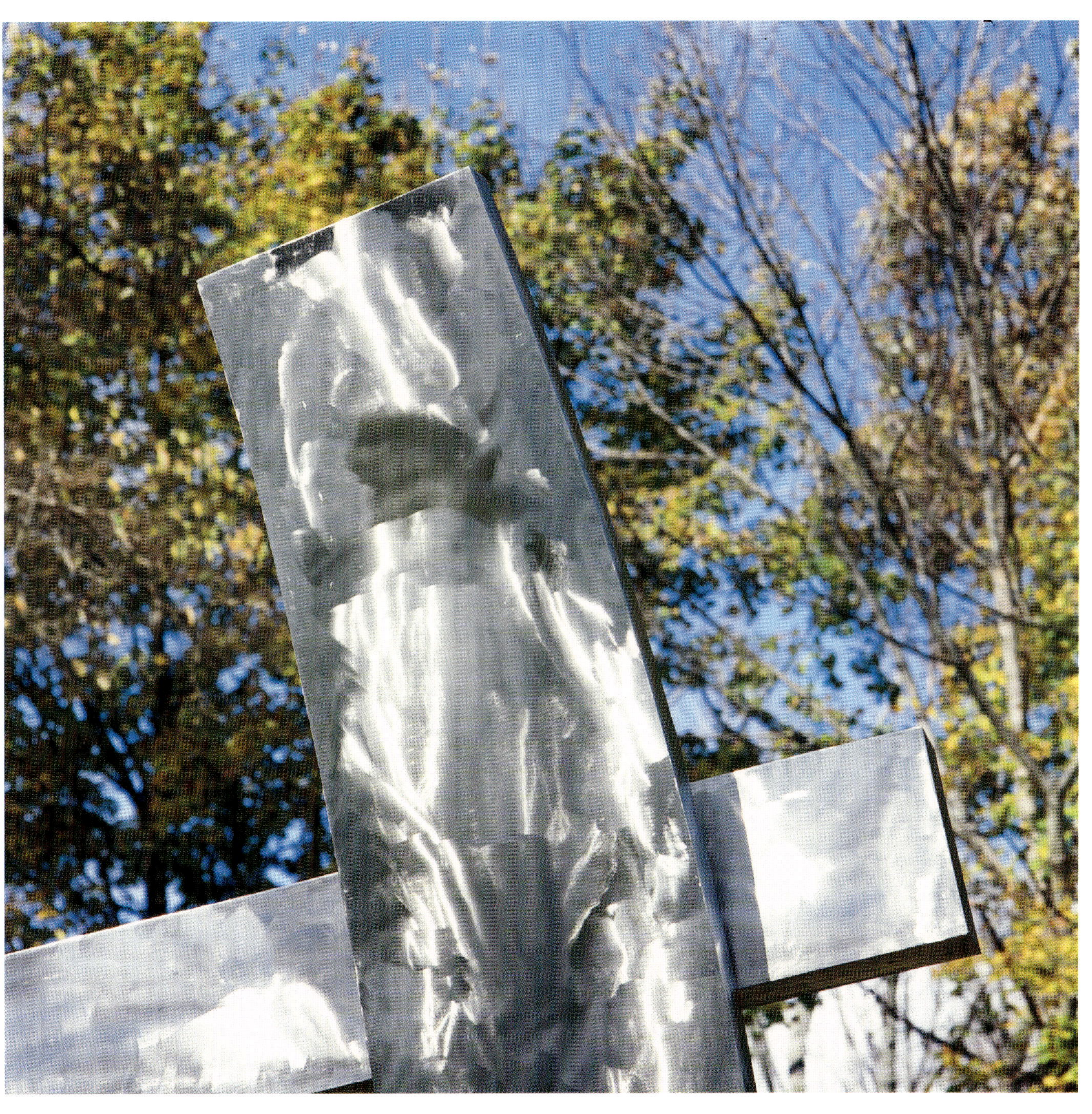

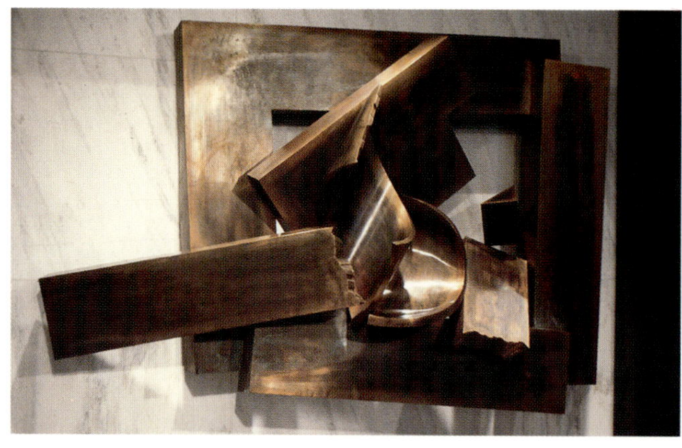 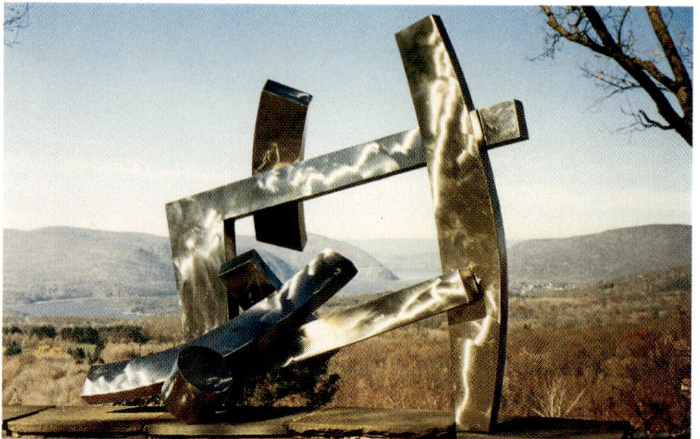

BREAKING AWAY RELIEF
1991
Bronze
7' x 11' x 3'6"
Durst Organization, NYC
733 Third Avenue, NYC

MUSCOOT MAQUETTE
1996
Stainless steel
24" x 30" x 14"
Collection of David Finn,
New Rochelle, NY

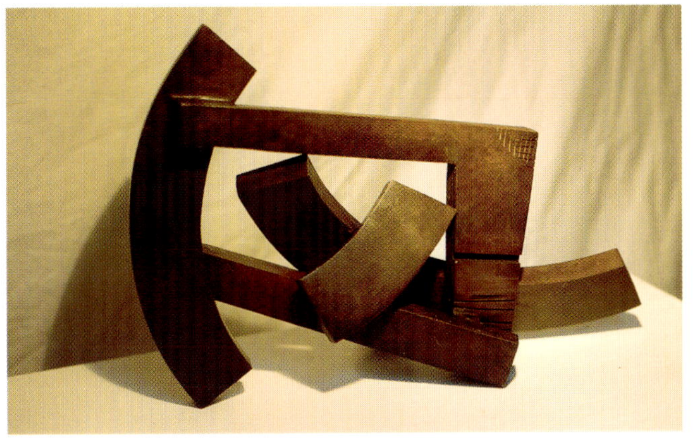

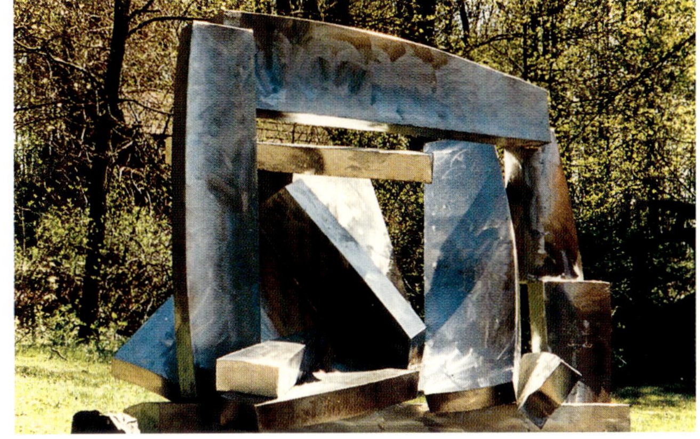

MUSCOOT (early maquette)
1990
Bronze
10" x 19" x 7"
Sold by Maxwell Davidson Gallery,
New York, New York

BREAKING AWAY VIII
1994
Stainless steel
61" x 74" x 42"
Collection of Martin Selig,
Seattle, WA

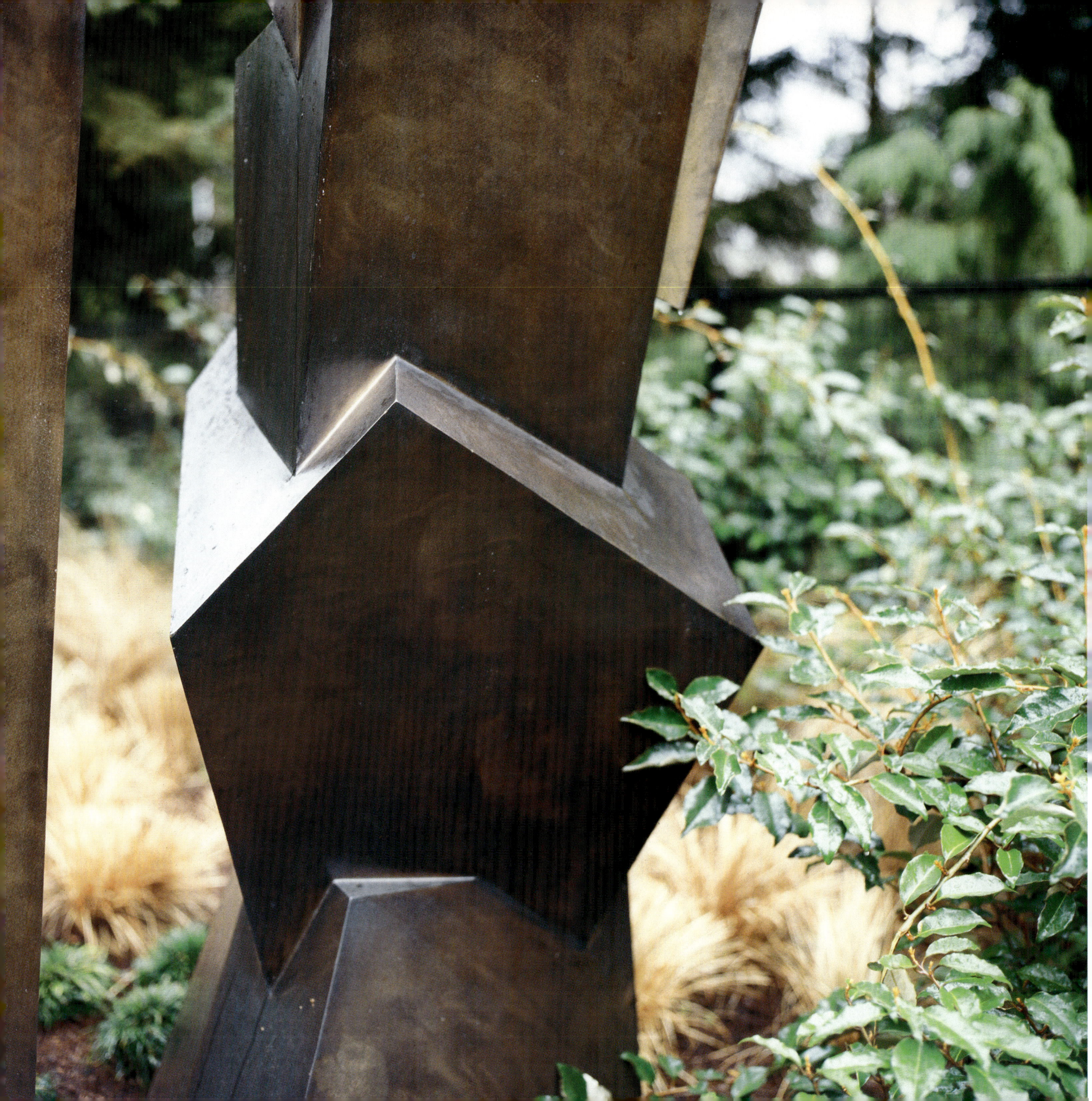

THE SECOND GATES OF PARADISE

When Jon and Mary Shirley gave me the opportunity to propose a set of gates for their wonderful art-filled estate in Medina, WA, I felt especially honored. Originally, we planned to make a single sliding gate. However, many considerations pointed toward a double swinging gate. Each side of the gate is a variation on the *Breaking Away* theme. The planes and angles were exaggerated to give the work a greater sense of depth. In addition, one side has a female symbol incorporated in its design and the other a male. Ends were added to the basic composition to conceal the hydraulic lift posts. Each side weighed almost a ton so the leverage was considerable. In addition, the gates had to rotate up about a foot to accommodate the rise in the driveway. The gates were meant to keep vehicles out while allowing the art works on the grounds to be seen through them. The architect, George Suyama, was very helpful in working out the driveway and landscaping components.

Opposite page: The Second Gates of Paradise

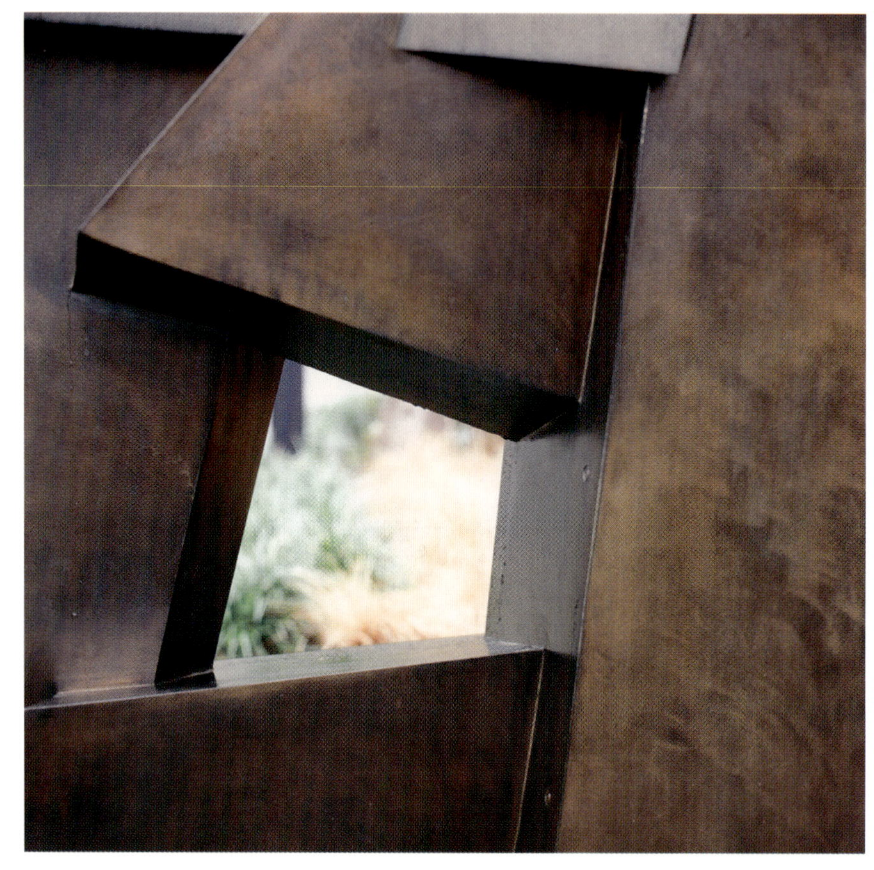

THE SECOND GATES
OF PARADISE

2002
Bronze
8' x 25' x 6'
Collection of Jon and Mary Shirley,
Medina, WA

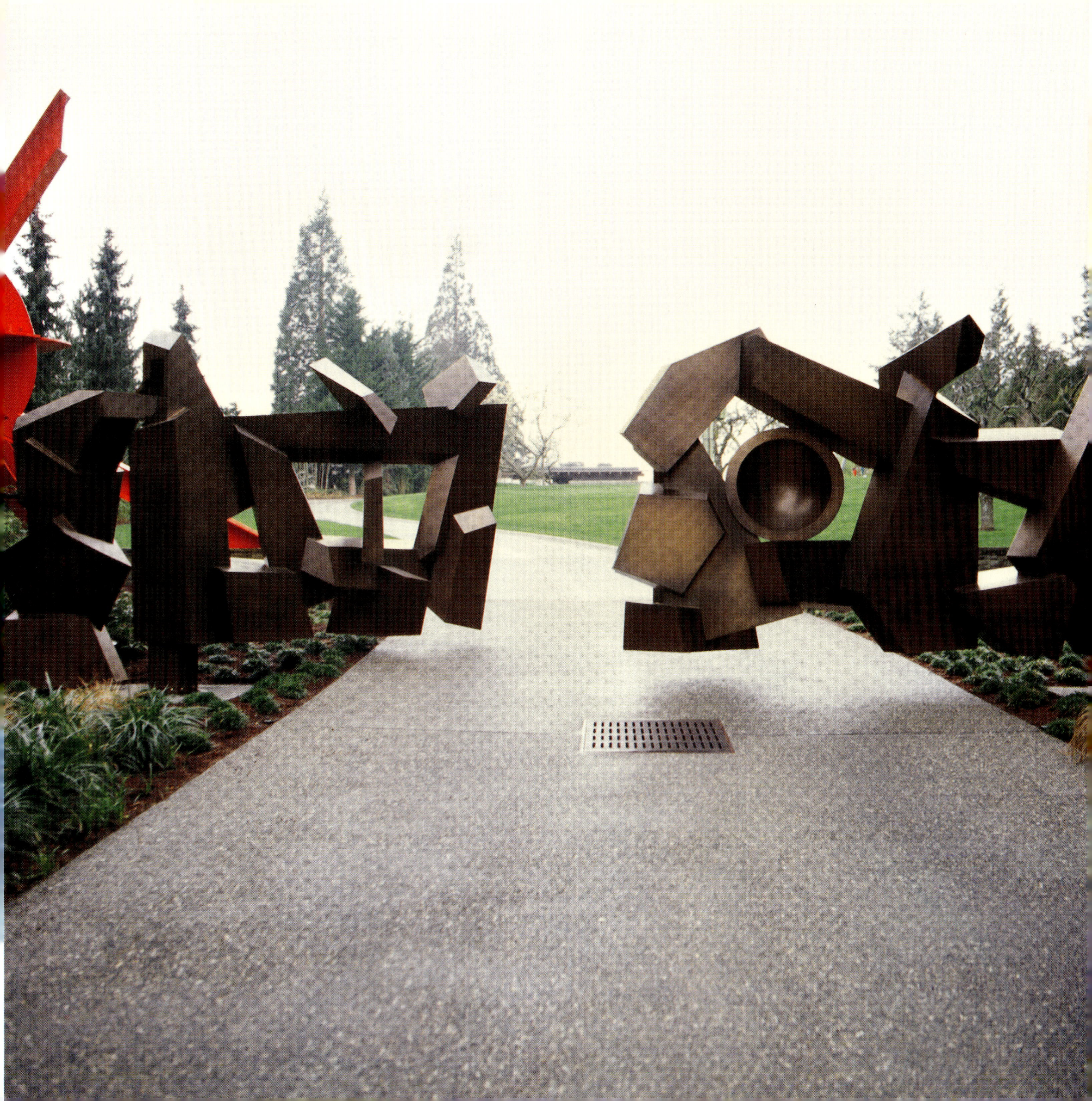

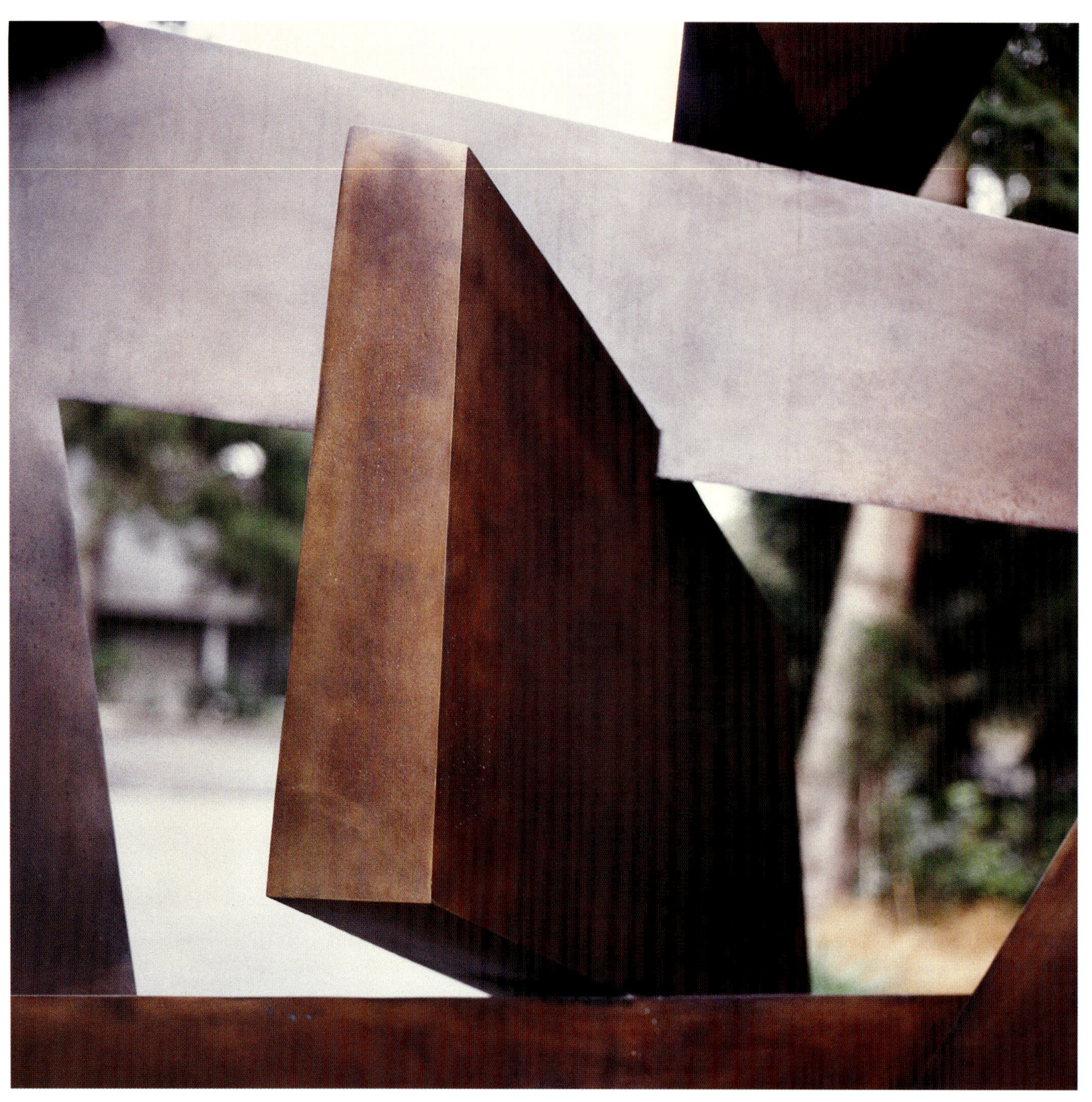

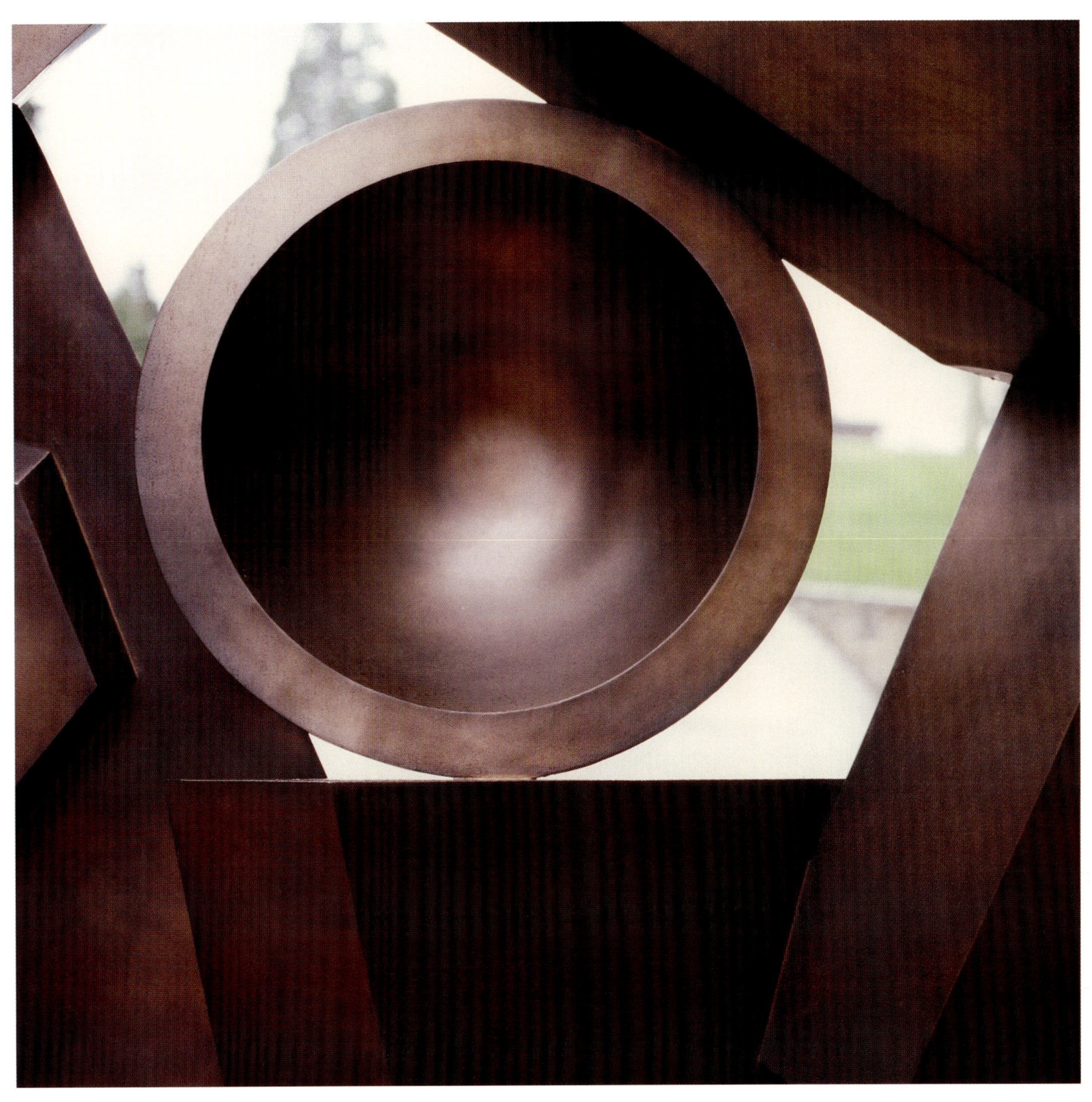

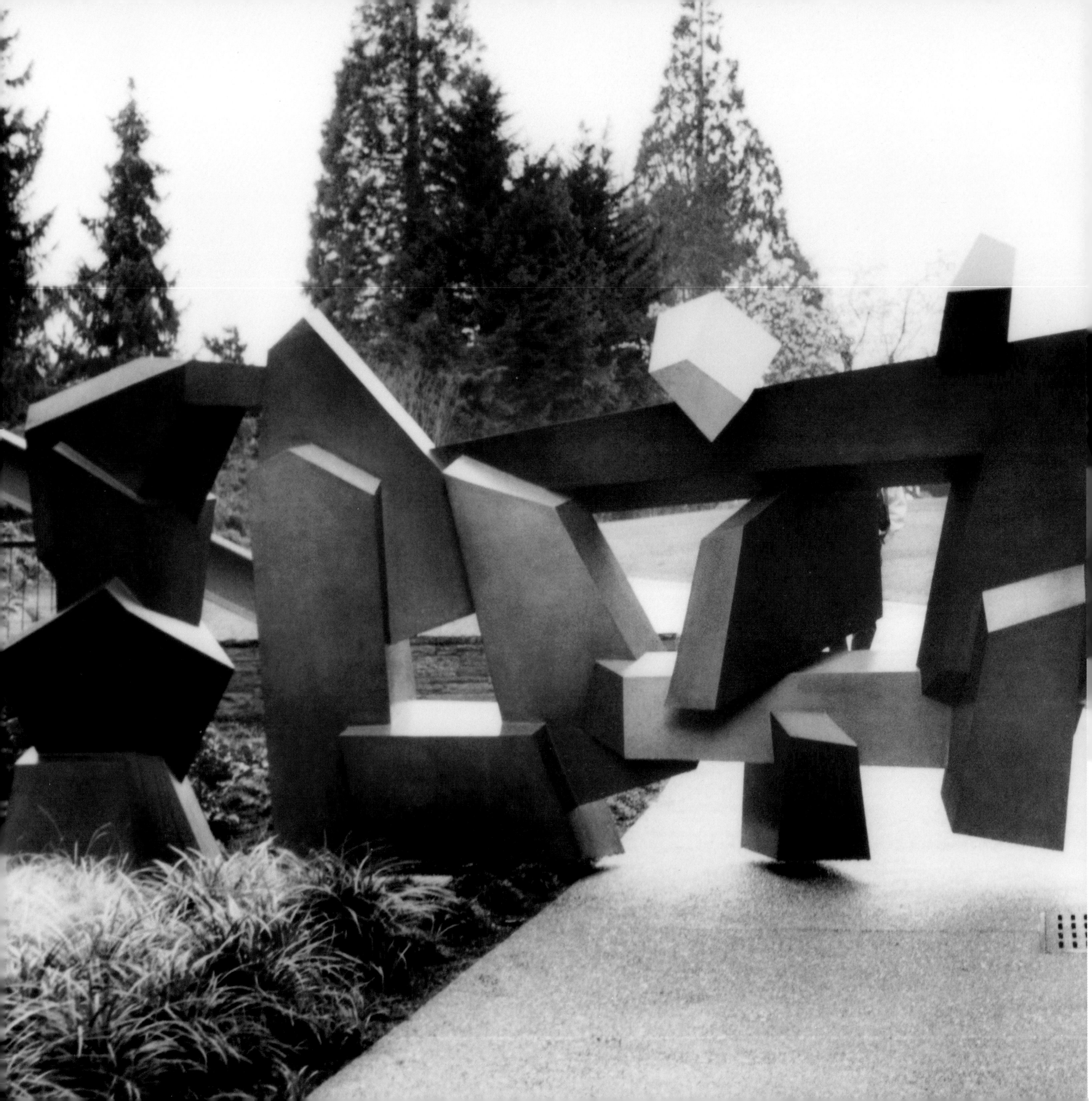

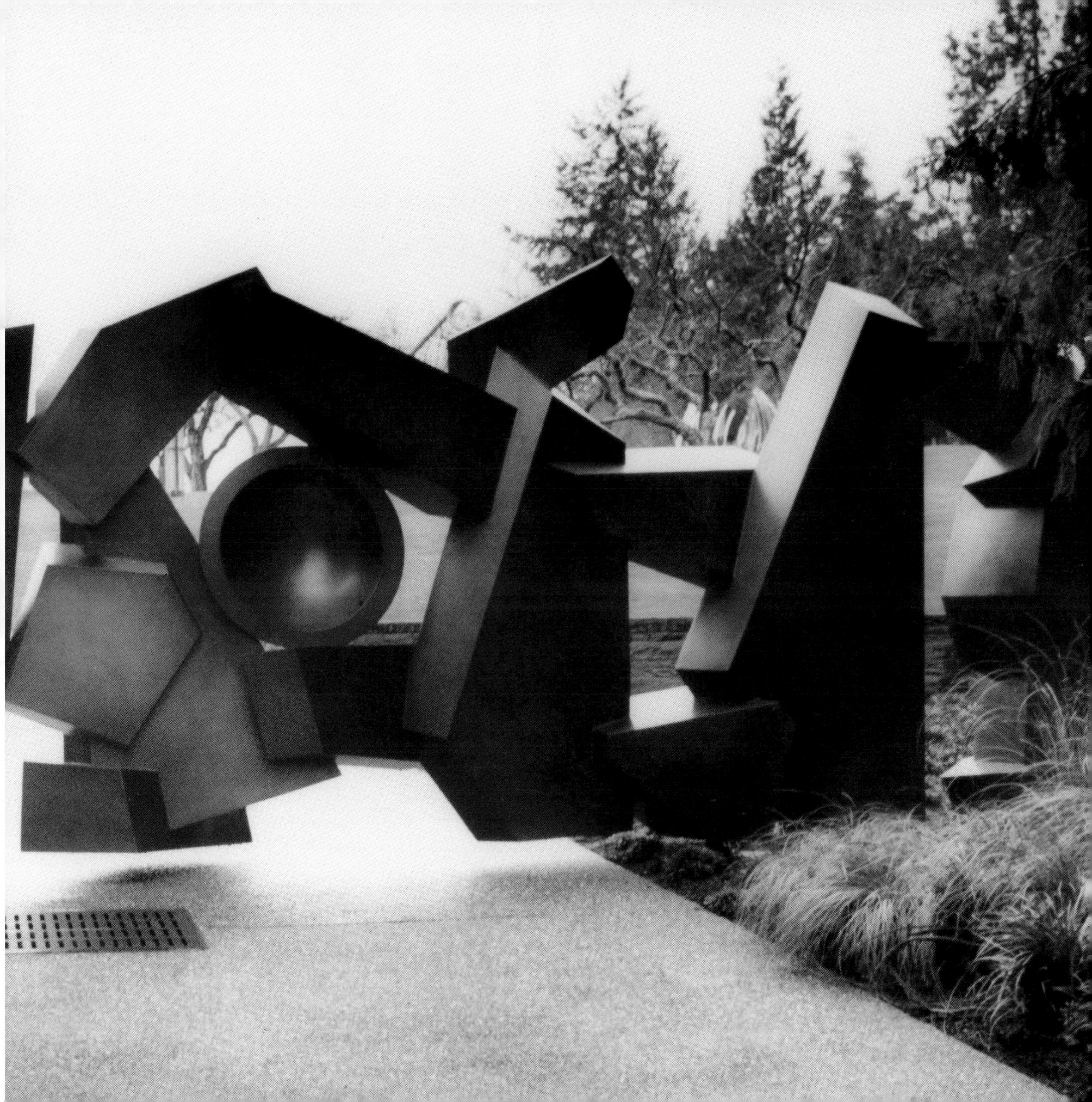

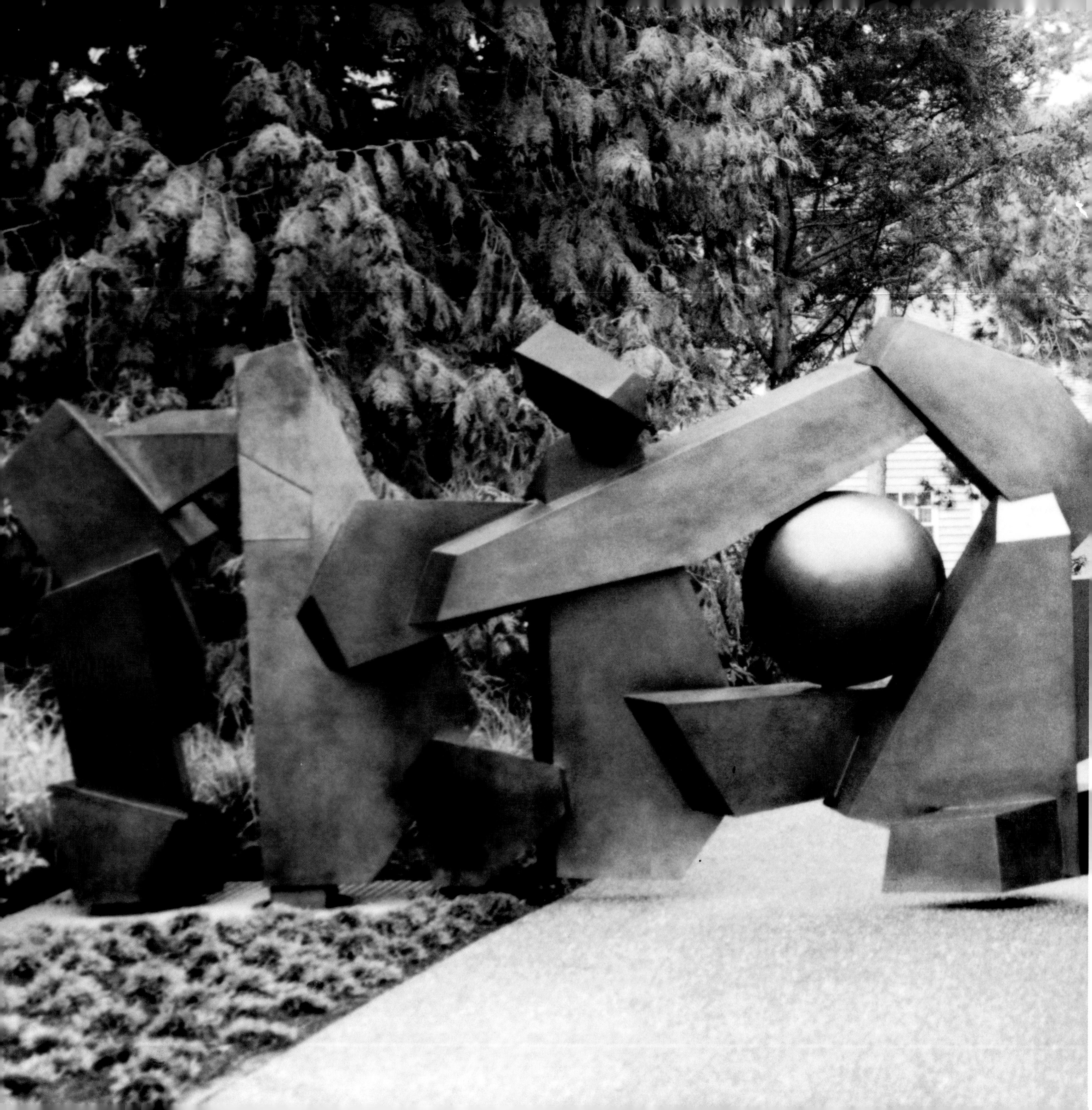

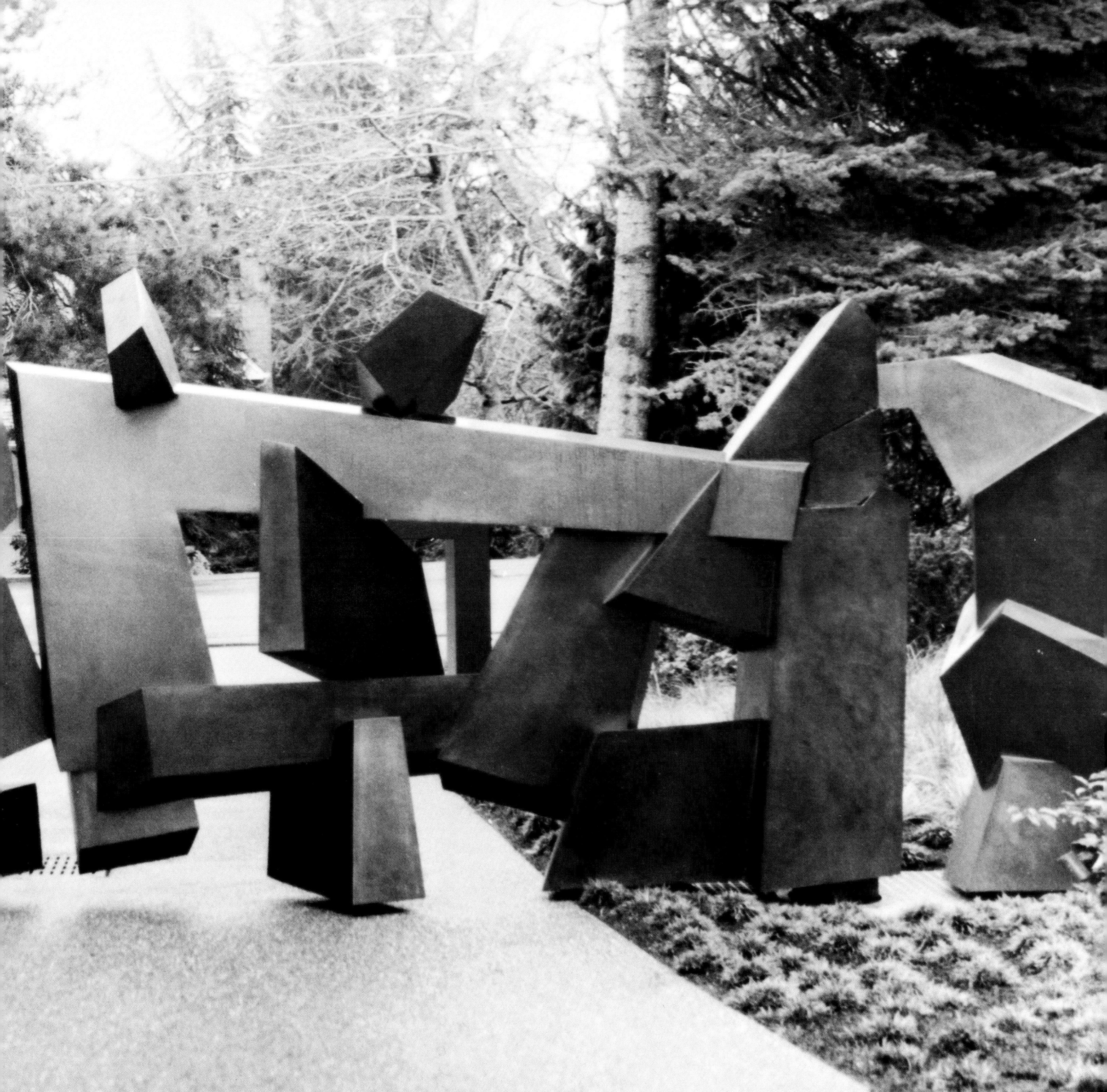

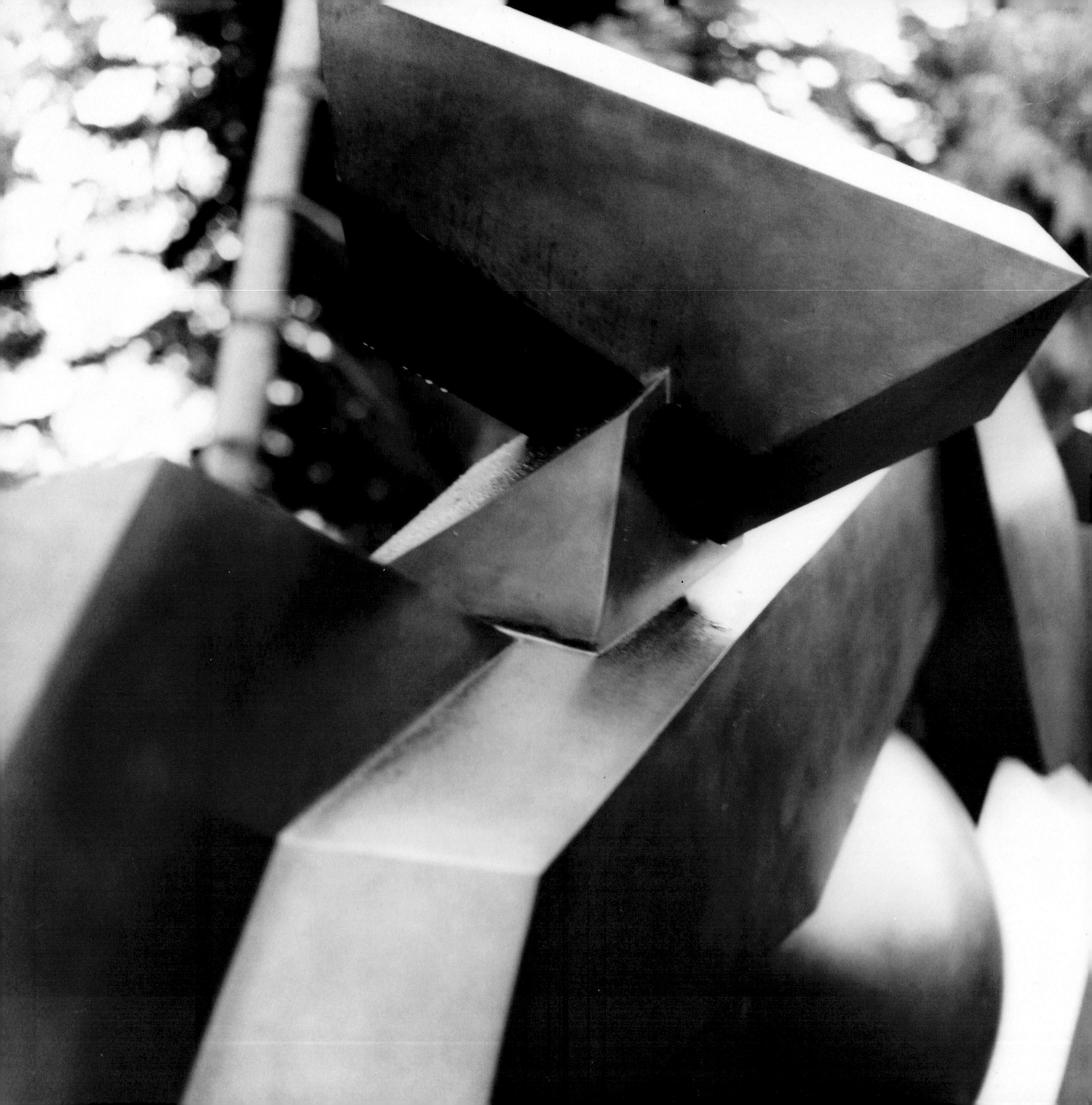

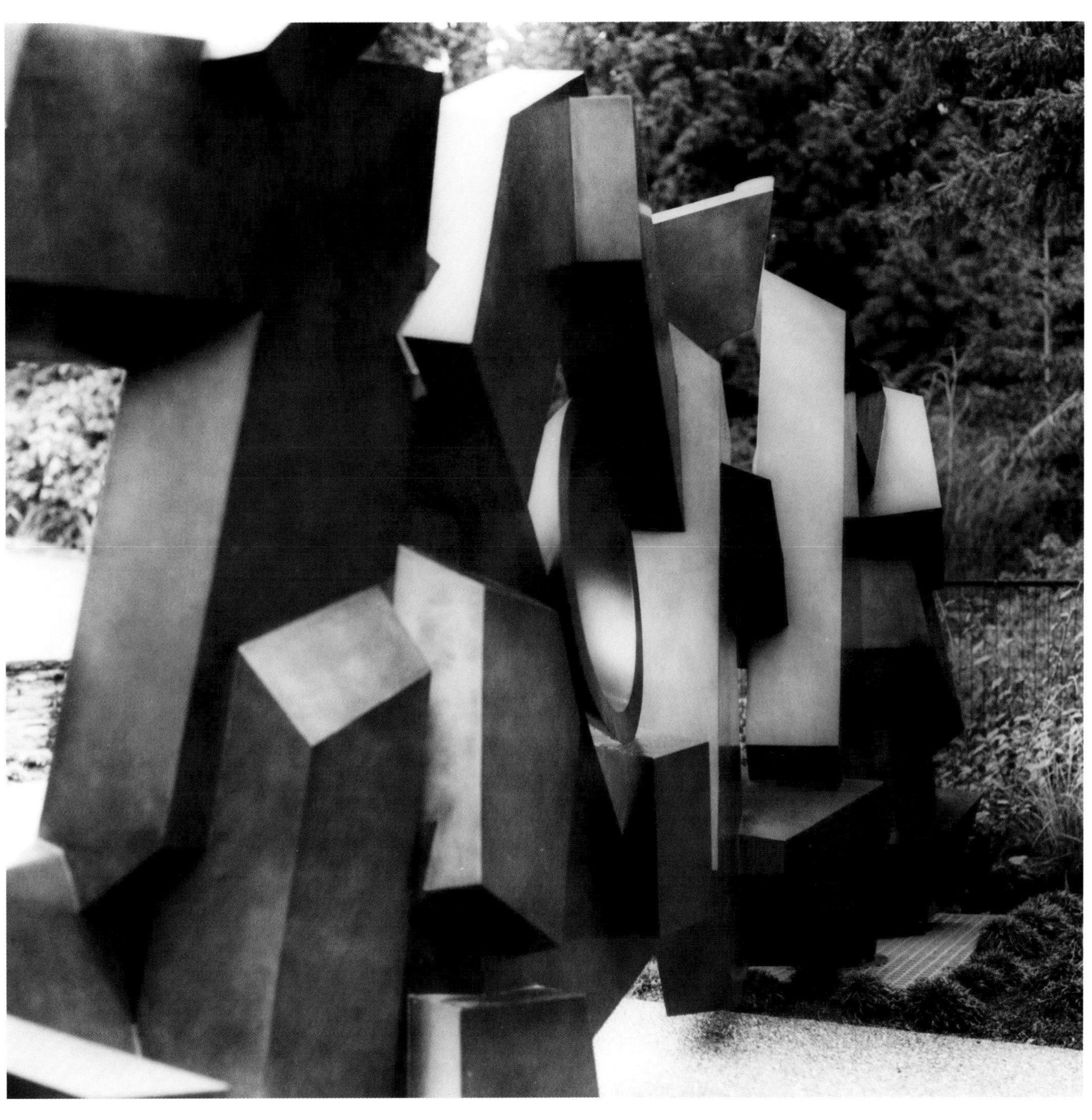

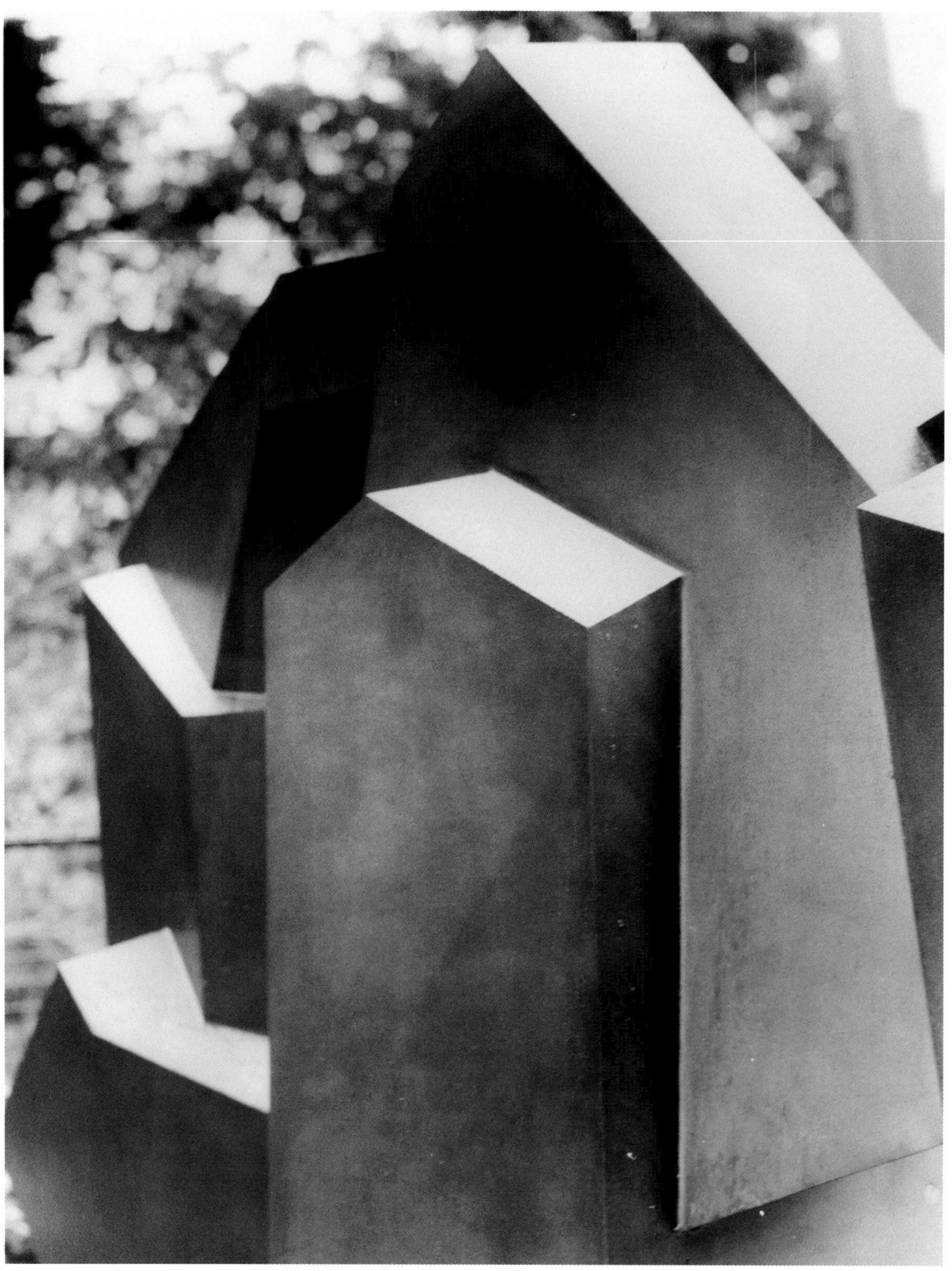

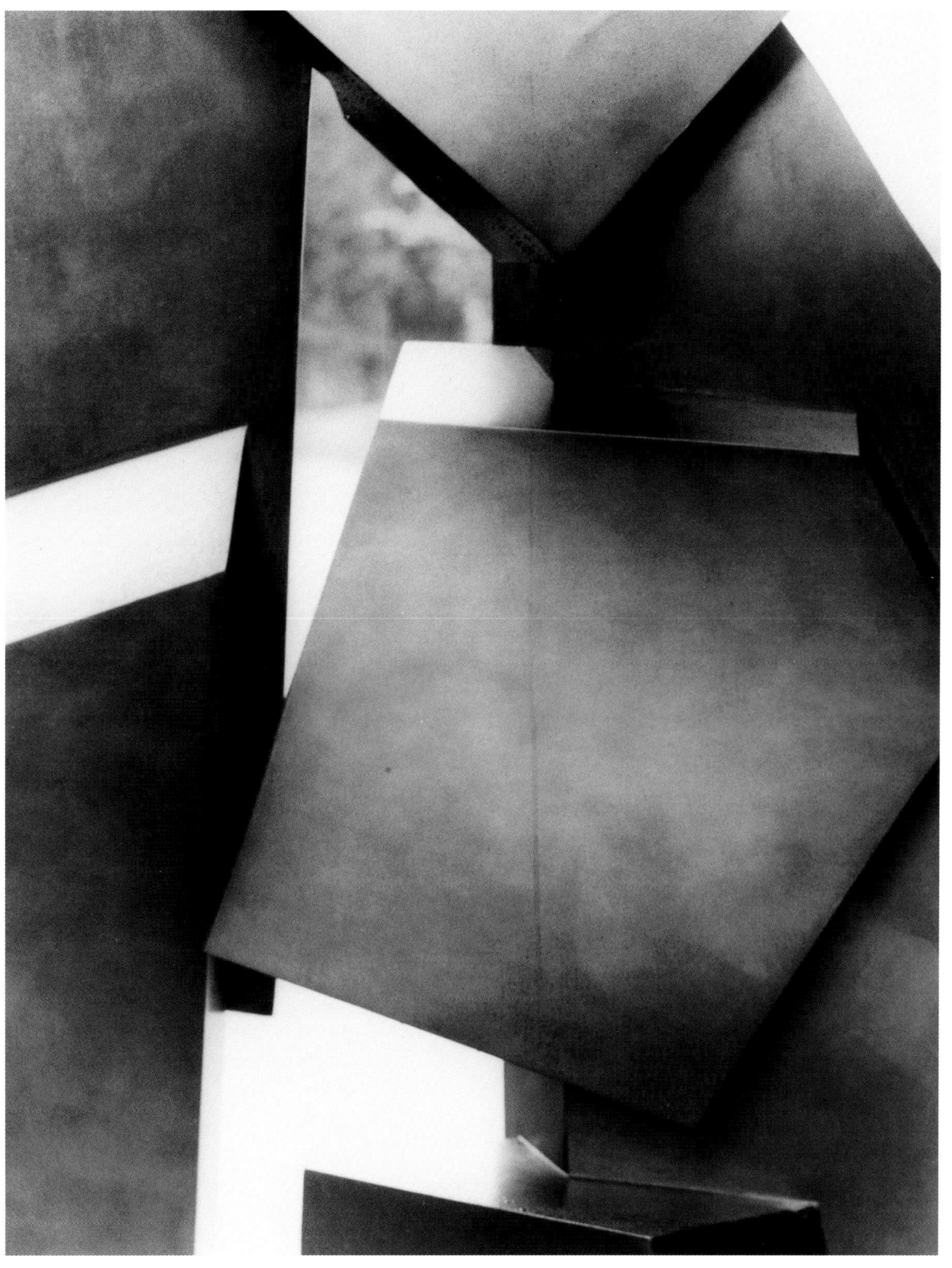

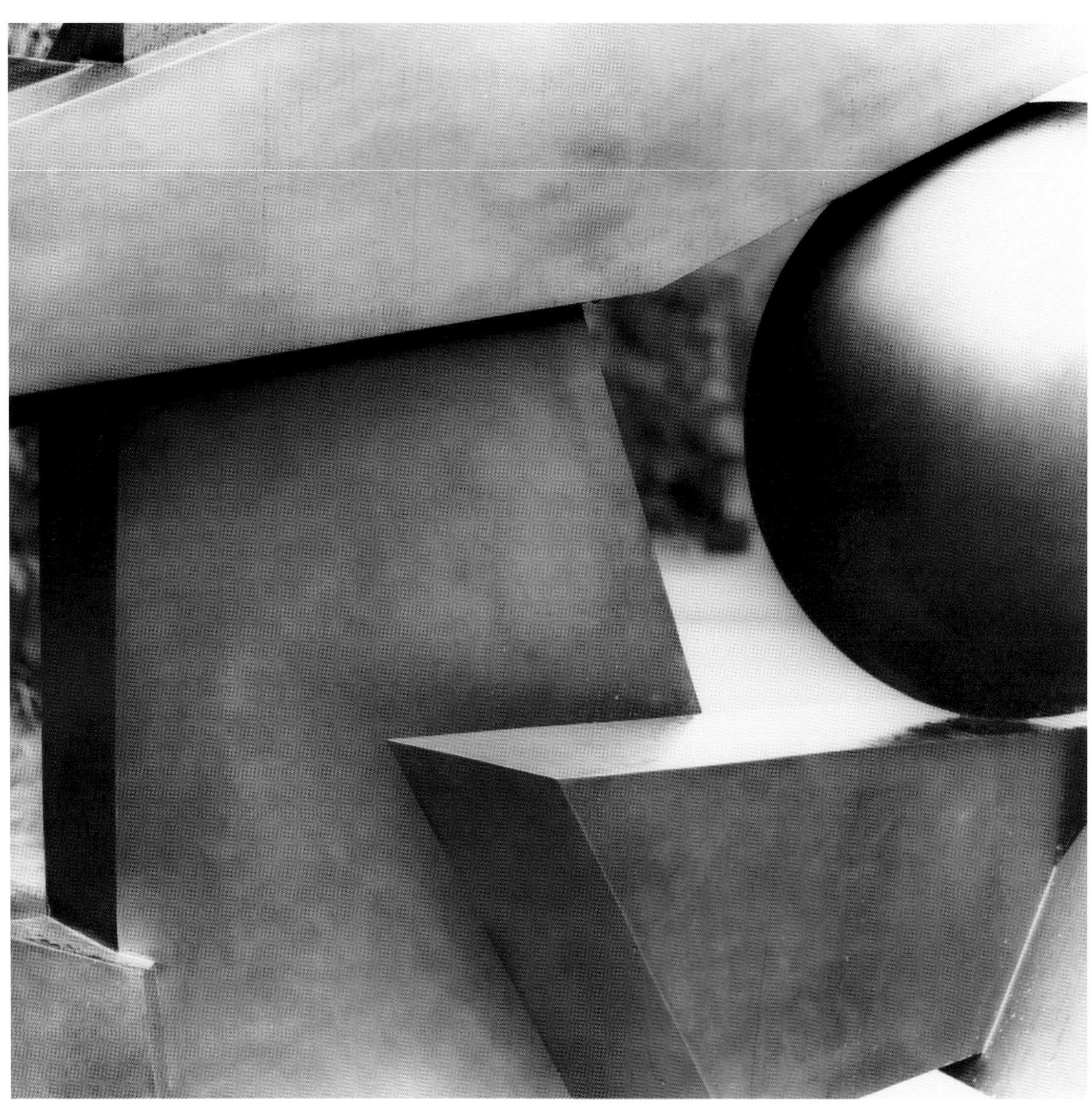

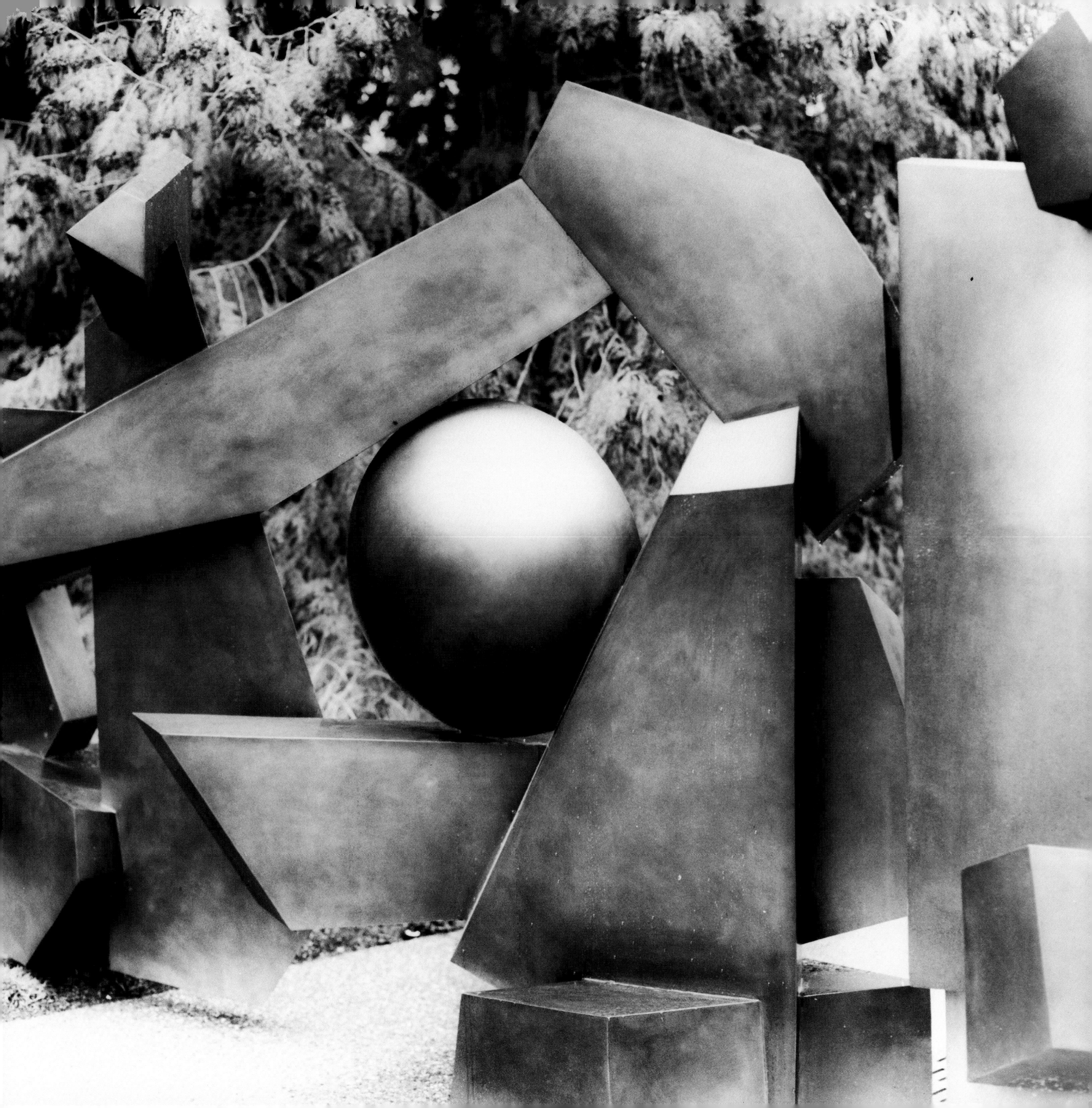

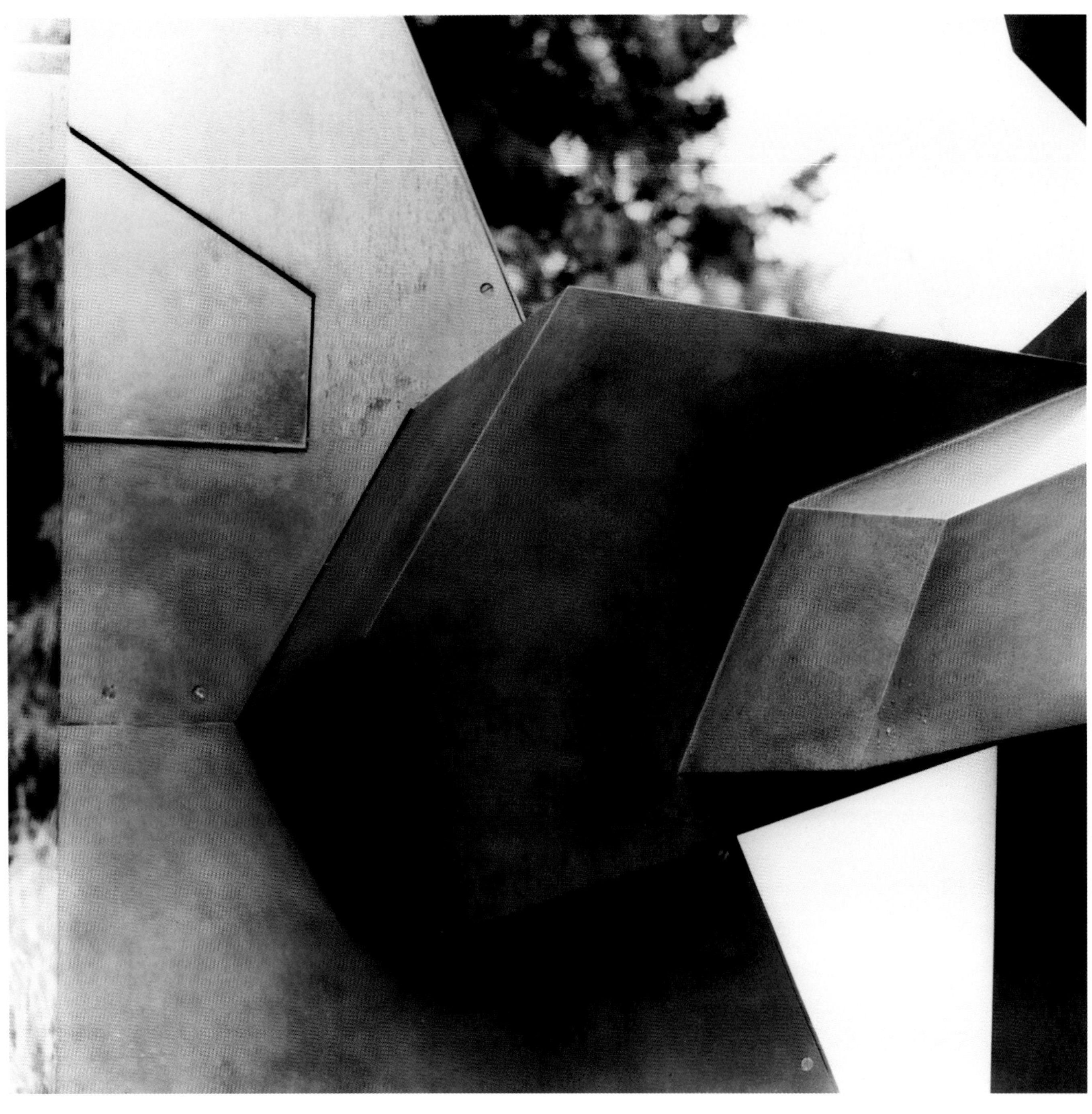

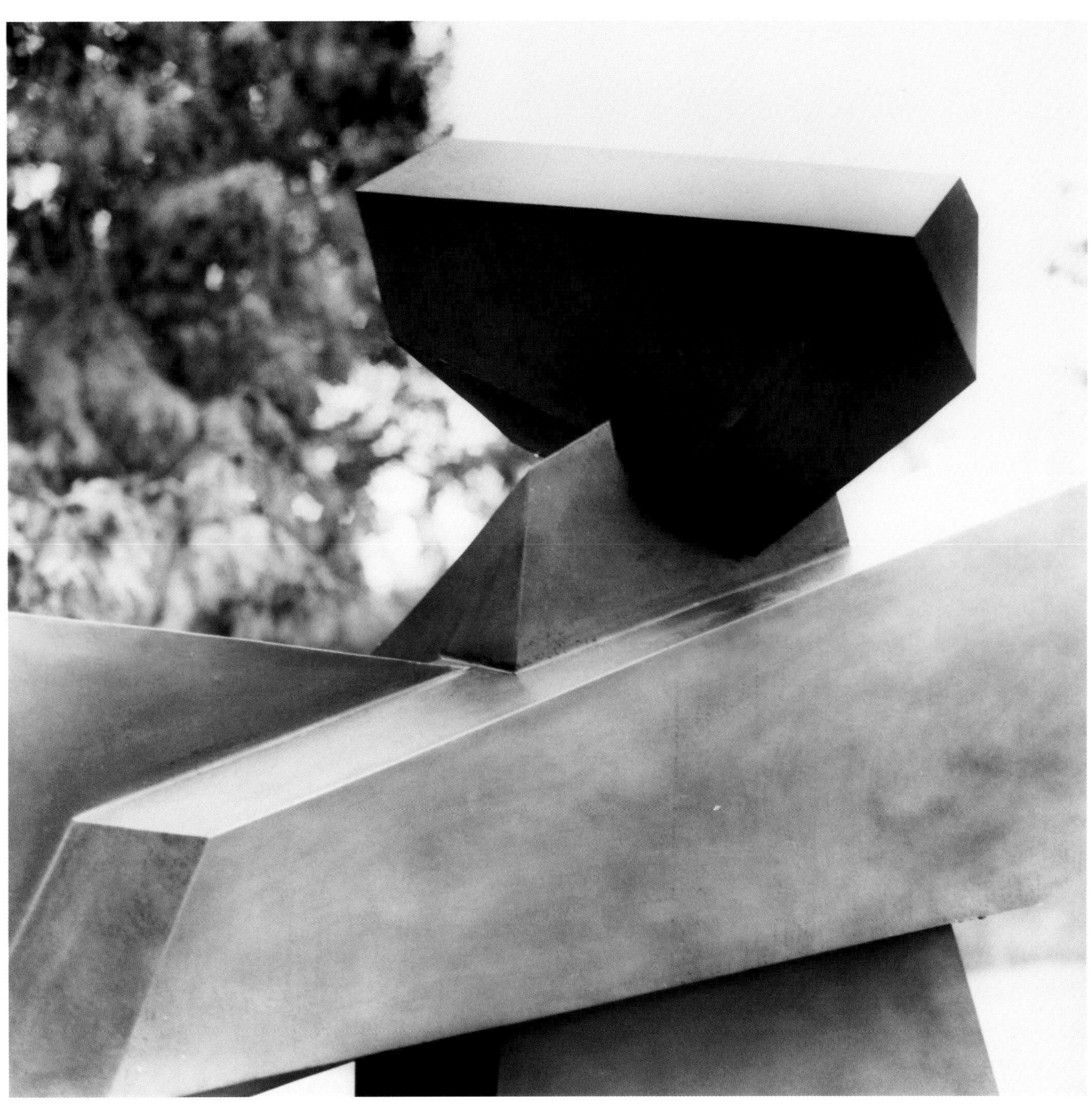

THE SECOND
GATES OF PARADISE,
MAQUETTE

2000
Bronze
collection of Jon and Mary Shirley

Here one can see how I combined the basic designs of *Breaking Away I and II.* The next model was executed in Styrofoam and measured 24" x 65" x 24". This allowed me to make many changes as the work proceeded.

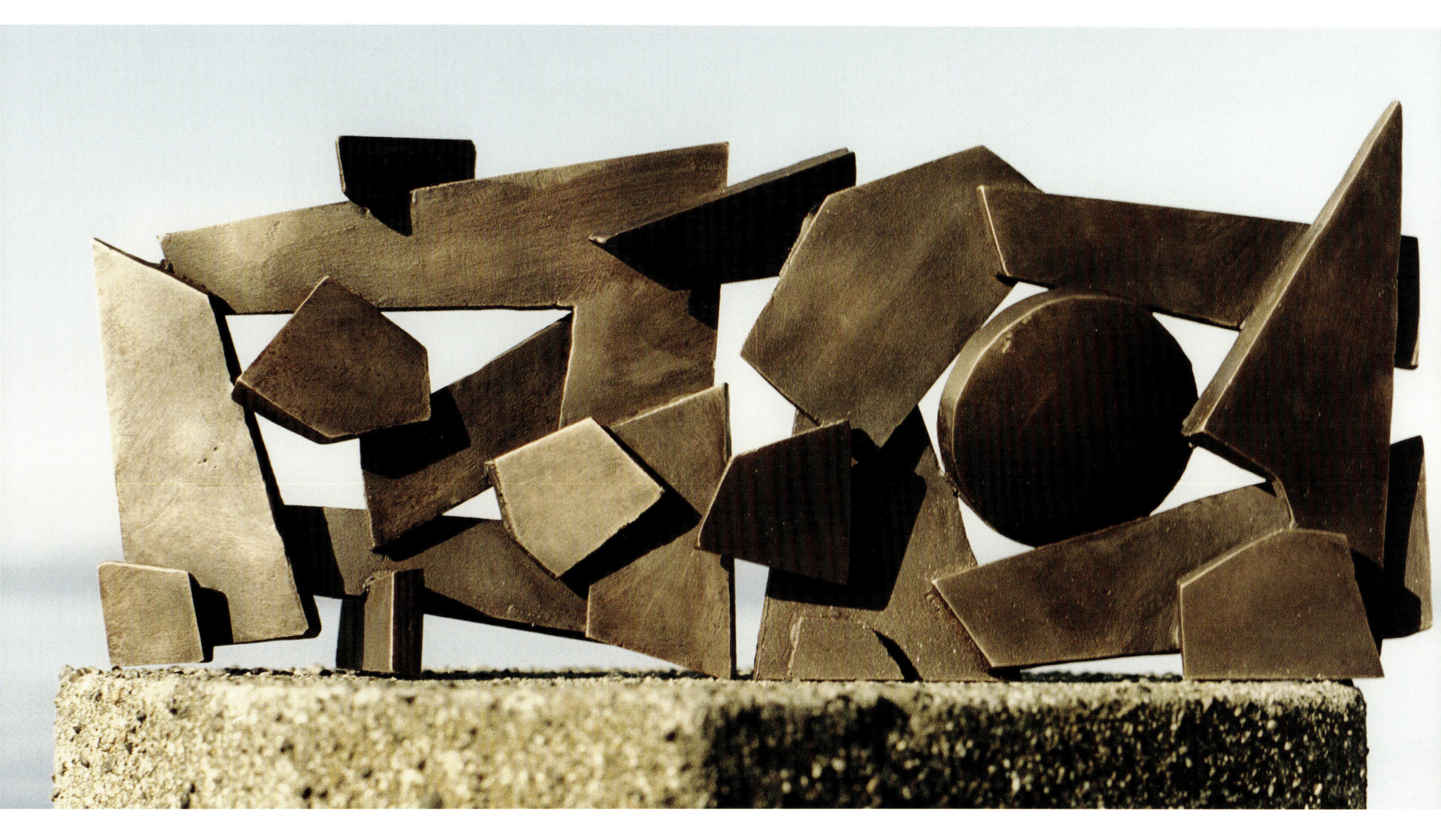

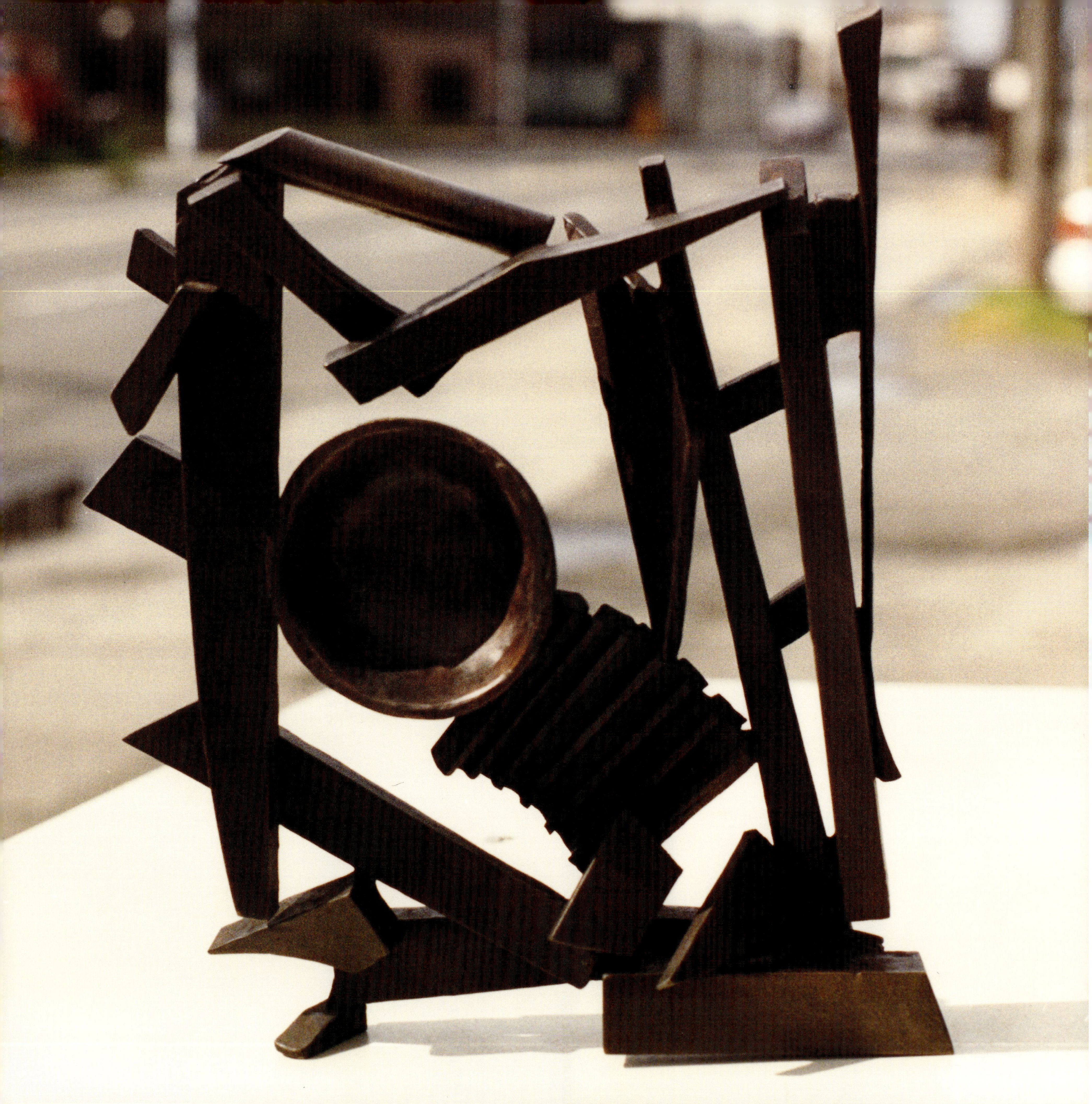

SMALLER BRONZES AND MAQUETTES

These bronzes, almost all unique castings done directly from wood models (except one, *Oracle*, which was cast from the original wax), are what I call "entertainments." In general, they were not necessarily created to be further developed into larger sculptures. Perhaps one or two will fuel an idea for a bigger version, but they were created to be finished and pleasurable objects in themselves. They can be handled with tactile satisfaction as well as viewed from many sides and directions. The titles mostly derive from my associations with the forms. Only *Danae* actually portrays a story. *Il Vento* is a semi-abstraction of my *Woman in the Wind* (1962).

HOMAGE TO KANDINSKY

1990
Bronze
18" x 16" x 6"
Collection of the artist

This piece was inspired by my many visits to the Guggenheim Museum in Manhattan, while waiting for my future wife, Maryann Jordan, who was working there. Some of the shapes came from the same cannibalized piece, *Triad,* used in *Breaking Away II*. These geometric shapes remind me of the wonderful paintings found in the Guggenheim collection of Kandinskys.

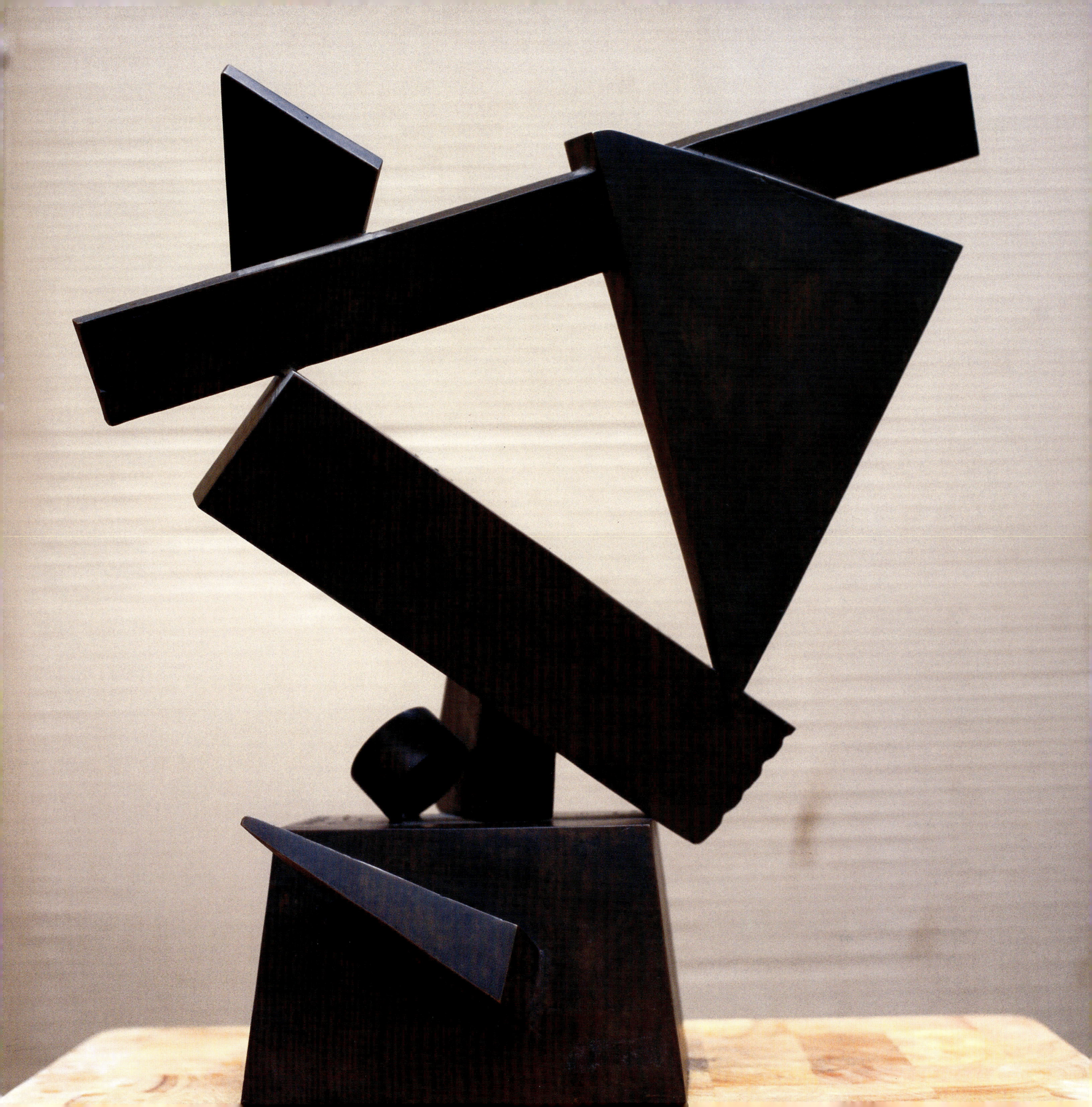

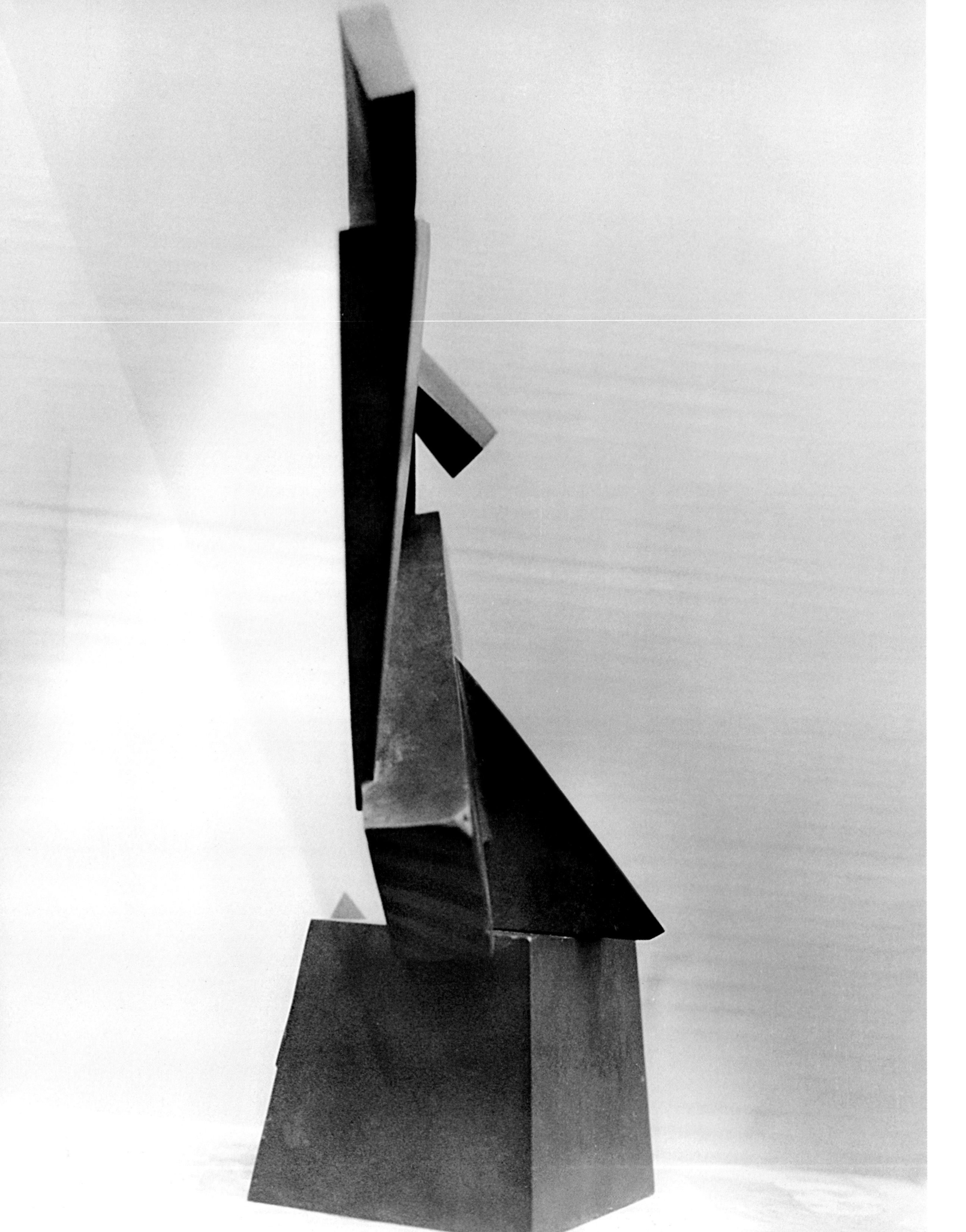

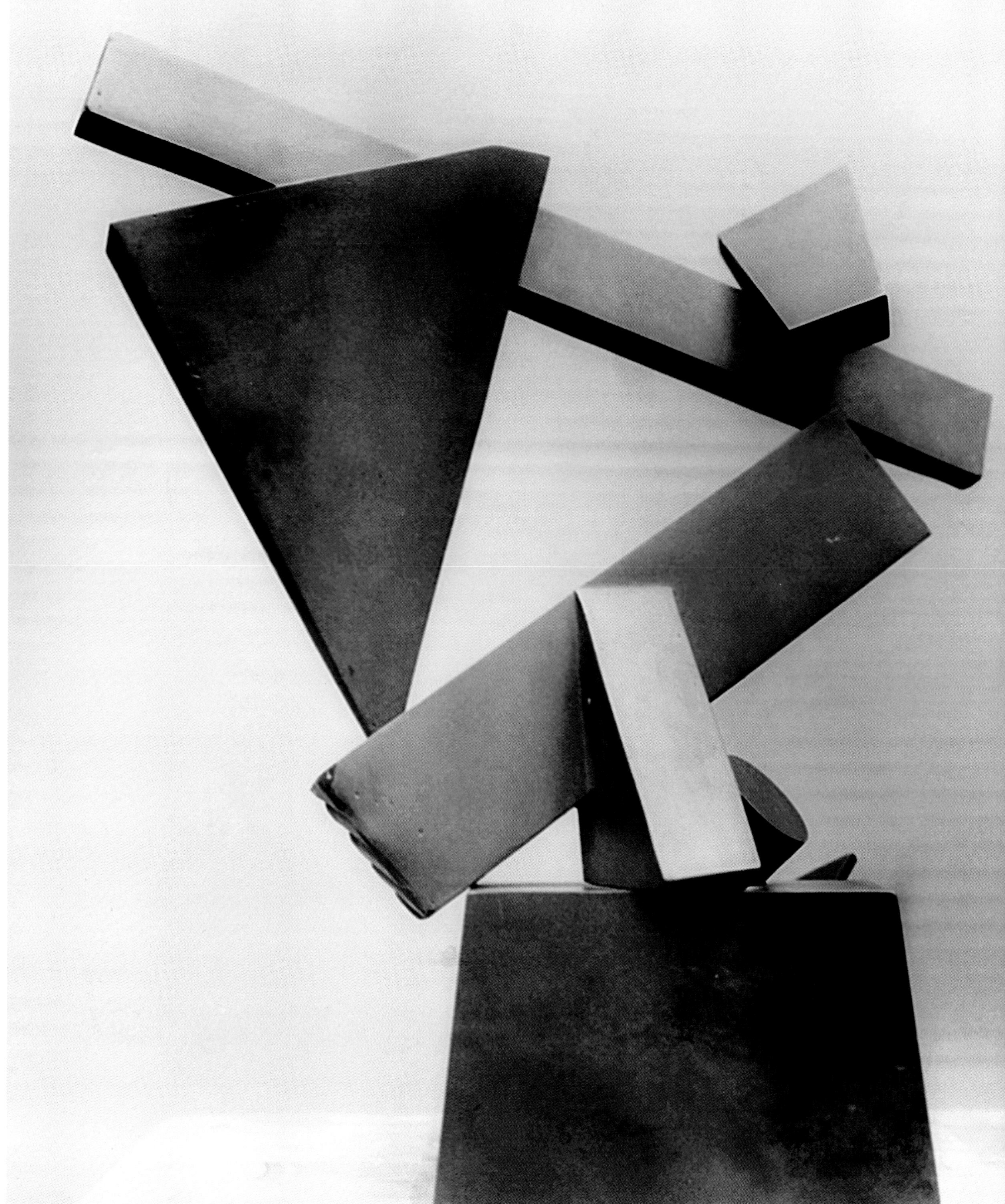

THE SOURCE

1990
Bronze
12"x 19.5" x 7"
Collection of Donald Kuspit, NYC

This was inspired by a Picasso painting of the same title. Actually it was a photograph of a stolen painting in an art journal. The composition of a draped, resting woman holding a large jug seemed ideal to translate into an abstract sculpture. I decided to use two discs instead of one and the extra "crow" on the knee seemed appropriate to finish the composition.

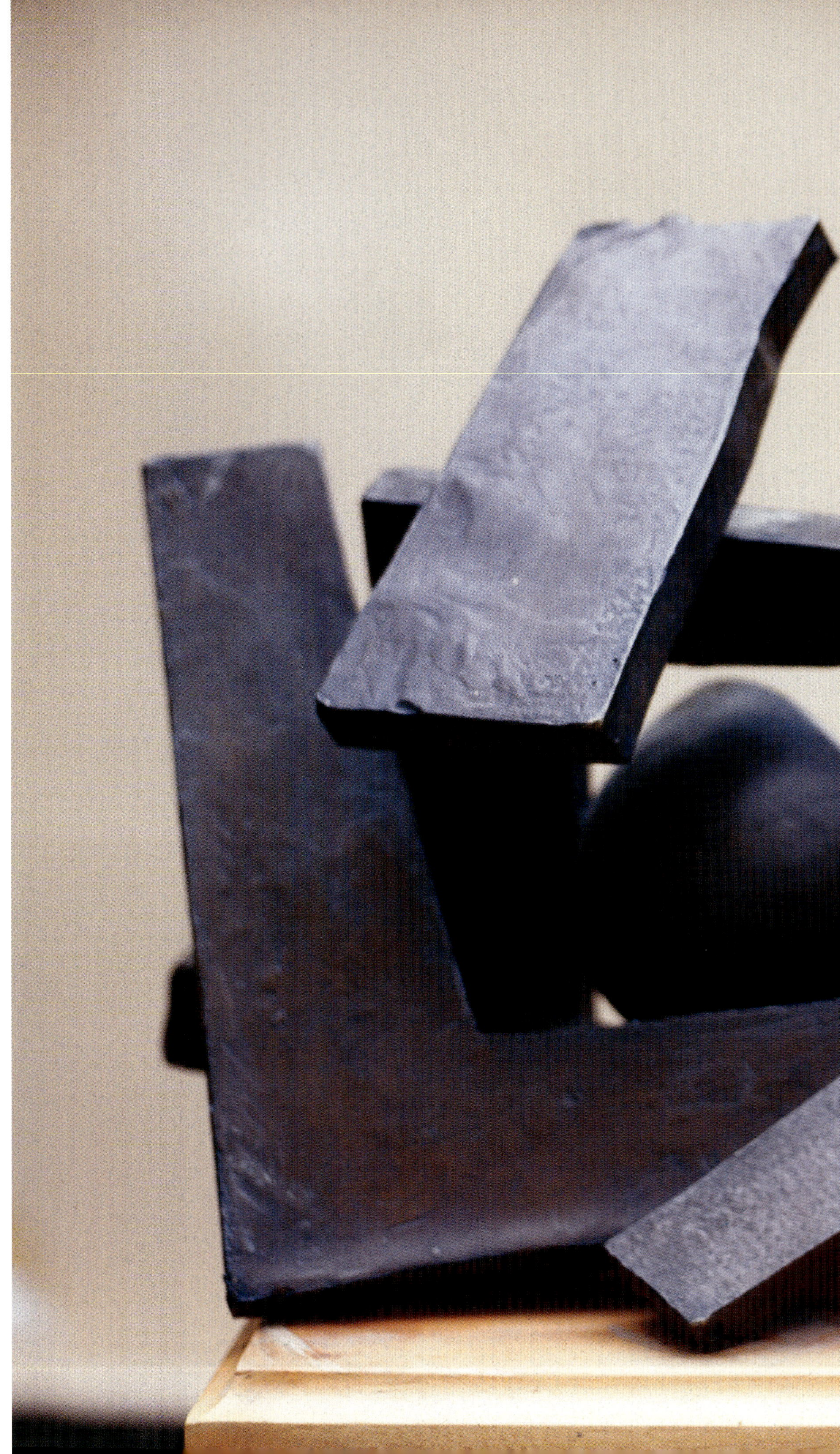

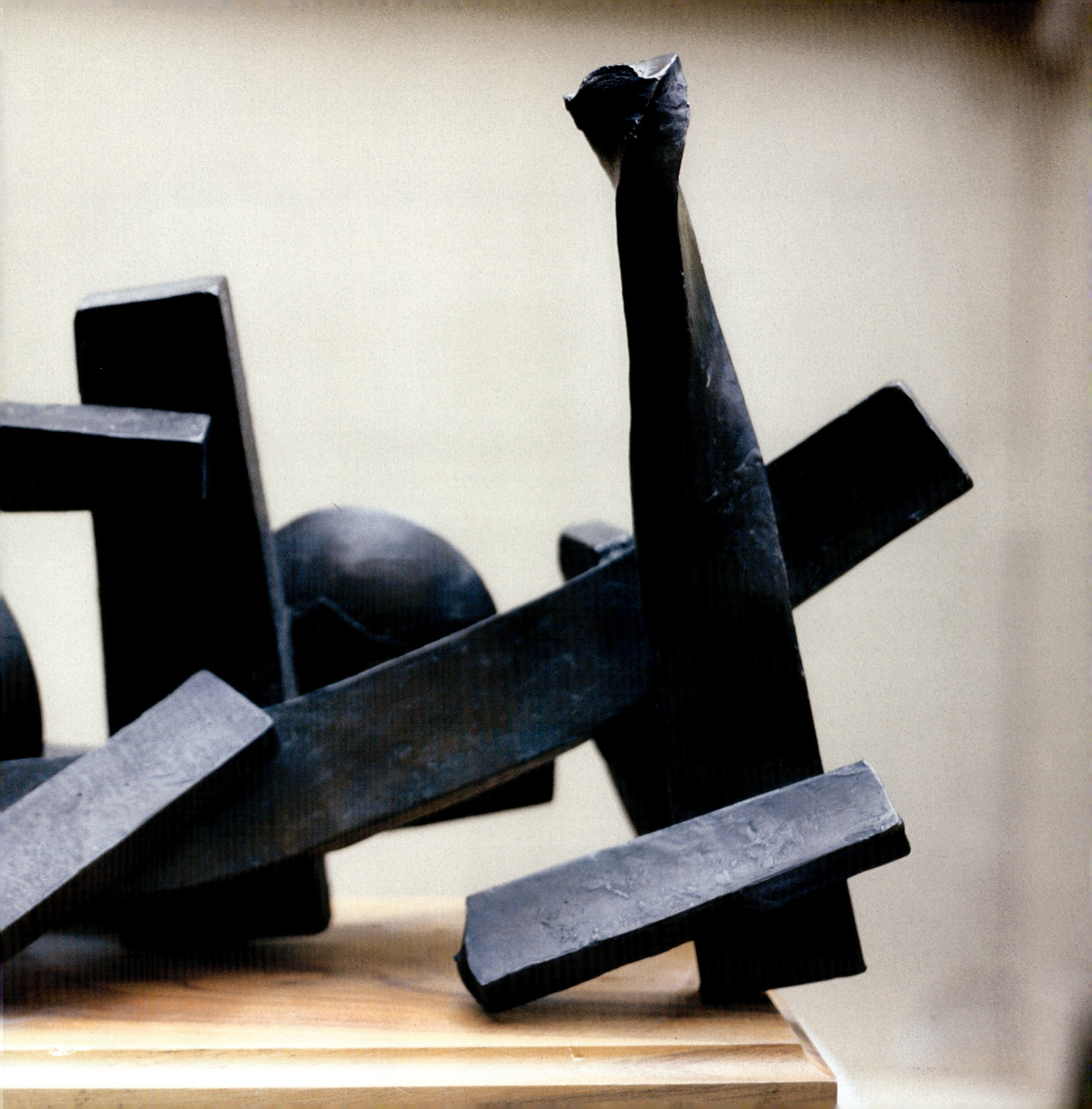

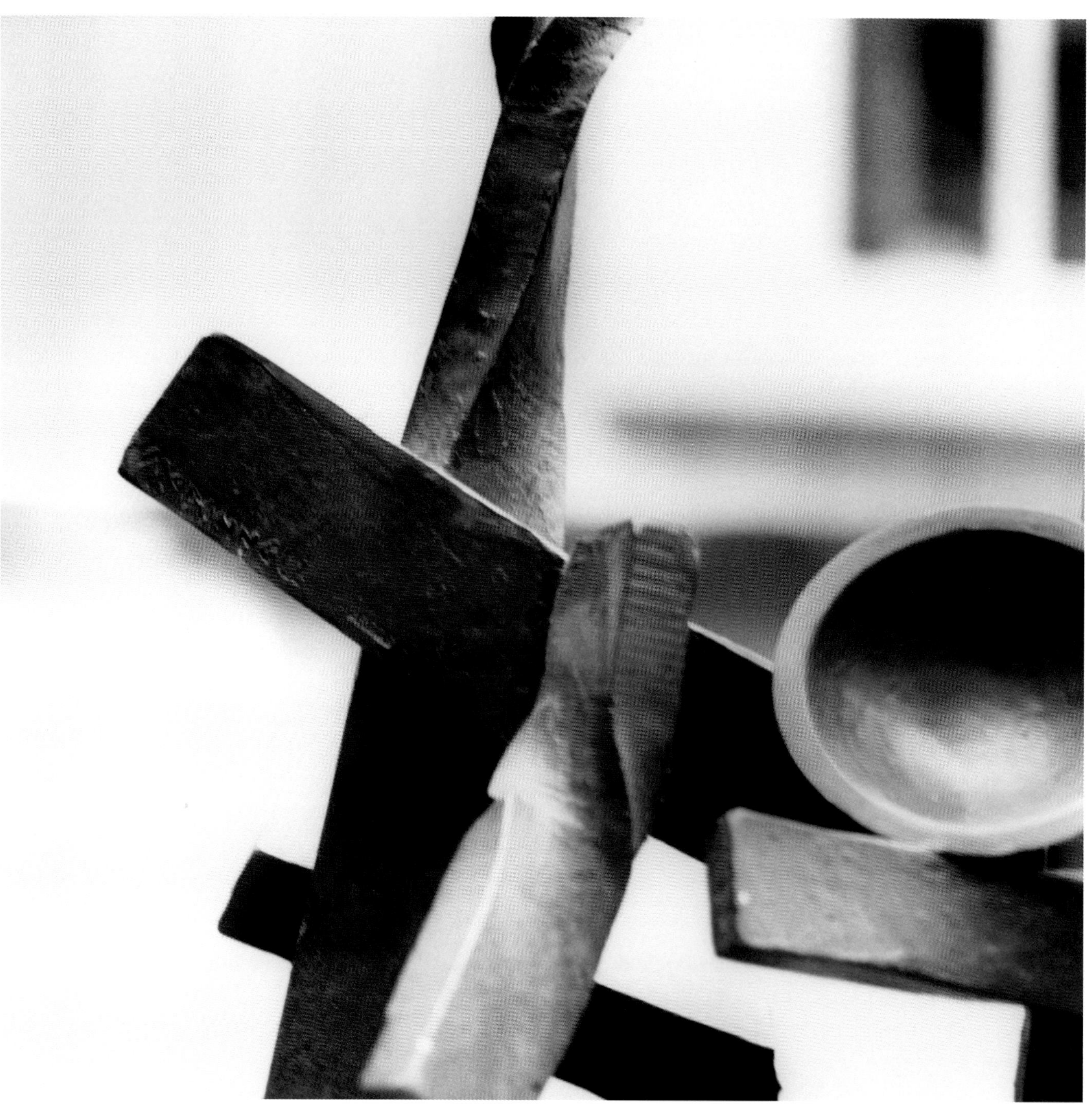

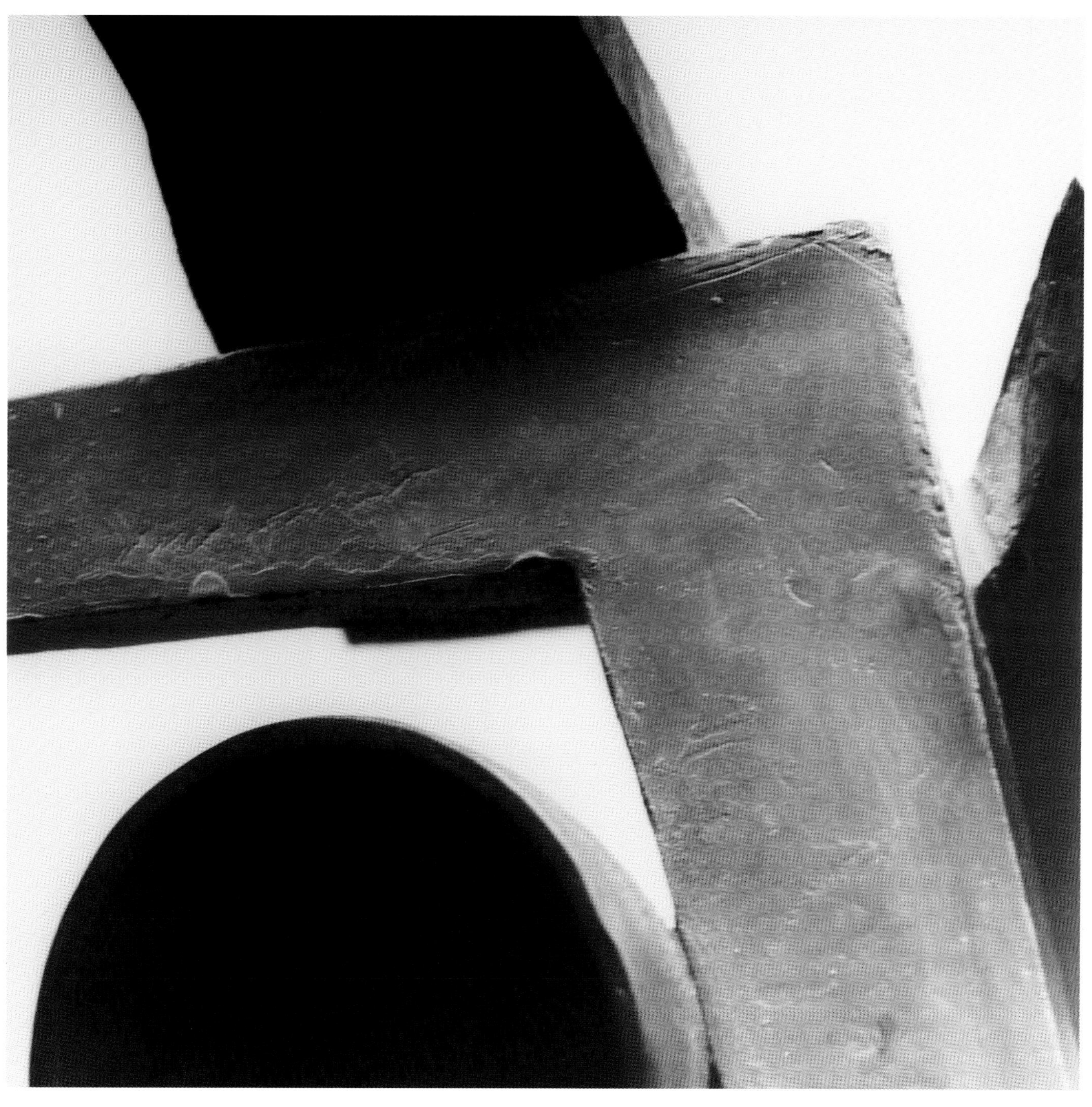

IL VENTO

2002
Bronze
15.5" x 7" x 4.5"
Collection of the artist

This is a constructed interpretation, forty years later, of my *Woman in the Wind*. It lacks the sensual quality of the earlier version but has much strength and determination.

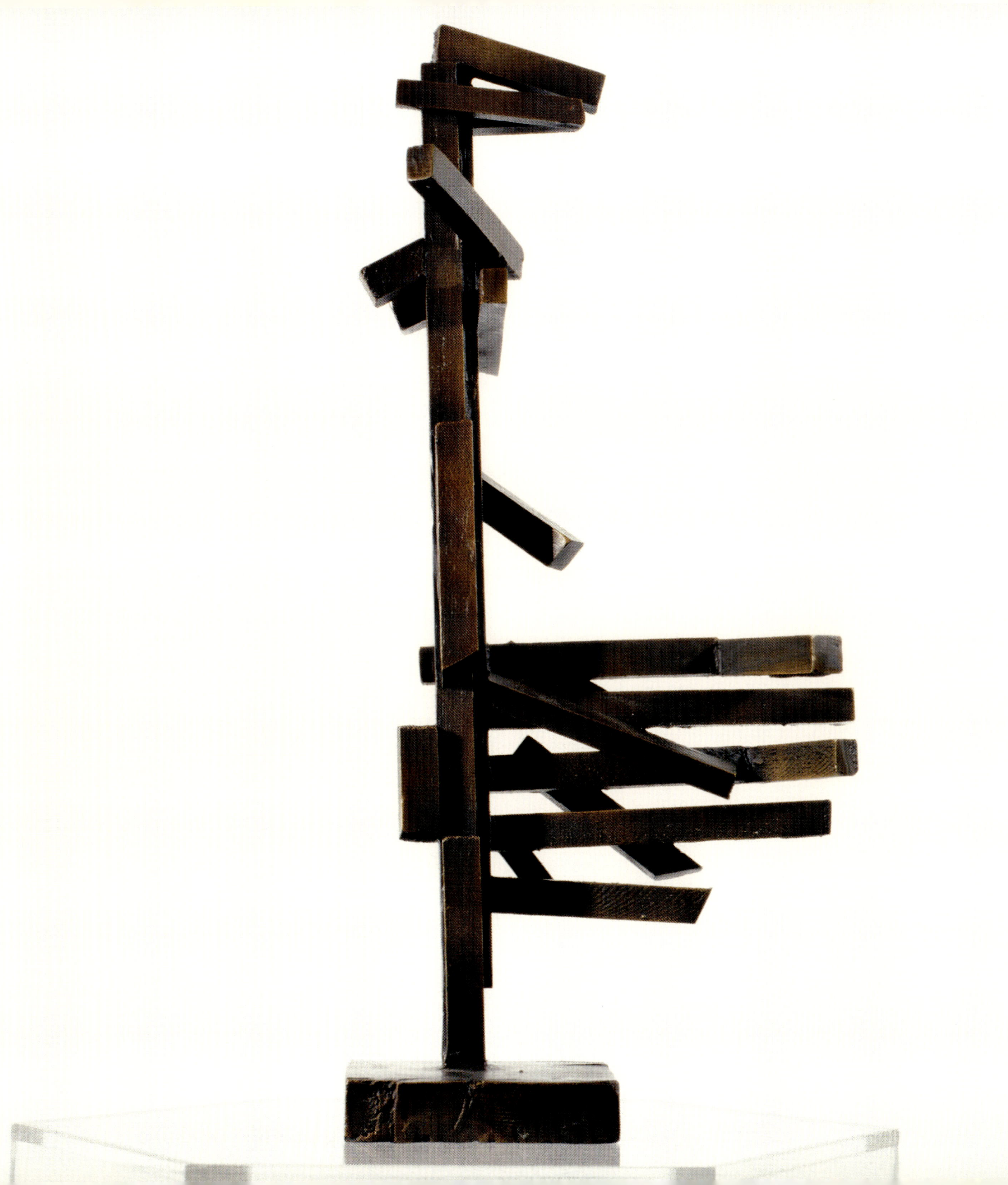

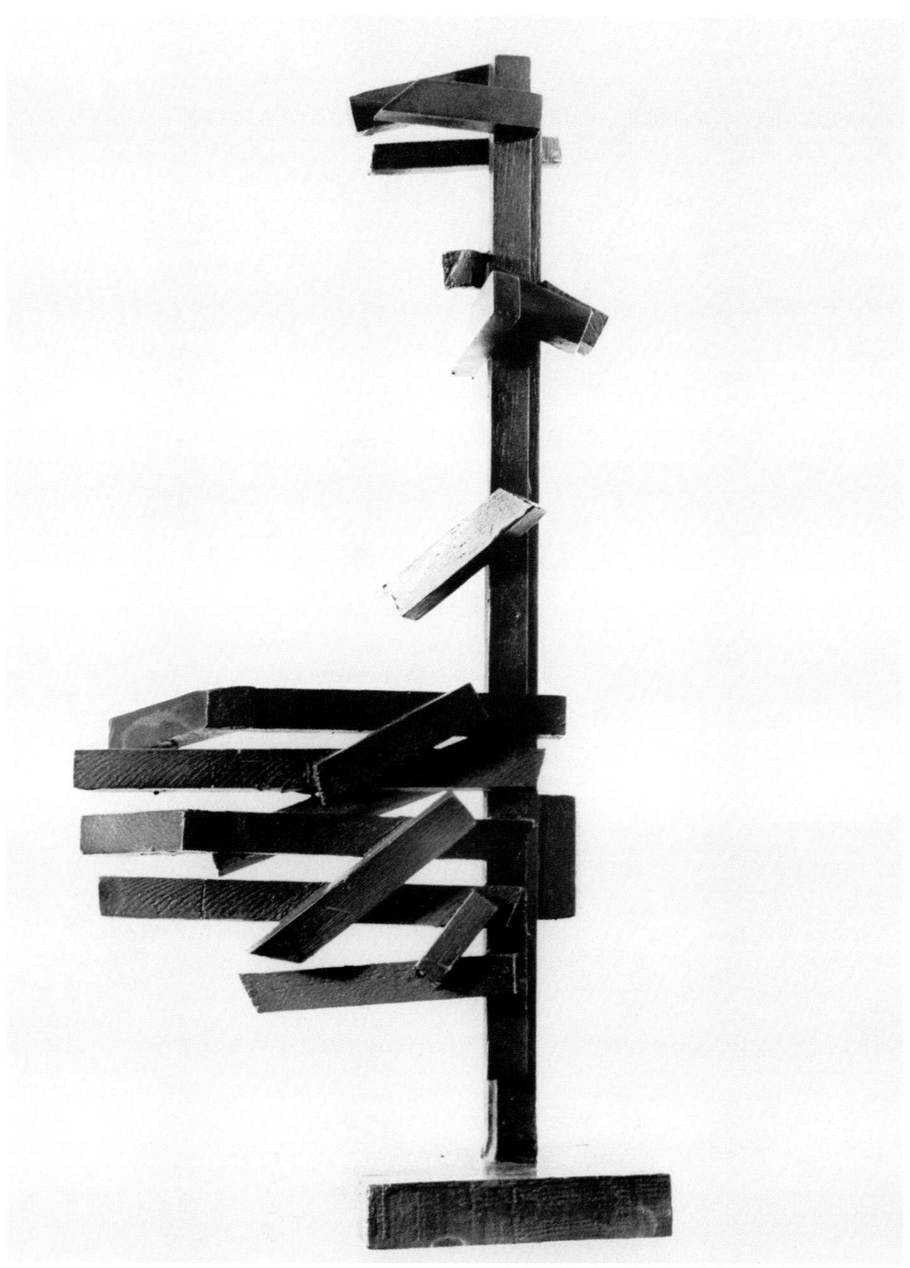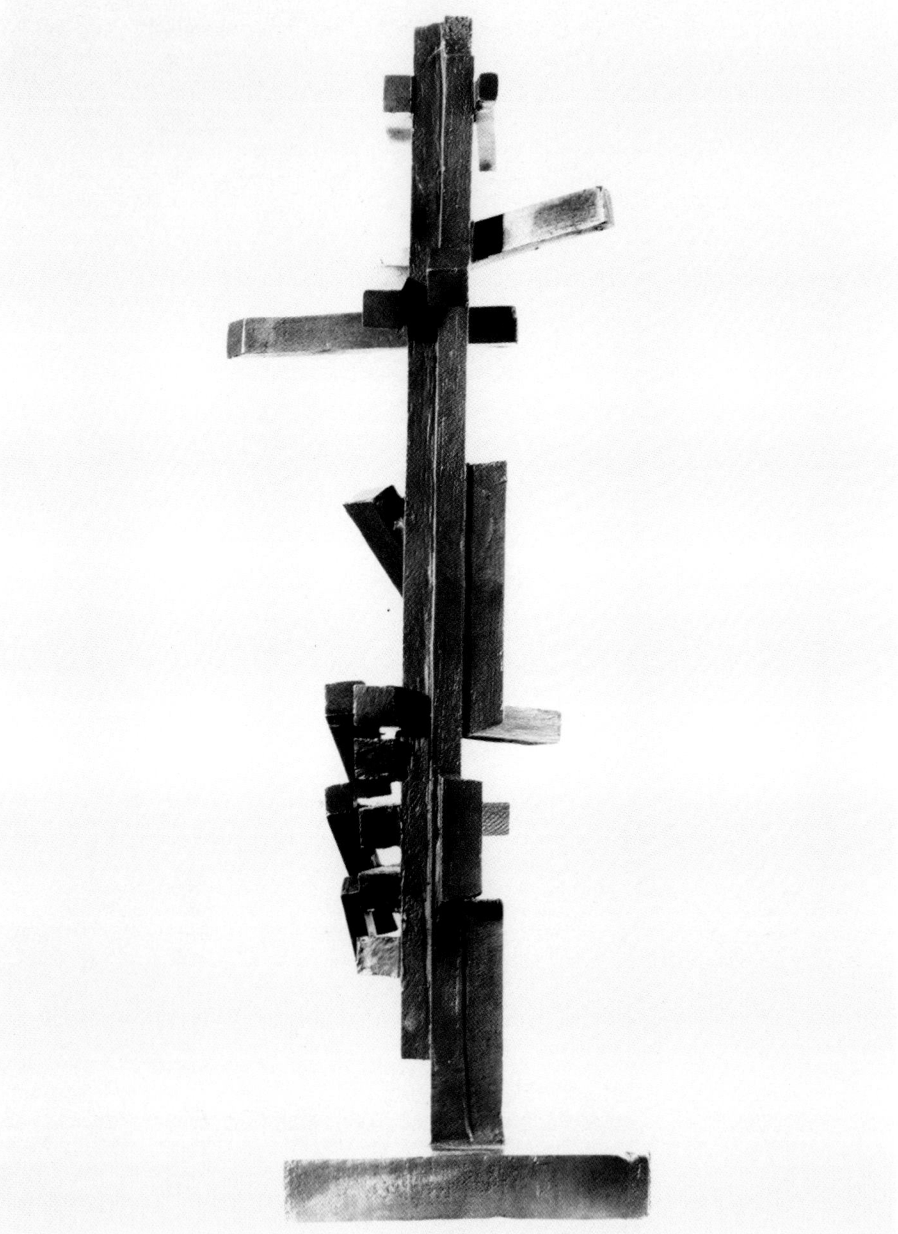

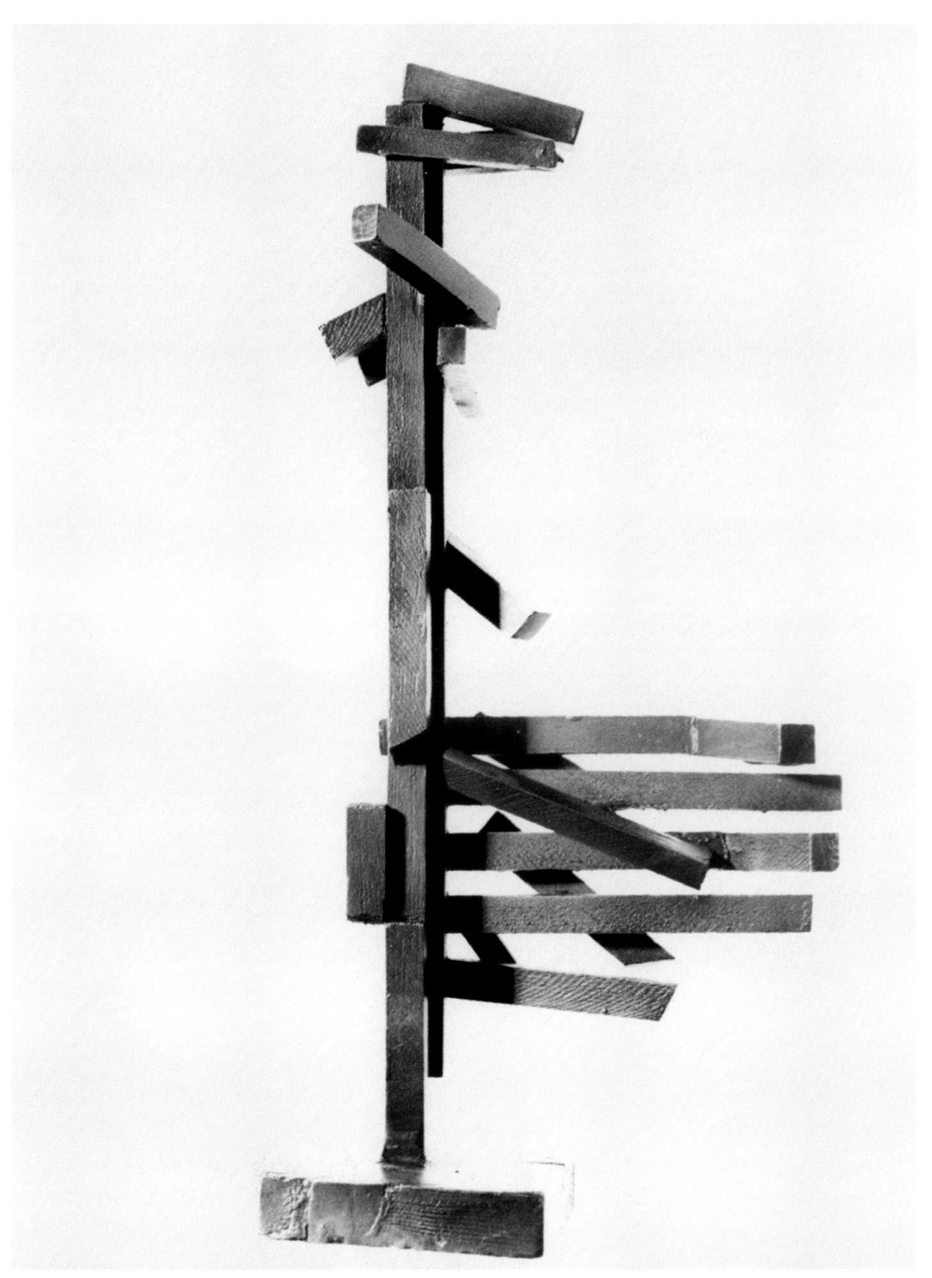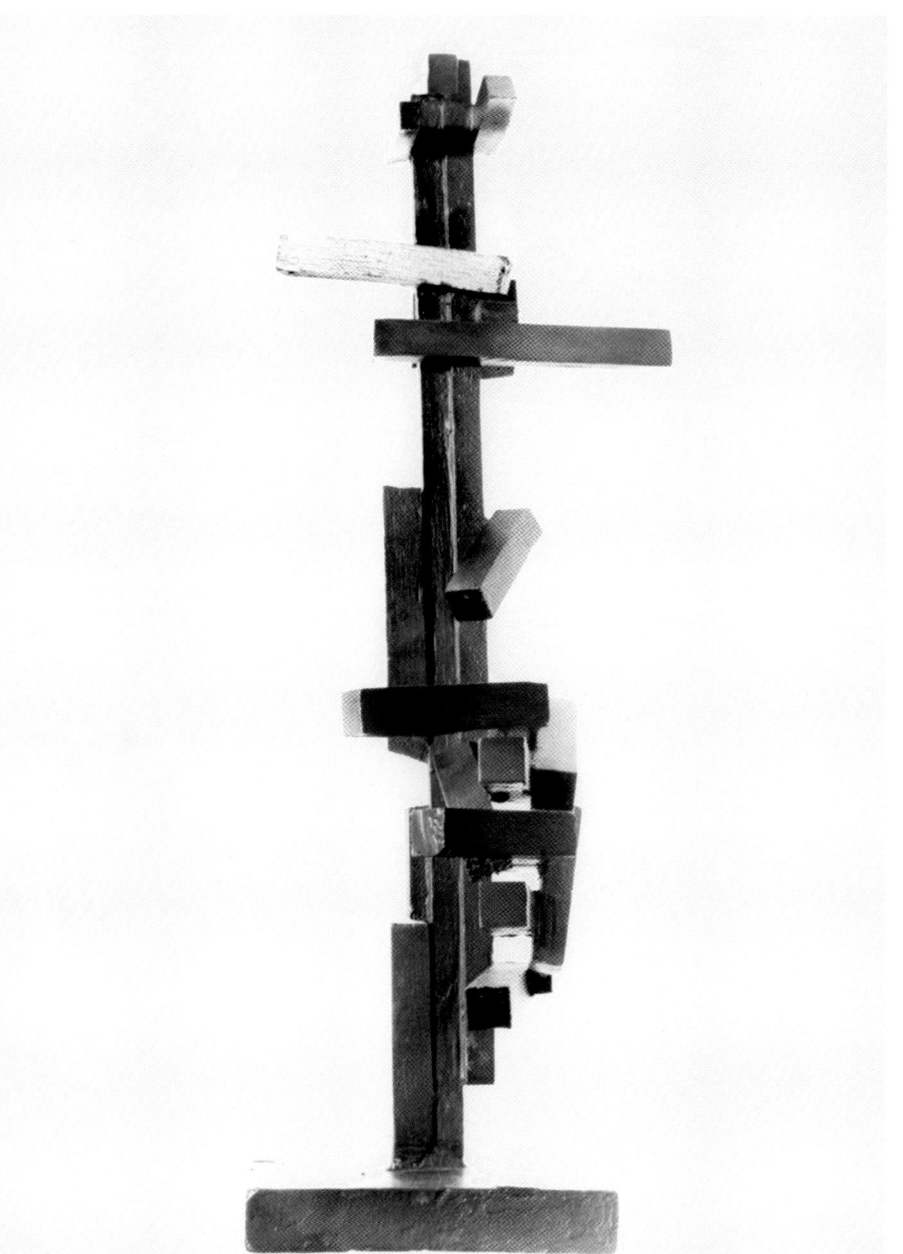

BREAKING AWAY

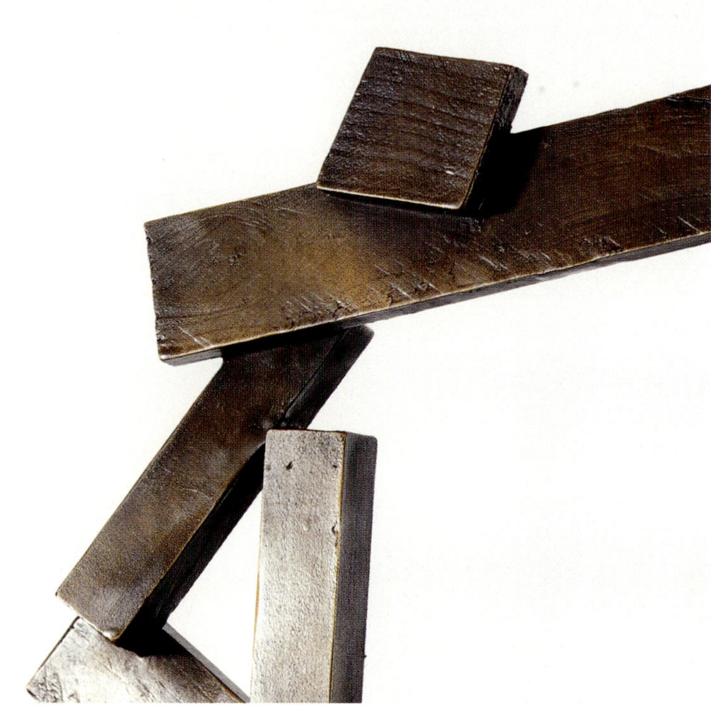

2001
Bronze
11" x 13" x 9"
Sold by Weber Fine Art, Scarsdale, NY

This is a much more open variation on my *Breaking Away* theme.

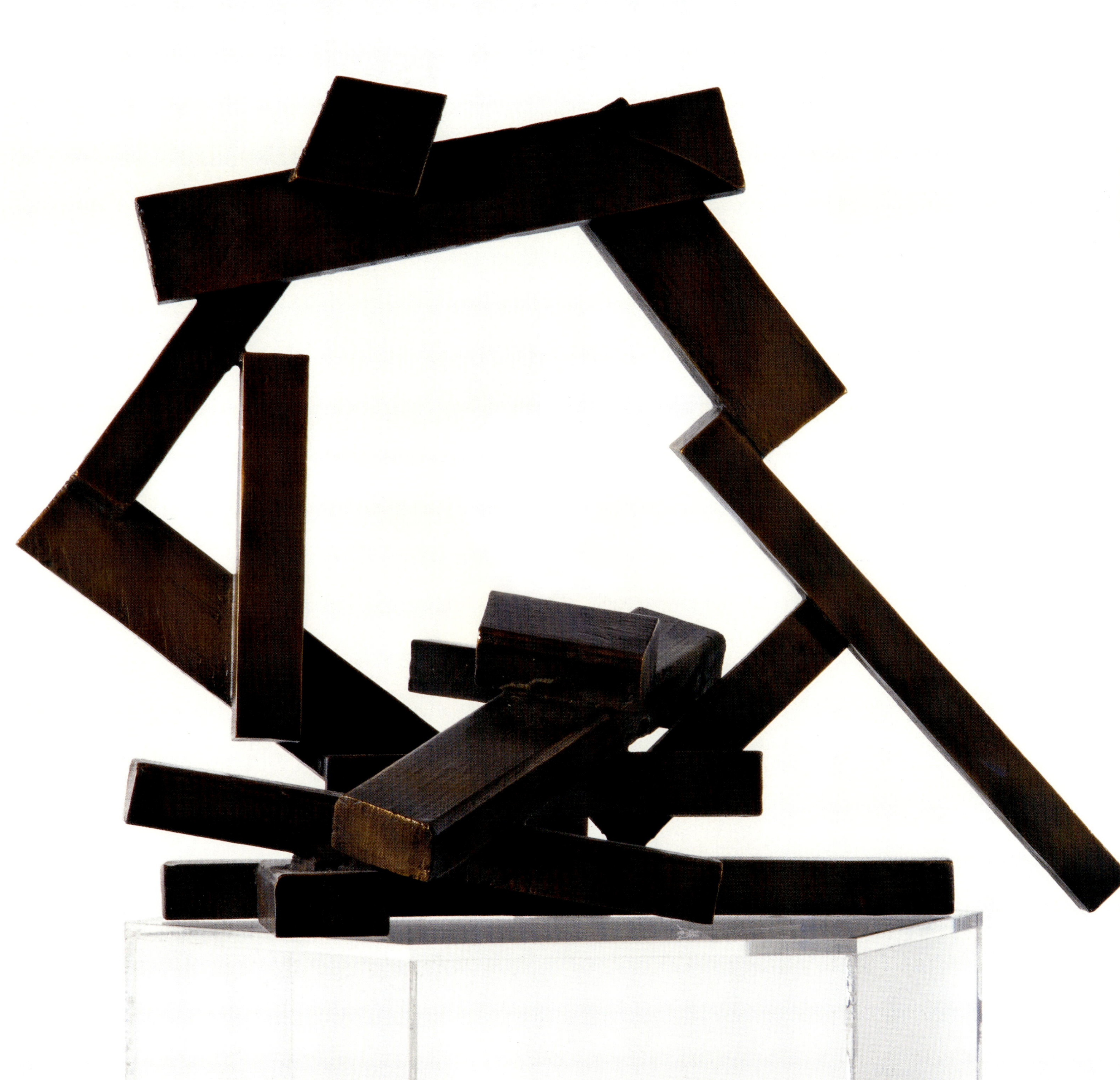

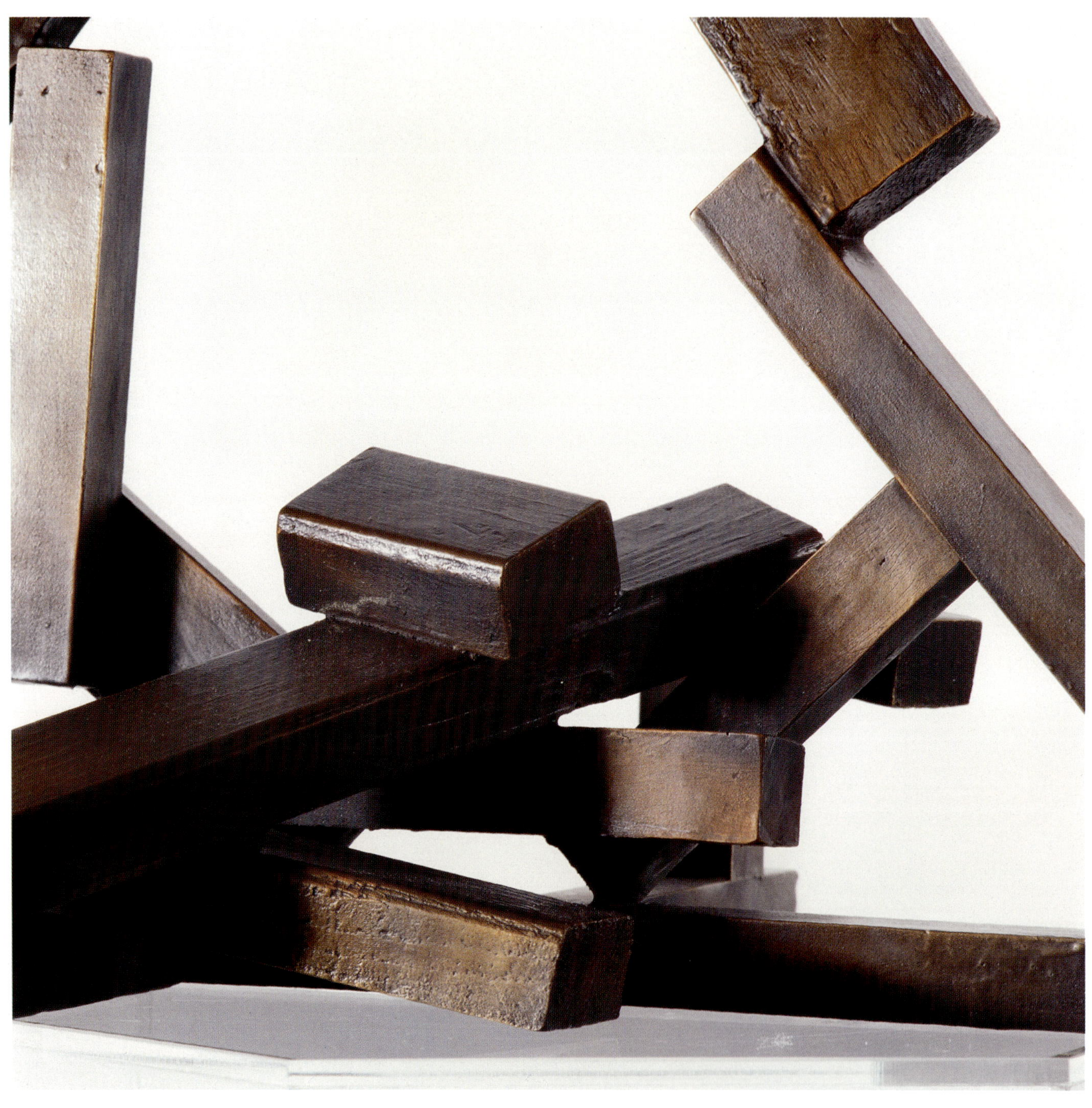

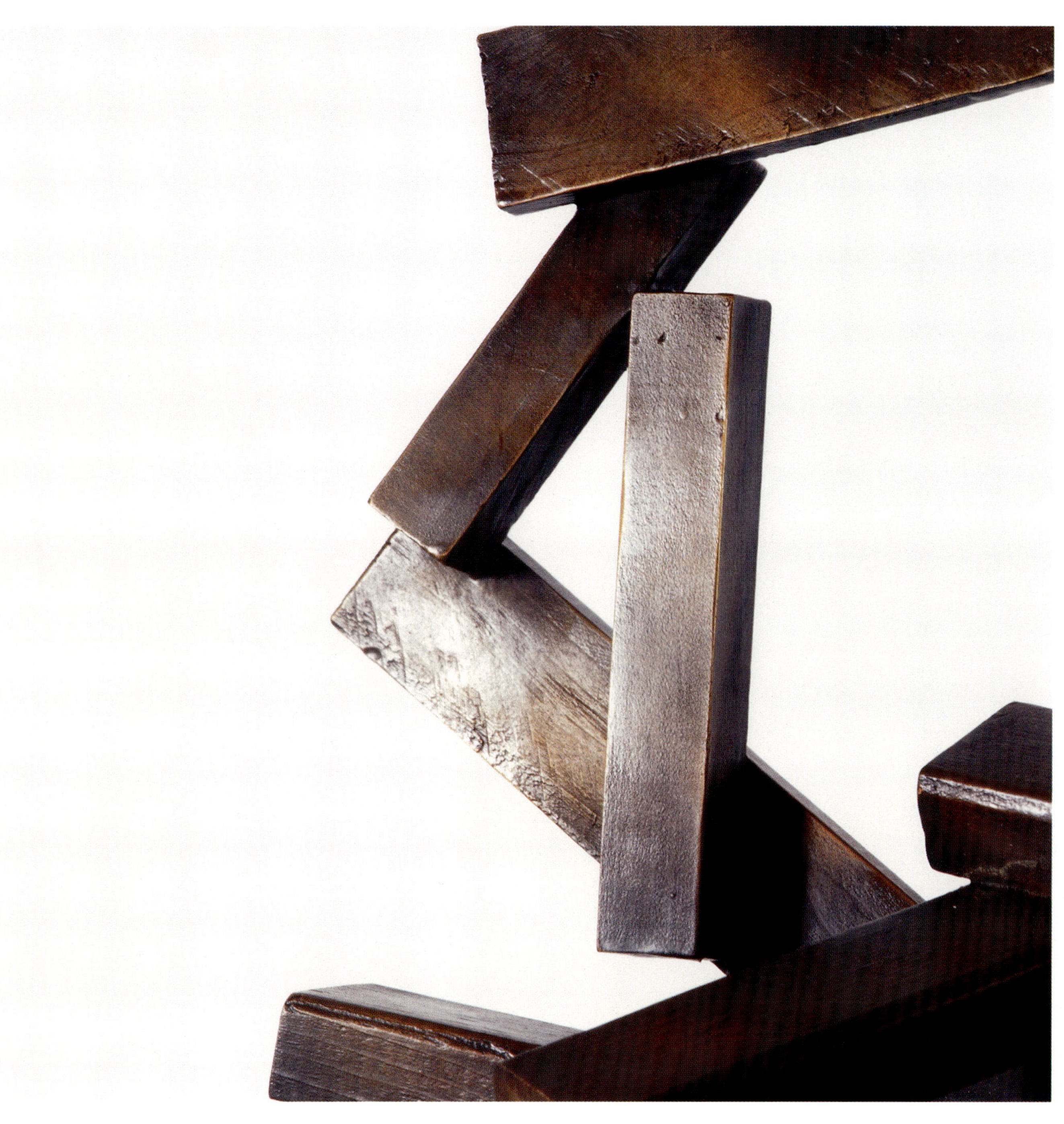

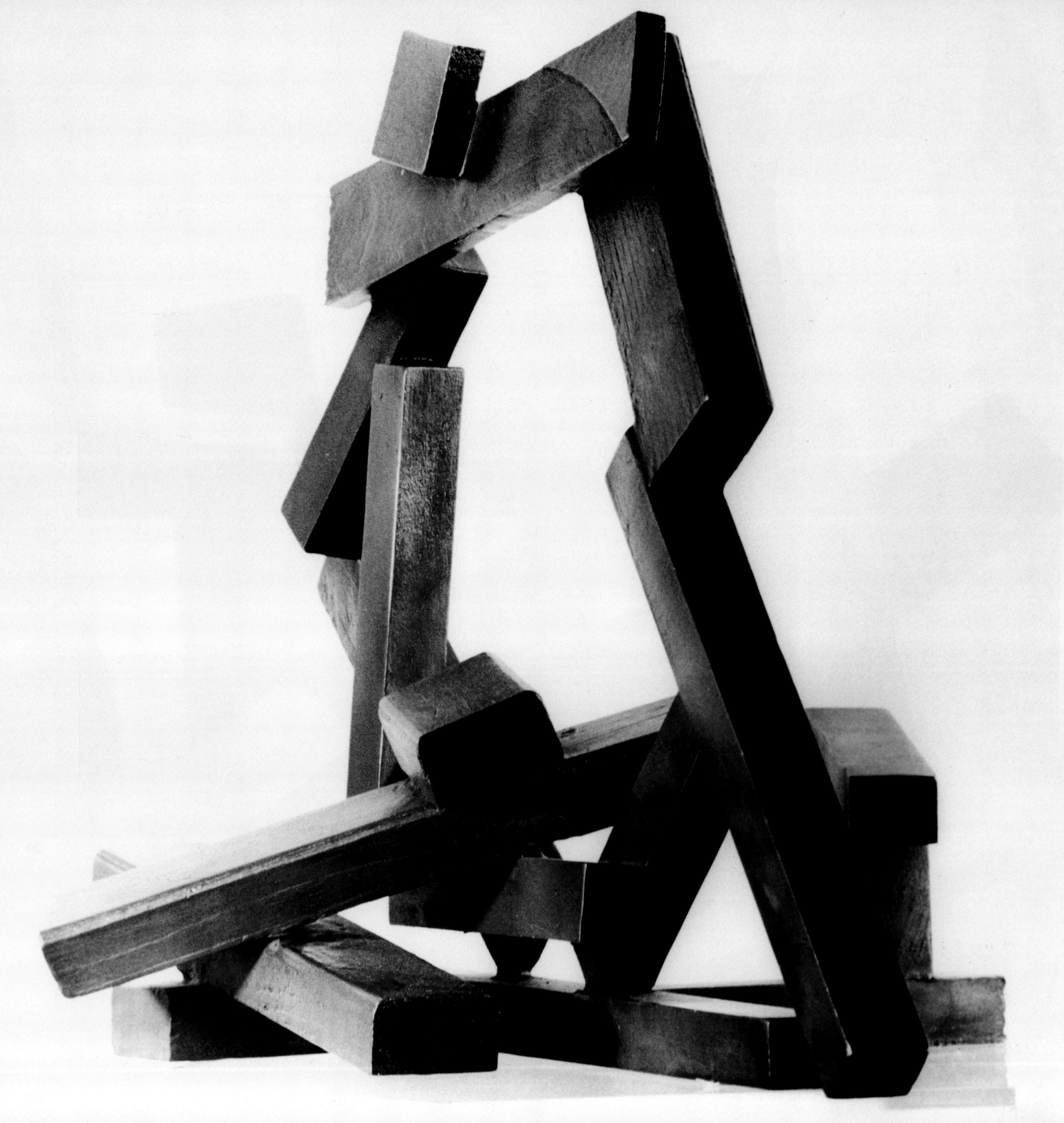

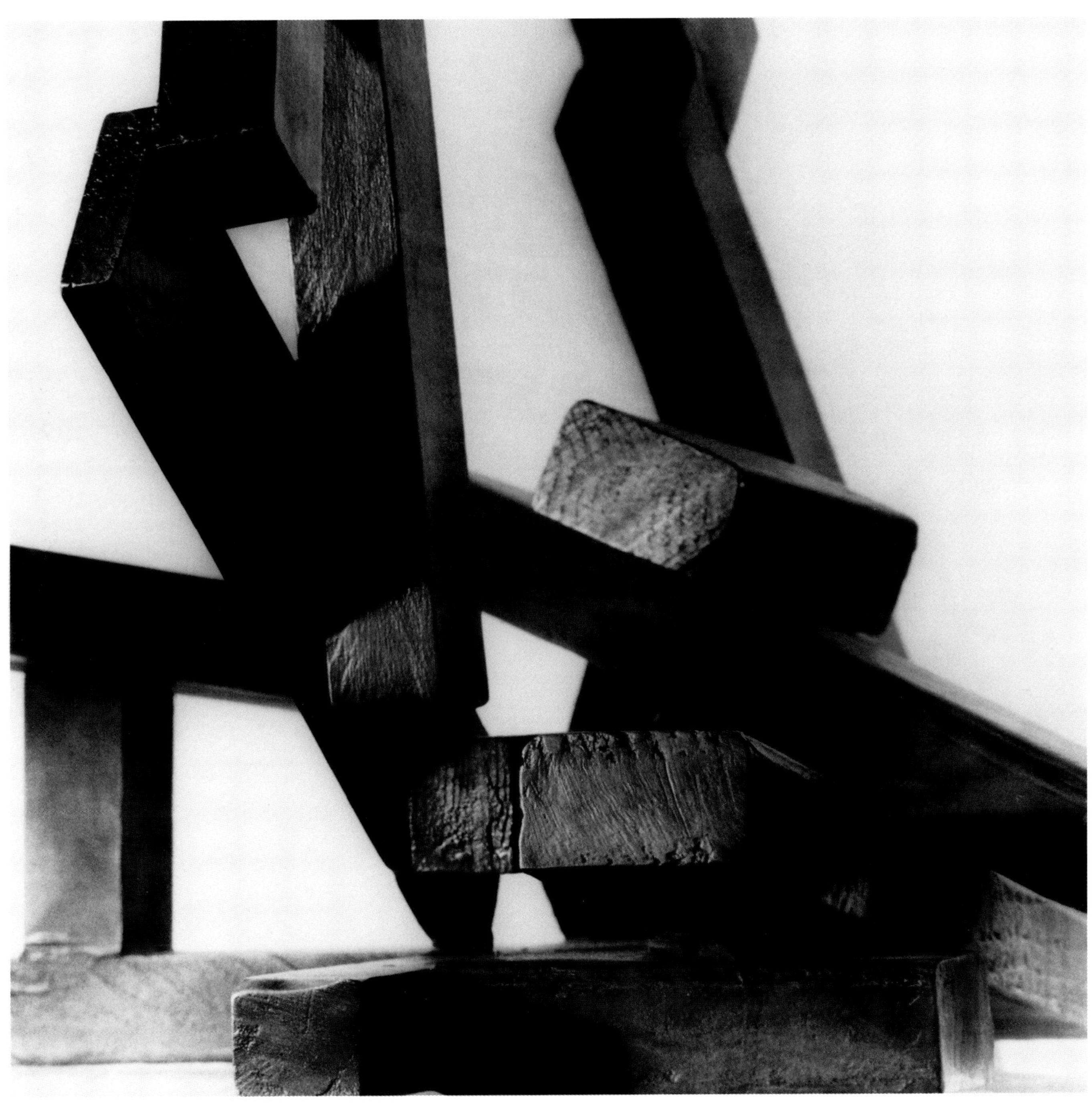

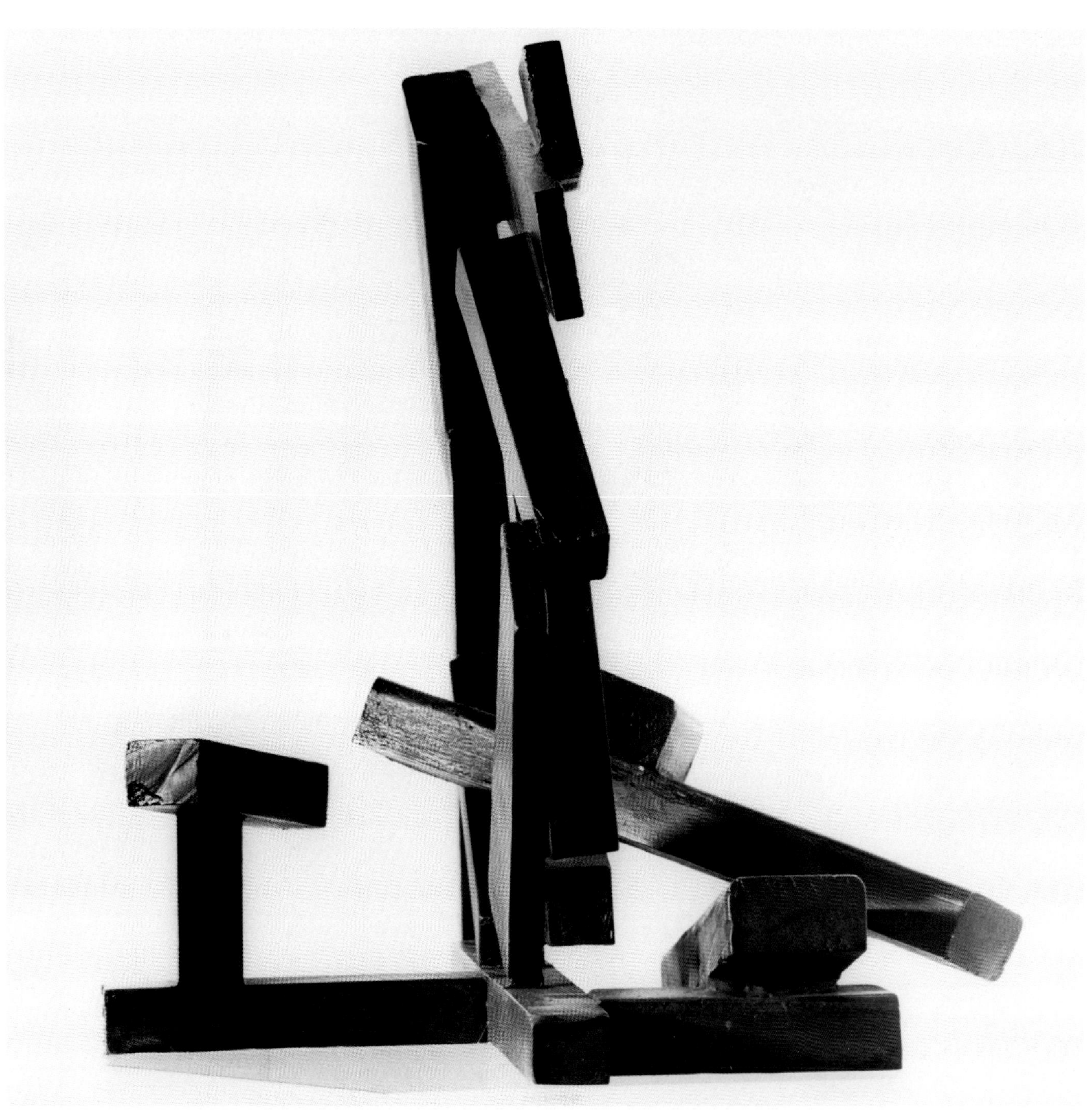

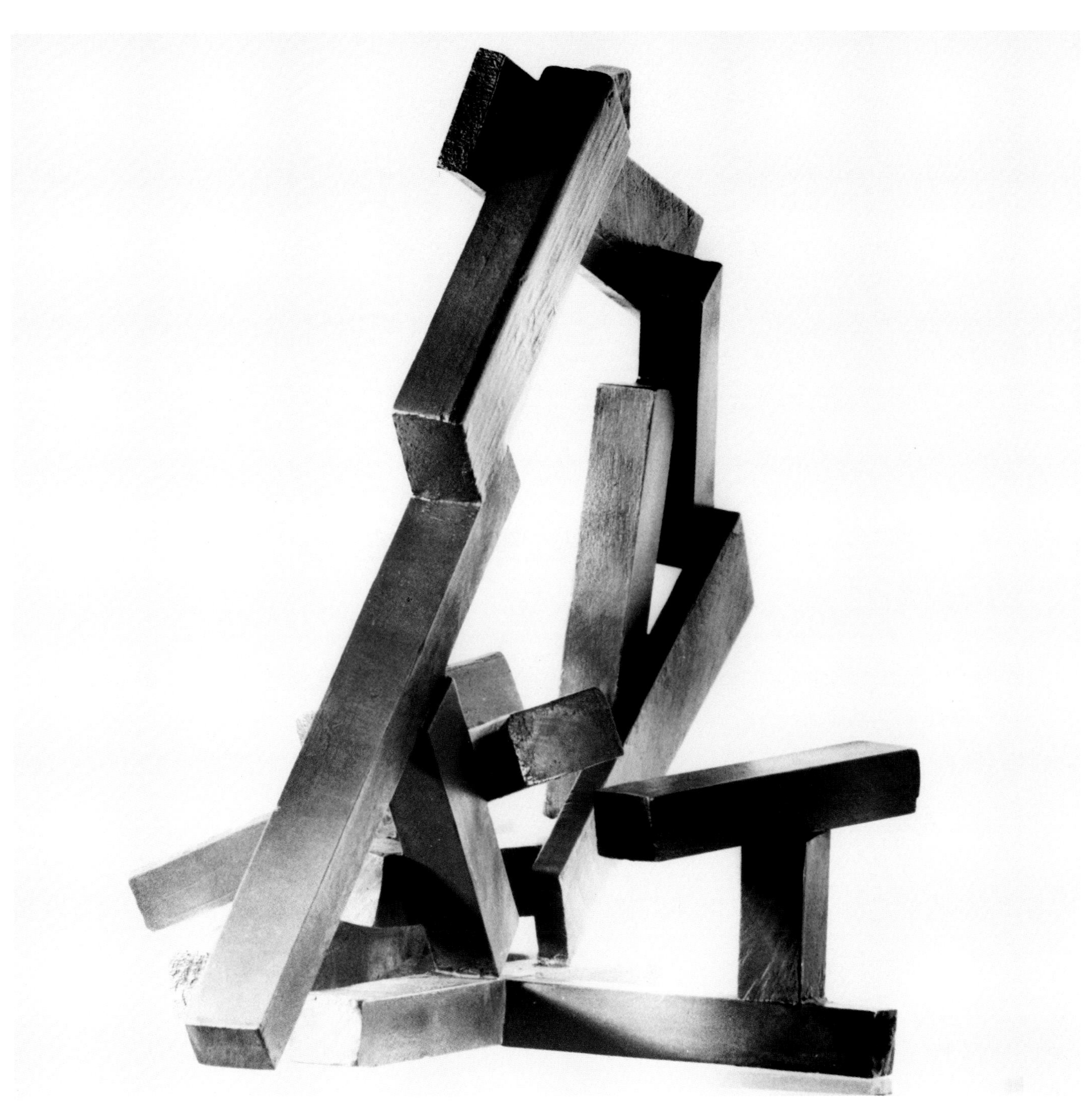

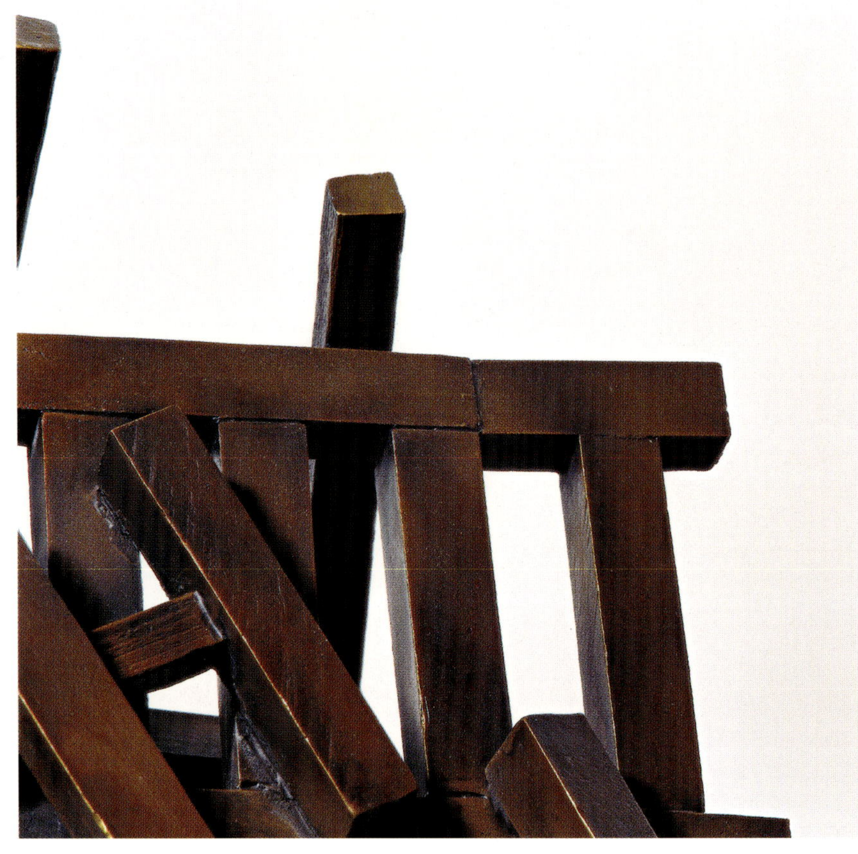

TOIN ME OVER

2001
Bronze
11" x 8" x 5"
Collection H. Stewart Ross, Everett, WA

Toin Me Over refers to the martyrdom of St. Lawrence, an early Christian saint, condemned by a Roman prefect to die by roasting on a grill. Supposedly St. Lawrence shouted, "I am roasted on one side. Now turn me over."

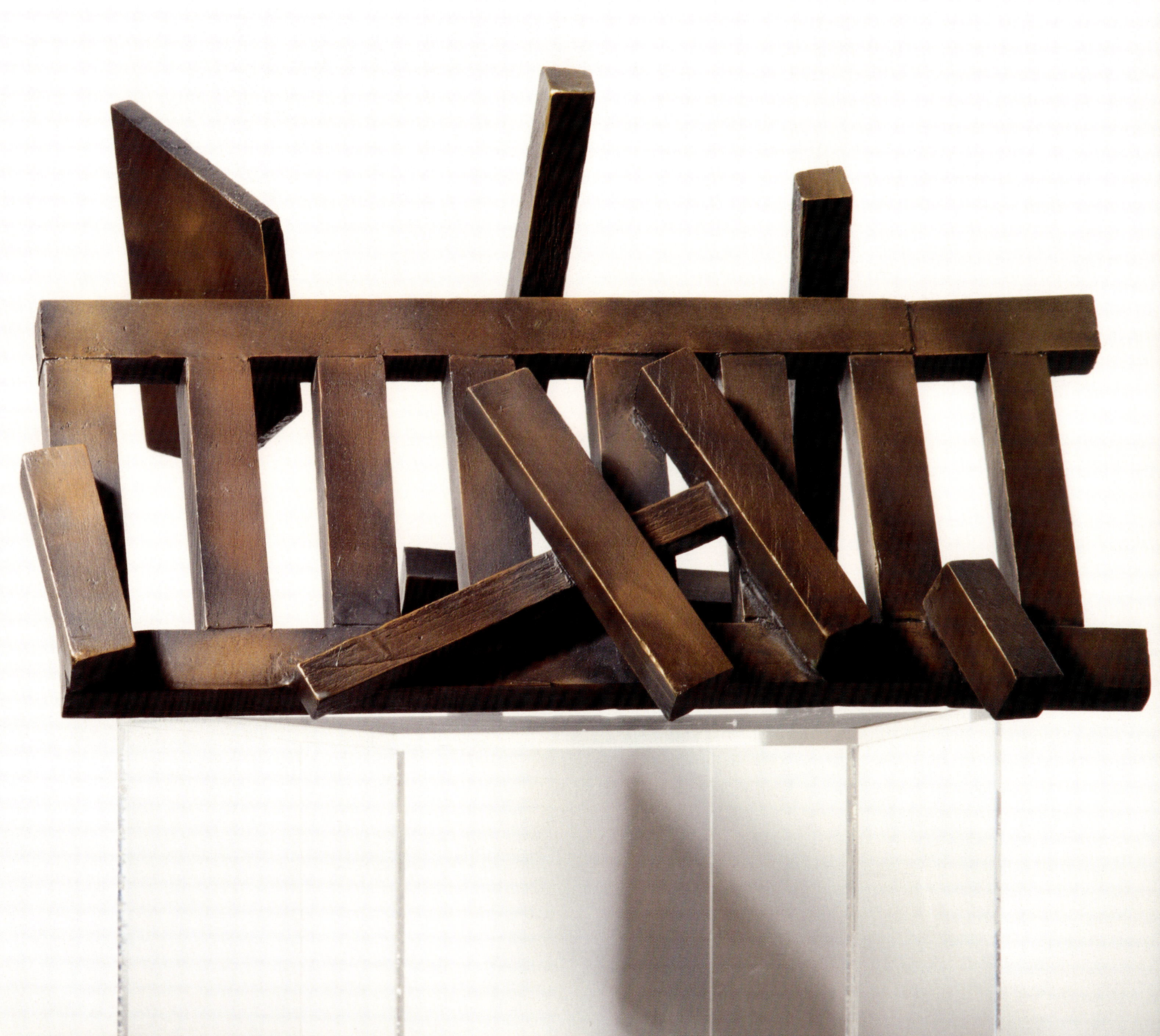

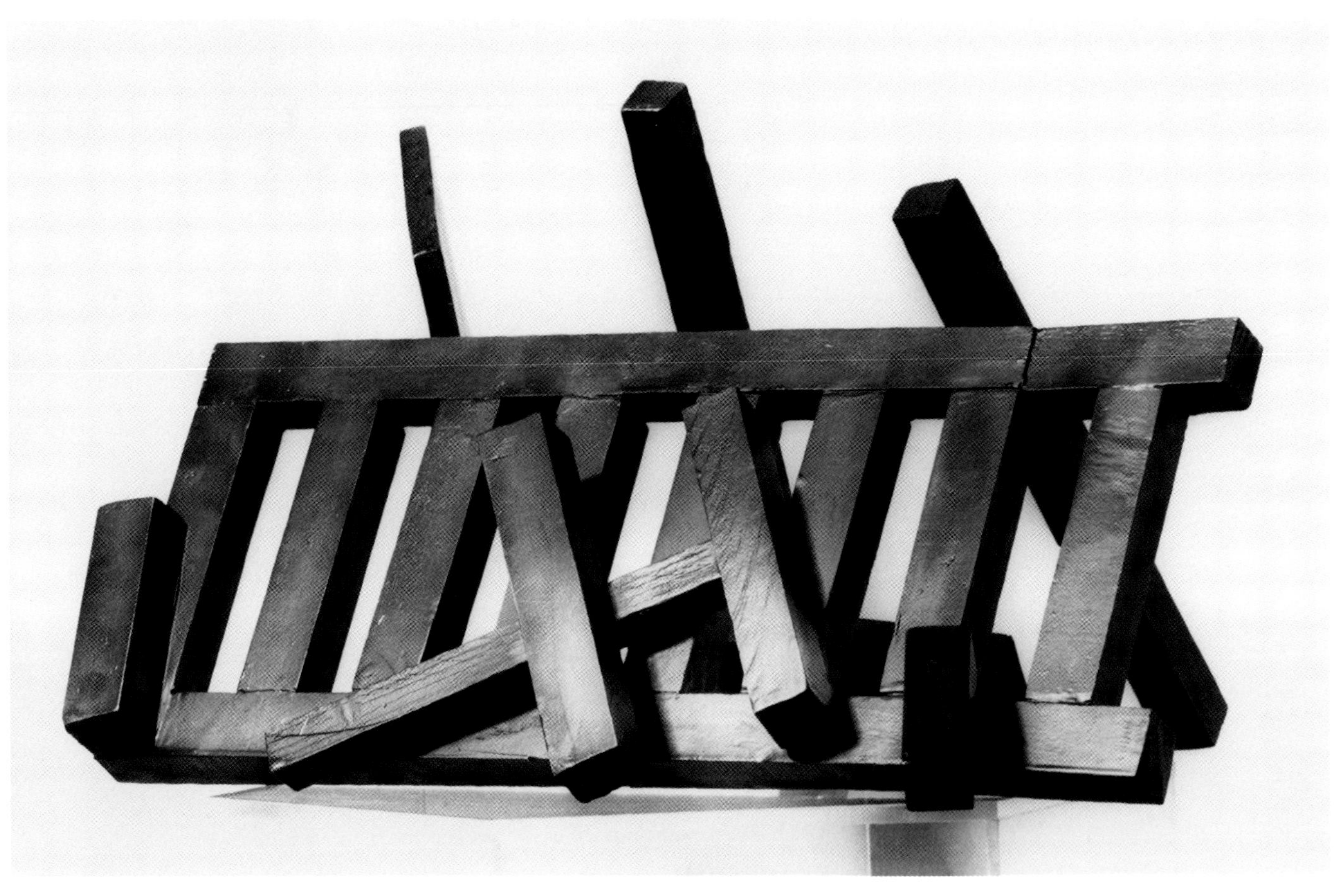

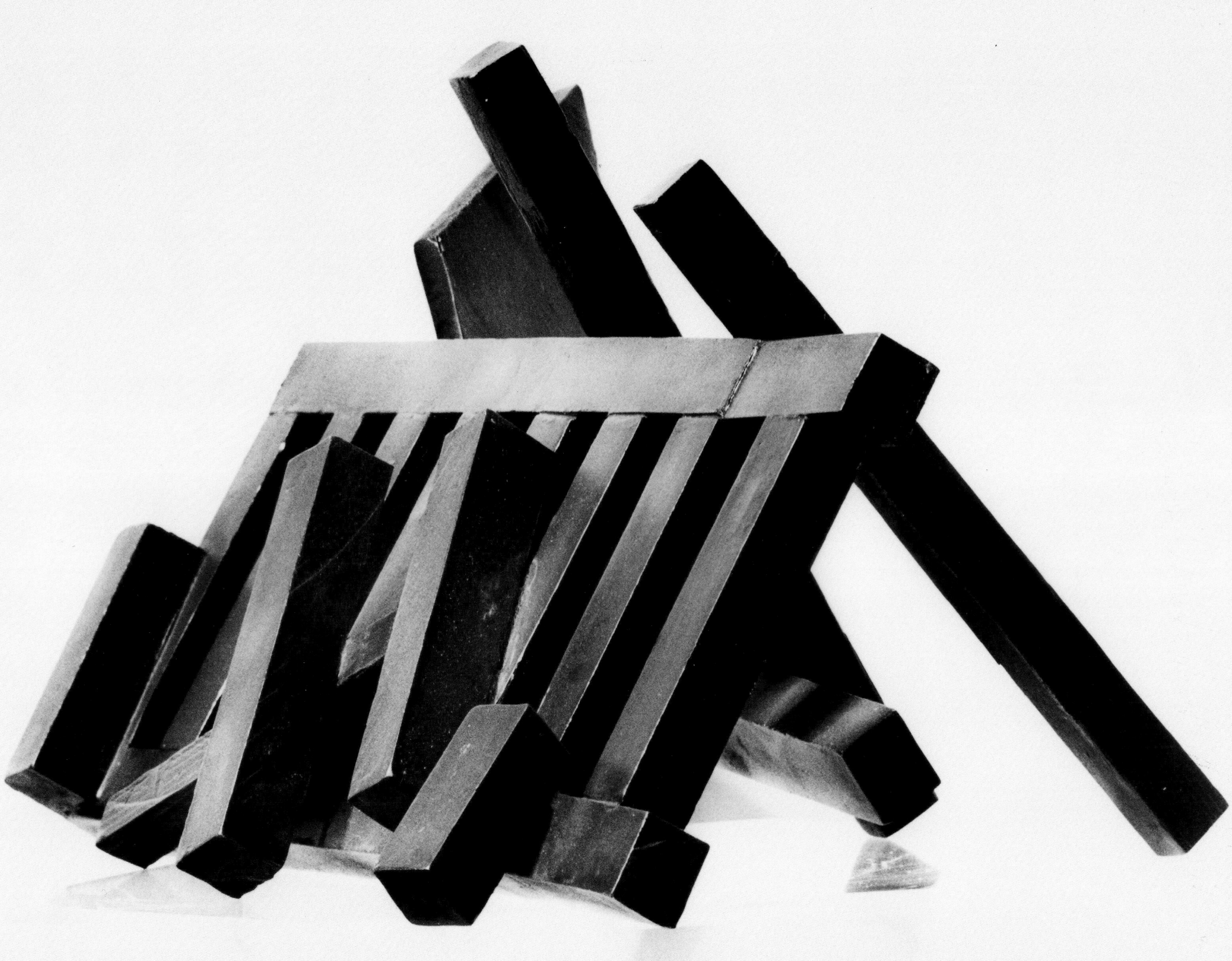

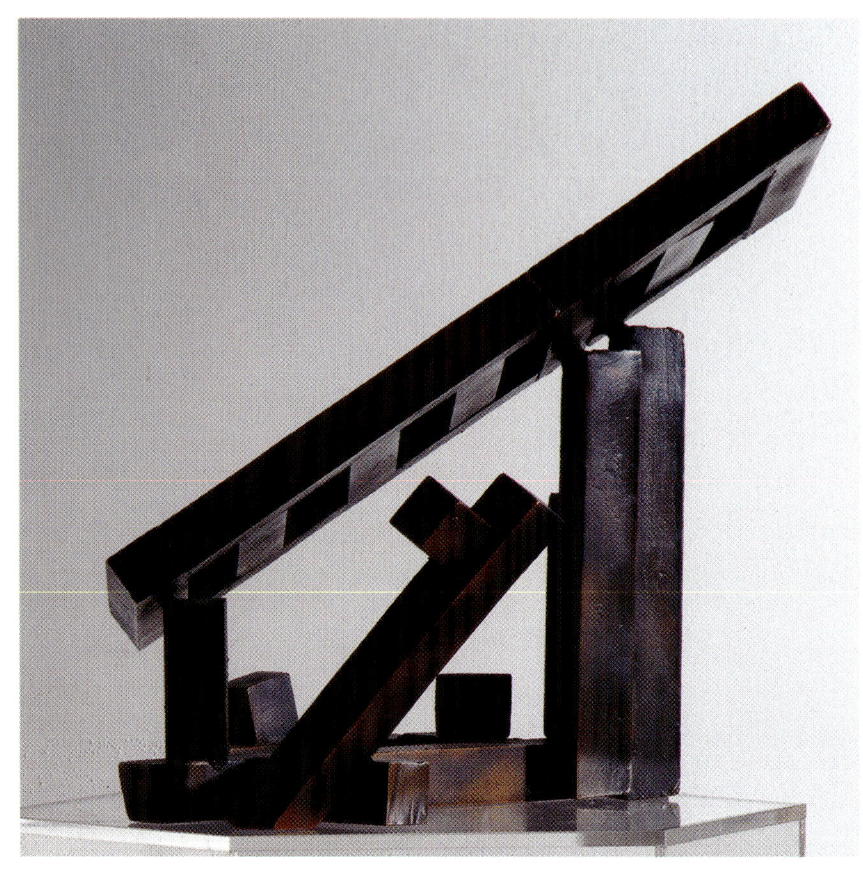

SAN LORENZO

2001
Bronze
9"x 9" x 7"
Sold by Weber Fine Art, Scarsdale, NY

This is symbolic of the grill upon which the martyr St. Lawrence was roasted. The grill is the emblem of the royal Spanish palace, the Escorial.

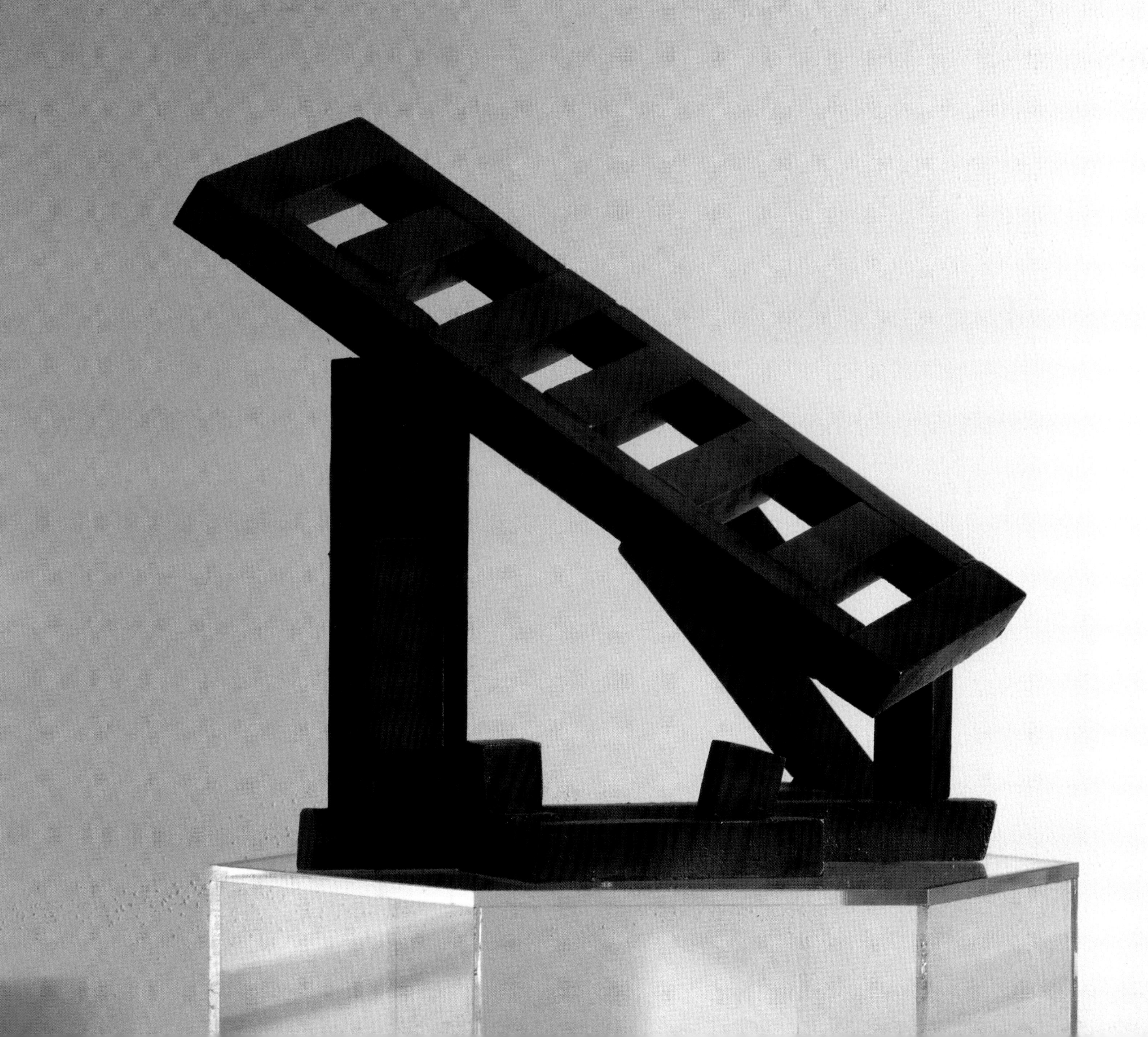

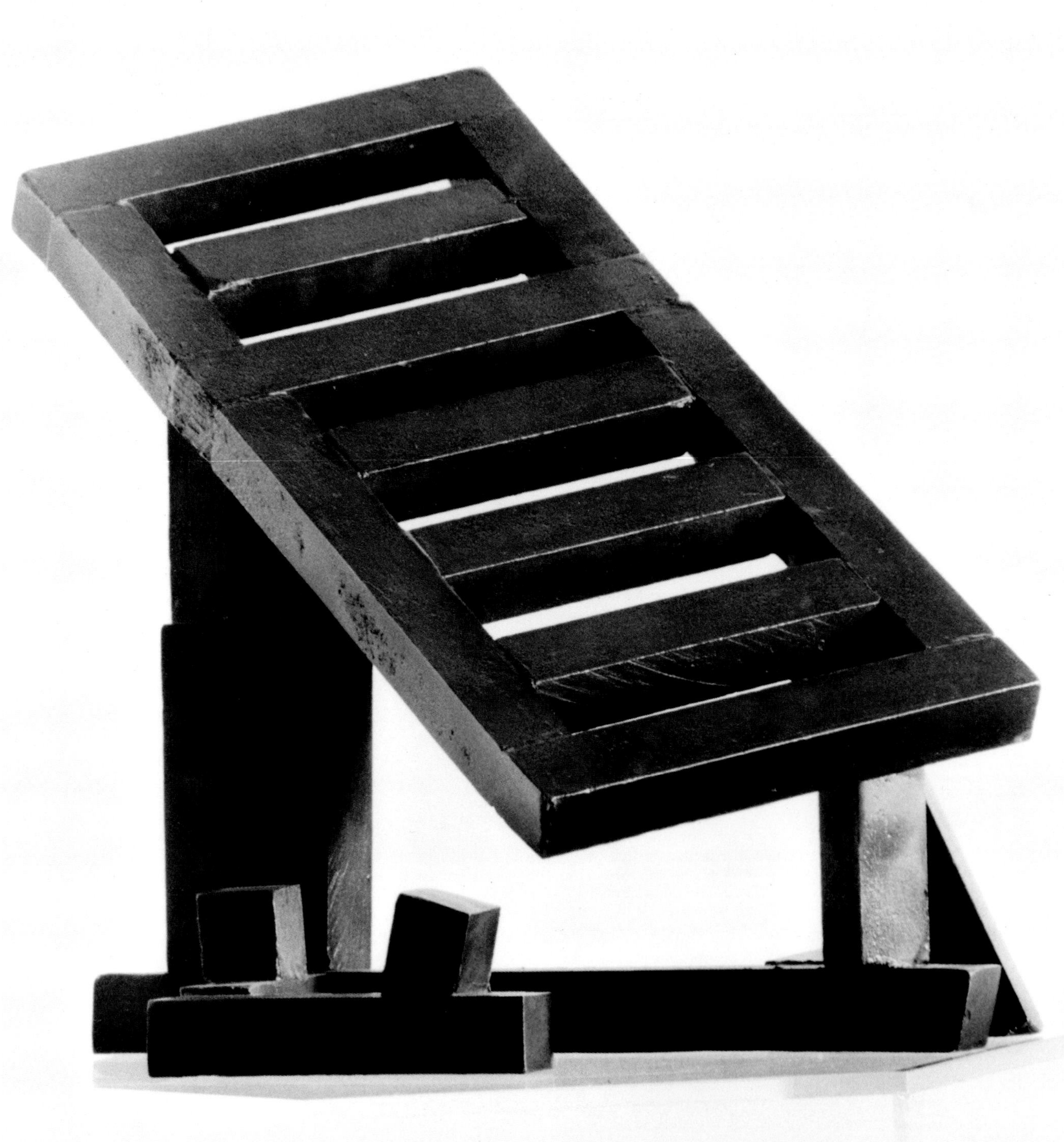

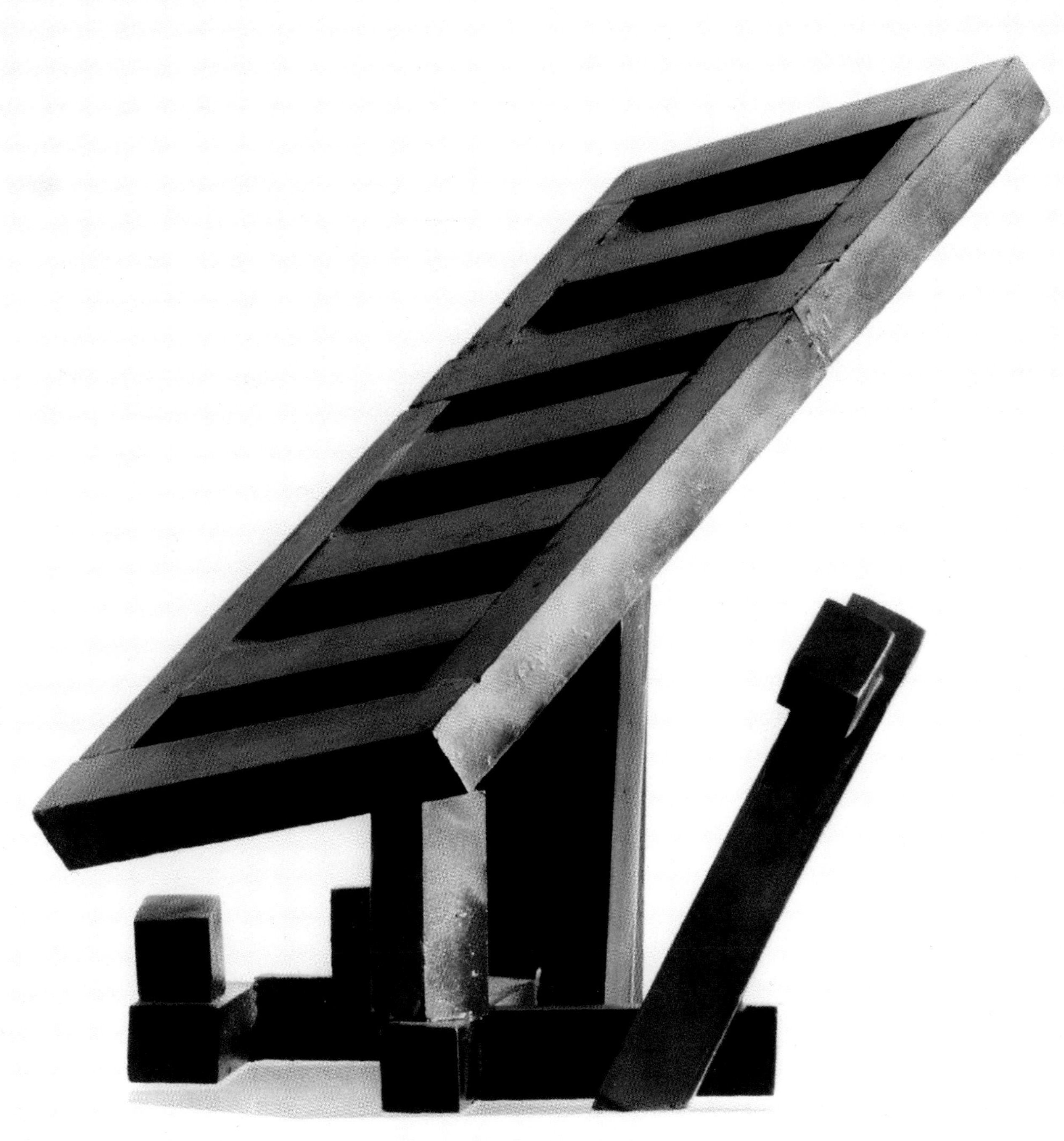

DANAE

Bronze
11" x 12.5" x 8"
Collection of the artist

In Greek mythology, Danae was the daughter of the king of Argos, who kept her locked in a large chamber so that Zeus could not violate her. Zeus changed himself into gold dust, floated into her room, and rained down upon Danae. She became the mother of Perseus.

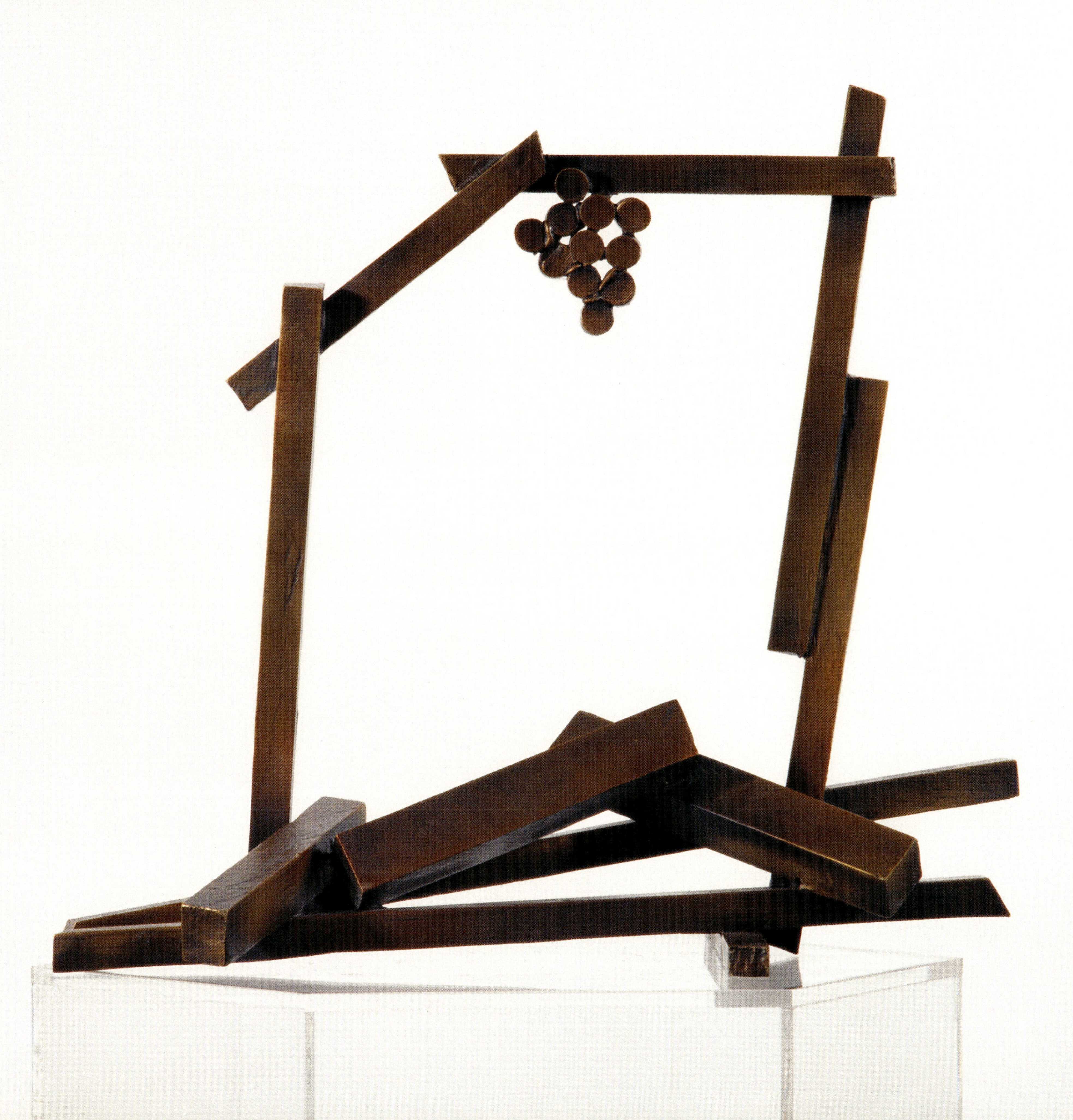

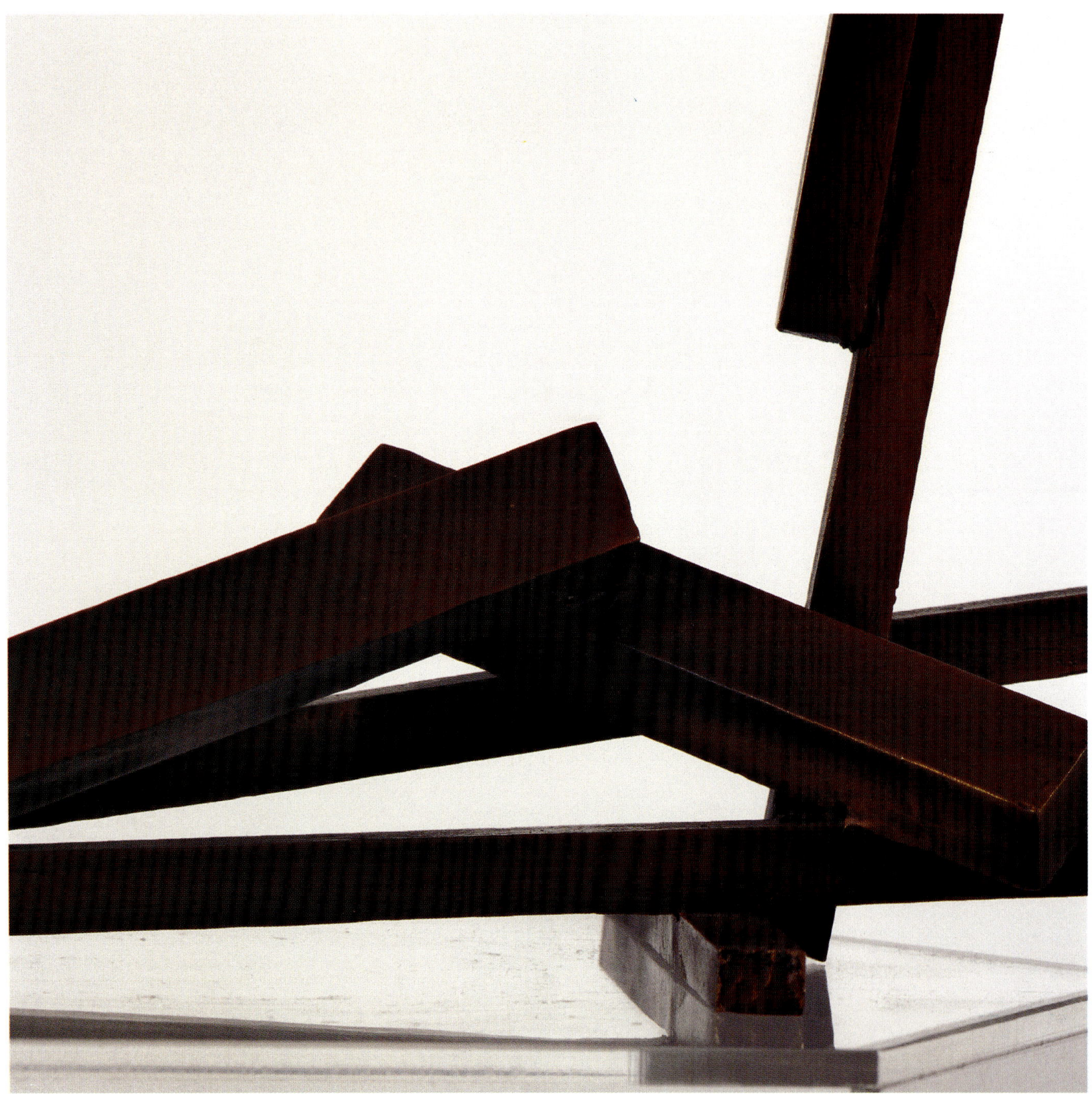

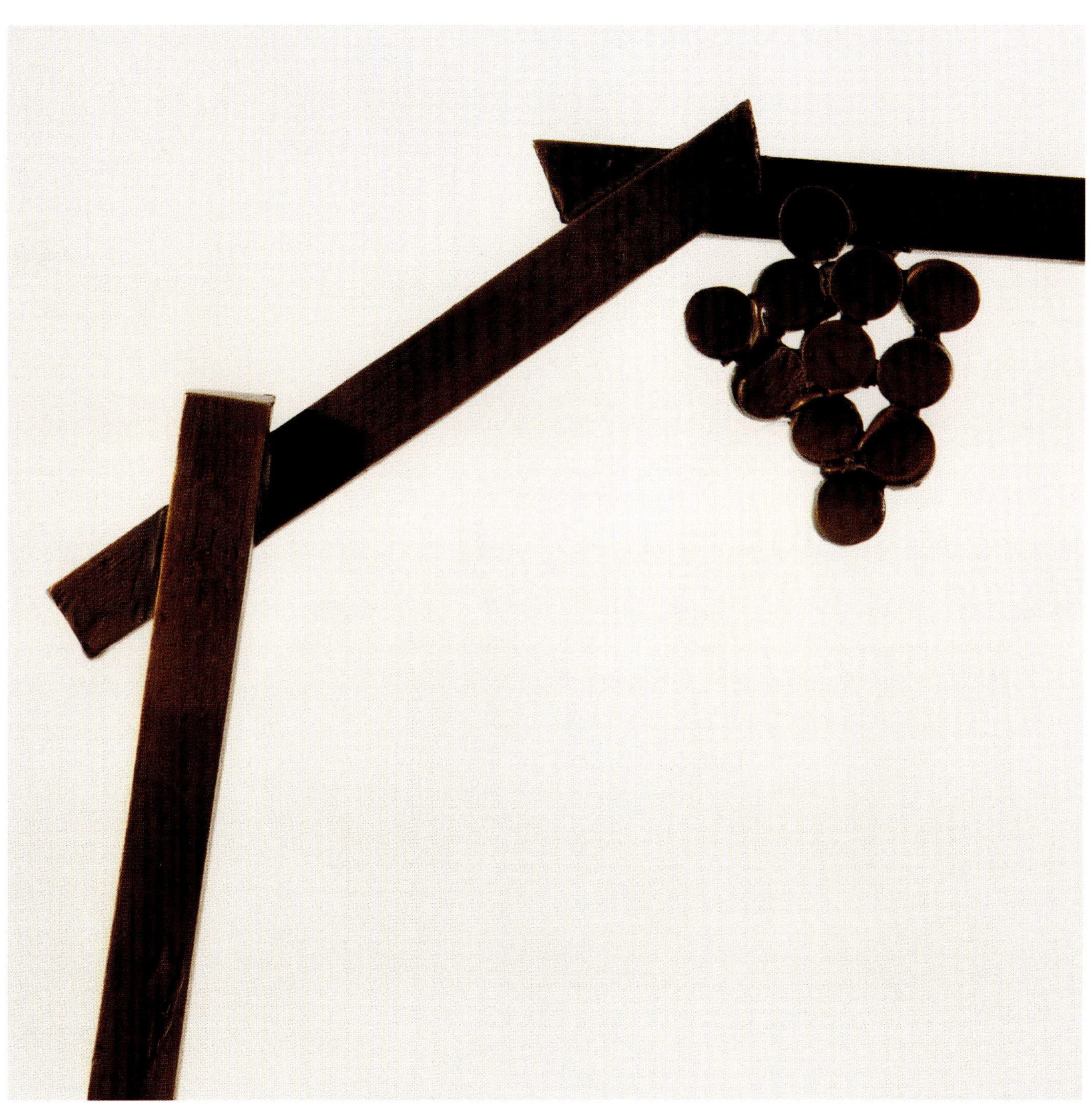

CYCLONE

2001
Bronze
9" x 9" x 6"
Sold by Weber Fine Art, Scarsdale, NY

Cyclone is very much like *Hurricane* except that I think the composition is freer and more chaotic. The terrible, fearful, force in these two acts of nature has always fascinated me.

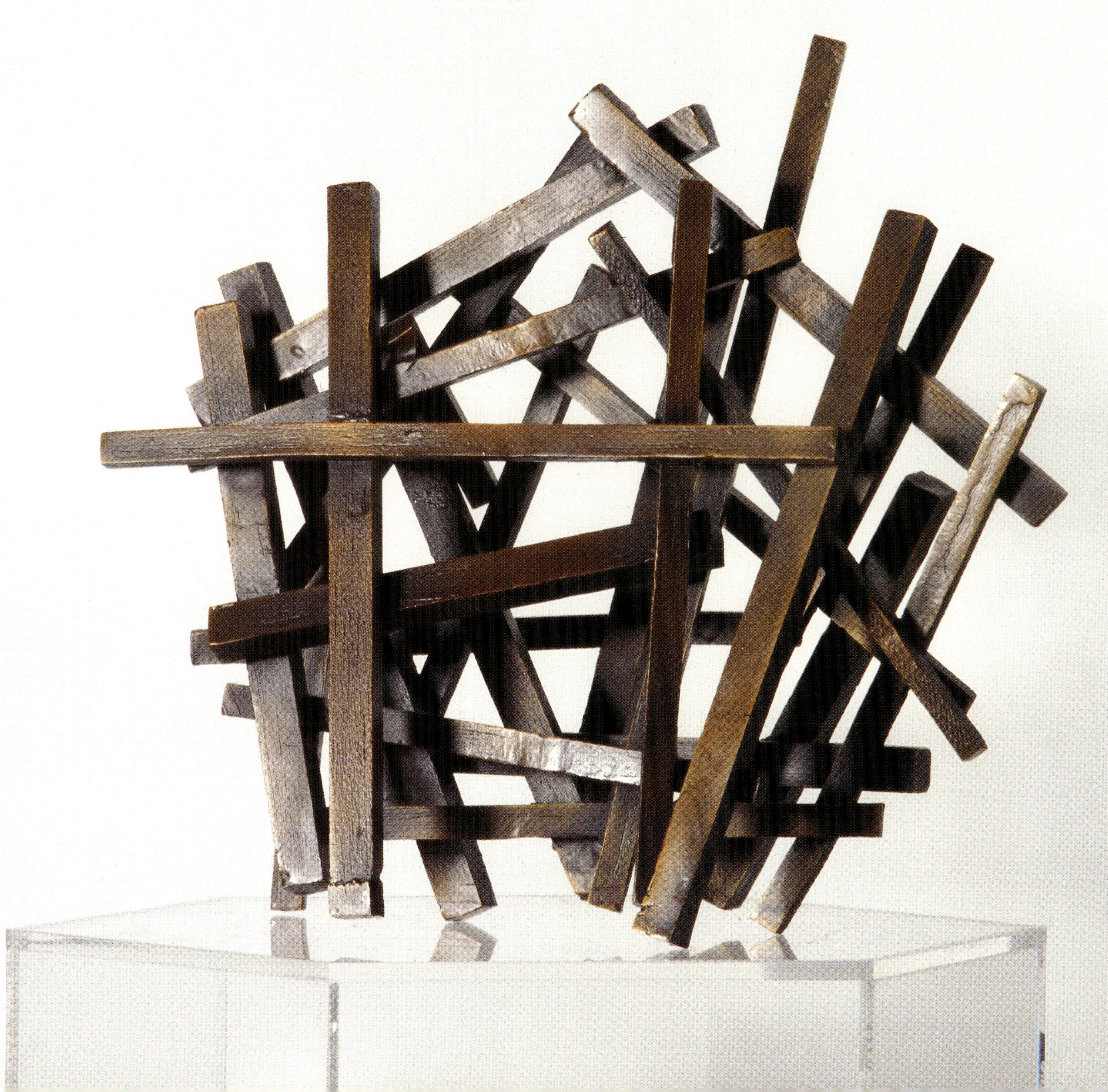

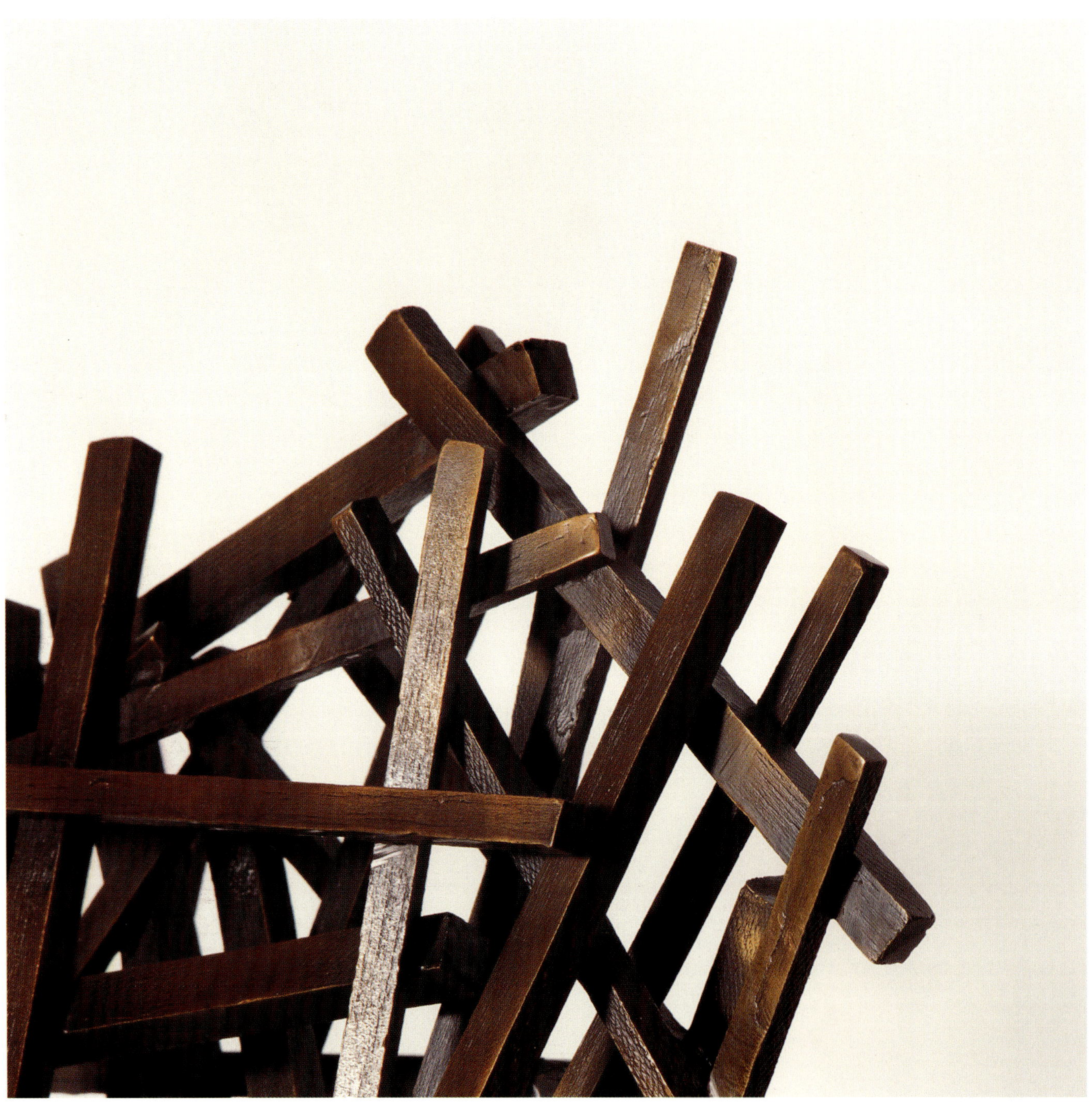

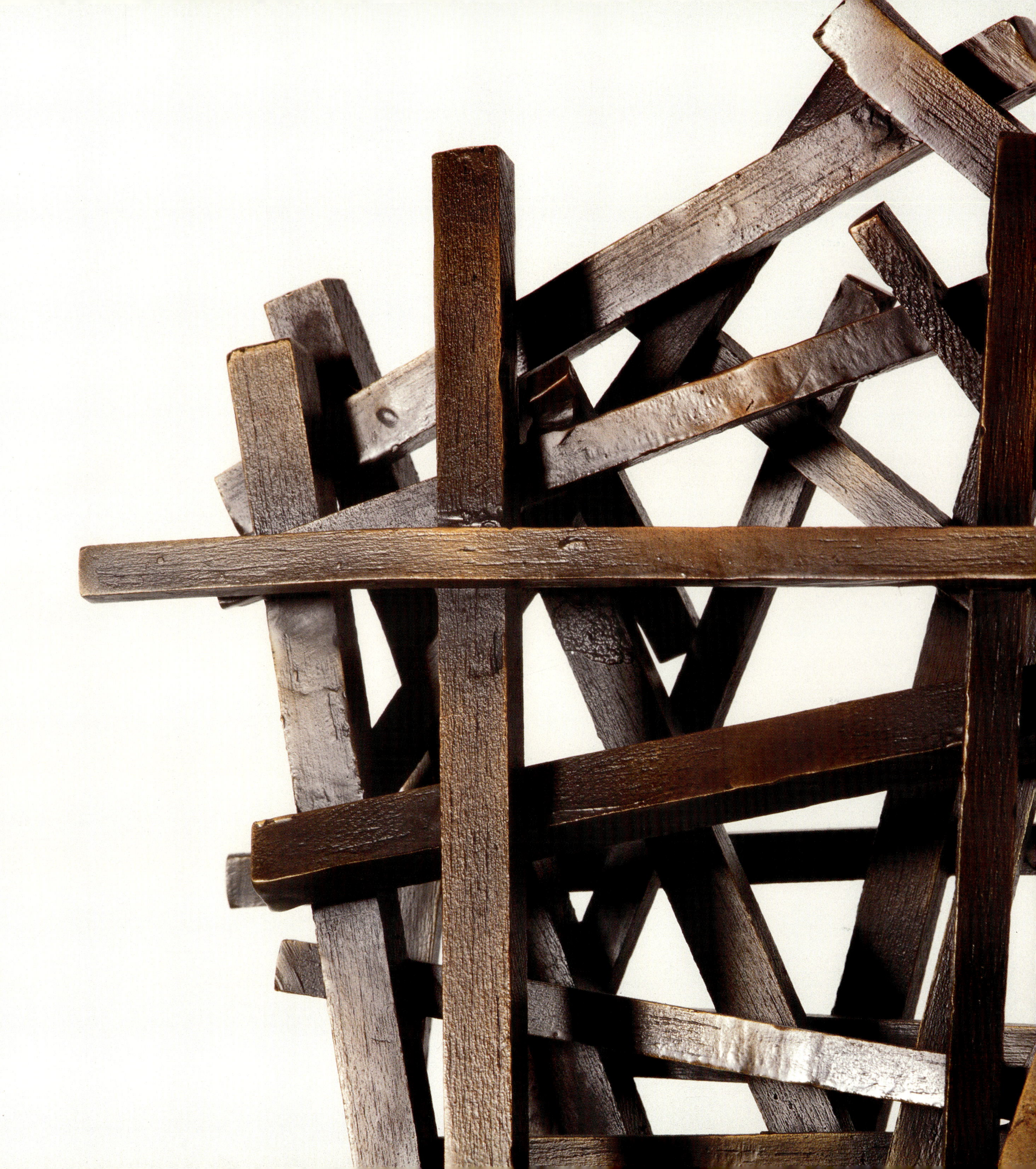

LOVE AIN'T EASY

2001
Bronze
10" x 6.5" x 4"
Sold by Weber Fine Art, Scarsdale, NY

This composition reminded me of a shearing tool.
Knowing, as we all do, that relationships are often
difficult, I came up with the title.

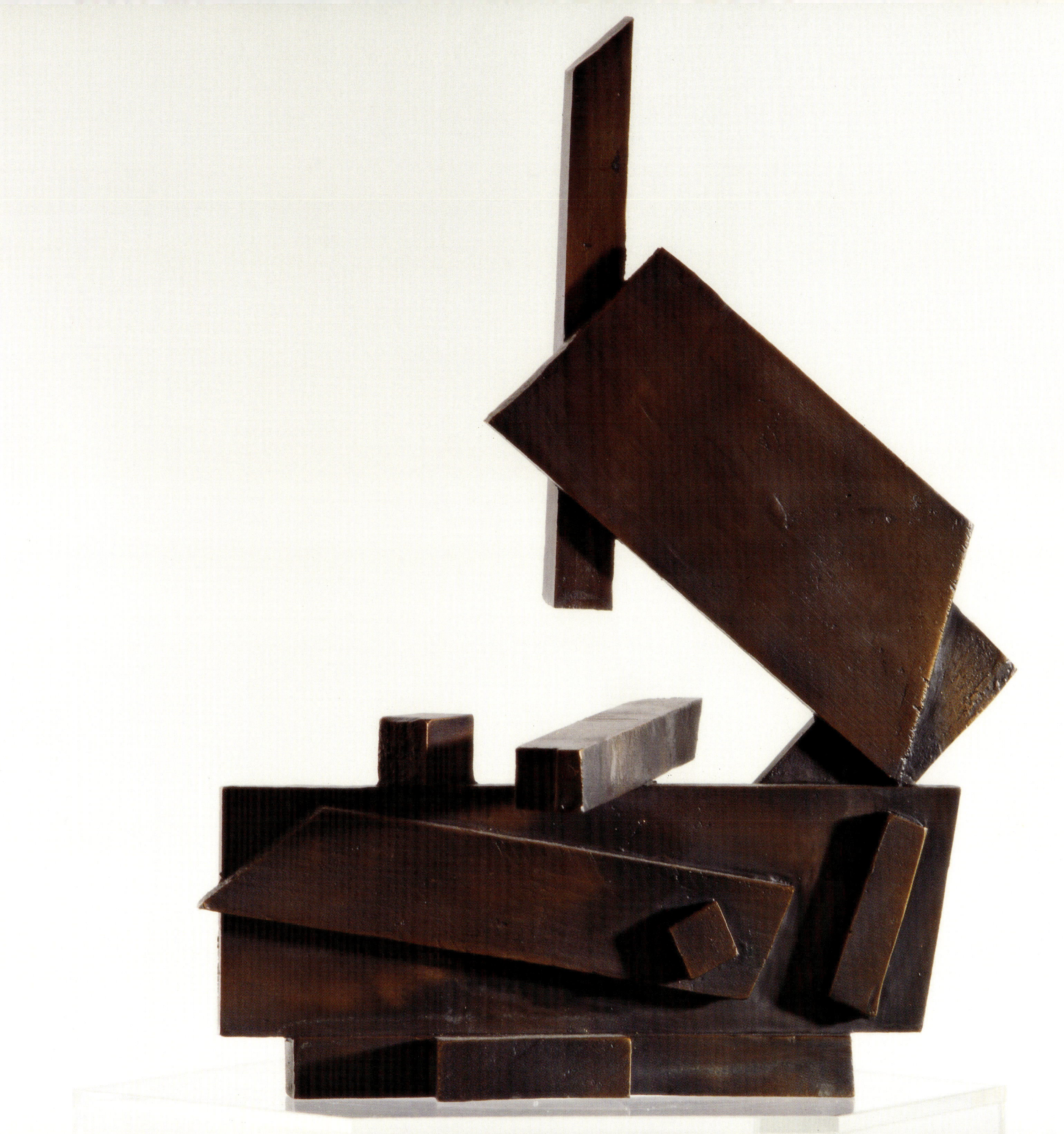

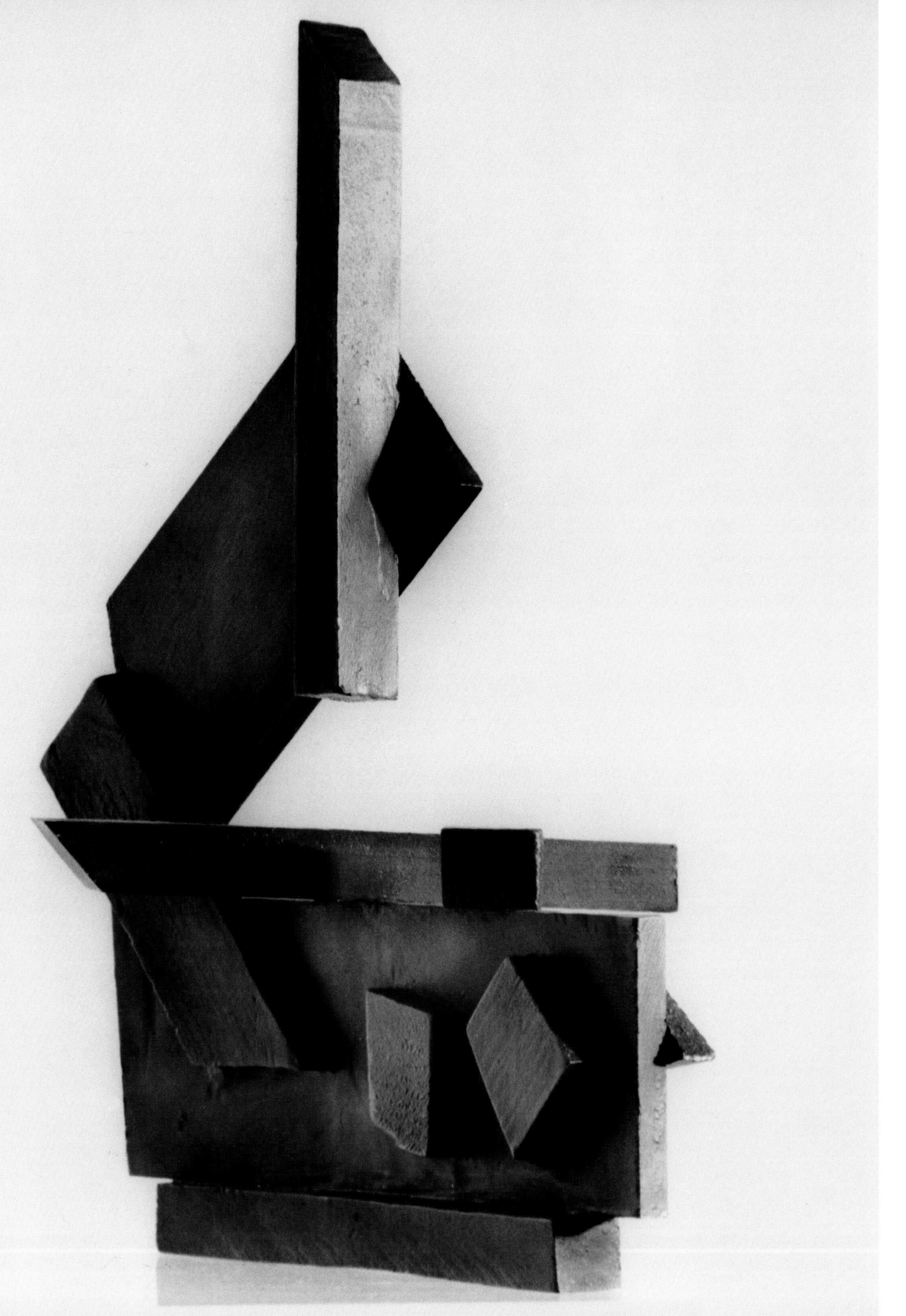

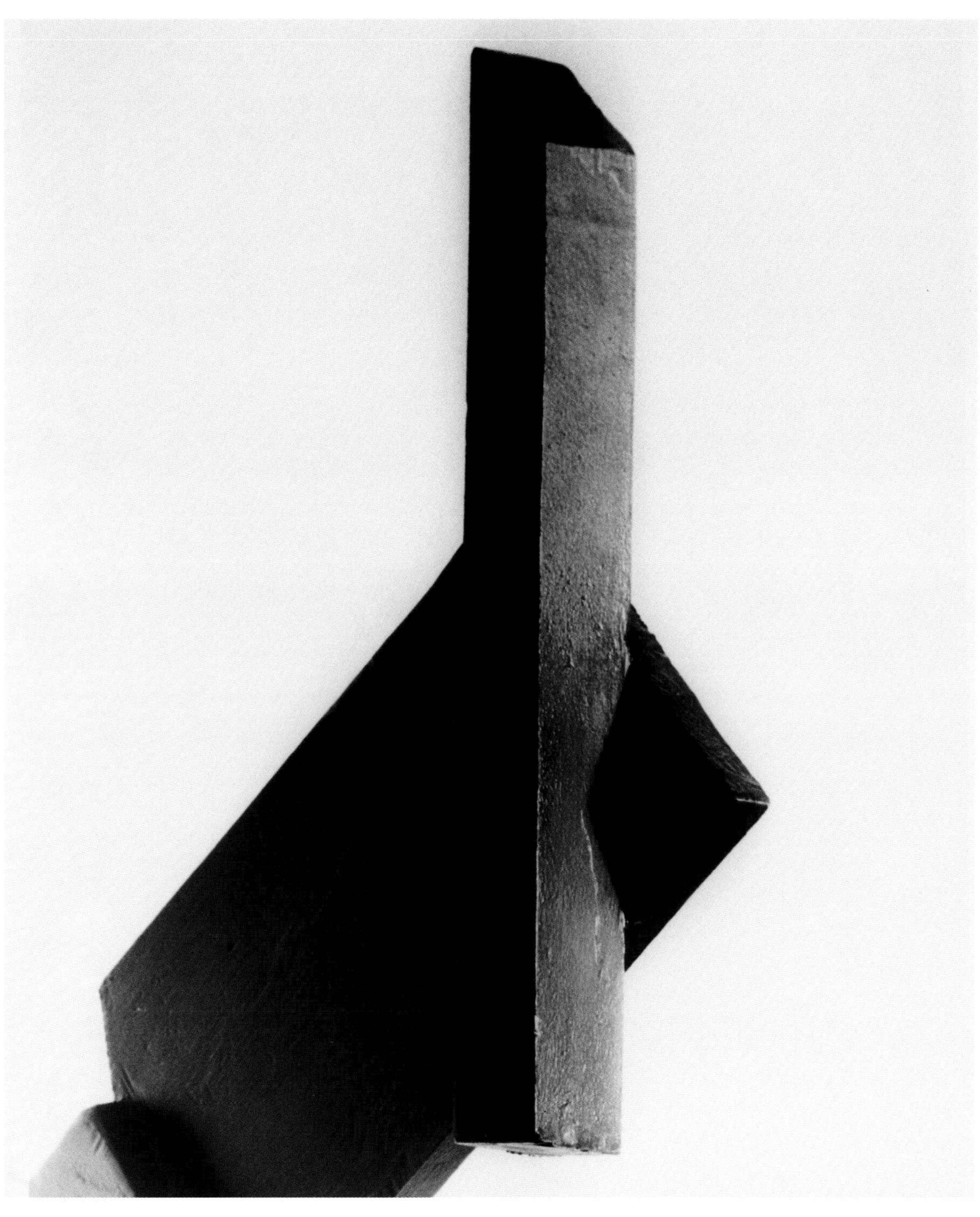

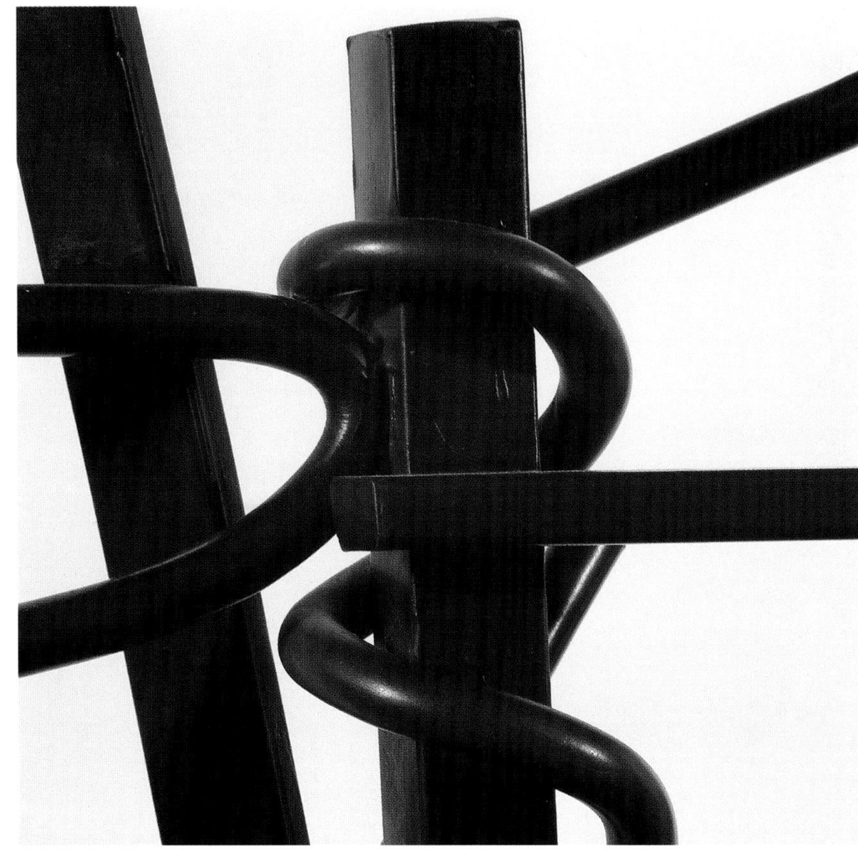

ALL TIED UP IN LOVE

2001
Bronze
8" x 4.5" x 4"
Collection of the artist

While at the foundry, I made some interesting small sculptures out of the wax used for the sprues and venting. The title followed the creation of the work.

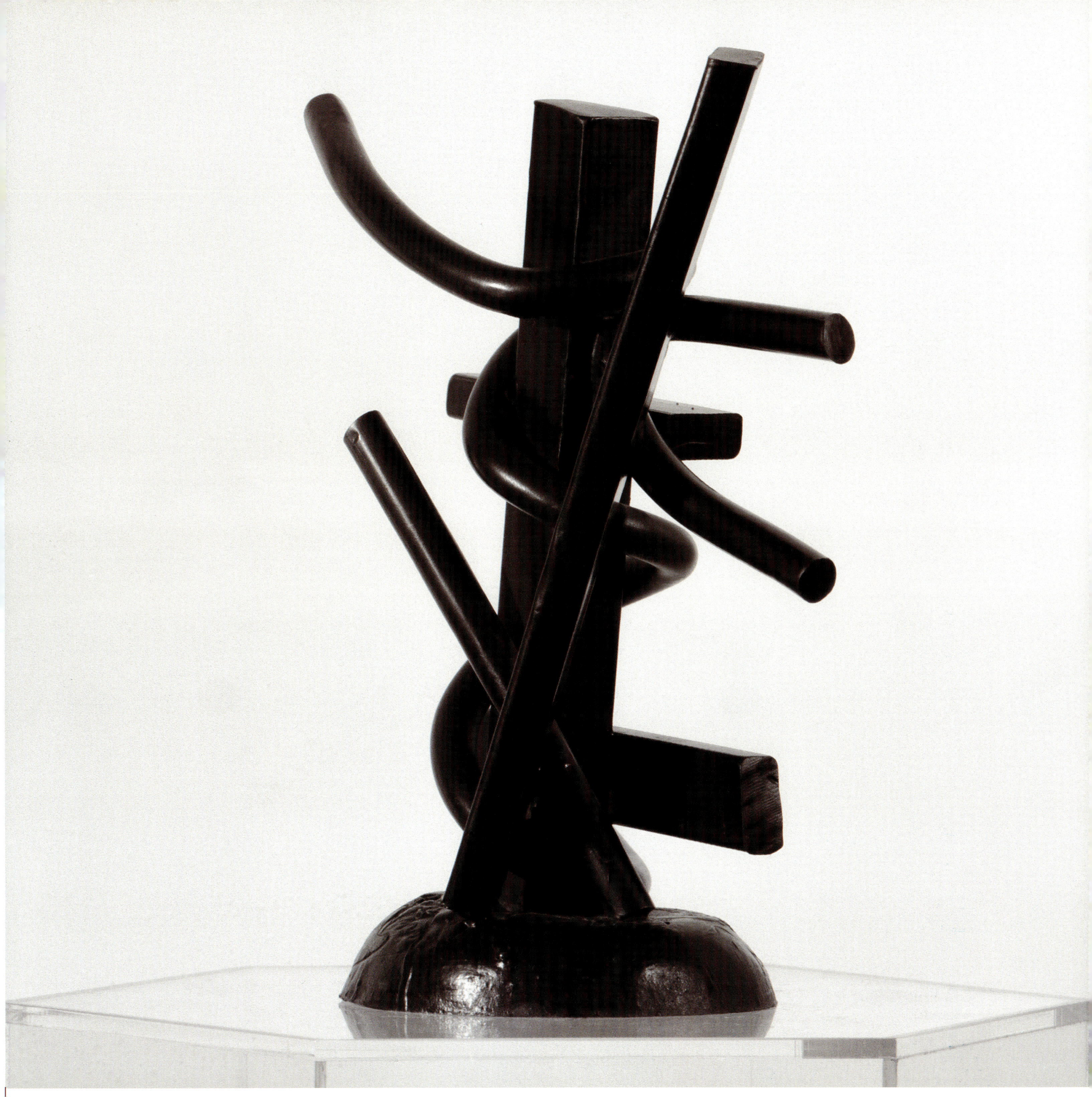

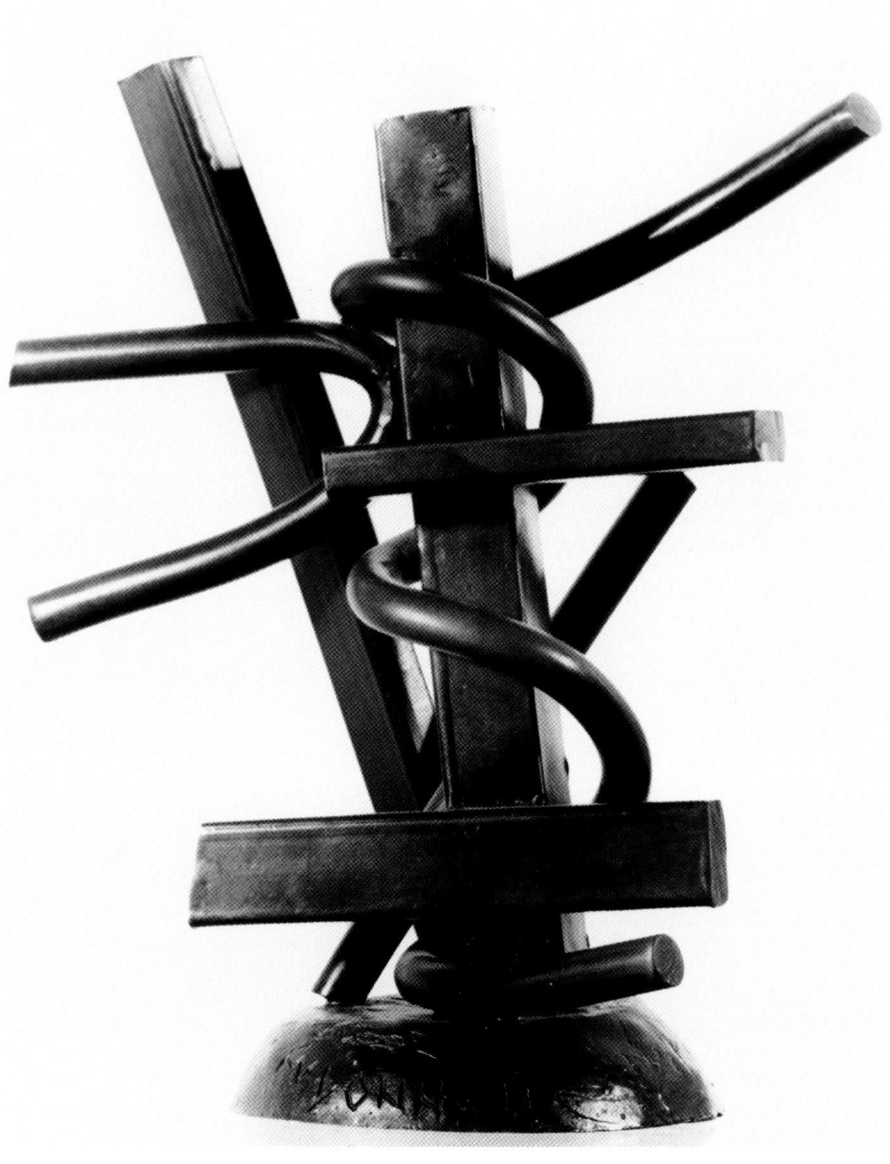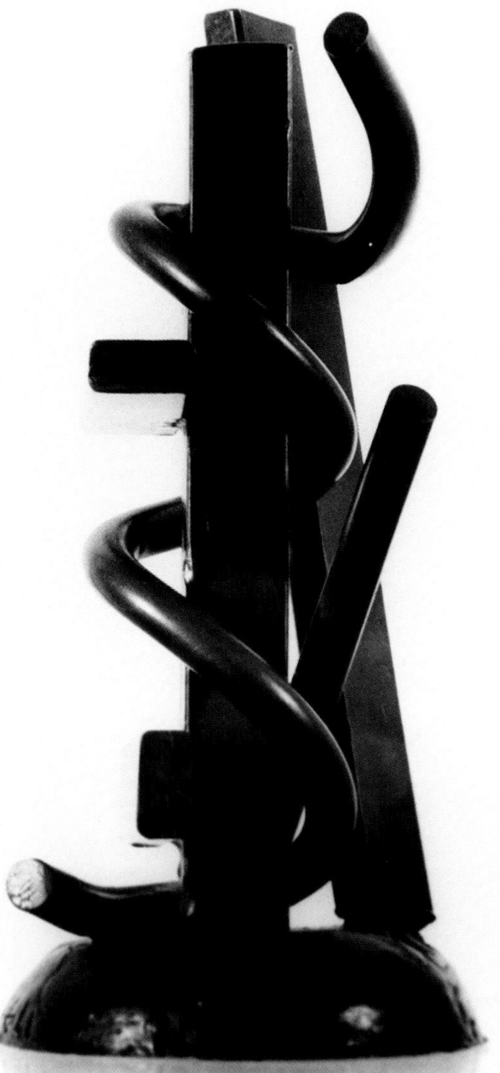

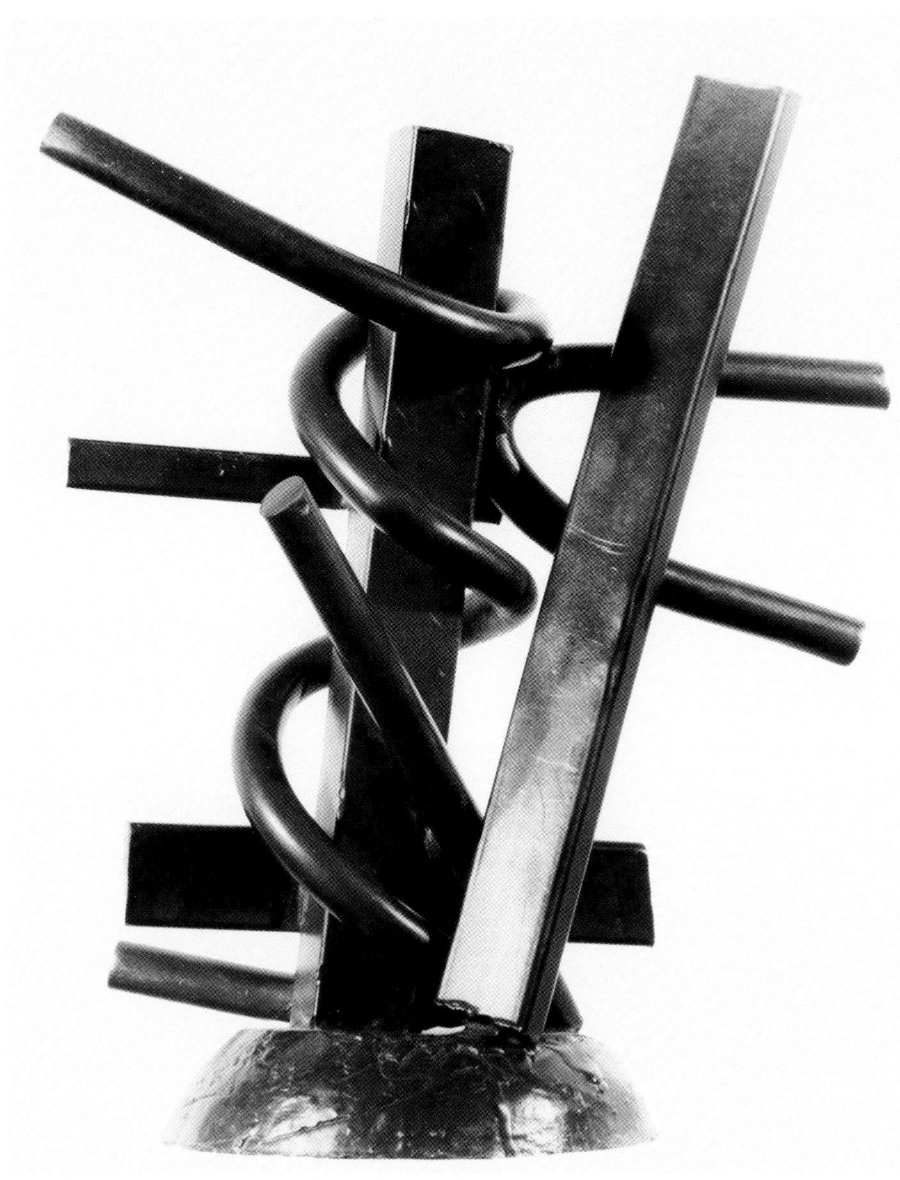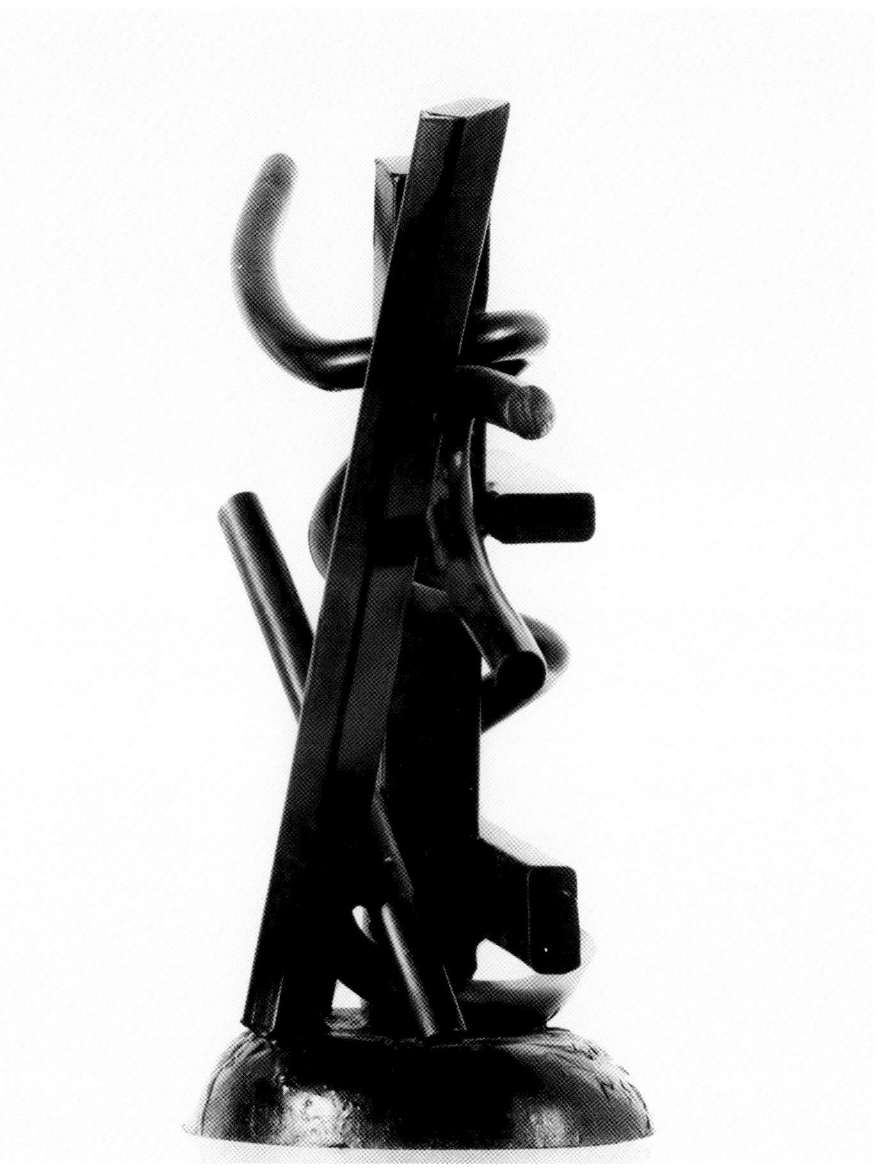

IRISH GATES, MAQUETTE

2002
Bronze
12.5" x 19" x 4.5"
Collection of the artist

In Leon Uris's book, *Trinity*, the main character is a blacksmith and metal worker who specializes in large, wonderful gates. With that in the back of my mind, I thought that these gates would be ones I should like to execute.

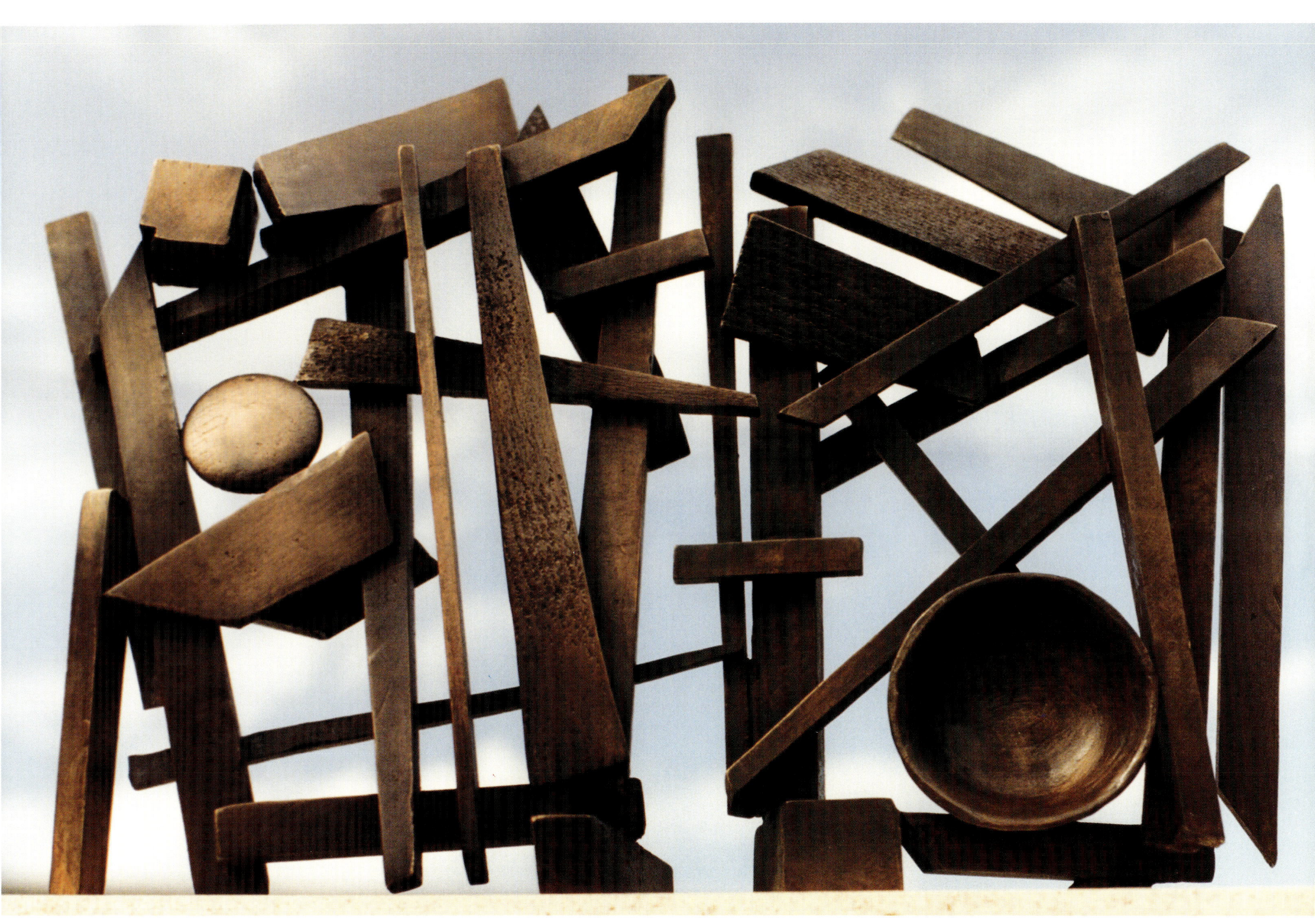

CHINESE BRACELET I

1999
Bronze
16" x 12" x 3"
Sold by Weber Fine Art, Scarsdale, NY

The catalyst for this sculpture was a Ming Dynasty jade bracelet in the Asian Art Museum of Seattle. The exquisite beauty of the bracelet intrigued me so that I studied it often. The opening and the overall shape was rather triangular. I made the second version thinner, which I preferred.

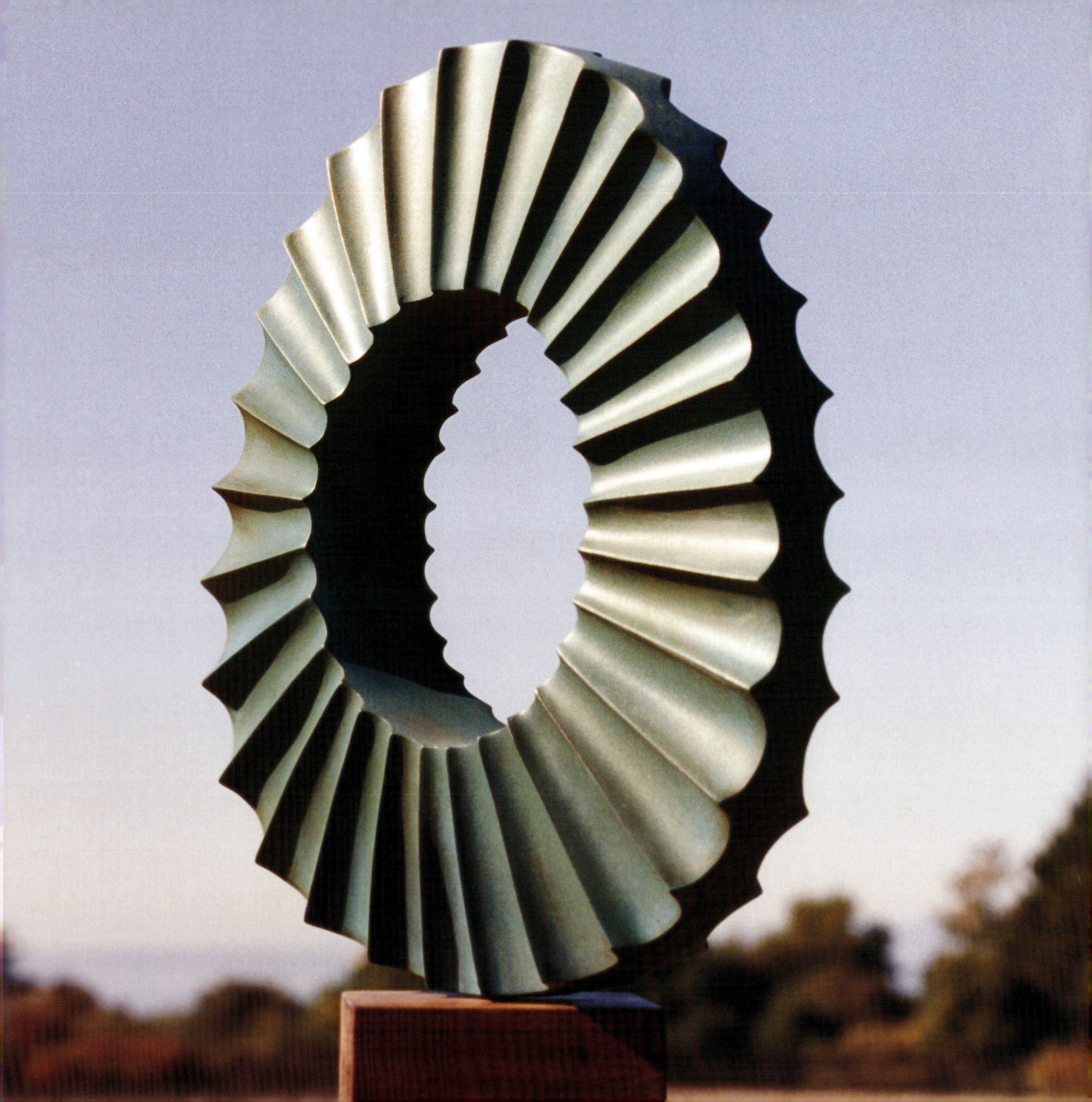

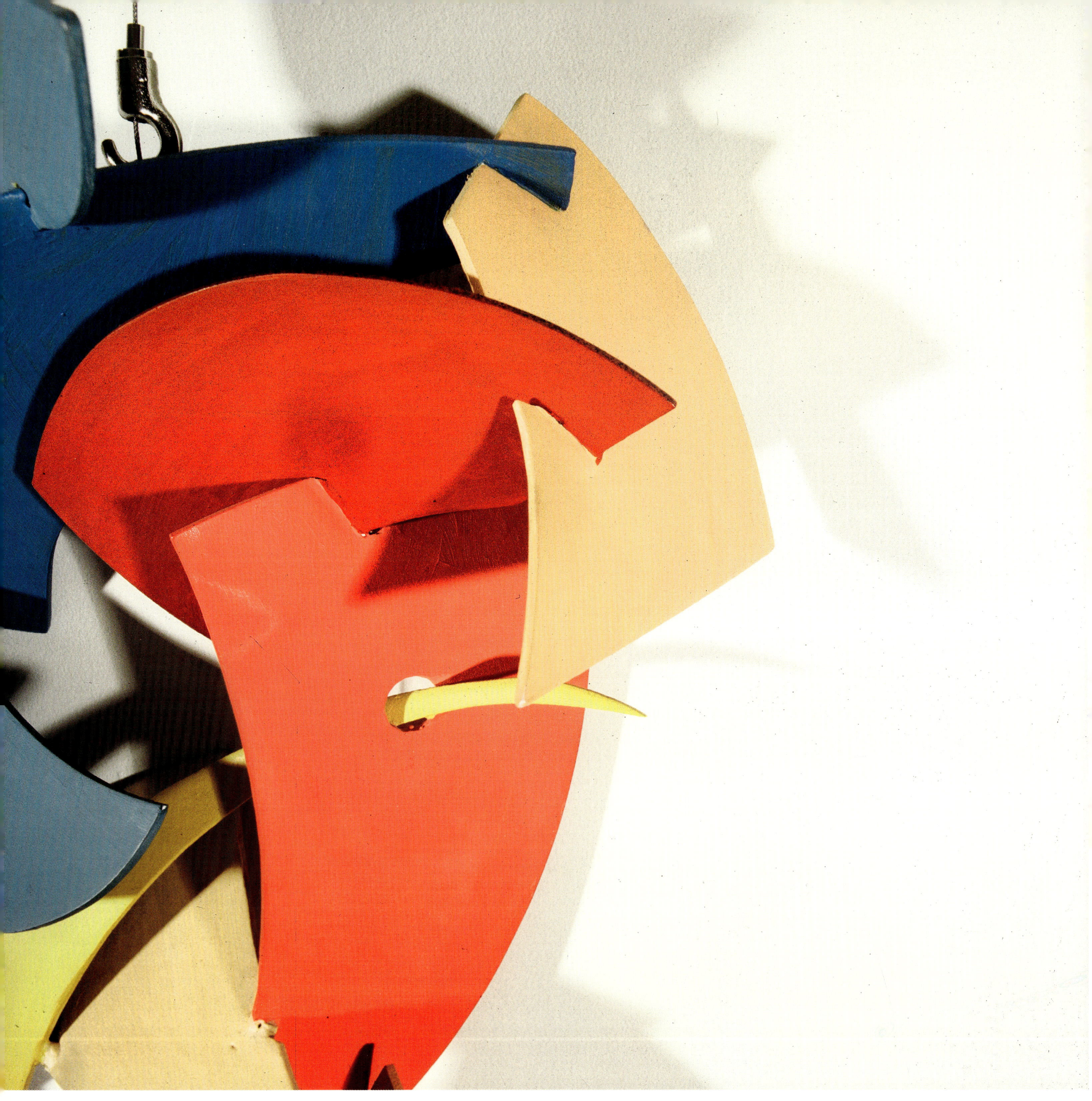

RELIEFS

Dealing with relief sculpture, that is one plane in front or behind another, the shadow edge, the lighting, and the angle of the planes, was something I became familiar with in college. My first public reliefs were in metal. The color was that of the metal. Sometimes I would add color to the background as in a series dealing with land, sea and sky. These early works were in bronze, brass, or stainless steel, all unpainted.

Eventually, a commission came along to do something large for a foyer in Stamford, Connecticut. Hugh Stubbins was the architect. The gray granite walls looked great with a red composition. Enamel on aluminum panels seemed the obvious choice. I would begin adding color, which would change the shapes, and their relationships, too. If the color works, it enhances the shapes. The process is a two way street.

Another relief had a lot of reflective, burnished surfaces so that the image seemed alive and created an incredible sense of space

Eventually, I tried painting some reliefs (this was actually before Frank Stella began painting his reliefs), which became three dimensional paintings floating on a wall like leaves before the wind. As I progressed, the paintings became more and more involved. They were very lively and seemed to evoke positive reactions. I believe people related to them more easily than to sculpture.

I would usually start off with a small watercolor or gouache sketch, and then cut the forms out of aluminum on a small scale, under two feet. The final versions were three or four times larger.

SHOOT THE MOON

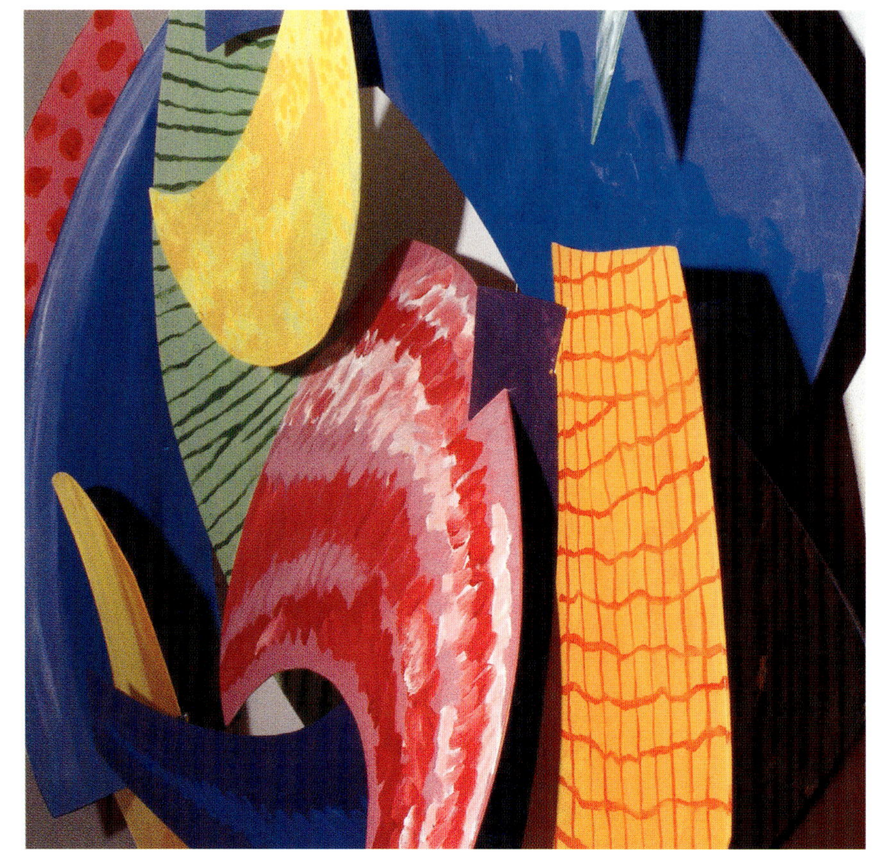

2002
Oil paint on aluminum
72" x 48" x 7"
Washington Mutual Conference Center, SeaTac, WA

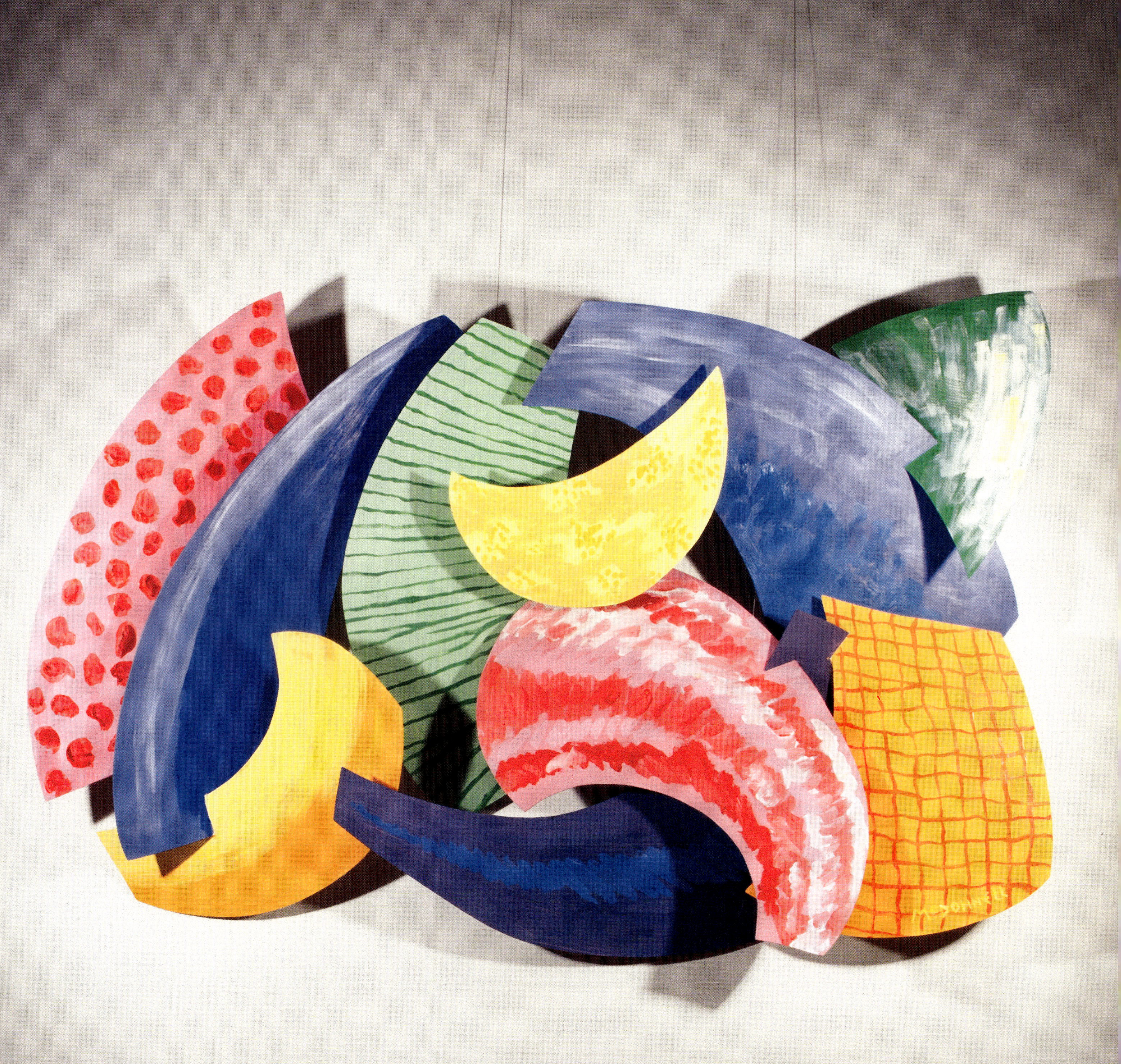

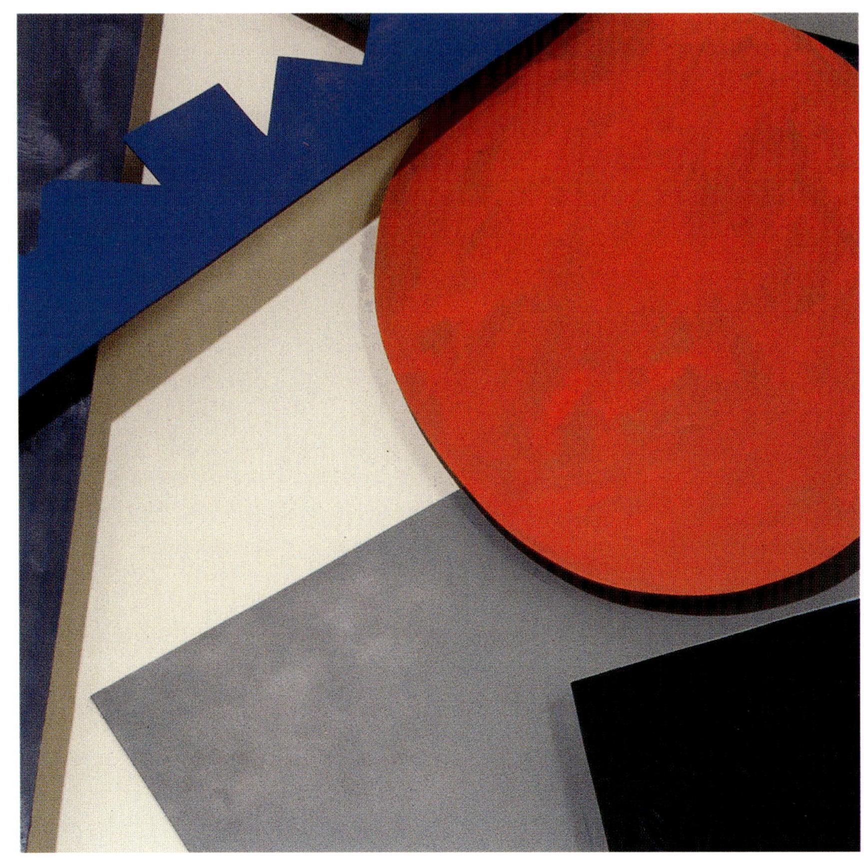

MEDITERRANEAN

2001
Oil paint on aluminum
66" x 49" x 4"
collection of the artist

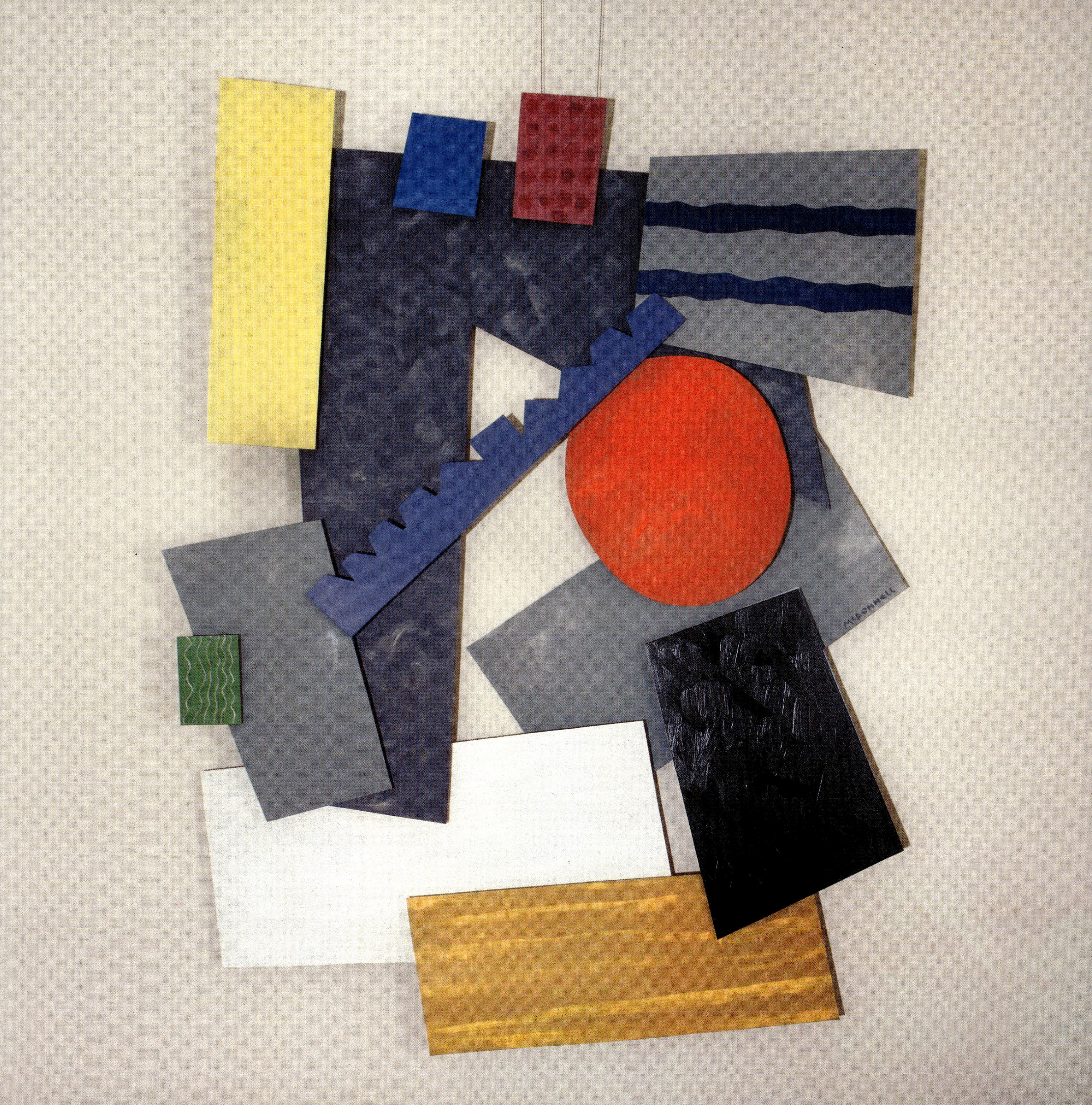

McDonnell

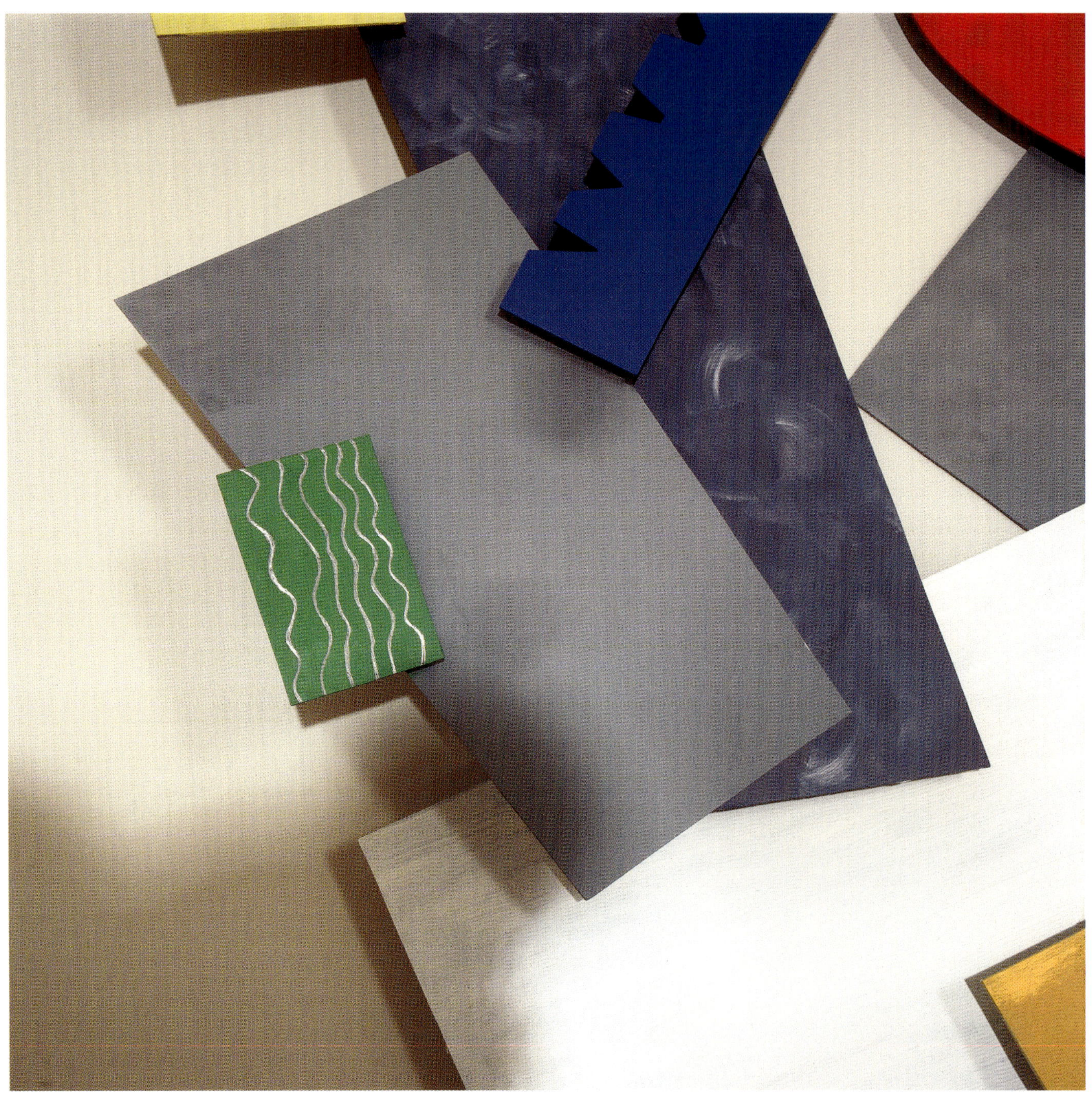

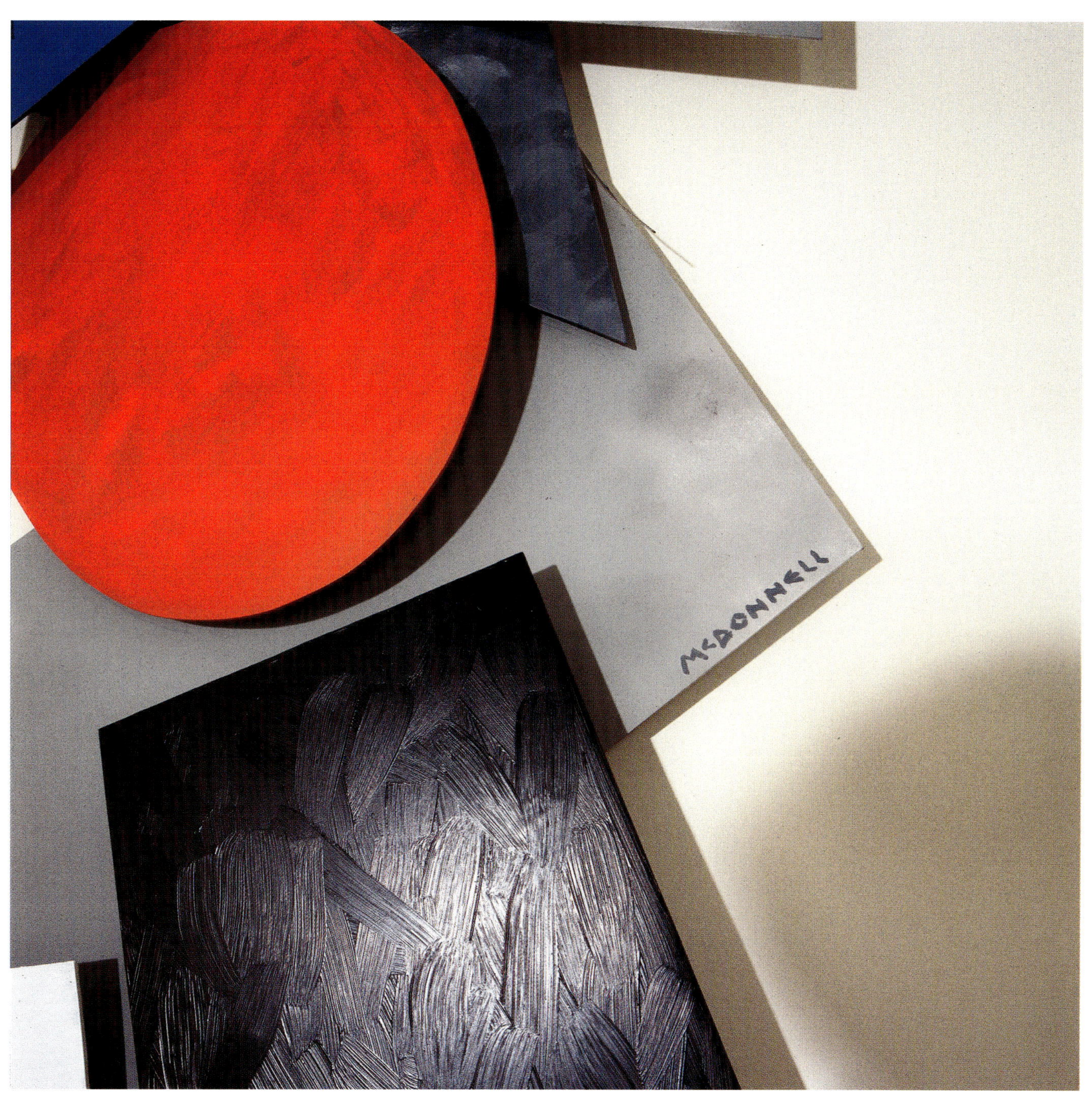McDONNELL

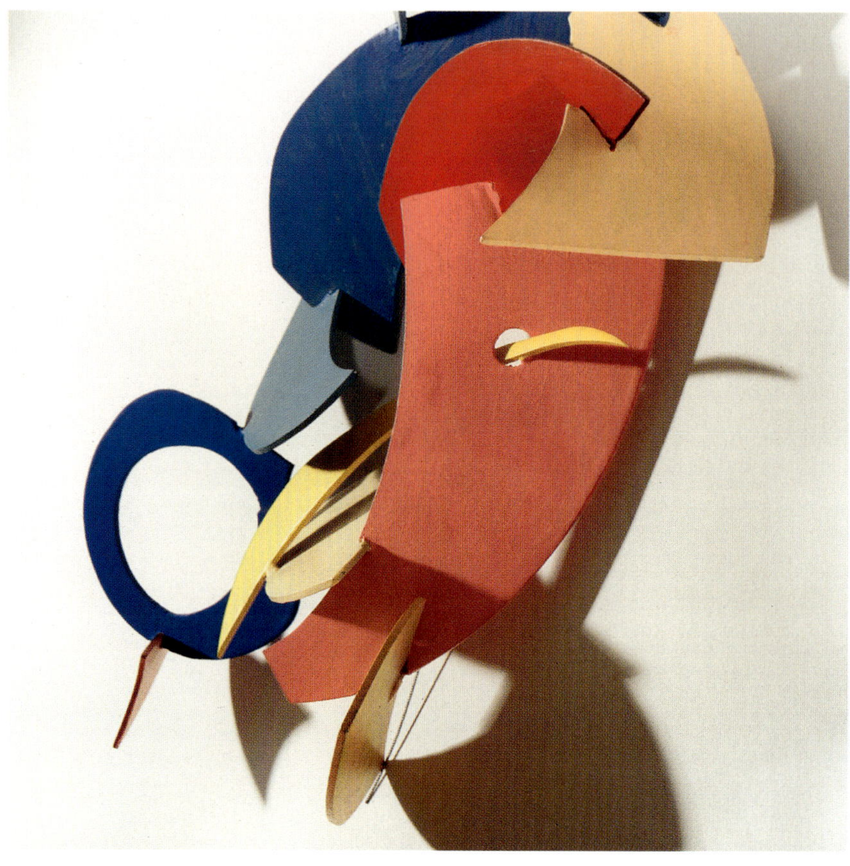

CIRCUS

1991
Oil on bronze
15"x 9" x 5"
Collection of H. Stewart Ross, Everett, WA

This little relief was constructed from bronze scraps in my studio. I tried painting it different colors on several occasions. Finally, I believe I got it right.

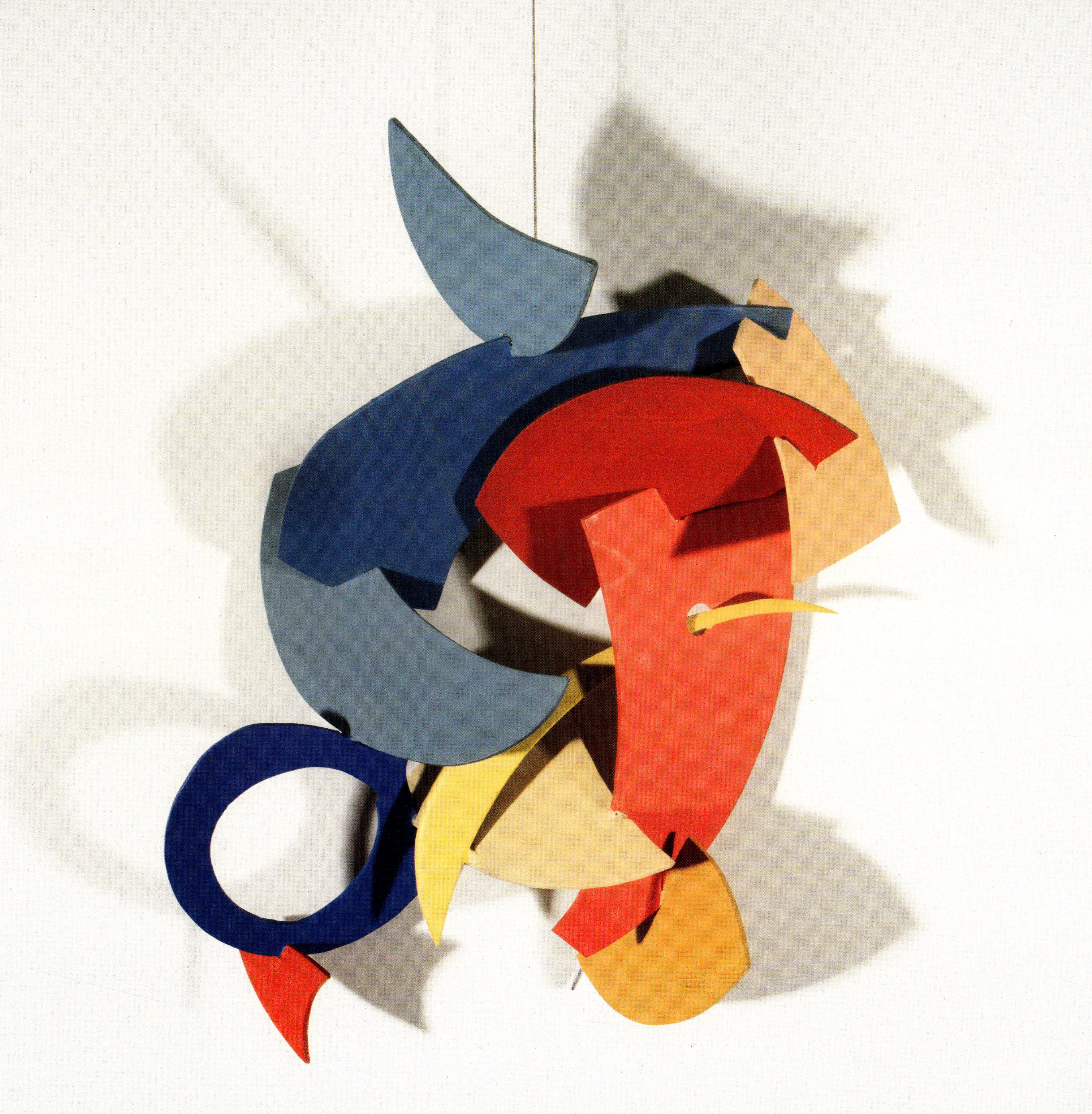

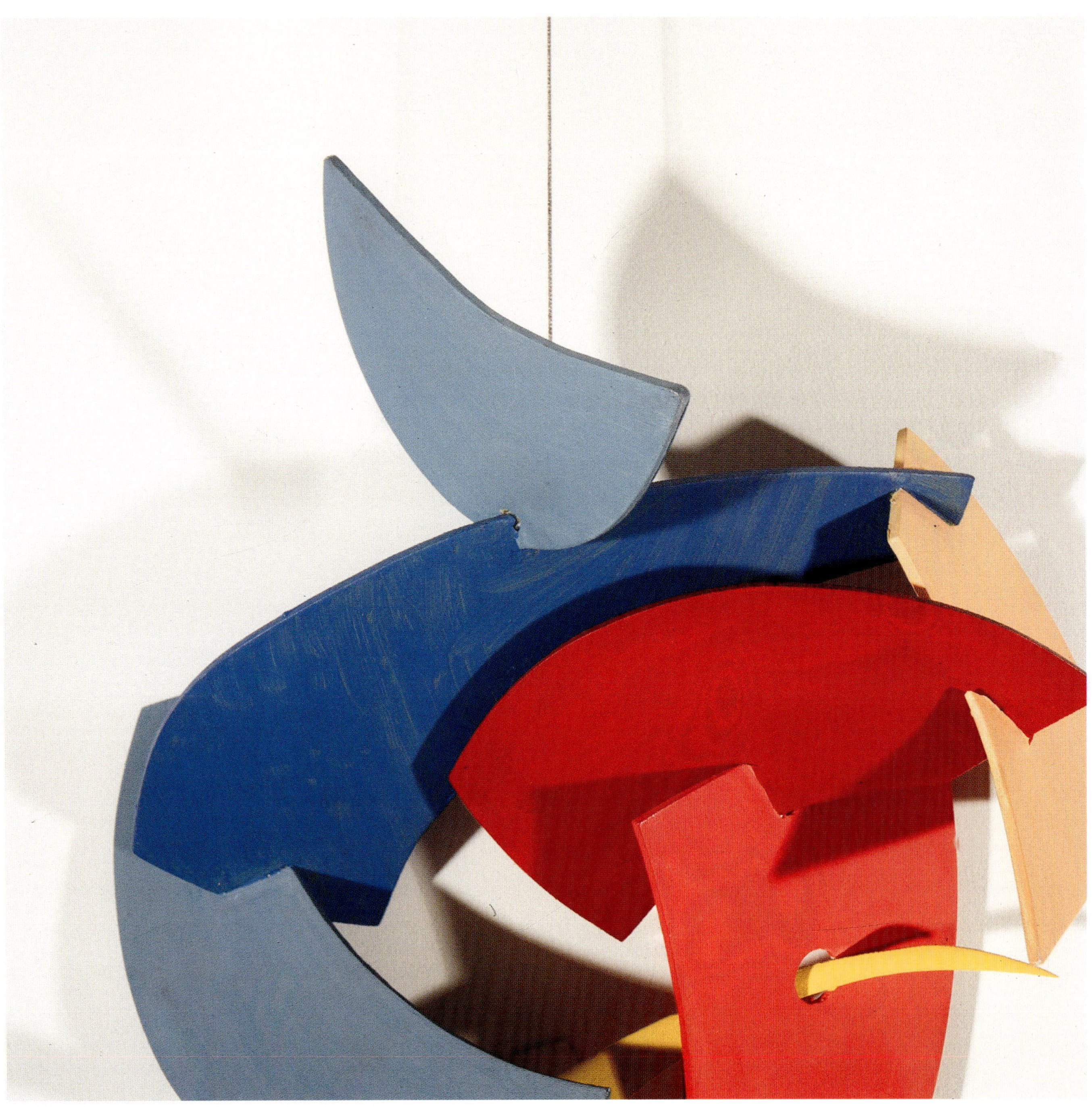

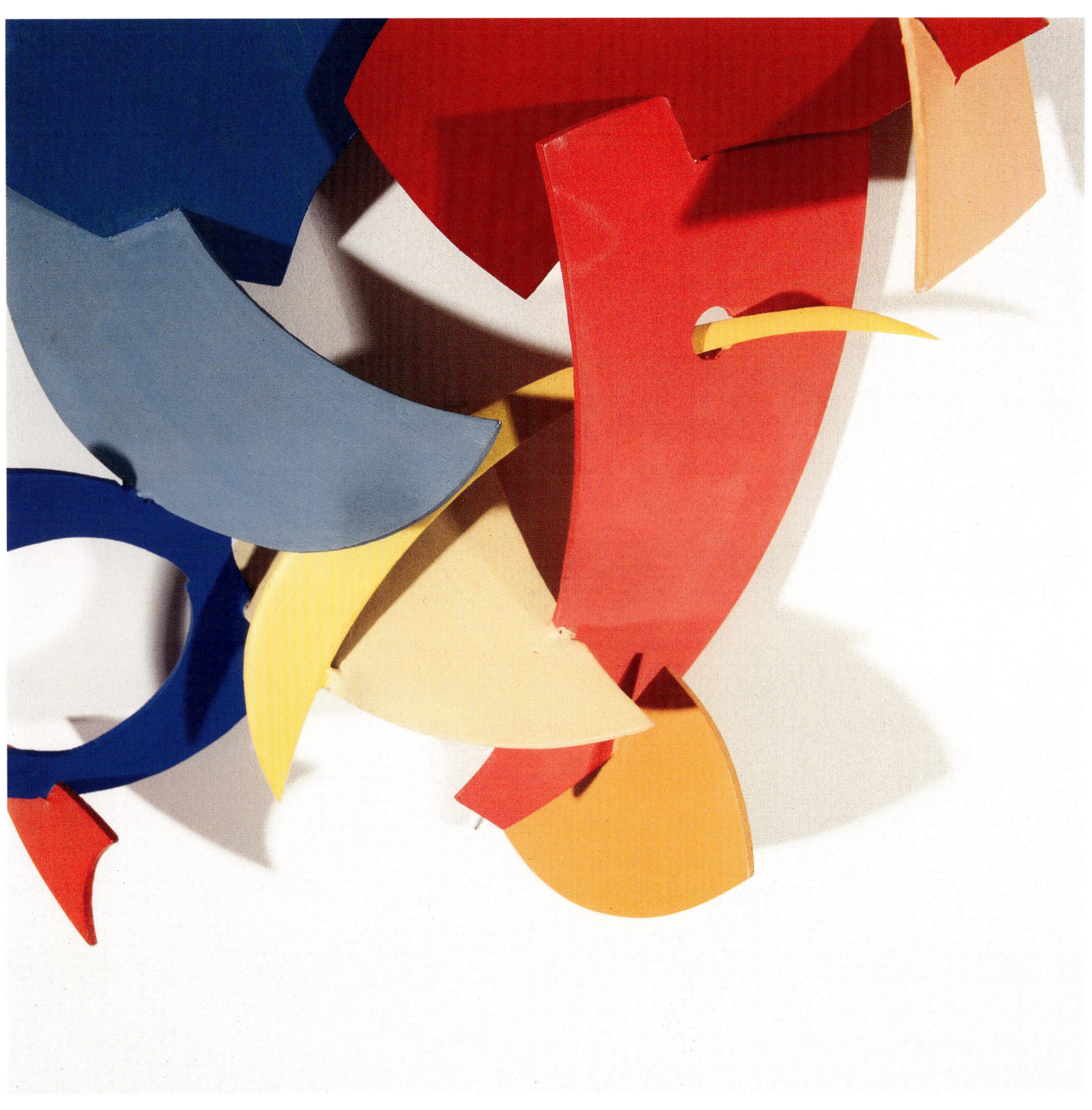

MEDITERRANEAN, SMALL

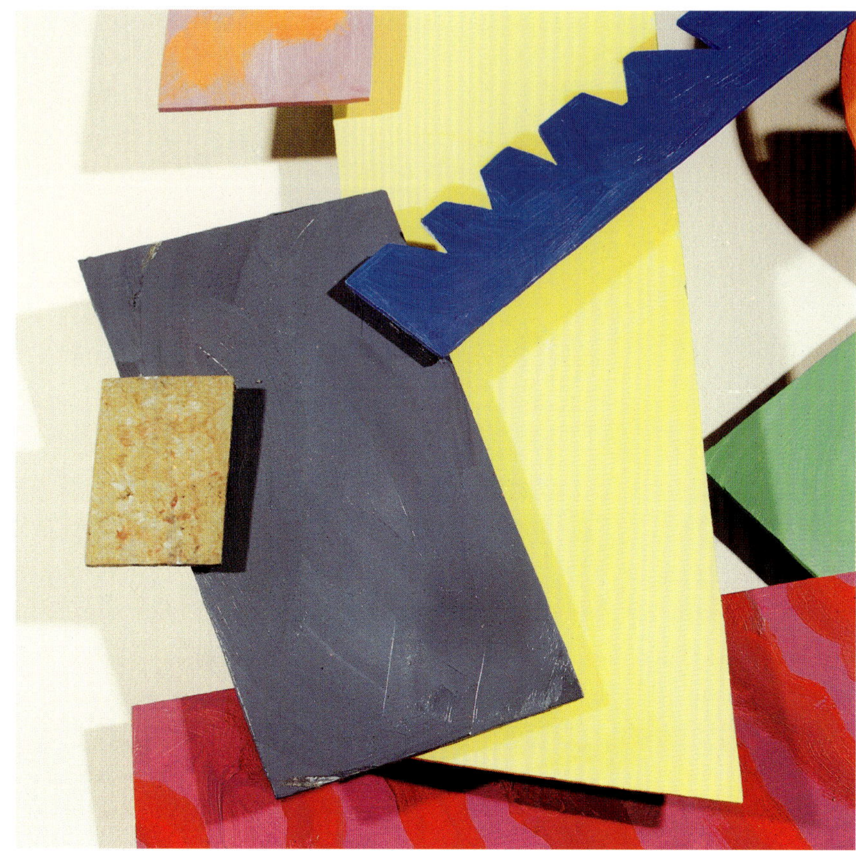

2001
Oil on aluminum
22" x 15" x 4"
Collection of Anthony Geraci, MD

This was my model for the larger version. Actually, I made a watercolor sketch first and then did this piece. This one is more lyrical and textural than the big one.

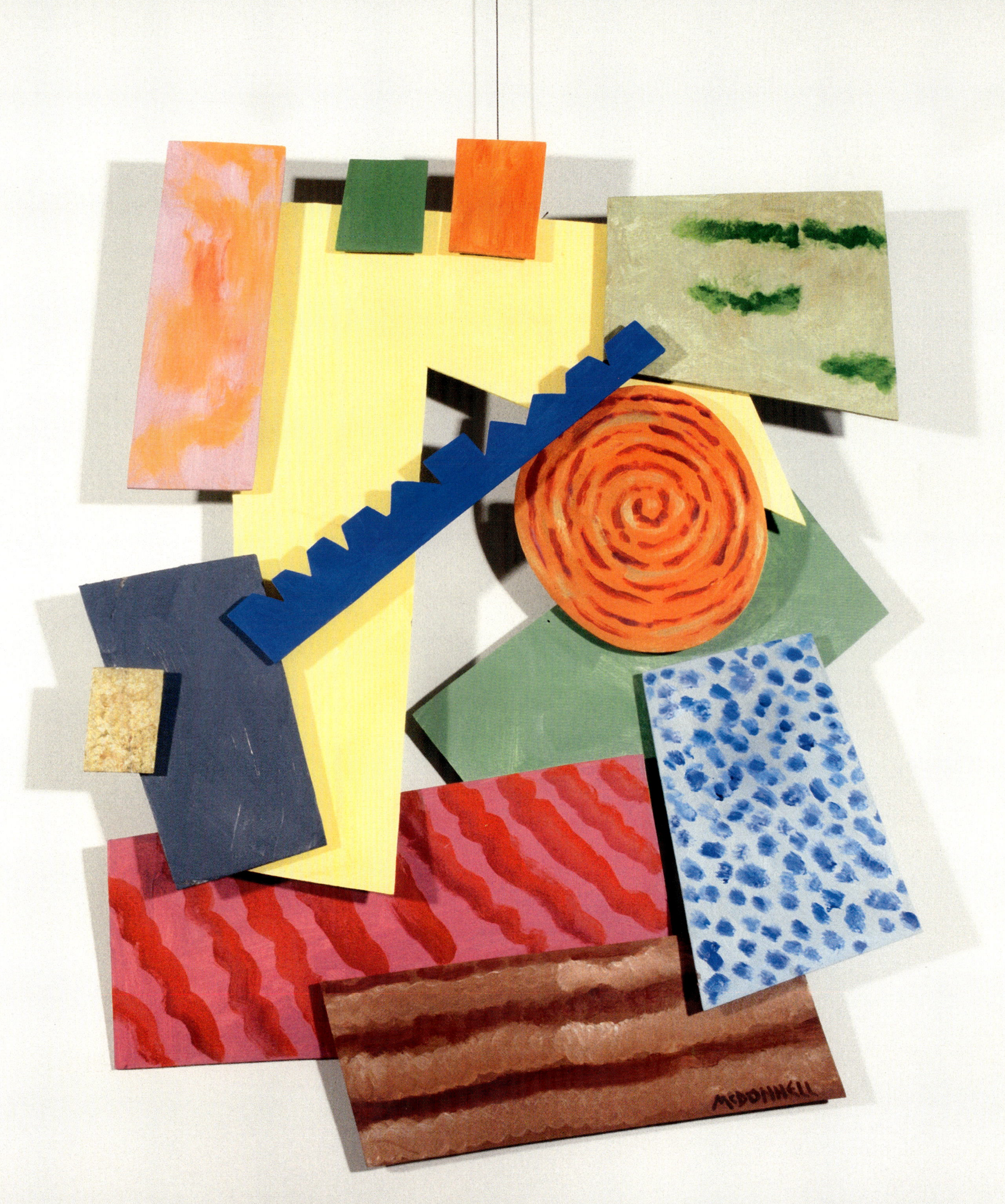

McDONNELL

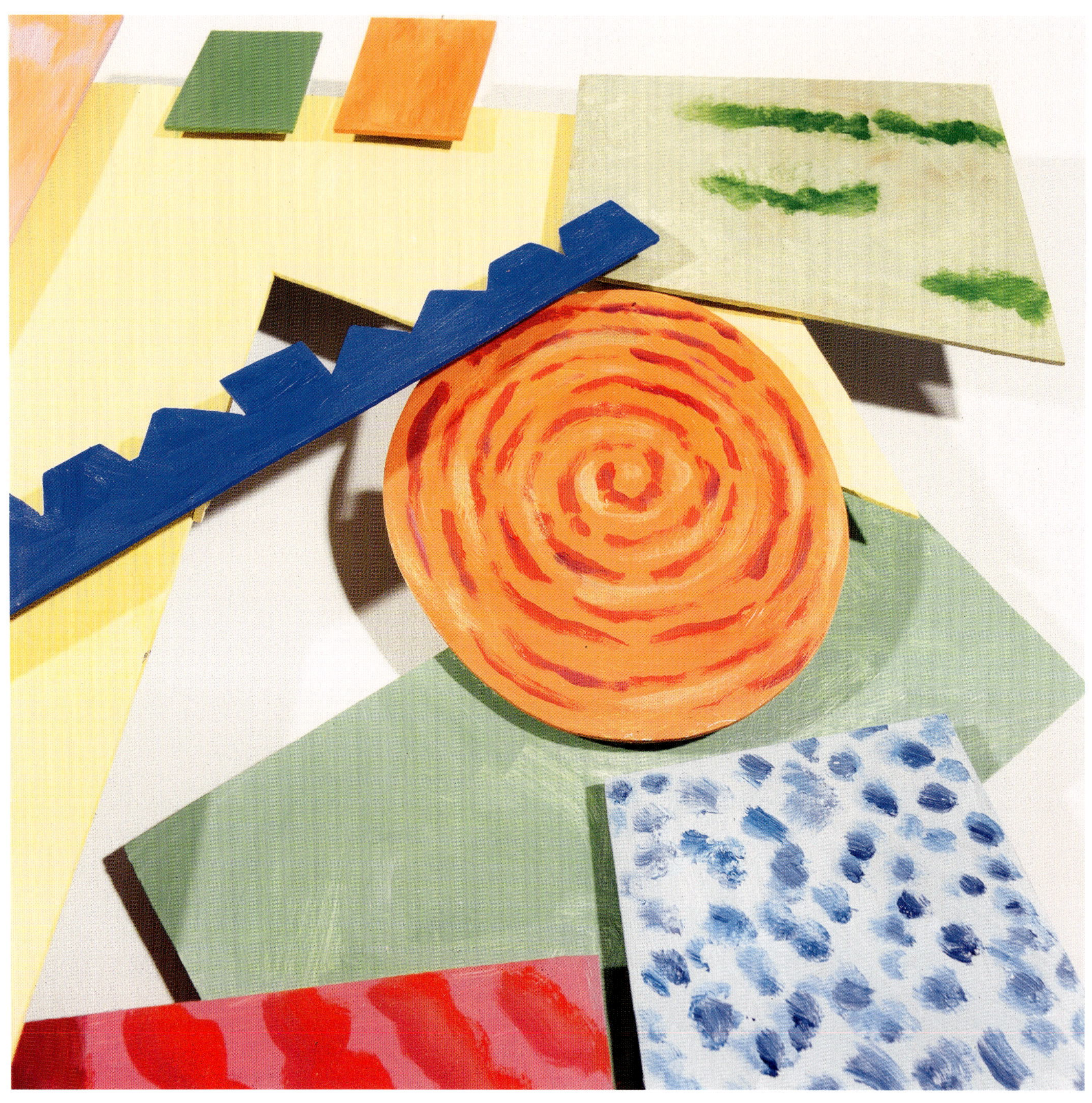

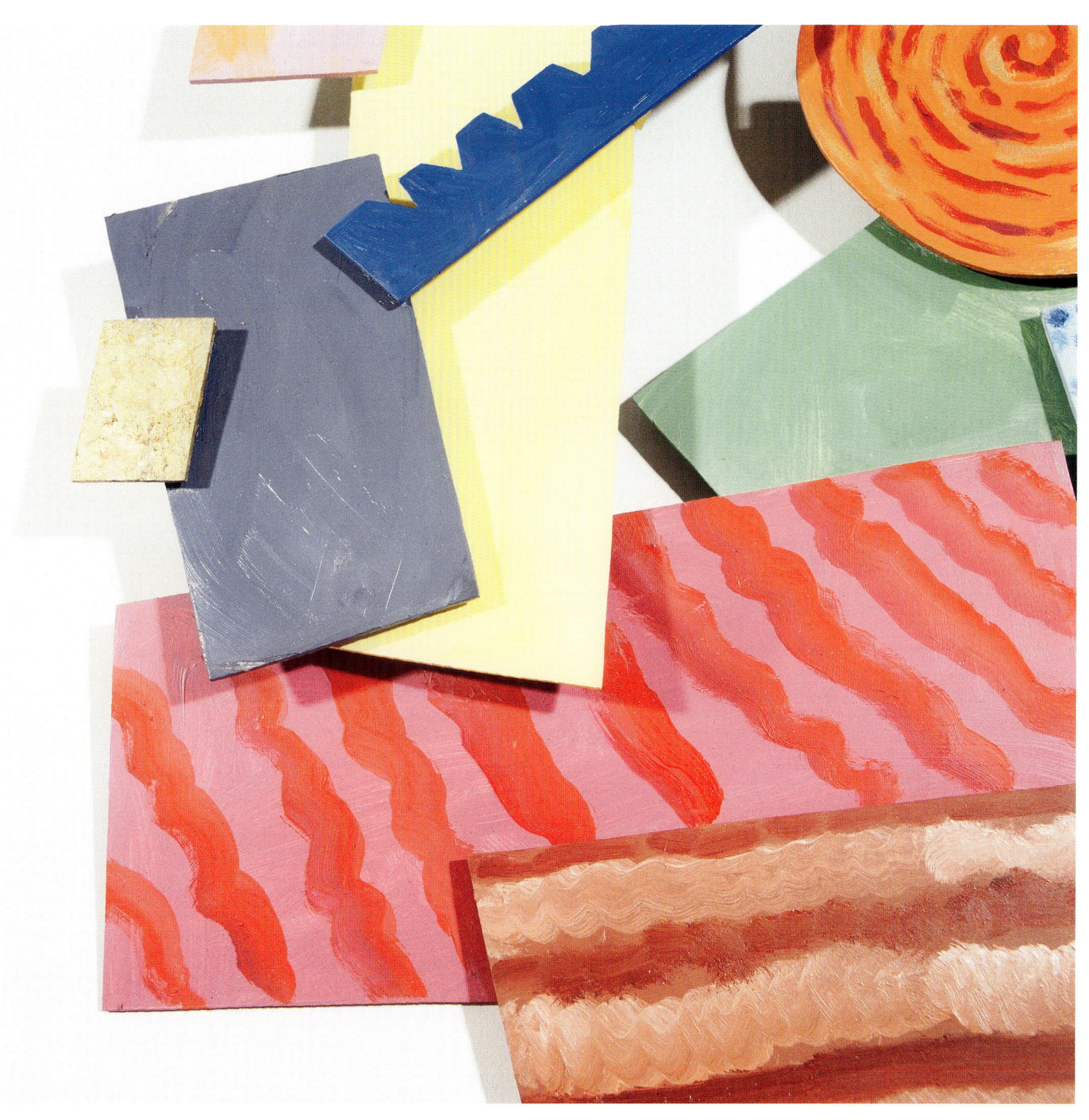

REQUIEM FOR
A MATADOR

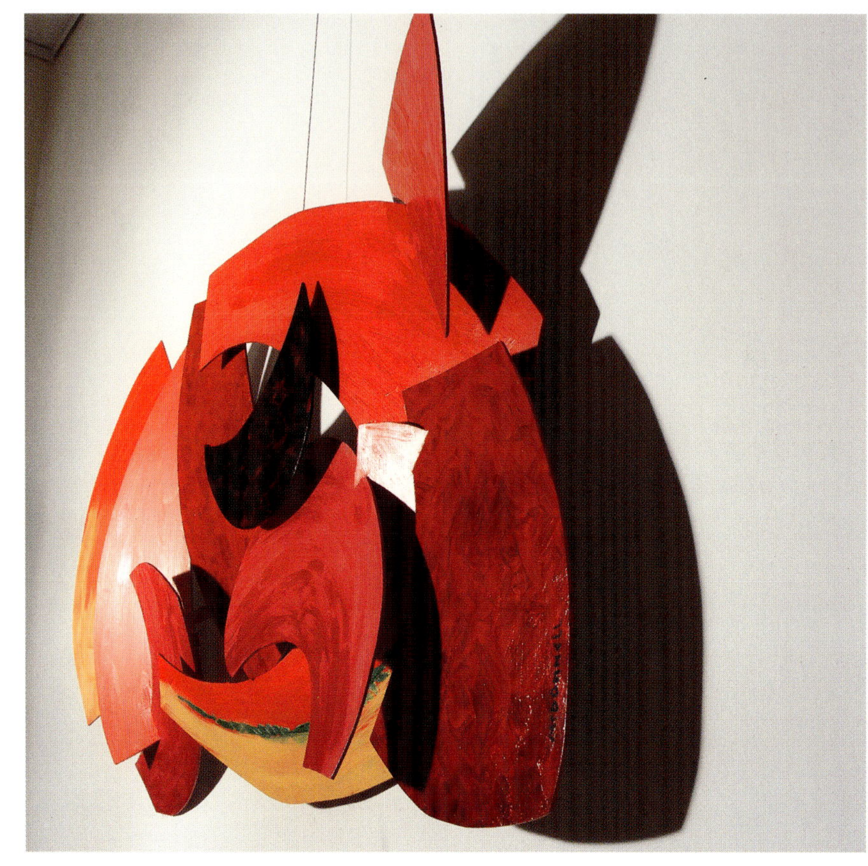

2001
Oil paint on aluminum
30" x 60" x 6"
Collection of Nancy and Dr. Buster Alvord,
Seattle, WA

This piece was later partially repainted with more dark
areas of transparent blues, greens, and blacks.

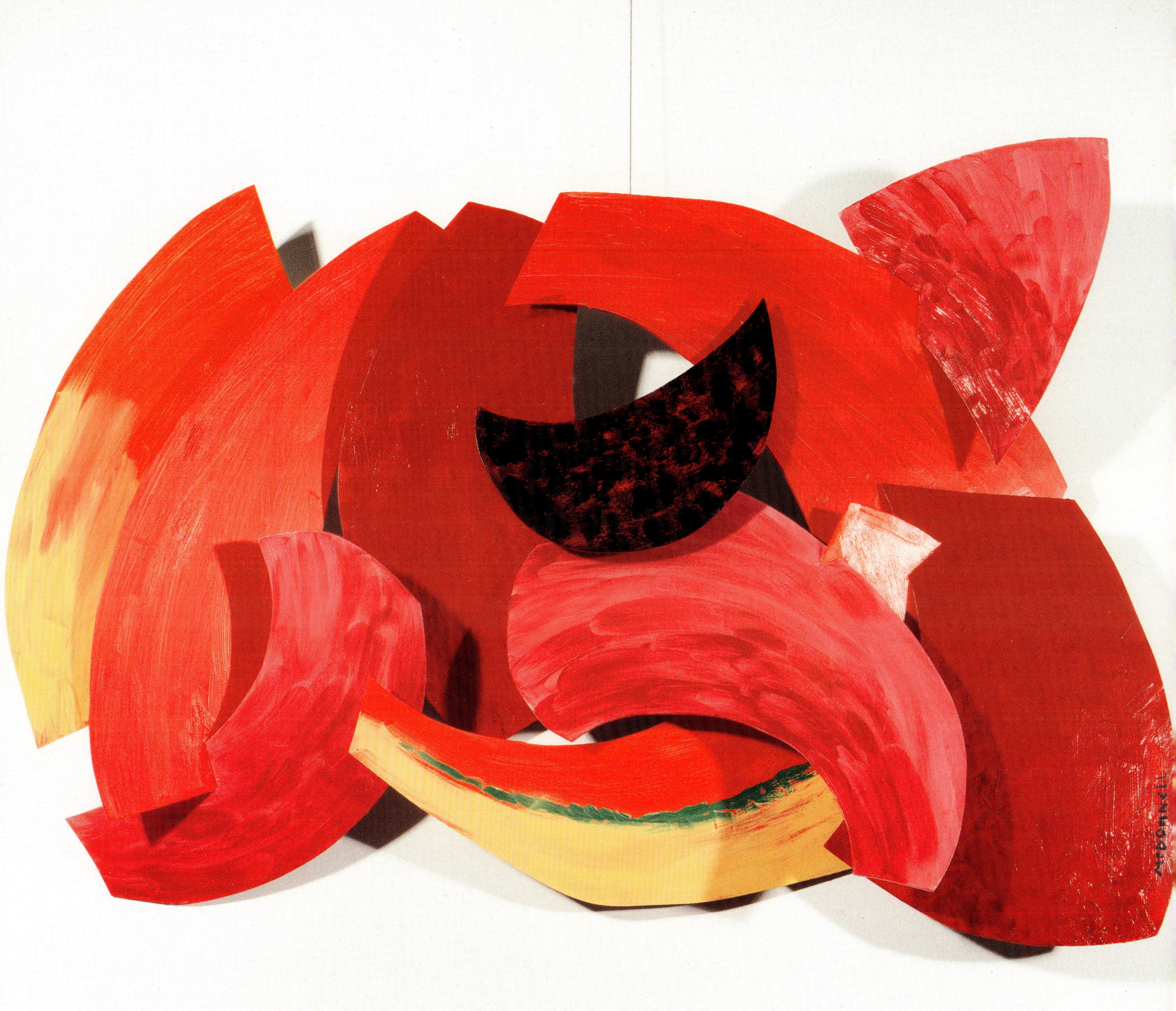

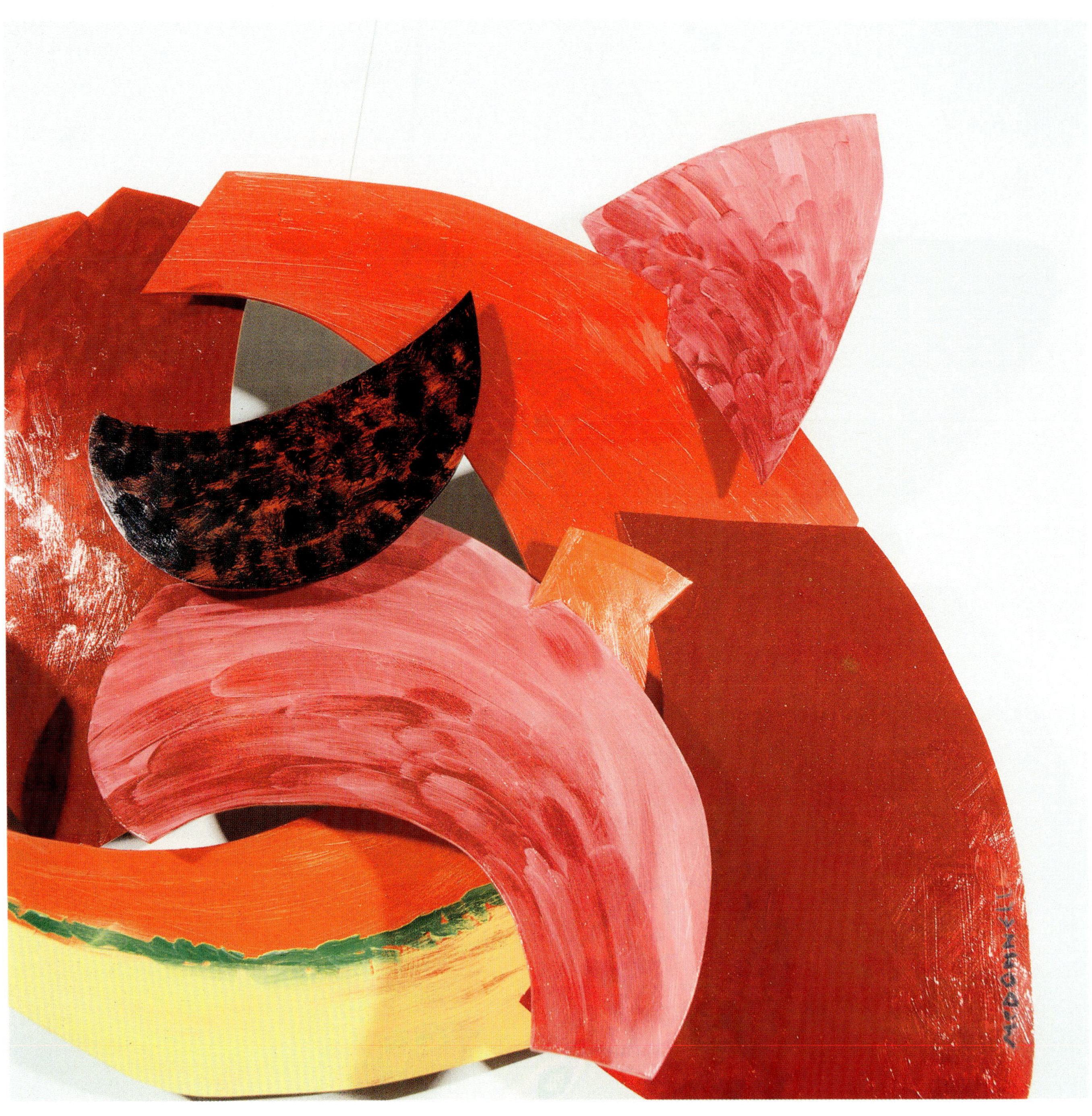

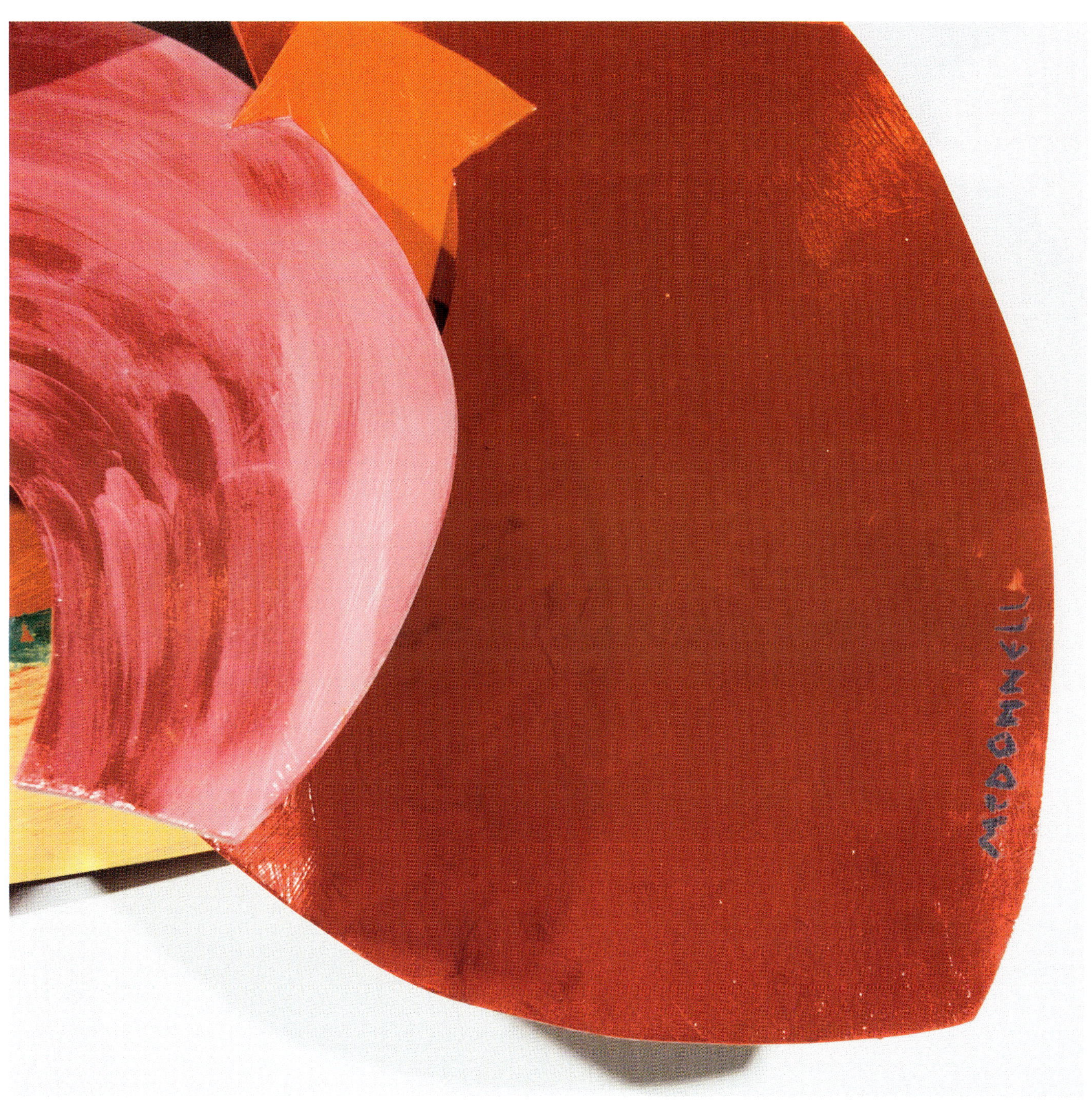

McDONNELL

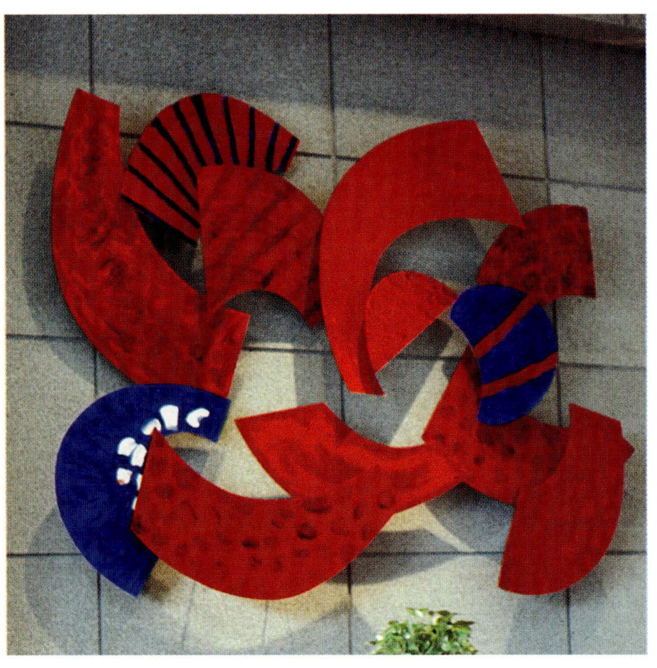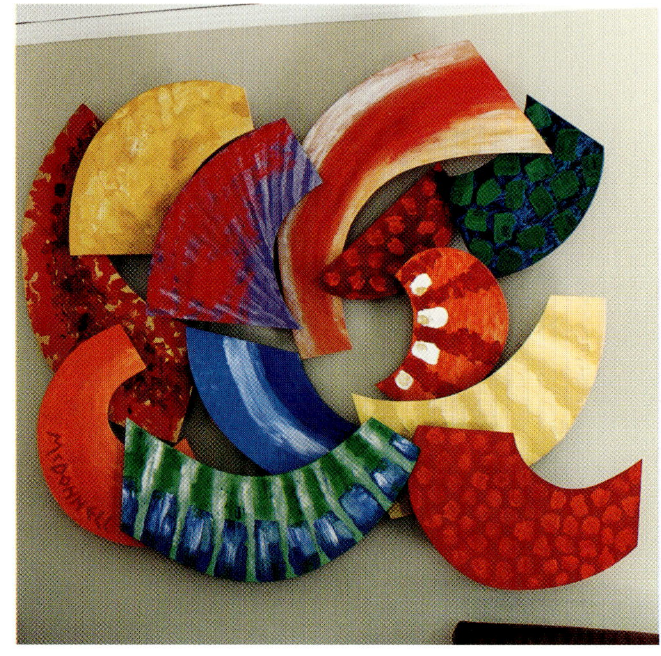

STAMFORD RELIEF
1994
Acrylic on aluminum
121" x 180" x 18"
owned by 1050 Washington Boulevard,
Stamford, CT

HAM, BACON, AND EGGS
2001
Oil paint on aluminum
60" x 70" x 7"
Collection of the artist

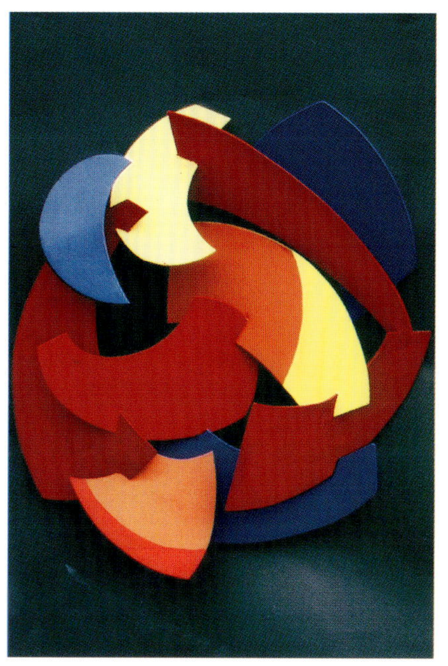

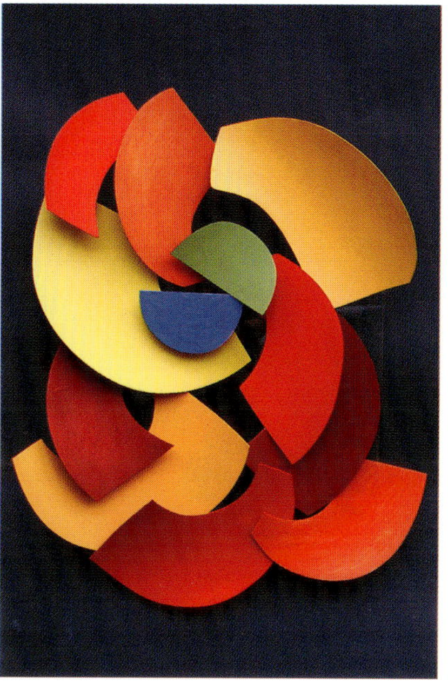

JUBILEE
2001
Bronze
20" x 14" x 5"
Collection of Susan K. Stern,
Scarsdale, NY

HOMAGE TO
EASTERN WASHINGTON
2001
Oil paint on aluminum
60" x 40" x 6"
Collection of Bill Gates,
Seattle, WA

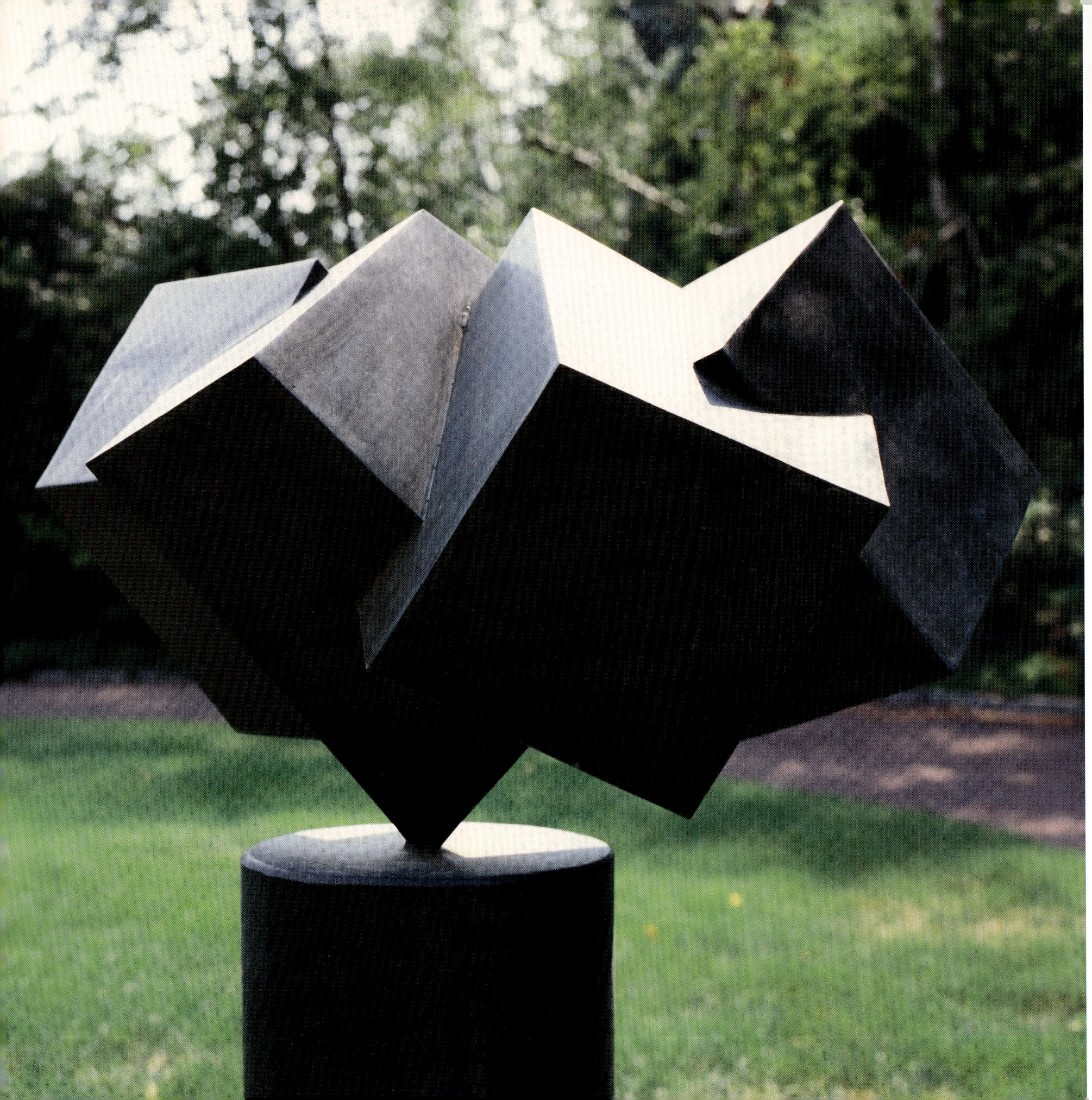

CUBE COMPOSITIONS

My inspiration for the cube compositions dates back to 1970. I had been in Italy working on several commissions, one of them a six-foot Mobius strip cast in aluminum. During a weekend foray to Umbria to visit friends who had a wonderful country house called Campo Sevole (wild field), my eye caught sight of the loveliest late Renaissance chapel. Its perfect setting was on a small rise surrounded by larger hills in a verdant landscape of cypress trees and fields. On investigation, I discovered that the architect was Danile di San Gallo, assistant to Michelangelo. Stopping to study this countryside jewel, I noticed that part of the cornices, and a number of adjacent blocks, had broken loose and lay smashed together in a rather dramatic composition on the ground. It seemed that one stone cube was emanating from the perfect form of another cube and another from that. The edges were beveled and true, the centers left rough in typical Renaissance fashion. Such a feeling of force and movement! I could not wait to interpret it in my own work.

Upon my return to Pietrasanta I developed a model for which some of the best local expert craftsmen cut out a large block of Noce (walnut colored) Travertine. The block was the size of a Volkswagen!! The finished sculpture was so heavy that it rested in front of my house in Bedford, NY for several years before being acquired by Mr. and Mrs. Spike Beitzel, who are among my strongest collectors. Spike was a top executive with IBM and Mary Lou a fine watercolorist.

My cube series ran all the way from single polygons to extremely involved compositions such as *Pyrite Piece*. In a way, the cube compositions opened the door for the *Breaking Away* pieces later.

Opposite page: Floating Cubes

FLOATING CUBES

1984
Bronze
30" x 28" x 14"
Collection of Arnold Cohen and Bren Robbins

There were a series of cubes created as a model for a very large piece I did in Houston for the Trammell Crow Company. I used what scrap bronze I had left around the studio and built one cube into the next. If you look carefully, you can actually see where there are seams making up the sides of some of the cubes. I called this one *Floating Cubes* because the cubes float on one point. I have done many sculptures using cubes. The round pedestal is part of the sculpture.

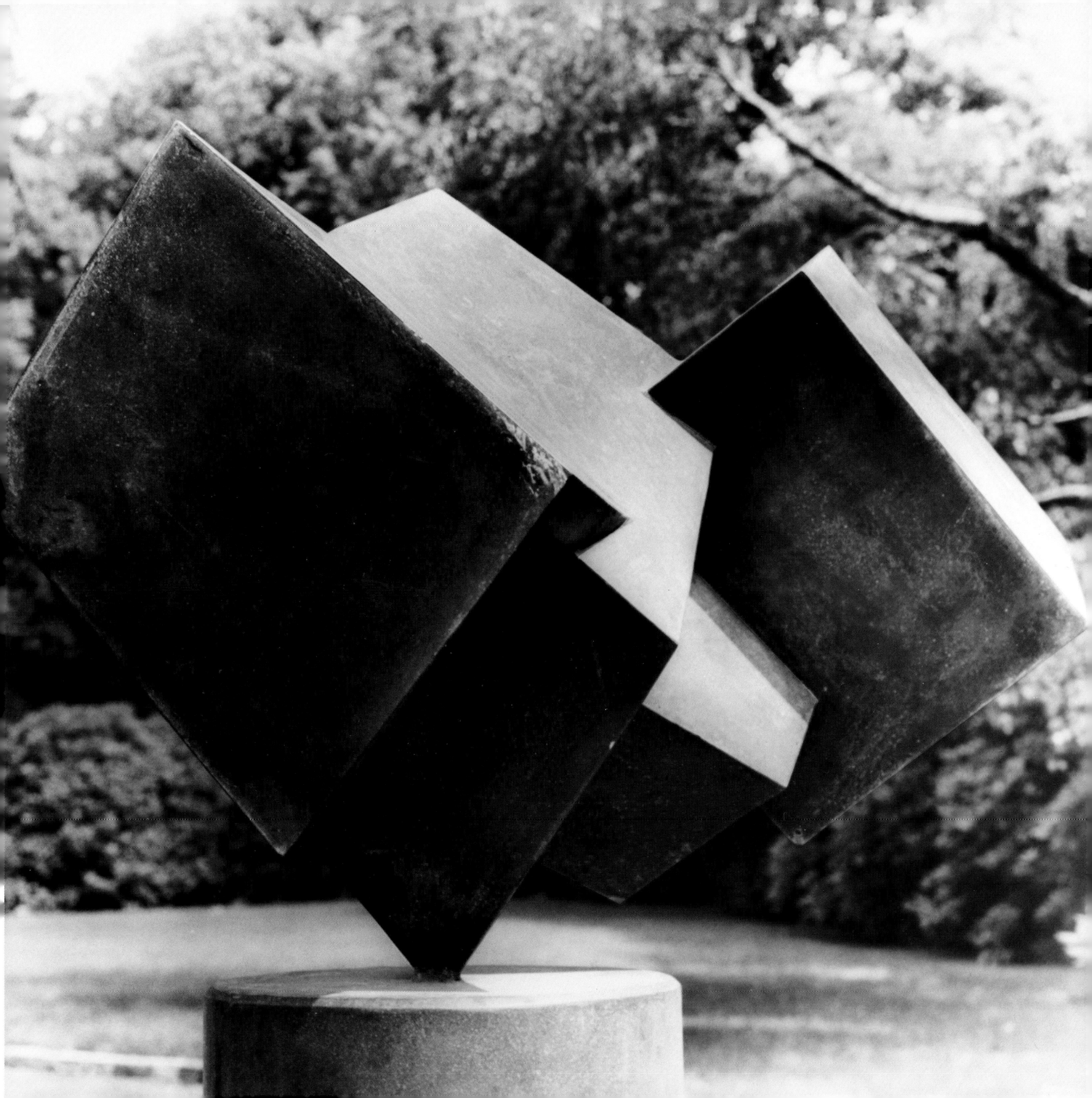

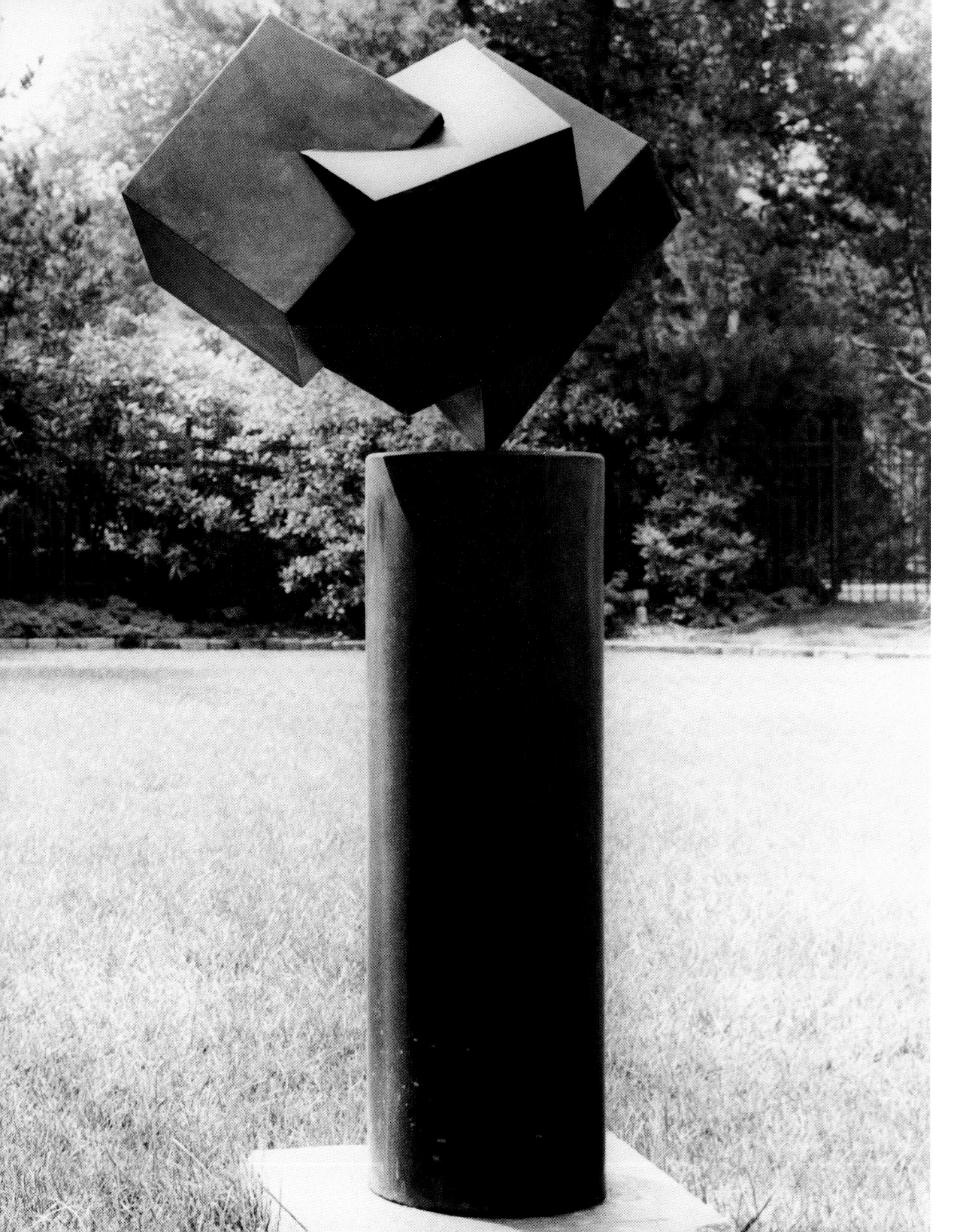

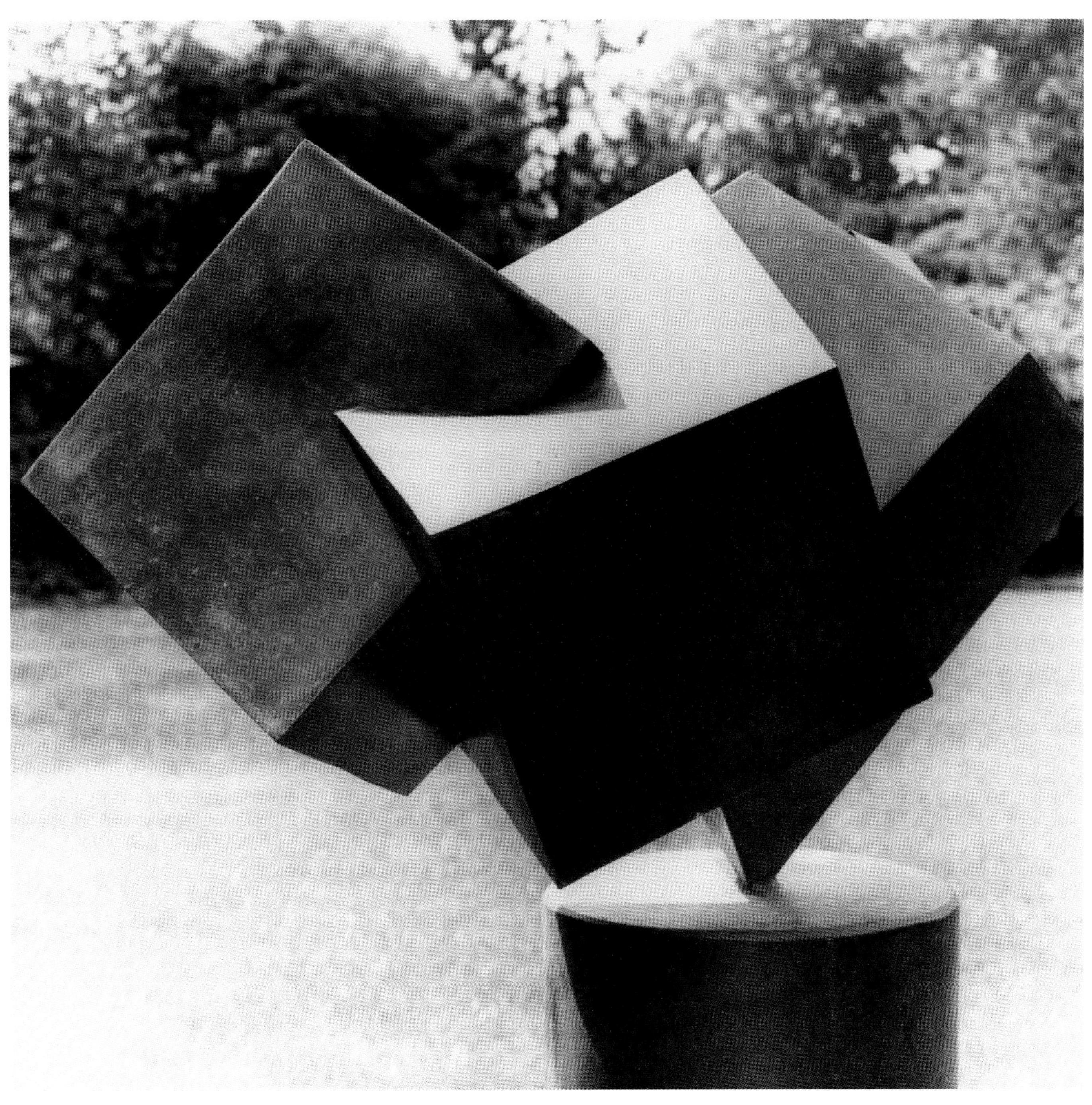

CROTON

1978
bronze
30' in height
Collection of Paul and Harriet Weissman

There is a huge dam at Croton Falls, NY that once was considered to be one of the seven modern wonders of the world. I saw that there were a number of stone blocks that had broken loose and tumbled down the hillside. This sculpture was inspired by those blocks, which is why I named it after the dam.

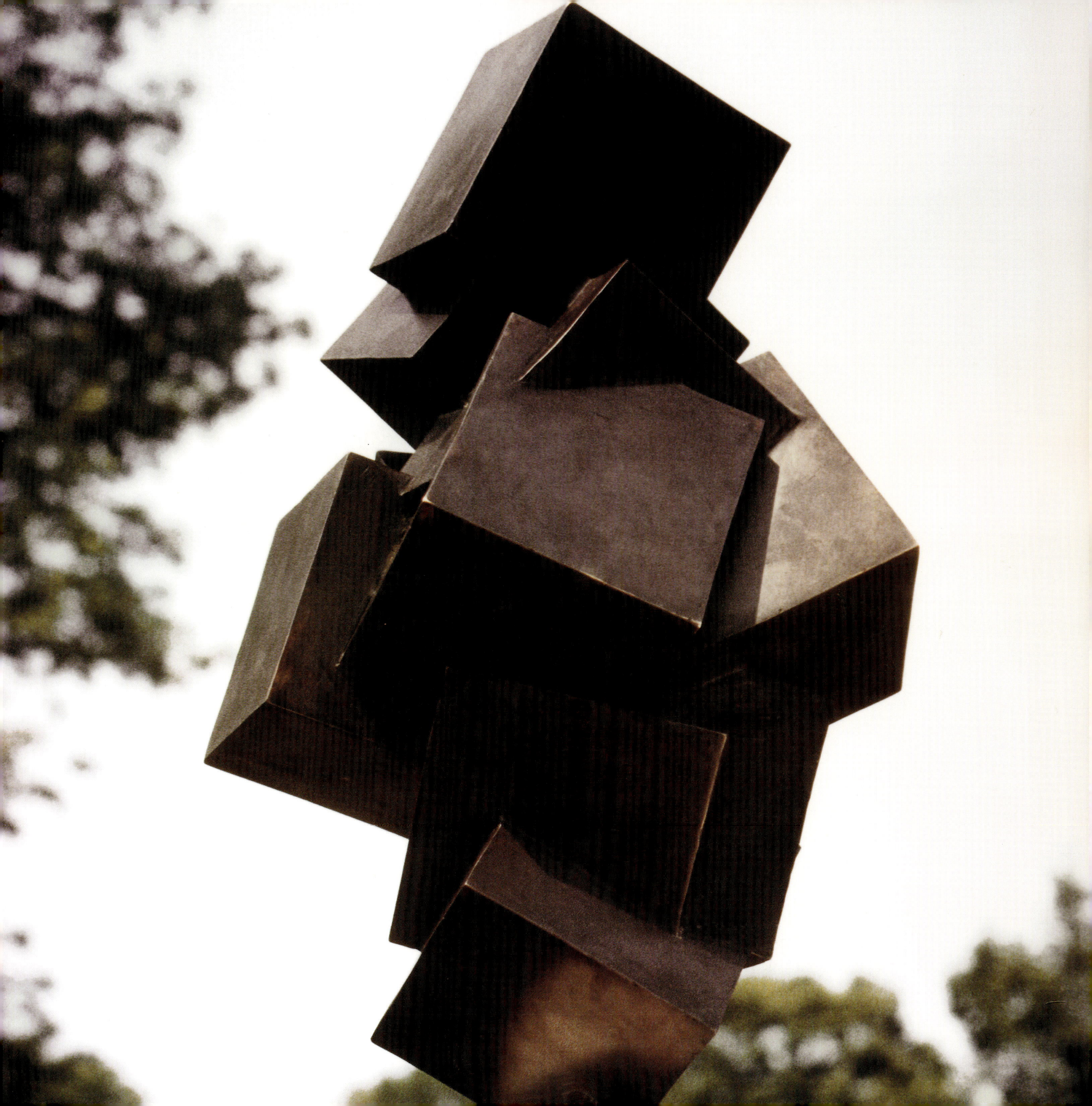

FLOATING CUBES II

2001
Bronze
9" x 16" x 9"
Collection of Martin Selig, Seattle, WA

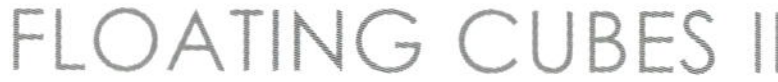

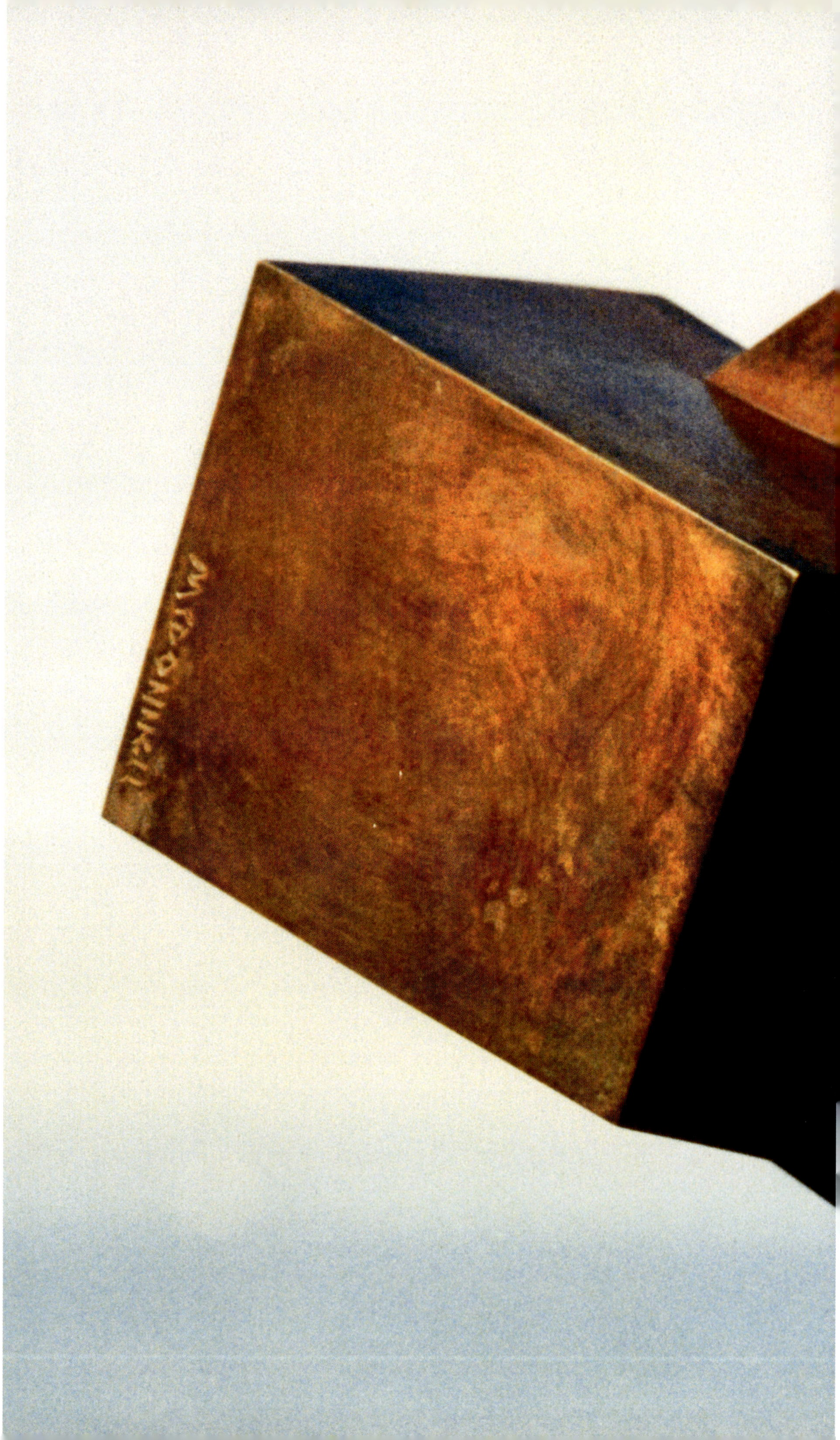

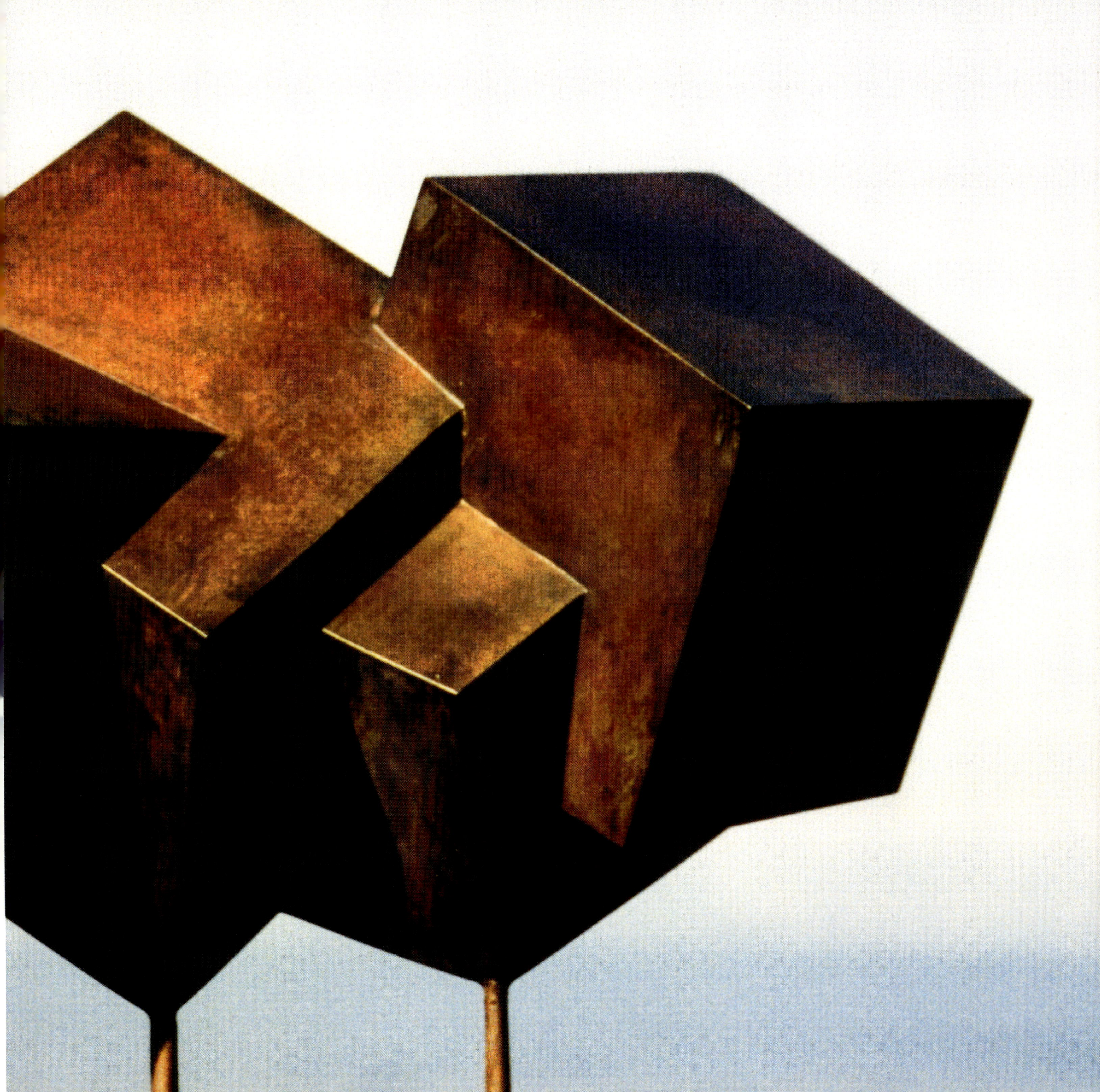

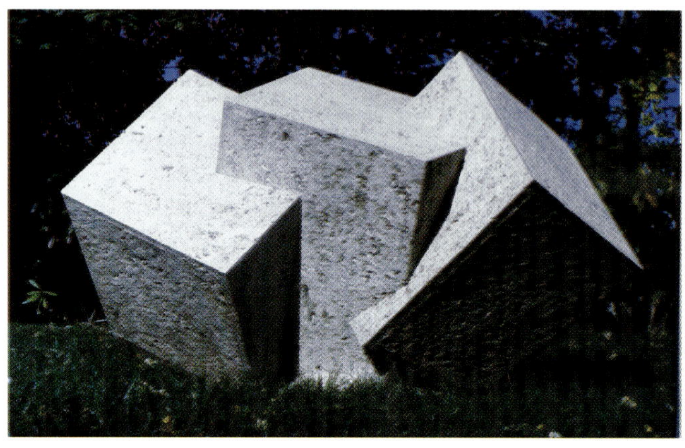

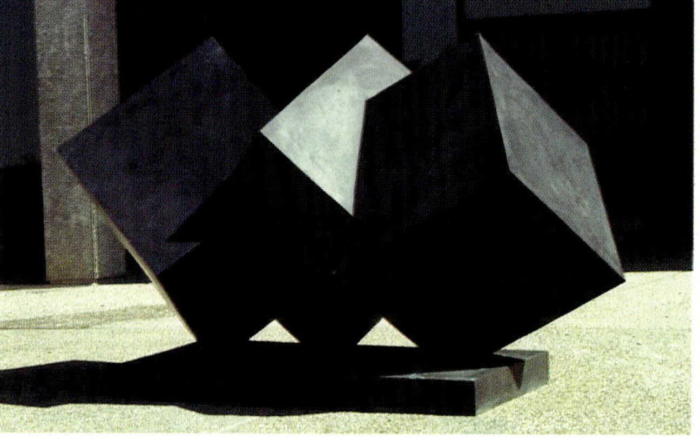

TRIPLE CUBES
1969
Travertine marble
32" x 65" x 34"
George and Marylou Beitzel,
Chappaqua, NY

TRIPLE CUBES
1972
Bronze
72" x 84' x 60"
Trammell Crow Company, Dallas, TX

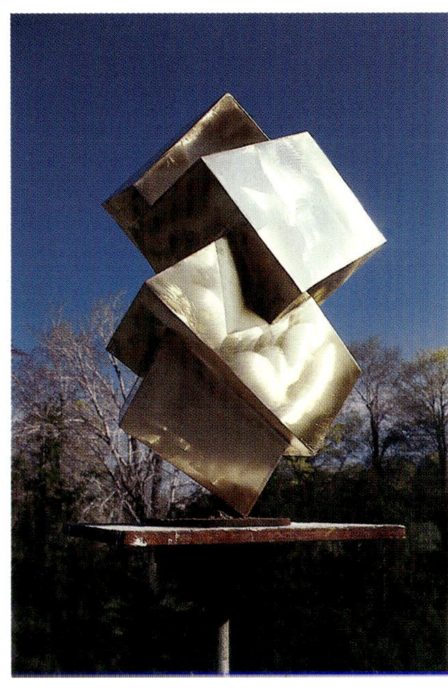

DIORITE
1980
Bronze
30" x 16" x 15"
Collection of the artist

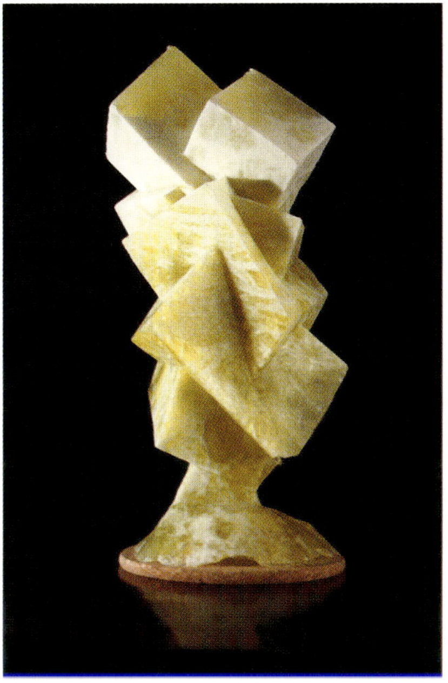

YELLOW CUBES
1999
Fused glass
17.5" x 8.5" x 9"
Collection of the artist

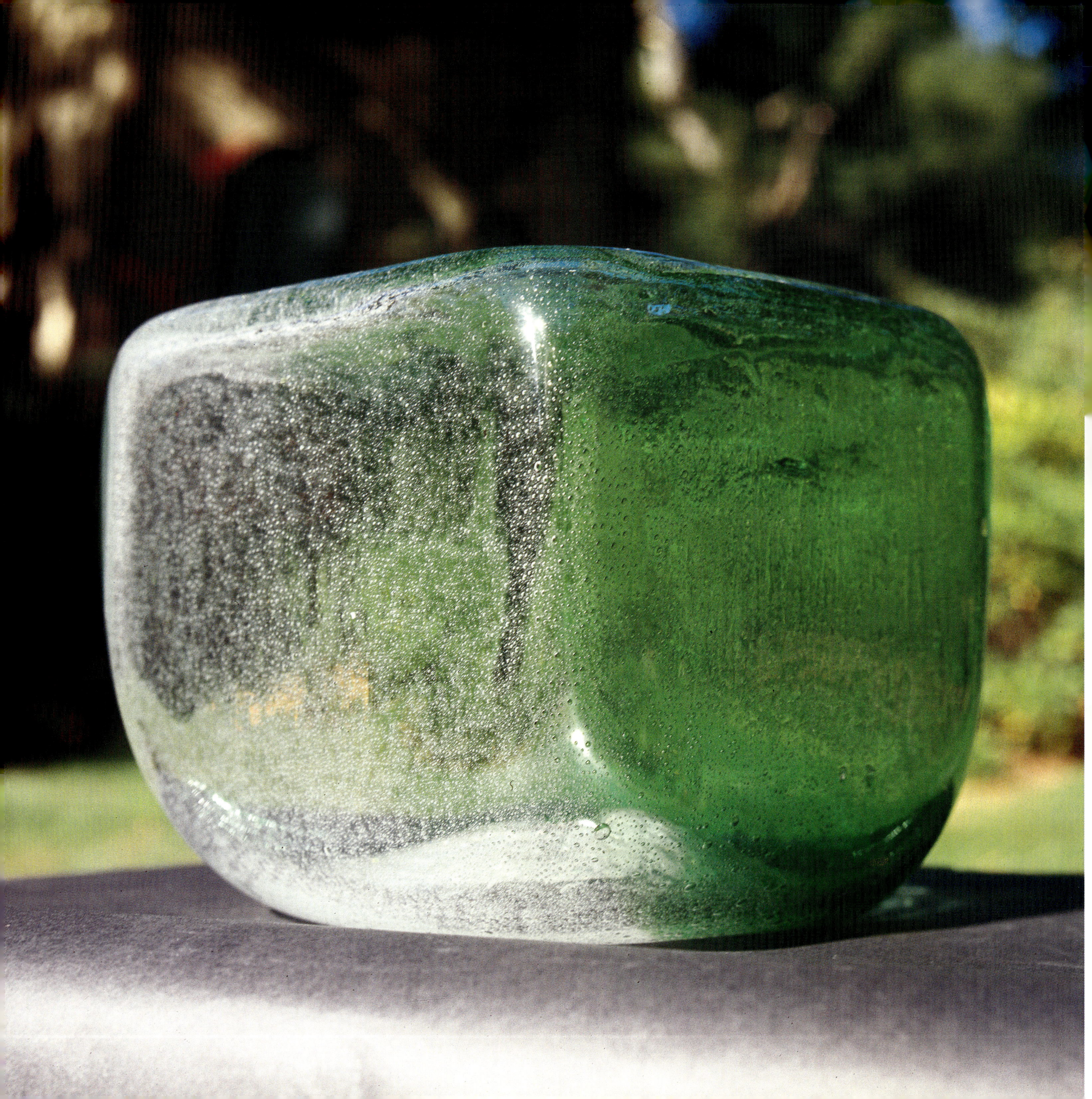

ICE CUBES AND GLASS

I grew up in Michigan and lived half my life around the Great Lakes. Things usually froze up around Thanksgiving and lasted through Easter. It seemed ice was everywhere. Most vividly, I remember huge dikes formed by enormous plates of ice, taller than several men, stacked along the shores of Lake Michigan and St. Clair.

Glass also had an early fascination for me. I recall melting glass straws over the stove to make knots and quirky animals, and in high school, my first term paper explored the production and use of glass in the time of Virgil.

That preoccupation was catalyzed during a visit to Seattle in 1991. We were invited to Dale Chihuly's Boathouse for a party and glass-blowing demonstration. His glass took on new form, and dimensions that I had never imagined. The more I learned about the potential, as well as the risk of the medium, the more intrigued I became.

I see the ice sculptures as a direct flow from my cubistic constructionist sculpture. However, there is also something akin to cubist paintings in the transparency and lightness of the blockish bubbly glass. By employing this new (to me) medium, I believe I have achieved another dimension and more flexibility in my work

Opposite page: Green Cube. 2004, Blown glass, 8" x 8" x 8", collection of Susan Slack, Long Beach, NY

BLUE CUBES

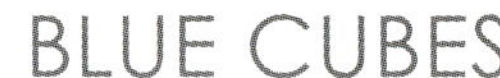

1997
Blown glass
6" or 8" each
Collection of the artist

My first effort at coloring my ice cubes was a series of these *Blue Cubes*. Some were opaque turquoise and others transparent cobalt. I especially liked them in groups where they were like a 3-D painting.

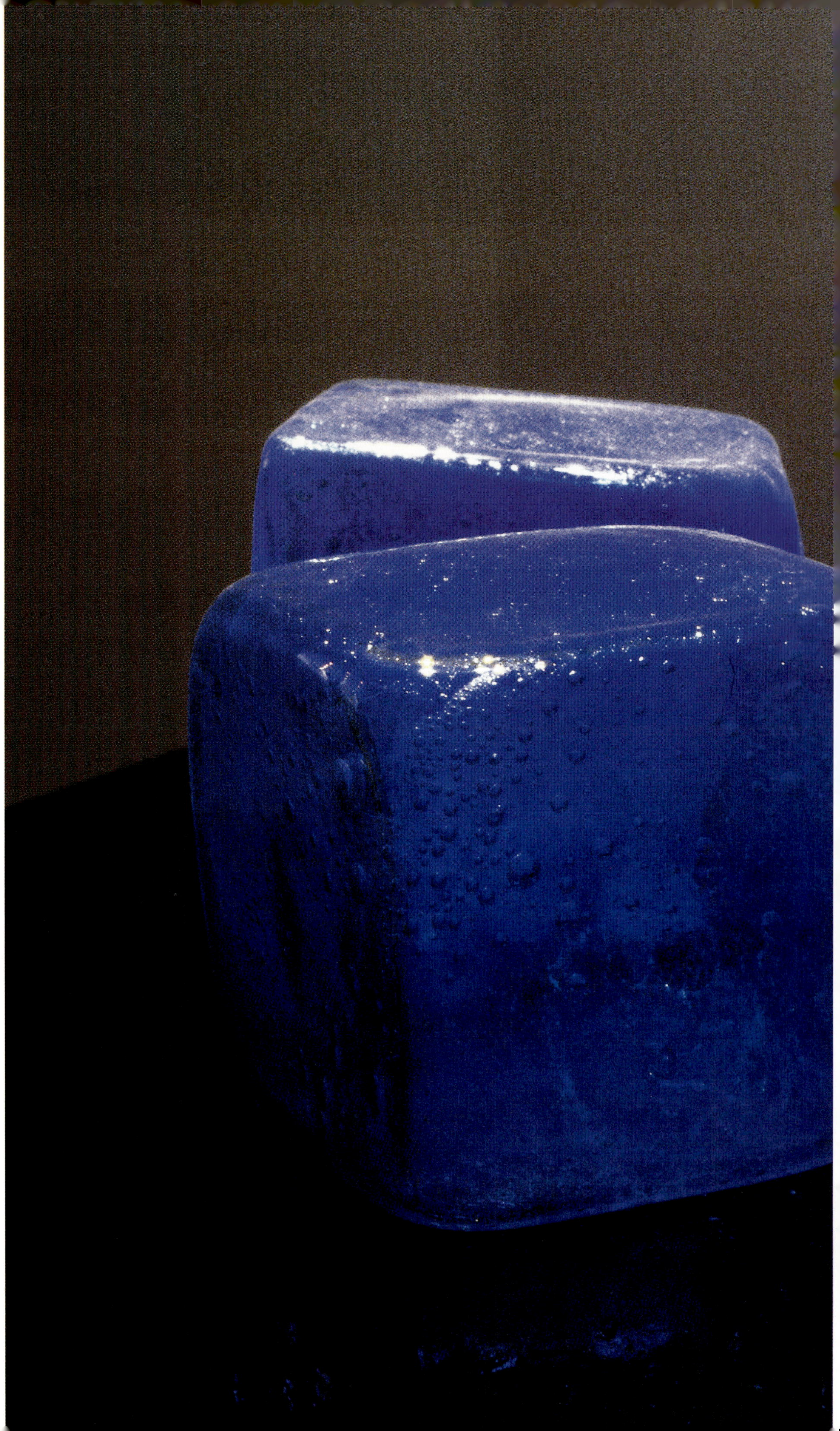

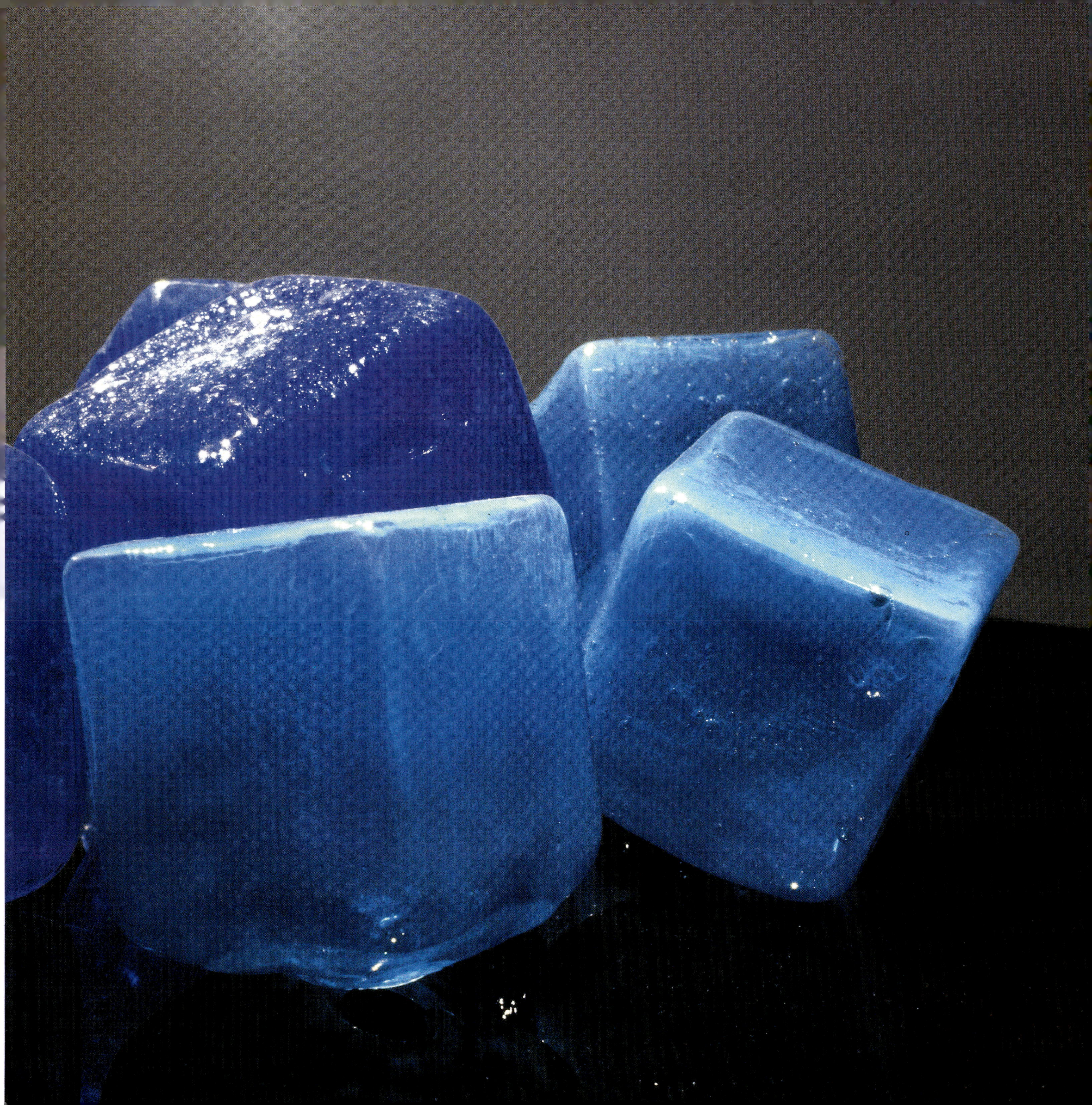

ON THE ROCKS

1996
Blown glass
60" x 60" x 60"
Collection of Donna and Cargil Macmillan, Palm
Desert, CA

When the collectors Donna and Cargill MacMillan told me about the new house that they were building in Palm Desert, they asked if I would be interested in designing something "kinda quirky, and preferably out of glass" for a water setting in the desert. It occurred to me, what is more quirky than ice in the desert? My suggestion of a large pile of glass ice cubes sitting in a fountain next to the swimming pool did not require much selling. However, turning this into a reality did require much advice and experimentation.

Technically making a medium that wants to be round into large cubes requires glass people of considerable experience, strength, and courage. Dale Chihuly kindly referred me to Ben Moore, who. suggested blowing into a wood box mold whose sides would fold out. He recommended Swedish glass blower and artist, Reno Bjork, at Urban Glass in New York. All told we lost about 50% of our production, mostly in the annealing kiln, but eventually we had our fountain and I liked the "ice cubes" so well that I began making them in various sizes and in various ways. To me they have their own aesthetic. They are a visual pun, somewhat "Pop," quite mysterious, and satisfying. I believe this is the threshold of what I would like to call my "ice age."

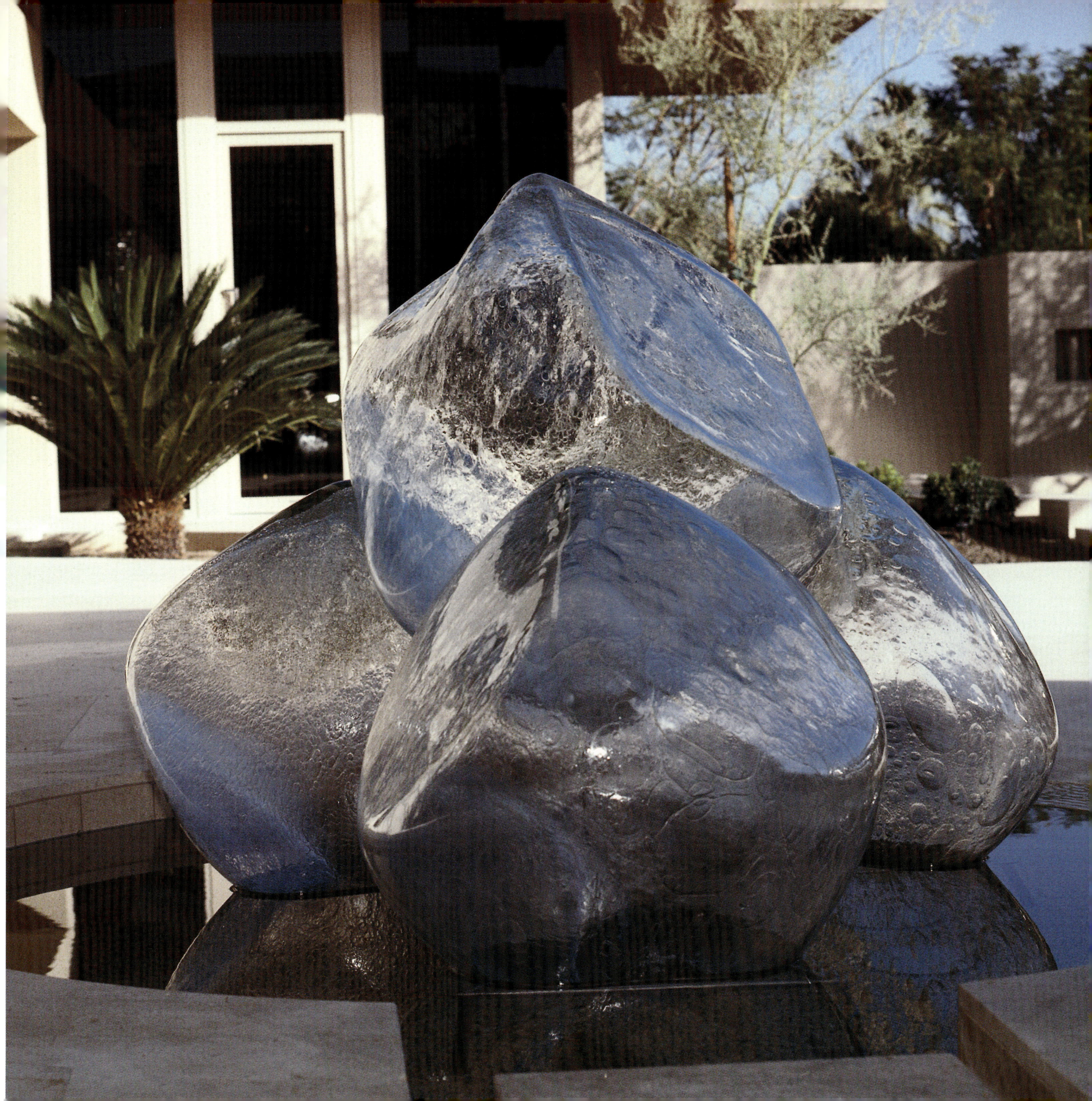

POLYURETHANE CUBES

2001
Polyurethane
18" x 18" x 18" each
Collection of Bonnie Kodis, Scottsdale, AZ

As glass could not safely be put in a swimming pool, I came up with the idea of creating my *Ice Cubes* out of plastic. Polyurethane was what we initially chose but we may also be able to use other types of plastic as the idea evolves. They have screw-on caps so that some water can be put inside to keep them from riding too high in the water. The cubes can also be used as seats, tables, or standing art objects.

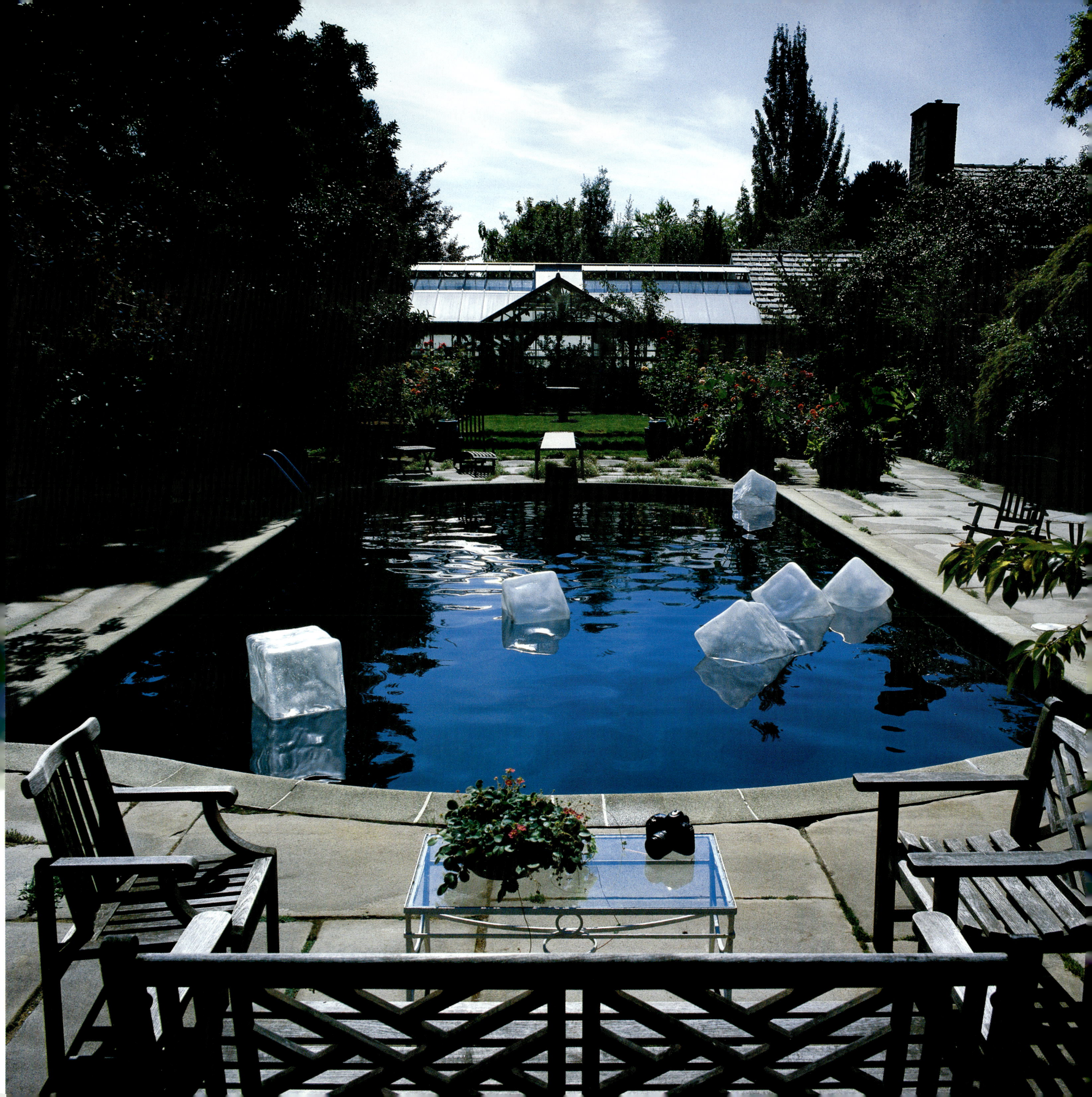

COOL

1998
Blown glass
40" x 120" x 40"
Durst Organization, New York City
1155 Avenue of the Americas, NYC

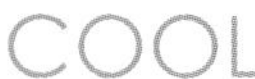

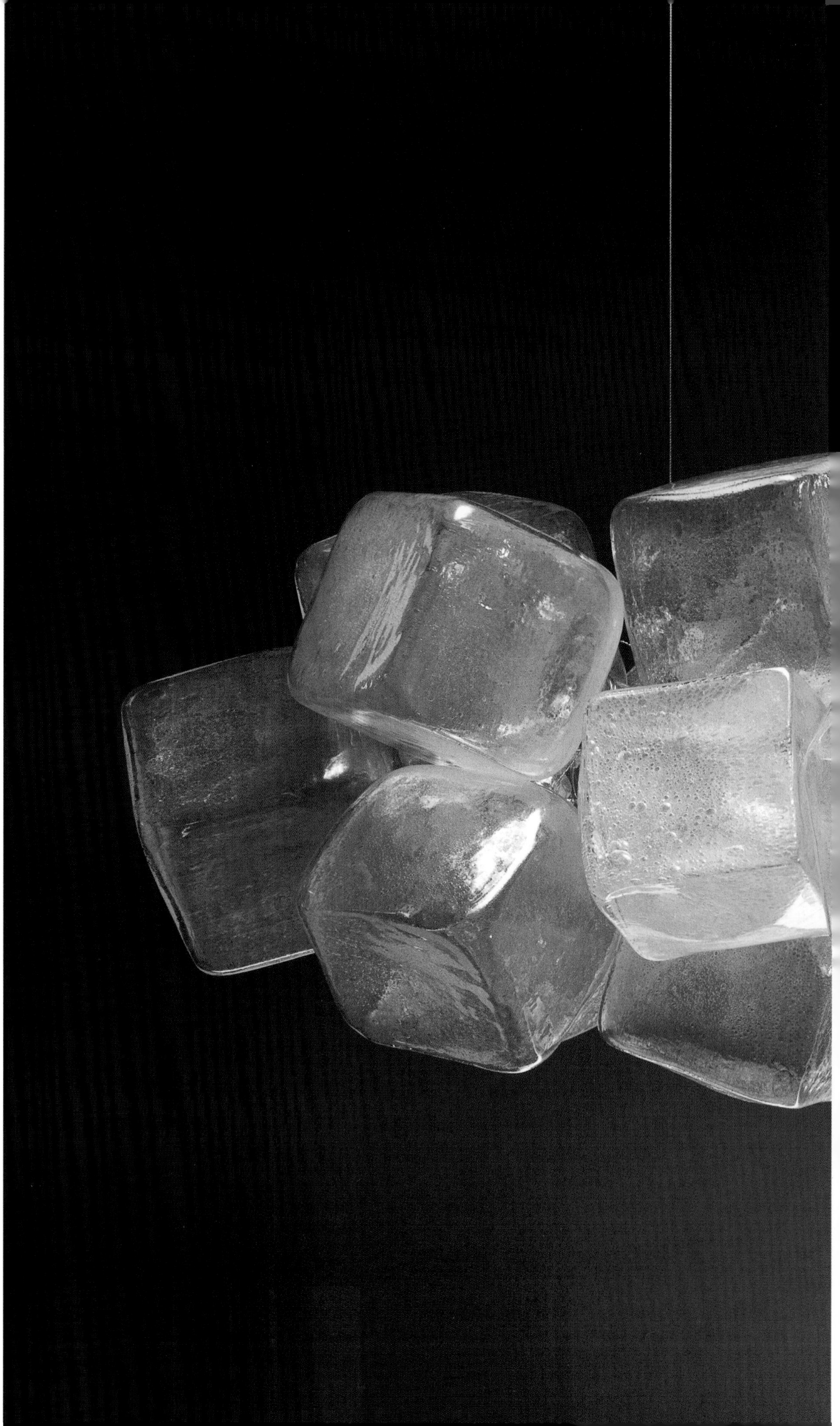

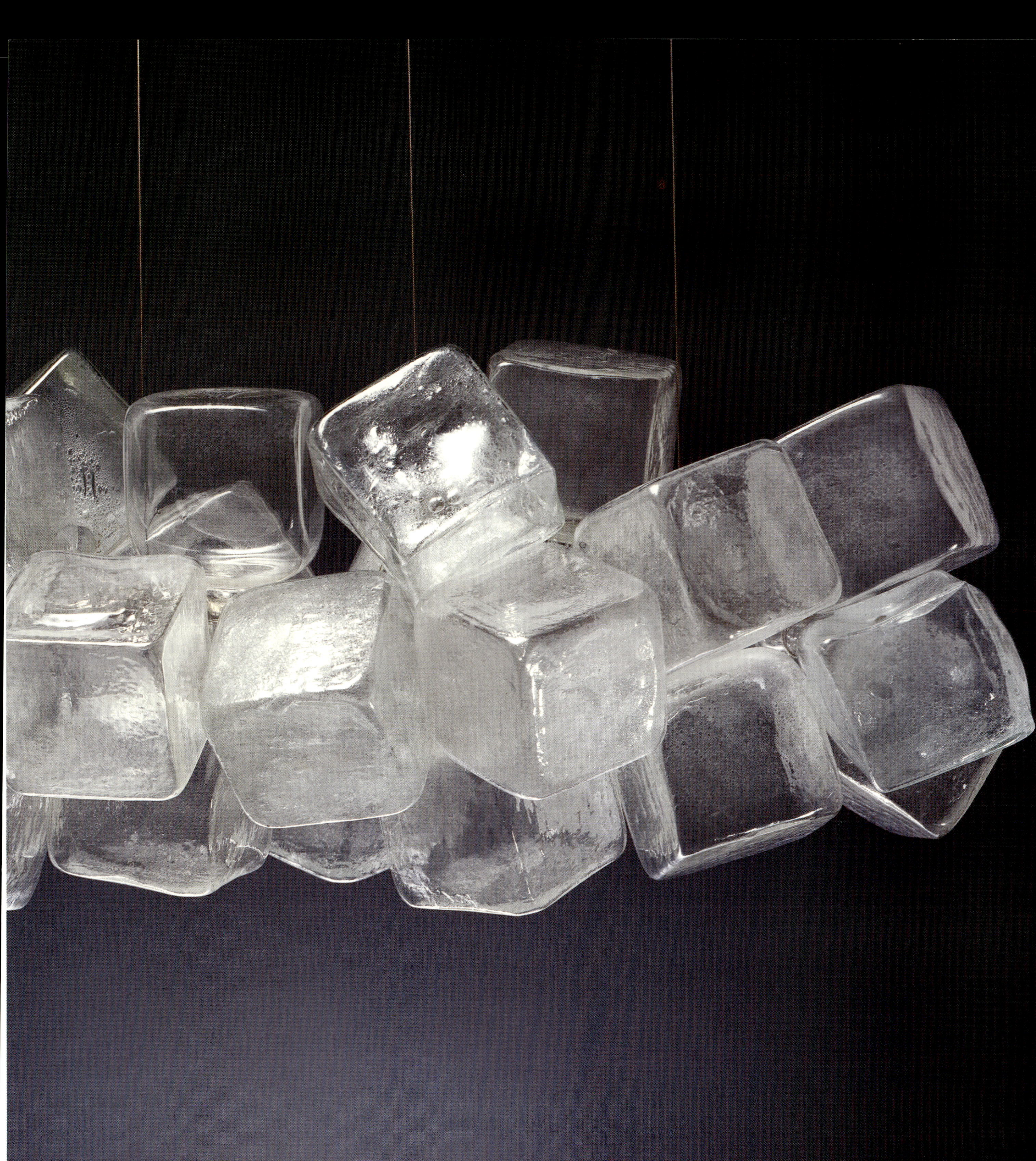

MERMAIDS' FORT

2004
8' x 14' x 4'
Gabion Water Wall of Glass and stainless steel
9th and Stewart Life Sciences Building, Seattle, WA

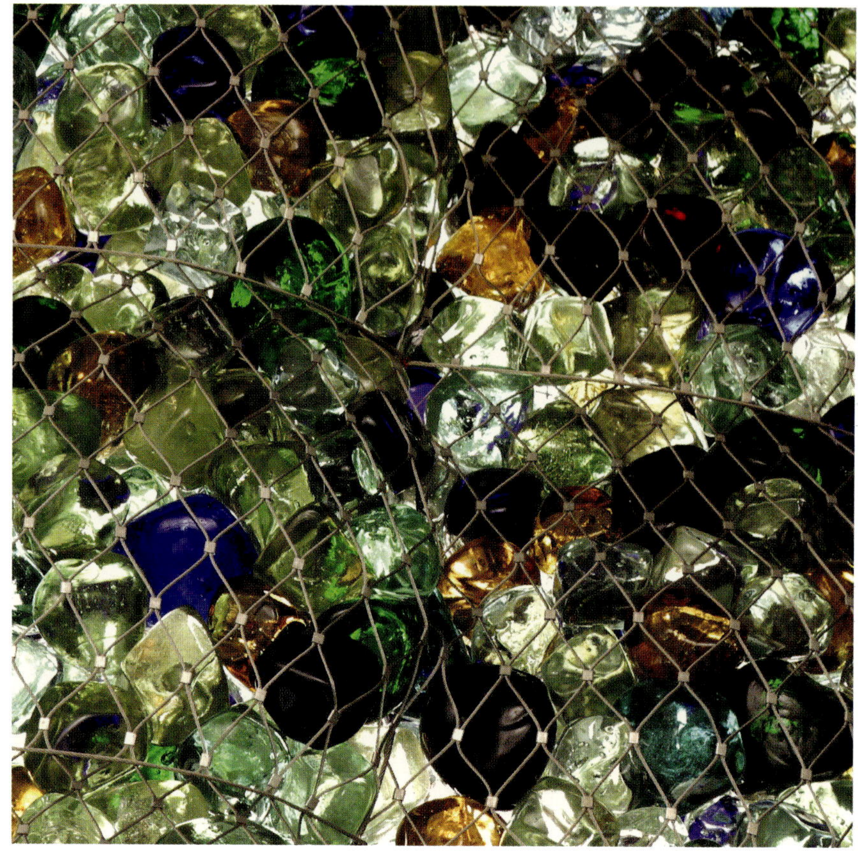

Gabions have always fascinated me, whether they were used as building blocks, retaining walls, or breakwaters. The word comes from the Italian, *gabbia*, meaning cage. I am also interested in wrapped forms like packages or bundles.

Henry Moore did a wonderful drawing of a crowd looking at a huge shrouded and trussed sculpture. It might be the feeling of weight and force that appeals to my sculptural senses. Something like Michelangelo's slaves pushing out from those strong blocks.

When my architect friend, Bob Bruckner, approached me with the idea of designing a water wall for the lobby of a new bio-tech building, I considered half a dozen possibilities. Eventually I decided on the idea of a Gabion water wall using large pieces of glass held in place with metal netting. The glass pieces were individually cast and flame finished, and the stainless steel retaining net had to be specially made.

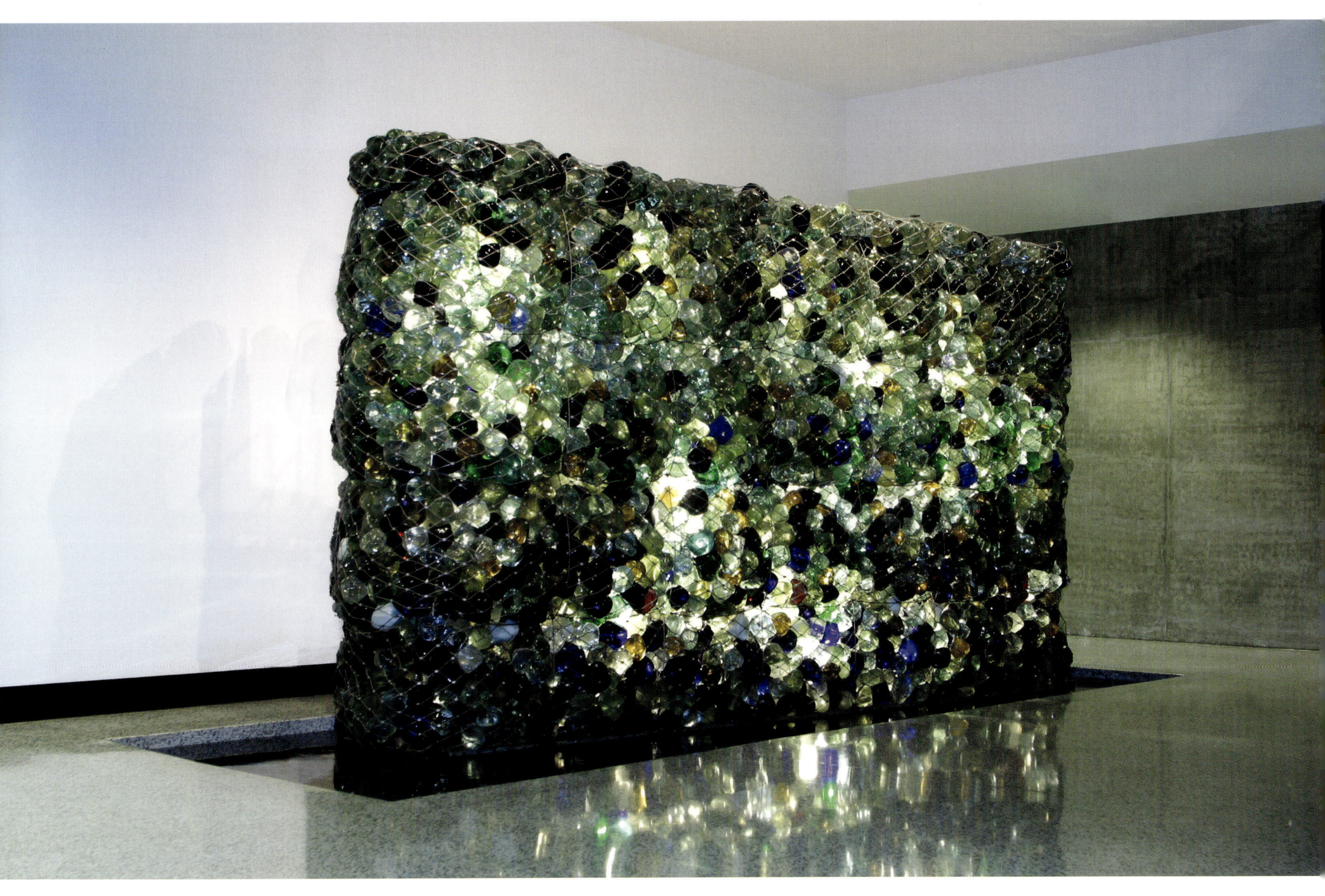

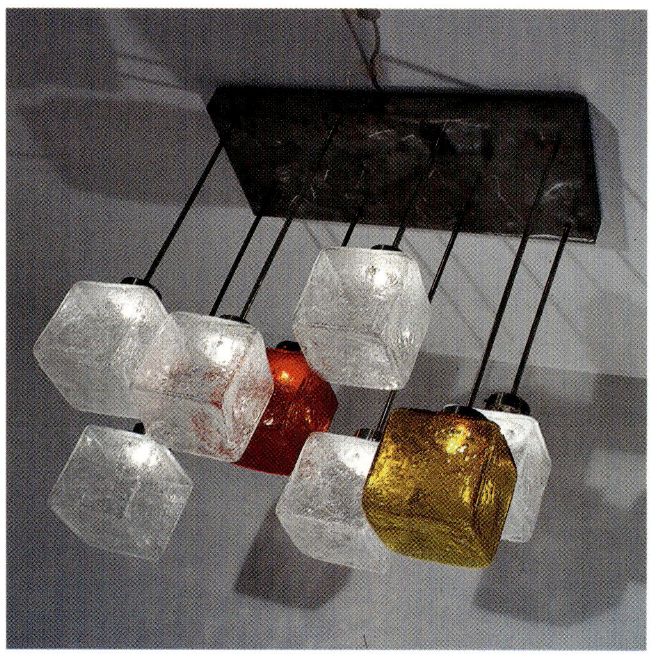

CHANDELIER III
2001
Blown glass and stainless steel
30" x 20" x 30"
Collection of Robert and Megan Bruckner,
Seattle, WA

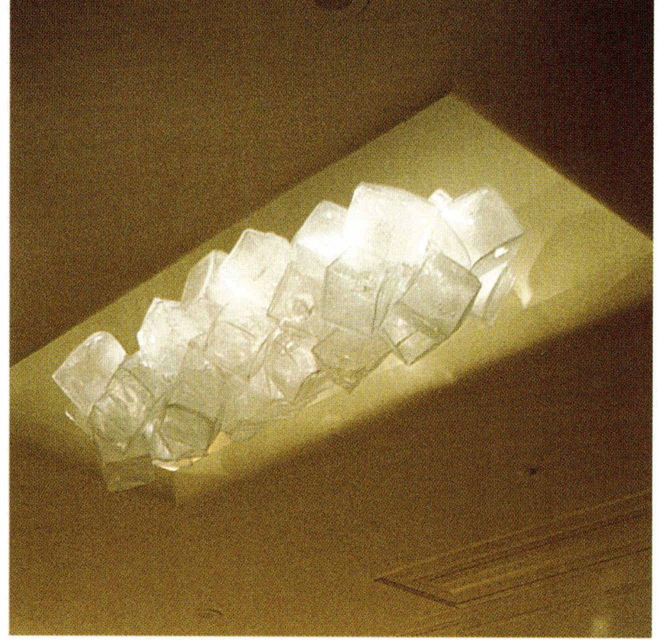

ROSA AYERS CHANDELIER
1996
Blown glass and stainless steel
220" X 96" X 48"
Seattle, WA

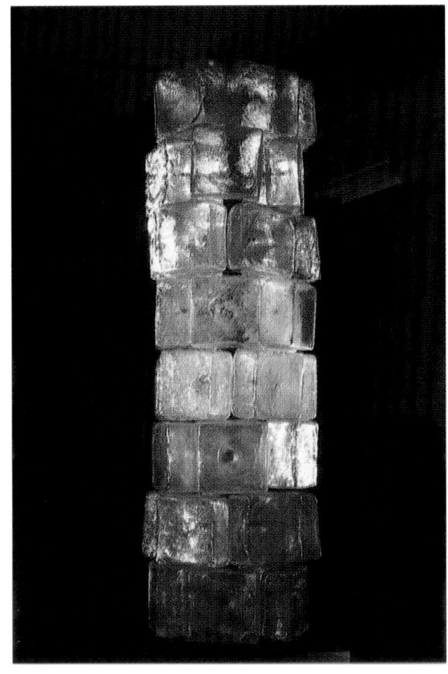

ICE COLUMN
2002
Blown glass, stainless steel and
neon light
96" x 32" x 32"
Collection of the artist

JOSEPH ANTHONY MCDONNELL

BORN

Detroit, 1936

EDUCATION

Harvard University School of Design, 1987

Accademia di Belle Arti, Florence, 1959-1961

BFA'58, MFA'59, University of Notre Dame

ONE MAN EXHIBITIONS

Foster/White, Seattle, WA, 2002, 2003

Weber Fine Art Gallery, Scarsdale, NY, 2002

Foster/White Gallery, Seattle WA, 2001

Nardin Galleries, New York, NY, 1997

Nardin Gallery, Somers, NY, 1995

Century Association, New York, NY, 1995

Paige Gallery, Dallas, TX, 1982

Ellsworth Gallery, Simsbury, CT, 1980

Westlake Gallery, White Plains, NY, 1978

John Wanamaker Fine Arts Gallery, Philadelphia, PA, 1970

Flint Art Institute, Flint, MI, 1964

Galleria Goldoni, Florence, Italy, 1963

McNay Art Institute, San Antonio, TX, 1964

Florence Art Gallery, Florence, Italy, 1962

Galleria Pater, Milan, Italy, 1962

Galleria Goldoni, Florence, Italy, 1961

Galleria L'88, Rome, Italy, 1961

GROUP EXHIBITIONS

Anne Reid Gallery, Sun Valley, ID, 2000-

Weber Fine Arts, Scarsdale, NY, 1999-

Maxwell Davidson, New York, NY, 1994-

Andre Emmerich, New York, NY, 1993-1995

National Academy of Design, NY, 1992

DeGraff Gallery, Chicago, IL, 1989-1990

Images Gallery, Norwalk, CT, 1988-1990

Shidoni Gallery, Santa Fe, NM, 1988-1990

Kouros Gallery, NY, 1985, 1986

Reece Gallery, NY, 1984, 1985, 1986

Campanile Gallery, Dallas, TX, 1985

Snite Museum, University of Notre Dame, 1980

Gallery at Hasting-on-Hudson, New York, NY, 1980

Audobon Artists Annual Show, NY, 1978

Katonah Gallery, Member Show, NY, 1976

New England Silvermine Exhibitions,
   New Canaan, CT 1976,1977

Yonkers Art Association Member Show, NY, 1976

Robert Kidd Gallery, Birmingham, MI

Barney Weinger Gallery, New York, NY,

Arwin Galleries, Detroit, MI

Detroit Artists Market, MI

The Contemporaries Gallery, New York, NY

Contemporanea, Florence, Italy, 1963

Mosta Mercato Nationale d'Arte, Italy,

USIS American Artists, in Florence, 1963

Houston Galleries, Houston, TX

Valley House Gallery, Dallas, TX

Florence Art Gallery, Florence, Italy

Galleria D'Arte "Lo Sprone," Florence, Italy

IX, X, and XII Piazza Dontello Exhibition, Florence, Italy

Donald Morris Gallery, Birmingham, MI

Galleria Schneider, Rome, Italy

Galleria L'88, Rome and Spoleto, Italy

Galleria XXII Marzo, Venice, Italy

Little Gallery, Birmingham, MI

COLLECTIONS

University of Michigan Museum, Dearborn, MI

Snite Museum, Notre Dame, IN

Museum of the Permian Basin, Midland, TX

AWARDS

Mural Competition, Bethesda, MD, 1988

Fountain Competition, Silver Spring, MD, 1985

New England Silvermine Exhibition, New Canaan, CT,
   1976 and 1977

SPECIAL COMMISSIONS

Bill and Melinda Gates Award For Global Health, Seattle, WA, 2001

Jazz at Lincoln Center Award, New York, NY, 1989-2001

Chicago Tribune Golf Classic, Chicago, IL, 1999

The Nordoff-Robbins Silver Cleft Award, NYC, 1996

The Hammond Awards, NYC, 1995

Westchester Golf Classic Award, NY, 1985-1995

Wanamaker Mile Award, NYC, 1971

PUBLICATIONS

Critic and Assistant Editor, *ARTWORLD*, NY, 1984-1995

Hospital Design for Healthcare and Senior Communities,
   Van Nostrand Reinhold, 1991

MR. McDONNELL IS INCLUDED IN:

Who's Who in American Art, (1973 to the present)

Who's Who in the East, (1975-76 to the present)

*International Who's Who in Art and Antique*s, (2nd Edition and on)

Art In Architecture, Louis G. Redstone, FAlA, (McGraw-Hill, 1968)

New Dimensions in Shopping Centers, Louis G. Redstone, FAIA
   (McGraw-Hill, 1973)

Outdoor Sculpture in Texas, University of Texas Press, (1996).

ARTICLES/REVIEWS:

L'Unity (Italy), May 30, 1961

II Telegraph (Italy), June 5, 1961

La Nazione (Italy), June 7, 1961

Giornale del Mattino (Italy), June 16,1961

La Nazione (Italy), June 25, 1961

Rome Daily American, September 28, 1961

Dallas Time Herald, June 26, 1963

The Villager, Greenwich Village, NY, August 1, 1963

San Antonio Light, February 5, 1964

San Antonio Light, February 16, 1964

Dallas Morning News, May 15, 1964

Milwaukee Journal, November 26, 1964

Milwaukee Journal, December 20, 1964

Milwaukee Journal, November 22, 1966

*Detroit New*s, May 23, 1969

Patent Trader, Mt. Kisco, NY, November 20, 1969

Evening Bulletin, Philadelphia, August 10, 1970

Madison (Wisconsin) Newspapers Inc. October 14, 1970

Philadelphia Inquirer, November 1, 1970

Chicago Today, August 13, 1971

The Detroit News, August 17, 1971

Madison (Wisconsin) *Newspapers Inc.* October 13, 1971

Chicago Tribune, January 5, 1973

Patent Trader, Mt. Kisco, NY, March 8, 1973

Reporter Dispatch, White Plains, NY, April 5, 1973

Patent Trader, Mt. Kisco, NY, May 10, 1973

East Hampton Star, May 31, 1973

South Bend Tribune, July 22, 1973

Chicago Daily News, August 8, 1973

Retail Directions (magazine cover), September, 1973

Patent Trader, Mt. Kisco, NY, November 22, 1973

Patent Trader, Mt. Kisco, NY, January 2, 1975

Gloucester County Times, Woodbuiy, NJ, May 29,1975

Building Design and Construction (magazine cover), April, 1976

Shopping Center World (magazine cover), June, 1976

The Courier, Champaign-Urbana, August, 1976

National Mall Monitor (magazine cover) February, 1976

Reporter Dispatch, White Plains, NY, April 22, 1977

New York Daily News, April 24, 1977

Patent Trader, Mt. Kisco, NY, April 28, 1977

Patent Trader, Mt. Kisco, NY, June 18, 1977

Reporter Dispatch, White Plains, NY, August 25, 1977

Traverse City (Michigan) *Record-Eagle*, October 13, 1977

Patent Trader, Mt. Kisco, NY, February 11, 1978

Traverse City (Michigan) *Record-Eagle*, October 13, 1977

The State Journal, Lansing, Michigan, August 22, 1978

Gannet Westchester Rockland Newspaper, June 4, 1985

New York Times, September 4, 1994

New York Times, September 19, 1995

The Albrightan, Reading, PA, November 12, 1997

University Week, University of Washington, October 5 and 10, 2000

On Center, Port Angeles Fine Arts Center, WA,
  October-November, 2000

Vero Beach Home and Design, January, 2001

New York Times, August 11, 2002

New York Times, October 16, 2003

Architectural Digest, August, 2004

ACKNOWLEDGEMENTS: to Don Ellegood, Director Emeritus of the University of Washington Press, who first conceived this book. His spirit lives on in the countless publications he produced. I would also like to express my sincere gratitude to Pat Soden, the current director of the Press, who made the book a reality, with such great support and enthusiasm. My heartfelt thanks also go to David Finn for orchestrating the production of the book by Ruder Finn Press, and especially for his magical photography and that of his granddaughter, Rebecca Binder. Special notes of thanks go to Susan Slack, Vice President/Editorial Director, Ruder Finn Press; Michael Schubert, Chief Creative Officer; Lisa Gabbay, President/Creative Director, Ruder Finn Design; and Winnie Chang, Art Director. I send enormous gratitude to my very able and tireless assistant, Corrie Befort Patnaught, who spent countless hours locating and organizing the material for this book. Finally, I extend my deepest thanks to Donald Kuspit, who dove deeply into my work as well as my soul to produce this essay, and to Andre Emmerich, my friend for many years, for his advice and his encouragement of my life in art.

To the collectors and patrons of my work, your faith and support have encouraged and sustained me.

WITH SPECIAL THANKS TO THE FOLLOWING FOR MAKING THIS BOOK POSSIBLE: Thomas and Amy Barwick, George and Mary Lou Beitzel, Al Clise, Donald R. Ellegood, Judith W. Evnin, William H. Gates, The Goergen Foundation, Barbara amd George Grashin, Douglas Howe, William and Storey John, Bonnie Kodis, Eugene and Sara Lipitz, Bruce and Shahara Llewellyn, Donna and Cargill MacMillan, John and Burdette McClelland, Barbara and Kevin McLoughlin, Thomas P. Moore II, Marianne and Robert Nestor, Richard and Ellen Perlman, H. Stewart Ross, Joseph Sanchez, Herman and Faye Sarkowsky, Martin Selig, Roberta M. Sherman, Jon and Mary Shirley Foundation, David and Amy Sidell, William Kelly Simpson, Carlyn Steiner, Leroy and Joie Soper, Robert M. Stahmer, Jeffrey and Susan Stern, Thurston Charitable Foundation, Touchstone Corporation, Paul and Harriett Weissman, Ann P. Wyckoff, Martha M. Wyckoff.